ARISTOTLE'S DIALOGUE
WITH SOCRATES

ARISTOTLE'S DIALOGUE WITH SOCRATES

ON THE
NICOMACHEAN ETHICS

Ronna Burger

THE UNIVERSITY OF CHICAGO PRESS

CHICAGO AND LONDON

Ronna Burger is professor of philosophy at Tulane University. She is the author of *The "Phaedo": A Platonic Labyrinth*, and, most recently, the editor of *Encounters and Reflections: Conversations with Seth Benardete* and, with Michael Davis, *The Argument of Action: Essays on Greek Poetry and Philosophy*, by Seth Benardete, both published by the University of Chicago Press.

The University of Chicago Press, Chicago 60637
The University of Chicago Press, Ltd., London
© 2008 by The University of Chicago
All rights reserved. Published 2008
Printed in the United States of America
17 16 15 14 13 12 11 10 09 08   1 2 3 4 5

ISBN-13: 978-0-226-08050-5   (cloth)
ISBN-10: 0-226-08050-1   (cloth)

Library of Congress Cataloging-in-Publication Data

Burger, Ronna, 1947–
Aristotle's dialogue with Socrates : on the Nicomachean ethics /
Ronna Burger.
    p. cm.
Includes bibliographical references and index.
ISBN-13: 978-0-226-08050-5 (hardcover: alk. paper)
ISBN-10: 0-226-08050-1 (hardcover: alk. paper)
    1. Aristotle. Nicomachean ethics.   2. Ethics.   3. Socrates.   I. Title.
B430.B87 2008
171'.3—dc22

2007034913

CONTENTS

ACKNOWLEDGMENTS

A book is produced by art; it does not grow by nature. Yet if one's work goes on for long enough—as in the present instance—that clear-cut boundary begins to be blurred. Under those circumstances, too many debts are accumulated to acknowledge individually and some too great to acknowledge in the way they deserve. In such cases, though—Aristotle speaks of gods, parents, and fellow participants in philosophy—one must pay back what one can, no matter how far it falls short of what one owes.

Writing, like thinking, is a solitary activity; but my own internal dialogue has been enriched and enlivened by discussion with friends and my expression of it enhanced by their responses, for which I owe special thanks to Michael Davis, Mary Nichols, and Stuart Warner. As my work on Aristotle developed I learned much from presenting it to receptive but challenging audiences at conferences and college campuses, including St. John's in Annapolis and Santa Fe, the University of Chicago, Boston College, the Catholic University of America, Assumption College, Roosevelt University, Howard University, the University of Dallas, Villanova University, Middlebury College, Boston University, and Fordham University. I am particularly grateful to my graduate students at Tulane, past and present, with whom I have worked out my understanding of Plato and Aristotle in ways that continue to feel like an adventure. In bringing this study to its present public form, it is my good fortune to have had the initial encouragement and ongoing support of my editor, John Tryneski, at the University of Chicago Press. The manuscript in its final stages benefited from comments and questions raised by readers for the Press and from the careful work of my copy editor, Mary Caraway.

The plan for this project began to emerge in the course of several summers of concentrated research and writing, supported by fellowships from Tulane University, the Earhart Foundation, and the National Endowment for the Humanities. It was a distinctive privilege to have a research fellowship at the Carl Friedrich von Siemens Foundation in Munich in 1999–2000 and, in particular, to share ideas with Heinrich Meier, director of the Foundation, whose interest in this project has helped sustain it over time. The prelude to that year in Munich was a public talk I presented at the Siemens Foundation in 1994. On that occasion, I had the honor of being introduced by my mentor, Seth Benardete, who made this remark: "Heidegger found Sophocles' tragedies to be a philosophic reflection on ethics superior to Aristotle's, but Burger promises to bring Aristotle's *Ethics* back into the fold of philosophy." If I have been able to pursue that promise, it is on the basis of an understanding of philosophy and the experience of its distinctive pleasures that I came to know over my years of study and conversation with Benardete. He is not here to see this project come to fruition, but his influence will be evident throughout.

My first discoveries of the treasures of Aristotle's *Ethics* occurred almost as long ago as the birth of my son, now a college student; watching his life take shape, while reflecting, in memory, on the place of my parents in my own, has kept me in touch with the reality of the questions this book addresses. My exploration of Aristotle's thought, and through it our own fundamental concerns, is something I have shared from the start with my husband, Robert Berman. We lived together with this study all along, and there are few ideas or arguments in it that were not clarified, deepened, and extended by his questioning and analysis.

I should acknowledge, finally, my appreciation of the unintended consequences of unwished-for circumstances. Forced by the aftermath of Hurricane Katrina to evacuate New Orleans during the fall semester of 2005, a generous family in Houston provided us a home away from home. Lucky to have my laptop computer stored with all my previous work and finding myself abruptly freed for a time from my usual academic responsibilities, I was able to complete a draft of the book that I now hand over to an unknown audience.

The Socratic Question of the *Ethics*

Aristotle sees the perfection of man as Plato sees it and more. However, because man's perfection is not self-evident or easy to explain by a demonstration leading to certainty, he saw fit to start from a position anterior to that from which Plato had started.

And it has become evident that the knowledge that he [Aristotle] investigated at the outset just because he loved to do so . . . has turned out to be necessary for acquiring the intellect for the sake of which man is made.

—Alfarabi, "The Philosophy of Aristotle," i and xix [1]

Aristotle's *Nicomachean Ethics* addresses a question of the utmost importance to us: What is the human good? Or, as the question comes to be elaborated, What is happiness? What is the good life for a human being? Its exploration of this question has made the *Ethics* one of the most influential works in the philosophical tradition, yet what exactly its teaching is has long puzzled readers and provoked much debate. The very arrangement of the text and the problems posed by it might lead one to wonder whether there is any underlying argument that makes the work a coherent whole. After grappling with its fundamental question about the human good in Book I, the inquiry enters upon what looks like a long, indirect path to its goal, beginning with an investigation of virtue; when, at the end of the tenth and last book, it finally returns to its original question, or something close to it, the answer proposed appears to leave behind much of the rich understanding of human life developed along the way.

Wherever the path of the *Ethics* finally leads, the question to which it responds sets Aristotle on a course following in the footsteps of Socrates. According to the history of philosophy that Aristotle constructs in *Metaphysics*

1

A, Socrates took a decisive step when he abandoned the cosmological speculation of his predecessors and turned his attention to the human things.[2] Socratic inquiry, whatever its specific starting point on any occasion, is directed ultimately to the question, What is the good life for a human being? In devoting itself to this fundamental question, the *Ethics* looks like *the* Socratic work in the Aristotelian corpus; whether it is a Socratic manner in which the *Ethics* proceeds, or a Socratic conclusion at which it arrives, is far less obvious.

Doubts might be raised, in the first place, by the manifest difference in form between the Aristotelian treatise and the Platonic dialogue as the exemplary representation of the Socratic practice of philosophy. The speeches of the dialogue belong to the characters who utter them; Plato remains hidden behind this representation and utters no view of his own within it. In the treatise, presumably, Aristotle speaks entirely in his own name; there should be no occasion and no need to interpret arguments or opinions as those of a character other than the author. In almost all the Platonic dialogues, the leading figure is the Socrates renowned for his practice of irony—in particular, the irony of a disclaimer to knowledge that, in the eyes of his interlocutors, is undercut by his conduct of the conversation.[3] The Platonic dialogue imitates the Socratic practice of irony in its own art of writing, using as its primary tool a contradiction or discrepancy between speeches and action.[4] The treatise, one would assume, has neither the need nor the means for such a practice.

Plato's Socrates discovers the importance of knowing what he does not know by reflection on the partial character of the knowledge involved in every art, which its own practitioners fail to recognize.[5] Of course, Socrates' knowledge of ignorance motivates in himself not satisfaction with the limits of a particular art but a quest for knowledge of the whole, which the Platonic dialogue imitates in its own form: while every conversation is differentiated from the others by the unique question it addresses, that question becomes only a particular lens through which the endeavor to grasp the whole is refracted. The treatise, in contrast, carves off a particular territory and respects the boundaries of its restricted subject matter and distinctive way of proceeding; Aristotle's political science, even if it seeks something as comprehensive as the human good, is only one discipline among others.[6] While the treatise looks like the fitting form for the presentation of a particular science, the dialogue always opens up the unlimited quest of philosophy.

That the form of the treatise is as appropriate to Aristotelian thought as the dialogue is to Socratic conversation appears to be confirmed in a particularly striking manner by the *Ethics*. Discussing the virtue of moderation (*sōphrosunē*), for example, the *Ethics* speaks of the right measure in our attraction to the pleasures of food, drink, and the *aphrodisia*. When Plato's Socrates raises the question, What is *sōphrosunē*? the discussion is driven to the radical proposal that it is a knowledge of itself and of all other knowledges.[7] Under the glaring light of his examination of opinion, Plato's Socrates finds the ordinary practices praised as moral virtue to be nothing but "demotic" or "vulgar" virtue and genuine virtue to lie only in philosophy. The *Ethics*, on the contrary, looks intent upon protecting the dignity of moral virtue as an autonomous sphere of human endeavor. If Aristotle is "the founder of political science," it is "because he is the discoverer of moral virtue."[8] Aristotelian moral virtue is supposed to supply the proper principles of action; those principles are the just and the beautiful, which appear as the desired ends only to the morally good man, while the discovery of the means to them is the work of prudence. The whole moral-political sphere, to which prudence belongs, thus appears to be closed by principles that are recognized only by the gentleman.

That understanding seems to be confirmed by Aristotle's remarks early on in Book I about the audience the *Ethics* is meant to address. After praising Plato for his perplexity about the right path of inquiry—from the principles or to the principles—Aristotle proposes a seemingly obvious solution: it is necessary, of course, to begin with what is first—not first in itself, however, but first for us. This inquiry, that means, has to start with certain long-standing opinions about the just and beautiful things;[9] it can address itself only to people brought up with those opinions. Such individuals already have the starting point, which is "the that," and if they are satisfied with it, they have no need for "the why" (1095b4–7). The *Ethics* speaks to the gentlemen, who are in principle not skeptics; they share an understanding of human decency and do not demand an answer to the question of what good it serves.[10]

But the invitation Aristotle extends to his audience is, in fact, a very paradoxical one: a prospective reader who does not already have "the that" should not even open the book, but one who has "the that" sufficiently should close it immediately. The gentleman for whom the inquiry is supposed to be intelligible would seem to have the least need for it. The inquiry is, apparently, inaccessible to some, and to the rest unnecessary: the *Ethics* presents itself from the start as a work for nobody. If that is not its real intention, the barrier it appears to erect at its threshold must be a test through which it sorts out the classes of its complex audience. The inquiry would be of the greatest need, it seems, and therefore of the greatest potential benefit, precisely for someone troubled by "the that" of his upbringing and seeking "the why." Such an individual may have been brought up to recognize that certain things are beautiful and just; but the beautiful and just things, Aristotle observes, being conceived of differently everywhere, display such "wandering" that they are sometimes thought to exist only by convention, not by nature. It is someone whose experience has led him to an awareness of this instability who would be seeking "the why" beyond "the that" of his moral education. The *Ethics* would offer itself to such a reader as a guide for the perplexed.[11] If, moreover, it is not passively awaiting such a reader, it must aim to create the requisite perplexity. It would do so by bringing to light whatever limitations or contradictions there might be in the self-understanding of ethical virtue; it would have to find a way, within the form of the treatise, to accomplish what Plato does by representing Socrates examining the opinions of his interlocutors.[12] The *Ethics* would have to present ethical virtue from the "inside"—as experienced by the person devoted to it—while occupying at the same time a perspective outside that horizon.

With this challenge in mind, Aristotle stages a debate with Socrates, represented as the proponent of a teaching that puts into question the common understanding of virtue. Over against that teaching, the *Ethics* sets out to develop a non-Socratic account, which begins with the separation of ethical from intellectual virtue, based on an analysis that divides the desiring from the reasoning parts of the human soul: a non-Socratic psychology provides the grounds for a non-Socratic account of the closed sphere of ethical virtue. Aristotle's debate with Socrates, which unfolds from that starting point, is marked by a series of seven explicit references from Book III through Book VII. No references to Socrates, but all the references in the *Ethics* to Plato—praising him for his wise insights—fall outside the boundaries of this debate. The pattern is reinforced by another striking feature: all direct references in the *Ethics* to "philosophy" appear, along with all references to Plato, outside the segment of the argument in which Socrates appears.[13] Of course, even then philosophy is mentioned only in passing and never as a subject in its own right: it is not one of the ways of life considered in Book I, nor one of the "intellectual virtues" in Book VI, and it is referred to in Book X merely to infer that the exercise of wisdom must be most pleasant, given the pleasures thought to belong to the mere pursuit of it (1177a23–27).

The apparently casual references to "philosophy," which lie outside the central Socratic territory of the *Ethics*, highlight the puzzle of the pattern that separates the views of Socrates from those of Plato. The tendency among scholars to assume that separation looks as if it must be traced all the way back to Aristotle, who seems to ignore, as much as that tradition does, the efforts Plato exerted, through his reliance on the dialogue form, to make such an independent identification of his own views virtually impossible. Of course, however problematic this separation may be, it alerts us to the question of what Aristotle's purposes are in his own argument for isolating from its original dialogic context the doctrines ascribed to Socrates. In the first such case, he extracts from Plato's *Laches* the thesis that virtue—in this case, courage—is knowledge, which happens to be put forward not by Socrates but by his interlocutor, and while it clearly has some Socratic provenance, it becomes obvious in the course of the conversation how far this "science of virtue" is from Socrates' understanding.[14]

Through the series of allusions to the Platonic dialogues beginning with this one, Aristotle constructs the figure of Socrates as a perfect foil against which to develop a different account of virtue of character. Traced back to their Platonic source, however, the doctrines Aristotle ascribes to Socrates are embedded in a complex set of problems—including the nature of true human excellence, justice in the city and in the soul, psychic conflict and pleasure, friendship and love, wisdom and the question of happiness—with which Aristotle wrestles throughout the *Ethics*.[15] In doing so, he engages in a dialogue in deed that extends beyond the boundaries of, and leads us to rethink the meaning of, the explicit debate with Socrates he conducts in the speeches of Book III through Book VII. It is that dialogue in deed to which the title of this study refers—not in the spirit of an empirical claim about what Aristotle had in mind when writing the *Ethics*, but as a tool of interpretation, to be judged by the philosophical results it yields, in particular, the underlying argument it discloses whose movement makes the work a whole.

The Socratic teaching that provides the initial target of critique for the argument of the *Ethics* is introduced in Book II, even before the name of Socrates is mentioned. Insisting on the indispensable role of habituation in producing virtuous dispositions of character, Aristotle charges the many with ignoring that need and instead "taking refuge in *logos*" (1105b12–14): he criticizes the mistaken belief that speeches are sufficient for acquiring virtue, employing the same formula by which Plato's Socrates describes his own distinctive practice of philosophy (*Phaedo* 99e). This allusion prepares for the first explicit reference in the *Ethics* to Socrates as the proponent of the thesis that courage is knowledge (1116b4–5). The thesis suggests the way Socratic philosophy entails the overturning of conventional morality; whether it captures the Socratic understanding of human excellence that takes the place of conventional morality is another question. What the figure of Socrates stands for in his first appearance in the *Ethics* is sustained by the last five references to him, clustered densely in the final chapter of Book VI and the opening chapters of Book VII. A single reference stands out from the rest in its identification of Socrates as the exemplar of the supposed vice of irony (*eironeia*), which is a form of self-deprecation: the momentary emergence of Socrates the *eiron*, who claims to know only what he does not know, compels us to rethink the whole string of references to a Socrates who believes virtue is knowledge. Aristotle thus quietly turns into the problem of Socrates what he has presented as the doctrine of Socrates: if it is not knowledge (*epistēmē*), what is the standard of human excellence of which ethical virtue falls short?

The debate with Socrates that drives the investigation of ethical virtue in the *Ethics* seems to be completed at the end of Book VI, with Aristotle's admission that there is something right in the Socratic view: there can be no genuine virtue apart from *phronēsis*, prudence or practical wisdom, which is supposed to belong to the independent sphere of intellectual virtue. This concession, which denies the status of ethical virtue as a separate and autonomous sphere, looks like a radical revision of the premise of the *Ethics*; yet, in retrospect, we find signs of its presence from early on. Why, then, was it necessary to stave off for so long this acknowledgment of the truth to be found in the Socratic view?

This pivotal moment in the argument of the *Ethics* raises another, equally perplexing question. Aristotle's acceptance, or partial acceptance, of the Socratic view overturns the cut between the nonrational and the rational parts of the soul, but it comes at the price of a new cut, within the rational soul: *phronēsis*, as the virtue of practical reason, is now separated from *sophia*, as the virtue of theoretical reason. In its mere concern with the good things for human beings, *phronēsis* is found inferior to *sophia*, defined as comprehensive knowledge of the whole cosmos or the most eminent knowledge of the highest beings in the cosmos. Pericles, as exemplar of the one, is ranked below Thales or Anaxagoras, as representative of the other. From the cosmic perspective, in which all things human look small and unimportant, *sophia* earns the title of happiness. This conclusion brings us back momentarily, for the first time, to the original question of Book I; why, then, does it not bring the inquiry to a close?

In fact, the argument is turned around from these lofty heights and pulled back down to earth, to reconsider the entire preceding account of virtue and the psychology on which it was based. Concern with the practice of praise and blame, which belongs to the task of molding character, is replaced in Book VII by the aim of healing, which requires a theoretical study of psychic illness. However important the perspective of the gentleman may have been throughout the investigation of virtue, at this point he is left behind. And the argument pushes beyond the boundaries that were supposed to determine the restricted territory of the *Ethics*, in content and in method. This new beginning is initiated by the same Socrates who appeared to bring the argument of the *Ethics* to a close at the end of Book VI; for in granting that virtue is or involves some kind of knowledge, Aristotle is compelled to face the consequences Socrates drew when he insisted that one cannot know one's own good and act contrary to that knowledge.

Aristotle's complex analysis of this issue leads him to the acknowledgment, once again, that Socrates in a sense got things right. This final stage in Aristotle's debate with Socrates results in a transformation of the inquiry, which seems to reflect the Socratic ground it has reached:[16] what began as political science now becomes the project of the political philosopher (1152b1–2). This is the first and only reference to the "political philosopher" in the *Ethics*, as attentive readers have noted;[17] yet it hardly seems fitting to the analysis that follows, which takes up an investigation of pleasure as that which all living things strive for by nature, from which point of view pleasure looks like *the* good. The progress of the inquiry beyond the investigation of virtue, which transformed it into political philosophy, appears to have freed it at the same time for the discovery of nature; but the naturalistic analysis of pleasure in Book VII can be only the first step in the unfolding of the argument out of which political philosophy must discover its way. The topic of pleasure itself will be taken up for reconsideration at the beginning of Book X—above all, in order to investigate whether there is a distinctively human pleasure, one that accompanies a distinctively human activity. What prepares for that reconsideration is the long discussion of friendship, which stands between the two accounts of pleasure along the path of return to the question of happiness.

Pleasure, according to the analysis in Book X, follows in the wake of, or is the very realization of, an activity of being aware, and that is being most fully alive; the importance of such awareness is introduced in the concluding stage of the discussion of friendship. Happiness, we discover in that context for the first time, involves more than a set of objective conditions; it requires an awareness of being alive and of the goodness of being alive, and that comes about through a reciprocal awareness, of oneself and of the friend as another self. This is what friends achieve by living together, which is a necessity for us as political beings; but living together for human beings means sharing speeches and thoughts, which is the exercise of our capacity as rational beings.[18]

The joint fulfillment of our nature as political and rational in the activity of sharing speeches and thoughts—which belongs, above all, to the friendship of those who "philosophize together"—hardly looks possible in light of the notoriously controversial conclusion the *Ethics* reaches at the end of Book X. The contest it stages for the title of the best human life recalls the conclusion of Book VI, which ranked the pure theoretical life of the pre-Socratic Thales or Anaxagoras over the political life of Pericles. In the language of the contemporary scholarly debate, the *Ethics* ends with an "exclusive" conception of happiness, to be found in the life most singly devoted to the activity of contemplation. And this conclusion stands in a problematic relation to the "inclusive" conception that seems to be implied by the inquiry as a whole, for which a life without ethical virtue or friendship, at the very least, could never be a good one for a human being. If there is a coherent underlying argument of the work as a whole, it would have to operate, apparently, like the plot of a tragic drama, wherein a reversal in the action, which overturns expectations, must be understood, finally, to belong to a sequence governed all along by probability or necessity.[19]

After presenting the thesis identifying happiness with *theōria*, Aristotle pauses to remind us that in matters like these, speeches must be measured by deed. What he proposes in response, however, is nothing but a conventional opinion: the theoretical life must be happiest because it is the one that would be rewarded by the gods, who suddenly appear on the scene after an almost complete absence from the entire inquiry. But Aristotle's warning about the limits of mere speeches should call our attention to a genuine deed—that which we have engaged in all along as participants in the inquiry. Of course, that activity is no more contemplation of the cosmos or the highest beings in the cosmos than it is political action; it is as conspicuously absent from those alternatives as Socrates, the founder of political philosophy, is from the contest between the pre-Socratic cosmologist and the political leader in the claim to represent the best human life. With its deliberate employment of a discrepancy between its speeches and its deed, Aristotle's treatise puts to use the basic tool of irony at work in the Platonic dialogues.[20] How is the teaching of the *Ethics* about human happiness to be understood when its speeches are interpreted in light of the deed that we can call the action of the *Ethics*? That is the question that inspires this study.

PART I

The Human Good

1

The Final End and the Way to It

SOCRATES: Well, then, let's make beforehand a still further agreement on some small points.
PROTARCHUS: What kind?
SOCRATES: Whether it's a necessity that the lot and portion of the good be complete and perfect or not complete and perfect.
PROTARCHUS: Surely, Socrates, the most complete and perfect of all.
SOCRATES: What of this? Is the good adequate and sufficient?
PROTARCHUS: Of course, and it differs in this respect from all the things that are.
SOCRATES: And it's most necessary, moreover, to make this further point about it, I suspect: everything that knows it pursues and desires it . . .
PROTARCHUS: It's impossible to contradict this.
SOCRATES: So let's examine and judge the life of pleasure and the life of thought by looking at them separately.
PROTARCHUS: How do you mean it?
SOCRATES: Let there be neither thought in the life of pleasure nor pleasure in the life of thought, for if either of them is good, it must not have any additional need of anything; but if either comes to light as needy, this is surely no longer the really and truly good for us.

—Plato *Philebus* 20c–21a, translated by Seth Benardete

FROM THE GOOD TO THE HUMAN GOOD

Politikē *as Architectonic*

Aristotle's *Nicomachean Ethics* begins with a seemingly preposterous contention:

OCT >

Every art [*technē*] and every way of proceeding [*methodos*], and likewise action [*praxis*] and choice [*prohairesis*], are thought to aim at some good; hence the good has been beautifully declared to be that at which all things aim. (1094a1–3)

Now, this might be acceptable, though it would not be saying much, if it were merely a formal generalization: the end at which anything purposive aims is "the good," whatever it might be in any particular case. But in light of the direction the argument is about to follow, the reference to that at which all things aim appears to be a more grand claim about a single end: from the opinion that there is some particular good for particular types of human endeavors,[1] a conclusion is drawn about *the* good as a comprehensive end. Of course, Aristotle observes only that this inference is "beautifully declared" (*kalōs apephēnanto*): *the* good as the unifying principle of the whole is a product of the beautiful as it operates through speech.[2] The beautiful certainly seems to be the right measure of a teleological cosmology, in which all parts are ordered in a whole by reference to a single highest end. The ambitious goal the *Ethics* sets for itself, if it is seeking knowledge of this ultimate principle, seems to erode in stages as the defining aim of the project slips from *the* good (1094a22) to the human good (1094b7), then to the practical good (1095a16–17), and finally to the sought-for good (1097a15). *The* good implies a cosmos within which the human has its natural place; the human good abandons that comprehensive whole; the practical good seems to impose even narrower restrictions by limiting itself to the sphere of action; and the sought-for good, in tying the end to our activity of seeking, makes us wonder whether the good, like being, not only was and is but will always be a question.[3]

Before addressing the question of the good, a preliminary analysis of kinds of ends (*telē*) is proposed—in what may well be the most abstract and obscure statement in the *Ethics:*

Some are activities [*energeiai*], some are works [*erga*] beyond them, and of those in which there are ends beyond the actions [*praxeis*], the works [*erga*] are by nature better than the activities [*energeiai*]. (1094a4–6)

Terms that are the subjects of lengthy examination in the *Metaphysics* and elsewhere appear here with no preparation or clarification, though they will play a central role in the argument of the *Ethics*.[4] What exactly is an *energeia*, what kind of *ergon* can be an end beyond it, and why, in such a case, should the *energeia* be understood as a *praxis*? Book I will return, in Chapter 7, to the notion of the *ergon* as the basis of an argument meant to establish what the good is that constitutes the final end in human life. The *ergon* of the sculptor, which is called upon there to illustrate the notion, is both the function of sculpting and the work produced by it; but only the work, his statue, would fit the present description of an *ergon* as an end beyond, and hence superior to, the action. Of course, that raises a question of why the activity exemplified by sculpting would be designated an "action" (*praxis*) and not, as one would expect, a "production" (*poiēsis*). The *ergon*, in any case, that Chapter 7 postulates as distinctive of the human being is itself an *energeia* of the soul, not a product to which an *energeia* would be subordinate (1098a13). How the *ergon* and *energeia* together determine the good for a human being will be suggested by their application to the relation of ethical virtue and intellectual virtue; but that will not be made explicit until the discussion of virtue as a whole is completed, at the end of Book VI (see 1144a5–7).

Leaving us for the moment in the dark about the point of the formal division of ends into *erga* and *energeiai*, the argument turns abruptly to a different basis for the division of ends and the problem of their unification. The plurality of "actions, arts, and sciences" entails a corresponding plurality of ends—health for medicine, ships for shipbuilding, victory for the military art, wealth for economics (1094a6–9); how, then, could there be a single unifying end? There is some ordered whole, Aristotle proposes, whenever several arts fall under a single "capacity," so that the ends of the architectonic arts are more choiceworthy than those of the subordinate arts. But the example offered—bridle making subordinated to horsemanship and that, in turn, to military strategy—might make us suspicious about the principle it is supposed to illustrate. While bridle making can be understood to be in itself for the sake of horseback riding, horseback riding is not necessarily subservient to military strategy. Doesn't the general's use of cavalry simply impose an end on an activity that by its nature could just as well be practiced for farming or racing, or just enjoyed for its own sake?[5]

A hierarchy has been proposed, however problematic, on the basis of an ordering of the arts and their ends, but it is without any explicit connection to the good. What brings us back to that final end is the consideration, in

Chapter 2 of Book I, of the structure of desire: *if* there is some end among actions that we want for its own sake and everything else because of this, and we don't choose everything because of something else,[6] it is clear that this end would be "the good and the best" (1094a18–22). Aristotle does not confirm the existence of such a final end, only the consequences that would follow from its absence: the chain of one choice for the sake of another would proceed to the infinite (*eis apeiron*), leaving all desire empty and in vain (*mataian*) (1094a20–21).[7] There is, apparently, no possibility of partial satisfaction in the fulfillment of any individual links in this chain; the restlessness of desire after desire without the closure of a final end supposedly makes every step meaningless. Aristotle still has not confirmed the existence of such a final end when he continues, hypothetically, with a question: wouldn't recognition (*gnōsis*) of it be the decisive thing in life, like a target at which archers could aim?[8]

If knowledge of the good is so decisive—the question of whether it exists has been bracketed—an effort should be made to grasp what it is in outline (1094a25–26): it is still only in outline at the end of the last book of the *Ethics* (1171a31).[9] But the "what it is" question quickly turns into another, which ties the hypothesized structure of desire back to the hierarchical division of knowledge: to what science (*epistēmē*) or capacity (*dunamis*) does the good belong? Presumably, it is the object of the most sovereign and architectonic, Aristotle reasons, and that appears to be *politikē*—either political science or a capacity for politics or both. *Politikē*, after all, lays down laws about what sciences are to exist in cities and what citizens are to study them. Besides that, it commands such honorable capacities as military strategy, economics, and rhetoric; hence, its end should encompass those of the others (1094a26–b6). Of course, it may do so only in the way the general's end contains that of horseback riding when he commands his cavalry for the purpose of achieving victory. *Politikē*, in its sovereign role, puts to use all the other arts in the city for its own purposes, without necessarily fulfilling the ends that might belong to those arts on their own. While determining the uses of all the subordinate arts, *politikē* at the same time imposes boundaries on them. It looks, as a result, like the political counterpart to Socrates' discovery of the partial character of every art, which no artisan could recognize from within the horizon of his art and which, consequently, led Socrates to realize the superiority of his own knowledge of ignorance. *Politikē*, in supervising a division of labor that regards every art as partial and binds them into a whole, is the city's replacement for philosophy.[10]

In its implicit claim to completeness, the city has made the structure of ends into a whole with its own end as the final and comprehensive one; it is in the course of this development that *the* good is replaced by the human good (1094b7).[11] As soon as it emerges as the defining end of *politikē*, however, the human good undergoes a split: while it may be the same for the individual and the city, its attainment and preservation for the city appears greater and more complete—acceptable even for a single person but more beautiful and divine for peoples and cities (1094b7–10). Aristotle does not defend the truth of this appearance. If the human good is a single end and if the good for the individual, as the conclusion of the *Ethics* will argue, lies in the activity of *theōria*, one must wonder how that activity could be "writ large" in the city, except perhaps as a metaphor.[12]

The establishment of the human good as its end determines the identity of the inquiry as a particular way of proceeding: "The *methodos*, then, aims at these, being some sort of political art (*politikē tis*)" (1094b10–11). The qualification—only "some sort," not *politikē* strictly—might seem intended to characterize the *Ethics*, in its concern with the good for the individual, over against the *Politics*, in its concern with the good for the city; but if the *methodos* aims at "these," that should mean the human good in its double form. *Politikē* without qualification, then, looks like it must be political practice or statesmanship, and "some sort of *politikē*" the art or science that comprehends the *Ethics* and the *Politics:* the one work, after all, is not engaged in laying down laws for the city any more than the other is in morally habituating individuals. Yet the purpose of the inquiry, Aristotle is about to insist, is not knowledge but action—or, at least, knowledge rendered useful because of its connection to action. "Some sort of *politikē*" cannot fulfill its aim through mere speeches any more than political practice can, even if the deeds required for each are not the same.

Methodos *and Audience*

Once the aim of the inquiry has been established, the path (*methodos*) it follows must meet the fitting degree of precision. Now, that aim is the human good, but the subject matter to be investigated is "the beautiful and the just things," about which opinions are at great variance (1094b14–16). Even if those opinions were consistent among one people in one epoch, they differ vastly from one place and time to another: one tribe deems it beautiful to bury their dead, another to burn them; different regimes might agree that justice requires unequal distributions to those who are unequal, but they disagree vehemently about what sort of inequality counts.[13] This "wandering," as Aristotle puts it, leads to the thought that the beautiful and the just things are such only by convention and not at all by nature (1094b14–16). The good things, too, are wandering, but in a very different way. Something may be good only for a particular subject in particular circumstances, and something good in itself can on occasion prove harmful; but though relative to a subject, the good things under certain conditions are indeed beneficial, and not just as a matter of opinion. It is not said of the good things, as it is of the beautiful and the just things, that they are so only by convention.[14]

What should be expected from this inquiry, given its wandering subject matter, is nothing more than the truth in outline (*tupō*): to demand more would lead to disappointment, which could threaten confidence in the power of reason altogether.[15] The proper expectation, in turn, determines the appropriate audience for this investigation. This is the first indication— it will not be the last—that the *Ethics* is not a treatise that can or must say the same thing to whoever takes it up. Aristotle's identification of his intended audience begins with a rather surprising restriction: young people are unfit for the study of the political things. Now, we might readily agree that politics, unlike mathematics, for example, is rarely if ever a field for child prodigies; but if the project is motivated by conflicting notions of the beautiful and just things, with the aim of discovering the good that should be our end in life, isn't it the young, above all, who stand in most urgent need of such an investigation? That is certainly what almost every Socratic conversation indicates; of course, it was, as Aristotle knows, the charge of corrupting the youth that brought Socrates to his trial and death.[16]

Aristotle justifies his exclusion of the youth on two grounds, both concerning the relation between speeches and deeds. The inquiry in "outline" amounts to mere speeches until it is filled in by "actions in accordance with life," but that is something the young are lacking. The participant in this project must have experienced enough of life to have put into question the fixity of the moral education with which he was brought up; but again, it would seem to be not children, admittedly, but young people who are most passionately undergoing just that kind of experience. It is, however, not just the experience in action one brings to these speeches that is required but a readiness to apply them in turn to action; hence, the young, who tend be led by their feelings, would listen in vain to speeches intended to guide action (1095a2–6).[17]

With this end in mind, Aristotle acknowledges finally that it is not merely, or not essentially, those young in years who pose the problem but any who live in accordance with passion rather than *logos*. The paradigm case would be the individual lacking self-restraint, whose actions are not guided by the *logos* he in some way possesses. The psychological problem that will bring Aristotle's debate with Socrates to a head in Book VII is thus present from the outset, in the question of the audience of the inquiry. Its fitting participants are determined by the purpose of the inquiry, which is not the acquisition of knowledge (*gnōsis*) but action (*praxis*); or, rather—(Aristotle restates the point with an almost unnoticeable but important change)—the knowledge this inquiry does indeed furnish is unprofitable apart from action (cf. 1095a5–6, 8–11). This apparently sensible claim begins to look more problematic as the *Ethics* unfolds and one realizes how little discussion there is of actions in any ordinary sense: it could hardly have a title like *Making Moral Decisions*. What exactly are the actions, we have to wonder, that would keep its speeches from being in vain?

The appropriate audience has been laid down sufficiently, Aristotle announces, although he is about to return to it with a supplement or revision, but only after the argument begins once again: since all knowledge (*gnōsis*) and choice (*prohairesis*) strive for some good, one should consider what the end is in the case of *politikē*. That end, which we thought was settled on as the human good, now becomes "the peak of all practical goods," which nearly everyone calls "happiness" (*eudaimonia*) (1095a14–19). They mean by that "doing well and faring well"—the convenient Greek *euprattein* has both senses at once; but there is the greatest dispute about what it consists in, especially between the many and the wise. The many—we hear nothing about the wise—take happiness to be something obvious, like pleasure or wealth or honor, though they disagree not only with each other but even with themselves at different times, always imagining the end relative to some perceived deficiency: for the sick, it seems to be health; for the poor, wealth; and for those who recognize their own ignorance, it is anything that sounds grand. Aristotle mentions the idea of some good by itself that is the cause of all good things being such (1095a25–28). Of course, this sort of grand-sounding idea might impress someone trying to hide, even from himself, the ignorance he senses in himself; but it would presumably be a question, not a doctrine to be admired, for someone whose knowledge of ignorance motivated a desire to know.

Having introduced the idea of the good, Aristotle turns to Plato, although not to identify him as the proponent of such an idea, but to praise him for being "well perplexed" about whether the proper way of proceeding is to begin from or lead to the principles, like running from the judges at the racetrack or to them (1095a30–b1).[18] It goes without saying, Aristotle grants, that we must begin from things well-known; but what is knowable simply is not necessarily what is well-known for us, although that must perhaps be sufficient as a starting point for us. Faced with the sophistic attack that denies the possibility of even getting started in inquiry, Socrates tries to encourage Meno by presenting a "doctrine of recollection." Aristotle offers a more sober proposal, though he says nothing at the moment about how we become aware of the need to move beyond the things more known by us, how we do move in that direction, or how we would recognize the things knowable simply if we did arrive at them.[19]

Aristotle's proposal about how inquiry should begin leads, in any case, to a new characterization of his intended audience: in order to listen sufficiently to speeches about the beautiful and just things and the political things generally, one must be beautifully habituated, for the starting point is "the that" (1095b4–6). To get anything from the *Ethics*, one might conclude, it is necessary to be familiar with the world it assumes as its starting point. Now, perhaps few of us today would recognize ourselves in the world of Aristotle's gentleman, as Churchill presumably did;[20] but would that really make the *Ethics* a closed book for us? Couldn't we begin, precisely under the guidance of the *Ethics*, from a "that" reconstructed to fit our own familiar world?[21] To begin from "the that" is to set out by examining the shadows on the walls of the cave as we know it; the *Ethics* provides a guide for examining those shadows, even in their variant forms.

Whatever the content of "the that" from which inquiry can begin, if it is sufficiently manifest, Aristotle goes on, there would be no need to look for "the why." If we have satisfied the conditions required to participate in this project, we have no need to pursue it; and if we do need to pursue it, we wouldn't have what is required to do so.[22] With this comically paradoxical invitation to a prospective audience that cannot exist, Aristotle compels us to rethink the purpose of the inquiry: must it not be of the greatest need, and therefore of the greatest worth, for someone who is not satisfied with "the that" of his moral education and is seeking "the why"? In doing so, he would be trying to understand what makes the beautiful and the just things good.[23] If the inquiry is meant to appeal to, or even arouse, desire for "the why," it must be prepared to bring to light the limitations, partial perspectives, or internal contradictions of the opinions assumed at the beginning—while trying to disturb as little as possible those satisfied with that starting point.[24]

Aristotle confirms the complexity of his intended audience by concluding his description with a quotation from Hesiod's *Works and Days:*

> He is the best of all who thinks out everything for himself,
> while he too is worthy who is persuaded by another speaking well;
> but he who neither thinks for himself nor takes to heart
> what he hears from another is a worthless man.
>
> (1095b10–13)[25]

There is a class structure of human beings, only it is not based on gender or race or wealth but on how one comes to understand. This is a distinction among different natures that shows up in different ways of listening, or reading. Hesiod's contrast between the person who relies on his own reasoning and one who accepts the well-spoken words of another articulates the divergent soul types to which the same speeches of the *Ethics* will be differently adjusted. The multilayered audience Aristotle articulates reflects, as the last chapter of Book I will indicate, a duality in the structure of the human soul, between self-initiating reason and the capacity for obedience to reason. Even Hesiod's third category, he who neither thinks for himself nor listens to another, will not be entirely forgotten: the very last chapter of the *Ethics,* which serves as a transition to the *Politics,* will insist that, for some, neither the force of reasoning nor the persuasion of beautiful speeches is sufficient but only the compulsion of law.

Opinions about Happiness

The Contest of Lives

After determining the fitting audience for the inquiry and its class division, Aristotle returns to an examination of the most prominent opinions about happiness. Now "the many and the most vulgar" are distinguished from—and seem to receive their designation from the perspective of—"the refined and active" (1095b16, 1095b22–23): the one sort embraces the life of enjoyment and identifies the good with pleasure; the other thinks of the political life as best for a human being and looks to honor as its end. A "theoretical life"—not "the philosophical life"—is mentioned, without any indication of what the good is toward which it is directed. Echoing the legendary Pythagorean contest among three lives, the discussion sounds so familiar that no question is raised about what exactly it means to speak of happiness belonging to a "life of something" and how that life is related to the good that constitutes its final end, although this question has important consequences for the argument of the *Ethics* as a whole.[26]

The life of enjoyment, which finds the human good in pleasure, is rejected with nothing but the disdainful remark that the many appear utterly slavish in choosing a life fit for cows. Behind this disdain lies the unexamined assumption that all pleasure is of one sort—the sort humans share with other animals—with no consideration of the various activities that can be a source of pleasure for human beings, or of the difficult problem of how pleasure is related to those sources. The steps required in the course of the *Ethics* to correct this starting point are, perhaps, the most prominent signposts of the movement of the argument of the work as a whole: most obviously, the concluding analysis of pleasure will criticize just the sort of unqualified rejection now being expressed (1172a28–b7).

In contrast to the private pleasure sought in the life of enjoyment, the end to which the political life is devoted, one might have expected, is the good for the city. But the question now at stake concerns the good for the individual who lives this life—and that is assumed to be honor. Honor, however, is thought to depend on those who bestow it, whereas the good is "divined" to be something proper to its possessor. The problem is especially egregious if those who consider themselves superior depend on honor from the many, whom they take to be living lives no better than cattle. This critique of honor as an end will be developed in the course of the examination of the ethical virtues, beginning with the description of political courage and culminating in the figure of the great-souled person. For now, the argument moves on to claim that it is not simply honor that people really desire but recognition of their worthiness. Hence the end of the political life might be thought to be virtue; of course, the end that has really been implied is a reputation for vir-

tue. Awaiting an objection of great importance, if virtue too is to be eliminated as a candidate for the human good, we are told only that it appears too
incomplete, or lacking in finality; it is possible, after all, to have a virtuous
disposition while asleep, or without being put into practice, or in the midst
of suffering great misfortune, which no one would call a happy life. It is not
obvious why this is an objection specifically applicable to virtue, though perhaps it is particularly important to confront the potentially powerful idea
that virtue is all that is required for happiness. Book I will soon return to the
question whether there is anything so sufficient that it guarantees happiness
even in the face of great misfortune.

Without clarifying the standard of completeness and finality, by which
virtue has been rejected as the end defining the best life, Aristotle turns to a
third possibility, the theoretical life, only to defer its assessment for later. We
will not get back to the theoretical life until the conclusion of the last book, $Bk\ 10$
with the surprising claim that its status as complete or perfect happiness has
been established before (1177a18). We wait until the end of the *Ethics* to fill in
what is missing from the current survey of opinion, and when we get there
we are told that it has been stated already—a statement readers have long
tried to identify.[27]

For the moment, consideration of the theoretical life is replaced by another possibility—the life of moneymaking (*chrēmatistēs*)—which seems to
be an unannounced fourth candidate, after the initial reference to the three
prominent lives. Moneymaking would not constitute another way of life altogether unless pursued as an end in itself; but wealth, it is assumed without
further argument, is properly understood only as a means. It is a necessary
condition, on some scale, for pursuing any of the lives under consideration,
though it might be thought to belong especially to the life of pleasure,[28]
which is taken seriously, Aristotle noted, only because it is sought by the
powerful and wealthy. But the very argument marshaled against wealth,
as essentially instrumental, could be turned into a defense of the claim of
pleasure to be the good. In fact, when that possibility is finally considered,
pleasure turns out to have a connection with theoretical activity that the
current survey of opinion has precluded.[29]

The examination of the foremost contenders to the title of the best
human life has eliminated all but one, and that one has been left in question. Pleasure is rejected as a final end on the assumption that it is all of one
sort, which makes the many *appear* slavish in choosing a life common to all

animals; honor is rejected because it is *thought* to depend on others, while we have *divined* that the good should be self-sufficient; and virtue *appears* inadequate because it is *thought* possible to have it in a state no one would *call* happy. The standards for whatever constitutes happiness have been distilled from the examination of opinion, which they are supposed to govern. The test Aristotle is conducting, like that of Socratic refutation, is for the coherence of ordinary opinion; and what he has discovered thus far is that the most common candidates for the referent of *eudaimonia* cannot live up to the criteria for *eudaimonia* that opinion already contains within itself.

The Idea *of the* Good

After putting off the investigation (*episkepsis*) of the theoretical life (1096a4–5), Aristotle suggests that it may be better to investigate (*episkepsasthai*) "the universal" and to become "thoroughly perplexed" (*diaporēsai*) about it (1096a11–12): with a Platonic formula, Aristotle introduces what is presumably his critique of a Platonic theory.[30] The investigation, he admits, goes against the grain of his friendship for those who "imported the forms," but he absolves himself before proceeding:

> It might be thought better, perhaps, and necessary to sacrifice the things of one's own with a view to preservation of the truth, especially being a philosopher; for while both of the pair are dear (*philoin*), it is holy to honor the truth in preference. (1096a14–17)

Friendship makes its first appearance in the *Ethics* here and with it, also for the first time, the philosopher along with truth.[31] The ideal behavior of the philosopher is holy, but the divinity he worships is the truth, which saves him from worshipping another human being.[32] Aristotle acknowledges here a conflict the philosopher faces between his devotion to "the things of one's own" and to the truth. This seems to mean that it may be necessary to give up allegiance to a friend with whom one disagrees in favor of the truth; but "the things of one's own" that might have to be sacrificed could refer instead to one's own opinion, whose inadequacy could be uncovered precisely through dialogue with a friend. While presumably describing the tension between friendship and truth, Aristotle speaks of them in the dual voice, as a bonded pair, both of which are dear, or a friend (*philoin*), to the *philo-sophos*, whose own name identifies him as a "friend of wisdom." This conjunction of friendship and philosophy will reappear at the end of the ninth book (1172a5), where it raises a question in advance about the final identification of perfect happiness with the essentially solitary activity of contemplation.

Aristotle conducts a critique of "the theory of ideas" without ever naming Plato, whom he had praised shortly before for his perplexity about how inquiry should proceed. The condensed and abstract investigation that follows, which certainly does not start from what is more known by us, could be seen as an almost comic illustration of why no Platonic dialogue represents two philosophers on an equal level.[33] The reader who is not satisfied with the discussion but is motivated to pursue the questions it raises would be led beyond the borders of political science; for all the perplexities in the notion of a universal good are shared by being as such. The good, like being, is "said in many ways"—dispersed among all the categories, in a hierarchical plurality that no single sense could comprehend. The division of sciences, furthermore, is based as much on the distinctive goods toward which each is directed as on the particular kind of being it carves off as its subject matter. The fragmentation of human knowledge, like the structure of speech, furnishes as much evidence against the unity of the good as against the unity of being, yet that fragmentation does not, apparently, prevent the search for a science of being as such.

Perhaps, Aristotle reasons, the intention of the theory is to collect in one class (*eidos*) all things pursued for their own sake, while anything else would have to be called "good" in some other sense. But is the good in the strict sense, then, constituted by the class of all things sought for themselves— such as prudence and sight and certain pleasures and honors? Or is there nothing good in itself except the *idea*? In that case, the class (*eidos*) of all intrinsically desirable things would be in vain (1096b20). This consequence echoes the earlier argument about the structure of desire, but there it was in the absence of a single final end that an infinite chain of desires would be in vain (1094a20–21), while now it is the *idea* of the good as such a final end that would make a class of intrinsic goods in vain.[34] While there is in fact, Aristotle maintains, no common notion of all things good in themselves, there may be one good from which all are derived, or perhaps they are connected analogically: the example he proposes—as sight (is good) in the body, so mind (*nous*) in the soul—will turn into a metaphor central to the search in the *Ethics* for the human good.[35]

However one tries to untie these ontological knots, a separate *idea*, Aristotle insists, would never be the practical good for a human being, which is what the present inquiry is seeking. Of course, he concedes, this *idea* might be thought to provide a pattern by which we can know the good things for us; he had already acknowledged the value of having such a target at which to aim (1094a22–24). But how, Aristotle now asks, would knowledge of the good itself, as a universal idea, help a weaver or a carpenter or a doctor or a general (1097a8–11)?[36] It looks, however, as if the same question could be raised about the *human* good, which is supposed to be the goal of the inquiry in the *Ethics*. Aristotle seems to invite that inference when he pushes his point by adding that the doctor does not even study health as a good for human beings generally, but only for the individual. Of course, it is his theoretical knowledge of health in general—or, at least, human health—that enables the doctor to carry out the practical task of healing the individual. And we would not be engaged in this inquiry at all if the same thing weren't true of the human good and its role in guiding our lives.[37]

THE STANDARD:

Finality and Self-Sufficiency

With the rejection of the universal *idea* of the good, we have returned to a plurality of "actions and arts," each directed toward its own particular end, but with this difference: the end we are trying to discover is now recognized as essentially a problem—"the sought-for good, whatever in the world it might be" (1097a15). If there were a single end of all our actions, Aristotle reasons now, this would be "the practical good." This qualification first appeared in identifying the end of *politikē* as "the peak of all practical goods" (1095a16–17), and it was followed by the deferral of "the theoretical life" as a candidate for happiness (1096a4–5); but now that the practical good has been designated "the sought-for good," we might infer that the *praxis* essentially tied to it is the action of seeking. If, however, there were no such single end but only the plurality of ends of our various actions, all those, Aristotle concedes, would be the good we are seeking, and the argument is brought back to its starting point (1097a24). No further progress can be made without discovering a hierarchical order of ends, which requires some standard. Aristotle discovers one in a quality that seems to belong almost by definition to the good—it *appears* to be something final (*teleios*), that is, chosen for its own sake. And that, in turn, entails another criterion—the final end is *thought* to be self-sufficient (*autarkes*) (1097a28, 1097b7–8).

The argument had arrived at an impasse in its search for a single final end when it was granted that if there were more than one end of our actions, all of them together would constitute the practical good (1097a22–24). Once finality is accepted, however, as a criterion of the good, and a different conclusion is drawn: if there were only one final end, that would be what we are seeking, while if there were more than one, it would be "the most final of those" (*teleiotaton*) (1097a28–30). Being *teleios* is to be understood, apparently, as a matter of degree. While some ends are only instrumental, it is possible for something to be chosen both in virtue of itself (*kath' auto*) as well as because of something else: while painful medical treatment is choiceworthy only as a means, health is desirable in virtue of itself and at the same time because of the good life to which it contributes. Any end chosen in virtue of itself is "more final" than one chosen because of something else, but only one that is never chosen because of something else is unqualifiedly final. That standard ushers *eudaimonia* back into the discussion as the only thing that meets the demand.

Happiness could not be simply identical with the good for a human being or there would be no need to have to establish that it meets the criteria entailed by the logic of the good.[38] The argument of the *Ethics* had identified its aim, by the end of Chapter 2, as the human good. *Eudaimonia* was first introduced, in Chapter 4, as the name agreed on by "nearly the greatest number" for that which is the peak of all practical goods, on the assumption that to be happy is the same as to live well and to do or fare well (*euprattein*, 1095a17–20). *Eudaimonia* then reappeared together with the good as the subject of examination in Chapter 5, where competing ways of life were each defined by a single end: while the good is the *telos*—pleasure or honor or wealth—*eudaimonia* belongs to the life as a whole. Another understanding of the good—the *idea* as a universal—was taken up in Chapter 6, before Chapter 7 returned to the "sought-for good," and only at this point, in looking for that which is unqualifiedly final, is *eudaimonia* reintroduced. Happiness is the one thing we always choose because of itself and never because of something other, while other ends that are desirable because of themselves—like honor, pleasure, mind, or virtue—we also choose for the sake of happiness (1097b1–6). We desire such goods in the belief they will make us happy, but happiness is the one thing we cannot desire for anything other than itself. It is unintelligible to ask for what further end we want *eudaimonia* while *eudaimonia* seems to be the answer to that question for everything else.

The same conclusion appears to follow from the consideration of self-sufficiency (*autarkeia*), which is a characteristic *thought* to belong to the final good (1097b8–9). Self-sufficiency, we are immediately warned, does not mean a solitary life, since the human being is by nature political. Our lives as individuals are bound up with those of family, friends, fellow citizens, . . . ; of course, some limit must be set, or such relations would proceed to infinity (*eis apeiron*, 1097b13)—like the chain of desires in the absence of a final end (cf. 1094a20). Aristotle implies a certain limit when he stops with fellow citizens;[39] but whatever it is for the political community to be self-sufficient, that could not be the *autarkeia* now defined as the characteristic of an activity that by itself makes life choiceworthy and lacking nothing. *Eudaimonia* meets the test of that standard because it is a condition that could not become better by the addition of any other good (1097b16–20).[40]

The interpretation of the criteria laid down for *eudaimonia* has been one, if not the, primary focus of contemporary debate about the teaching of the *Ethics*. This debate is set in motion by the observation that "in speaking of the good for man Aristotle hesitates between an inclusive and an exclusive formulation."[41] Do the standards of finality and self-sufficiency imply a conception of *eudaimonia* as incorporating a plurality of ends or as a single highest end? To explain why happiness is thought to be simply final, Aristotle argued that every other end we desire because of itself—like honor or pleasure or mind or virtue—we also choose for the sake of happiness; happiness itself, however, has not been identified with any other single end for which everything else is chosen. *Eudaimonia*, some have inferred, if it is the only thing that is simply final, must be so because of its inclusiveness, and the whole set of intrinsically choiceworthy ends, like those just referred to, would be not means to but constituents of it.[42] What would guarantee, however, that these intrinsically choiceworthy ends are compatible in one life? And if it is necessary for those ends to be not merely compatible but shaped in a hierarchically ordered whole, wouldn't that require their being directed toward a highest end internal to that whole, which would only push the problem back a step?

However *eudaimonia* as a final end is understood, its being *teleion* is supposed to entail its self-sufficiency, and that criterion seems to provide the strongest support for an inclusive conception of happiness: how could any single activity be capable all by itself of making a human life complete? If, as most readers agree, the activity of *theōria* as presented at the conclusion of Book X exemplifies an exclusive conception of happiness,[43] it is hard to understand how *eudaimonia* so construed could be thought to be lacking in nothing or to be such that nothing could be added to it to make it better. But if it is an inclusive conception of *eudaimonia* that meets the standard of self-sufficiency, what kind of life would exemplify it? If ethical virtue and *theōria* each prove to be determined by an end that cannot serve as a means to the other, how could they be directed to an inclusive final end in a single life while remaining what they are in themselves?

The problem of an inclusive or exclusive interpretation of the criteria for *eudaimonia* will soon reappear in the *ergon* argument, which defines the human good in connection with the virtue that is most *teleia* (1098a16–18)— either the most comprehensive or the highest excellence. It will come to a head when Book X brings the argument to a close with the claim that *theōria* is the single *energeia* that counts as *eudaimonia* in the primary sense. Does the characterization of *eudaimonia* in Book I as final and self-sufficient prepare for the thesis of Book X or put it into question from the outset? Is that thesis anticipated by the account of the human *ergon* as an *energeia* in accordance with virtue that is *teleiotatē*, meaning "most perfect"? Or does the thesis of Book X about *eudaimonia* conflict with the account of the human *ergon* if the virtue that is *teleiotatē* means "most complete"?[44] The reasoning offered in support of various positions in this debate provides evidence for the ambiguity of Book I's account of happiness and the human good; it does not follow, of course, that this is a result of confusion on Aristotle's part or an unintended failure to clarify his thought.[45] It is in fact precisely the ambiguity of the account in Book I that allows, or requires, the argument of the *Ethics* to follow the indirect route it takes through an investigation of virtue, followed by an examination of pleasure and friendship, before it returns to the question of human happiness.

The problems introduced by the discussion of *eudaimonia* have arisen, in any event, not from an Aristotelian doctrine but from an examination of opinion: Why should happiness more than anything else be *thought to be* simply final? And why should the final good be *thought to be* self-sufficient so that happiness would *appear* to have that status? Rather than clearly endorsing these criteria, Aristotle has pointed to what at least in part motivates them. In the finality ascribed to it, happiness would be that which puts an end to one desire for the sake of another; in its self-sufficiency, it would put an end to the possibility that life could always be better with some other good added to it. The issue in the one case concerns the relation of means and end, in the other the relation of part and whole, but in both the demand for some kind of closure that would preclude an endless series. Finality and self-sufficiency seem to be the criteria for happiness that opinion holds up in the face of this double threat, or what is perceived as a threat, of the infinite.

The argument is about to take a further step when Aristotle comes forward with a proposal of his own in an attempt to attain greater clarity about happiness as a final and self-sufficient end. Yet the analysis that follows leads to a definition not, strictly speaking, of happiness but of the human good; the standard of self-sufficiency is never invoked, and the feature of being *teleios* is applied not to the human good but, on the one hand, to the virtue that accompanies it and, on the other, to the life characterized by it. The human good, as this argument will define it, is an *energeia*, an activity or condition of being-at-work, that cannot be measured over time; only after the human good has been defined does happiness come back into consideration, bringing with it the requirement for the completeness of a lifetime.

The Human Good and the Human *Ergon*

Happiness has been found to meet the criteria of finality and self-sufficiency, but that only arouses "a longing for something more manifest to be said about what it is" (1097b24).[46] To satisfy this longing, Aristotle suggests a consideration of the human *ergon*, a work or function distinctive to the human being as such; for in the case of any subject with an *ergon*, like a flute player or a sculptor, "the good and the well" are thought to lie in that *ergon* (1097b25–28).[47] If a subject is defined by a particular job to be done, it may be clear enough what it means to do it well; but is doing it well necessarily the good for the one who performs it?[48] If the shoemaker performs his task well, the beneficiary would be the one who uses his service, being in need of shoes.[49] Of course, one might say that doing his job well is the good for the shoemaker not as a human being, with needs to be fulfilled, but the good for him as an artisan, who thereby realizes what he is qua shoemaker. Is there, then, an equivalent for the human being as human? If there were, in this one case there would be a convergence of the good for the individual as defined by his functional role and the good for him in fulfilling his need as a human being.

Aristotle raises the question of what such an *ergon* would be without demonstrating that there is one, relying instead on two "rhetorical questions":

Are there, then, certain *erga* and actions of carpenter and shoemaker but none of the human being, who is naturally idle [*argon*]? Or just as there appears to be some *ergon* of eye and hand and foot and generally each of the parts, should one thusly posit also some *ergon* of the human being beyond all those? Whatever, then, would this be? (1097b22–33)

The model is a twofold one—the arts in the city and the organs of the body. While the *ergon* of the eye is nothing but the actualization of its natural capacity, the artisan produces an *ergon* that is, according to the opening argument of Chapter 1, an end beyond the action that brings it into being. Aristotle provides two models without explicitly differentiating them or asking which furnishes the proper model for the human *ergon*.

What both models share, in any case, is a structure of whole and parts. A division of labor, either social or biological, assigns to each subject a defining job, which, if done well, allows for the flourishing of the whole to which that subject belongs: when the shoemaker does his job well, it benefits the community of which he is a part; when the eye does its job well, it benefits the whole body of which it is a part, or the individual whose body is doing its work well. The human being, accordingly, would have a distinctive *ergon* if it belonged as a part to a greater whole for which it was assigned a unique purpose; and when the human being did his job well, that whole would flourish. The whole in question cannot be the city, because its division of labor assigns a role to each individual as artisan or citizen, not as human being. If, on the other hand, the division of labor were a natural one, the whole would presumably have to be the cosmos or, more precisely—as Aristotle soon implies by separating human from plant and animal—whatever is alive in it. With the *ergon* argument, in that case, Aristotle would be attempting to fulfill the Anaxagorean promise, as Socrates interpreted it, of a teleological cosmology: the whole ordered by mind looking to the good would provide the necessary support for a human function.[50] Aristotle does proceed to inquire about the activity that appears to be unique to the human, as opposed to other natural beings; he never states, let alone defends, the premise that there is a whole of "life" to the good of which the human species makes a unique contribution. Our question, in any case, concerned the good for the individual human being, not for the city or the cosmic whole of which human life may be a part.

Whatever the whole may be to which it belongs, the distinctive human *ergon* is to be discovered by stripping away the functions human beings share with other forms of life. Nutrition and growth appear to be common to all living things, including plants, while sentience appears common to all animals;[51] what remains—Aristotle offers no proof for the exhaustiveness of the alternatives—is "some practice (*praktikē*) of that which has *logos*" (1097b33–1098a4). The formula seems to highlight some function of practical reason in particular: though reason as such separates human beings from plants and animals, the exercise of theoretical reason might not be unique to human beings. The argument goes on to acknowledge a twofold sense of "having *logos*"—not, however, as practical and theoretical but as that which is merely obedient to reason in contrast with that which initiates the exercise of reason, and in the sovereign sense that should mean not just as a potential but the exercise of reason in *energeia*. The conclusion can now be drawn that the human *ergon* is itself an *energeia* of the soul in accordance with *logos,* or at least not without it (1098a7–8). That last, apparently slight, qualification would, of course, expand significantly the range of activities that could meet the standard.[52] The *energeia* of soul is an activity expressing our rational nature, but Aristotle has gone out of his way to characterize what it is to be rational in two ways: self-initiating reason and obedience to reason in another source. That twofold characterization echoes the two human types in the citation from Hesiod by which Aristotle described his intended audience (1095b10–11); it will be supported by the soul structure presented at the close of Book I, which locates the capacity for obedience to *logos* in the desiring part of the soul, separated from that which has *logos* in itself.

Aristotle proceeds to draw the consequences about the human good that follow from the postulation of the human *ergon,* but only hypothetically, resting on a series of unconfirmed conditions:[53]

(1) If the *ergon* of a human being is an *energeia* of the soul in accordance with *logos,* or at least not without *logos;*

(2) and we say that the *ergon* of a member of a genus and that of a serious one [*spoudaios*] are the same (like a cithara player and a serious

cithara player), adding the superiority in accordance with excellence to the *ergon* (to playing the cithara, playing it well);

(3) if this is so, and we lay it down that the *ergon* of the human being is some kind of life [*zoē*] and that is an *energeia* of the soul and actions with *logos*,

(4) and in the case of the serious man, doing this well and beautifully, each thing accomplishing something well in accordance with its proper excellence;

(5) if this is so, the human good becomes an *energeia* of the soul in accordance with excellence [*aretē*];

(6) and if more than one excellence, in accordance with the best and most perfect or complete [*teleios*].

(7) And, furthermore, in a complete lifetime [*en biō teleiō*]—for one swallow doesn't make a spring, nor one day make a man blessed and happy. (1098a7–20)

The claim that the *ergon* of the human being is an *energeia* of the *psychē* raises one question immediately: why the abstraction of soul from the living being as a whole? [54] If, in any event, the human *ergon* is itself an *energeia*, it cannot be the external product of an action (which, according to the opening argument of the *Ethics*, would be superior to the *energeia* of the action in itself): the human *ergon* must be much closer to what sight is for the eye than to the work the artisan performs to produce an artifact. The initial characterization of this *ergon* is at first minimal—an activity "at least not without *logos*." But a higher, more demanding standard is immediately introduced: to know what the *ergon* is that defines any member of a class, one should see it performed at its best by the exemplary member of that class. Virtue, which consists in aiming at a mean, is itself preeminence or superiority (*hyperochē*) in performance of the *ergon*. Once one takes one's bearings from that standard, of course, it threatens to eliminate all inferior instances as members of the class at all: if Aristotle exemplifies what it is for a human being to have *logos*, there will be few who really count as human beings. In this context, Aristotle refers to the exemplary member of the class as "the serious one" (*ho spoudaios*). This figure will be called upon repeatedly in the course of the inquiry as a "role model" (in the following chapter, for example, at 1099a22–24); of course, such an appeal to the authority of the *spoudaios* would presumably satisfy someone content with "the that," not someone searching for "the why."

The first two steps of the argument—(1) identifying the human *ergon* with a certain *energeia* of the soul, and (2) appealing to the exemplary subject who performs that *ergon* well—look as if they should suffice to arrive at the conclusion about the human good (5). It is far from obvious what necessitates the intervening steps, which begin by identifying the *ergon* as some form of life (*zoē*) (3). The *energeia*, then, must be the exercise of a natural capacity that defines what we are as living beings; but, at just this point, the *energeia* ceases to be the sole expression of the human *ergon* as a form of life. Instead, "actions with *logos*" are added to it (3), and with that addition the argument reverses its direction entirely. Instead of defining the superior human being as one who performs the single human *ergon* well, it derives what it is to perform well—and beautifully—from "the proper excellence" of the subject, "the serious man" (*ho spoudaios anēr*) (4). When the human good is at last defined as an *energeia* of the soul in accordance with *aretē* (5), excellence has become an independent standard and is no longer a mere adverbial modifier of the defining *ergon*—"doing it well." Of course, for an activity to be "in accordance with" virtue does not imply that it *is* virtue, or even that it flows from virtue—coincidence with what virtue requires could be sufficient. What it means for the human good to be an activity "in accordance with" virtue might depend, then, on what kind of virtue is being held up as a measure.

In opening up this question, the argument anticipates the debate Aristotle will conduct with Socrates. If the human *ergon* is "some practice (*praktikē*) of that which has *logos*," the distinctively human virtue would seem to be the perfection of practical reason, or the deliberative function of the soul, and that is prudence, or *phronēsis*. Instead, excellence is released from the unique human *ergon*, which opens up a plurality of virtues and, with that, the need to single out the "best and most *teleia*" (6). This is the decisive moment in the argument; it provokes the debate over the inclusive versus exclusive conception of happiness, for which "the most *teleia*" virtue is now a standard. If this qualification meant "most complete," the good for a human being would be an activity of the soul in accordance with the virtues of all its parts together, or at least all that share in any way in rationality. But since it was a plurality of virtues that made it necessary in the first place to identify the highest, "the best and most *teleia*" would seem to have to mean "the most perfect."[55] If the *ergon* defining the human species, however, is some kind of "practical rationality," its virtue should be prudence, and that will not prove to be the single highest excellence to which the human being can aspire.[56]

The difficulties raised by the ambiguity of "most *teleia* virtue"—most comprehensive or highest—are compounded by the abrupt attachment of one last requirement (7): happiness must be "in a *teleios* life (*bios*)." The human *ergon* was first identified as a certain form of life (*zoē*), but the argument arrives in the end at a different notion, of a lifetime (*bios*) in its span from birth to death, which could be "*teleios*" only in the sense of complete in time:[57] Aristotle soon explains the phrase by referring to the misfortunes of Priam before his death, which make it impossible to ascribe happiness to him (1100a5–9). The human good was found to be an *energeia*—an activity that must be complete at any moment of its existence and cannot be measured as a temporal extension;[58] it is the introduction of *eudaimonia* that brings with it the requirement for duration through time. According to the original twofold model for the argument, when the *ergon* that belongs to each part is performed well, it is good for the whole; and the whole to which the human being would make its unique contribution looked as if it would have to be the cosmos or, rather, what is alive in it. That cosmic whole will undergo a transformation, through a kind of synecdoche, by the end of Book I, when the whole divided into functionally different parts becomes the human soul. At the moment, however, it is the lifetime of an individual to which the requirement for completeness is being applied, but if that is the whole, its parts must be temporal ones—years, days, or moments—not uniquely differentiated functions. The *ergon* argument began with the search for a final end of human life, in the sense of a single unifying goal; it seems to have concluded, although nothing in the argument prepared for it, by looking to the end of life in the sense of its termination.

Aristotle warns that he has furnished only an outline (*tupos*), which needs to be filled in with time as our co-worker (*sunergon*). The task should set the appropriate degree of precision: a carpenter studies a right angle with only as much precision as is useful for his product (*ergon*), while a geometer does so as a "contemplator of the truth," looking for the "what it is" and "what sort." We should not allow digressions (*parerga*), therefore, to interfere with our deeds (*erga*) (1097a29–33). Our *ergon* at present is to consider the human *ergon* in our search for the human good. But if what we are doing is the equivalent to the carpenter's task, what is the equivalent to the geometer's?[59]

Whether we should, in fact, be satisfied with the carpenter's standard may depend on how we understand the measure of precision. We might readily grant that there will be no mathematical algorithm to fill in the outline of the human good. But Aristotle raises some doubts about the limits being set in making our task analogous to the carpenter's when he goes on to remind us that the subject matter should determine the appropriate demand for knowledge of cause, since sometimes "the that" suffices if it is beautifully established (1098b1–3): the reader who is satisfied with having reached an answer at this point is, once again, invited to close the book. The questions Aristotle seems to be discouraging are precisely the ones that would have to be addressed by the reader who is not satisfied with the "outline" provided thus far: What is an *energeia* of the *psychē*? Or, more fundamentally, what is an *energeia*? If it is the unique *ergon* of a human being, how can there be more than one perfection of it? In what way is it a form of life (*zoē*)? And how is that related to a lifetime (*bios*)? The outline of the good is a principle, or starting point (*archē*), that may contain "more than half the whole" (1098b7–8);[60] but it could shed light on the things being sought, as Aristotle now promises, only if the consequences unfolded from it can throw back their reflected light on it—like traveling back on the circular racecourse from the judges' position to the starting line (cf. 1095a32–b1).

Happiness in a Complete Life

As soon as he has completed the outline of the human good based on the postulation of a human *ergon,* Aristotle pulls us back from being satisfied with it. The conclusion is not to be trusted merely on the basis of the argument from which it is drawn; it must be brought back to the sphere of opinion and tested for its harmony with the things commonly said about such matters (1098b9–12). Through a masterful act of diplomacy, Aristotle proceeds to encompass his own proposal in a net so broad that all the opinions about happiness rejected before the introduction of the function argument are now restored and found perfectly compatible with it. He finds himself in agreement, in the first place, with the ancient opinion—shared by "those who philosophize" (1098b18)—ranking the class of goods of the soul above corporeal and external goods. Of the several candidates commonly proposed for the title of happiness—virtue, prudence, some sort of wisdom, one or all in combination with pleasure, or with external prosperity as a condition—none is incompatible with the proposed definition. Nor are these views assigned any longer to the "many and vulgar" over against "the more refined," but now to the "many from of old" and "the few distinguished ones," neither class of which is likely to be entirely mistaken. That the good is "in accordance with excellence" is close enough, Aristotle now maintains, to the claim that it *is* excellence or some virtue in particular—although, he confirms, as a mere disposition it would be incomplete. The proposed definition of the human good is supported, finally, by its connection with pleasure, which, in sharp contrast with its original treatment, is now admitted to be as versatile as the things by which one can be pleased—including, or especially, actions in accordance with virtue.

Aristotle summarizes the comprehensive status of his definition of happiness by attacking the inscription at Delos, which declares "Justice the most beautiful, and health the most welcome, but what one desires most pleasant." Happiness, Aristotle counters, is at once best and most beautiful and most pleasant (1099a24–28); that it should also be most just would, apparently, be demanding too much. Justice is problematic in part because *eudaimonia,* as Aristotle now admits, appears to need certain external goods, which are not necessarily distributed by desert. The human good may be simply an *energeia* of the soul, but *eudaimonia* cannot be reduced to that. For it is difficult, or impossible, Aristotle admits, to do the beautiful things without a sufficient "chorus," that is, instruments like friends, wealth, or power: for the performance of beautiful deeds, friends are as instrumental as wealth and power. Nor is blessedness attainable without certain advantages, like good birth, good children, or beauty (1099a31–b6). The test for harmony has gone further than one would ever have expected in reconciling Aristotle's definition of the human good with ordinary opinion, but the consequence is that happiness now appears to require a coincidence of excellence of character with good fortune that could never be guaranteed.

The admission of factors beyond our control brings in its wake the question of how happiness comes to be—whether by learning, habituation, some other kind of practice, some divine portion, or simply by chance (1099b9–11). Aristotle applies to happiness the question Meno addressed to Socrates about virtue, and his response echoes that of Socrates: if there is anything that is a gift from the gods to humans, it would be reasonable to think it is happiness.[61] Whatever the role of the gods may be—Aristotle puts off the question for another investigation—happiness appears to be one of the most divine things; and to leave the greatest and most beautiful of things to fortune would be contrary to the fitting (1099b24–25). But what evidence is there that reality adheres to the standard of what we find fitting?

To whatever extent *eudaimonia* depends on certain necessary conditions or requires "instruments," it is vulnerable to all the unpredictable turns of the wheel of fortune. This vulnerability seems to bear a special weight at the end of life, if only because there is no chance to recover from what might have otherwise been only a temporary phase of misery. The problem was anticipated with the demand for happiness in a "complete life" at the close of the *ergon* argument, though nothing in the account of the human good entailed such a requirement (1098a18–20). That demand is about to be pushed to such an extreme that it puts into question the possibility of considering any life a happy one. Yet it does seem true that even someone who lived a long time in great prosperity would not be said to have a good life if he fell into terrible misfortune before he died. Offering Priam as an example, Aristotle calls attention to how much this theme is at home in poetry, tragedy in particular; in doing so, he leads us to wonder if the requirement for a "complete life" is somehow imported from the standard of a poetic work, which aims to represent a "complete whole" by means of its plot, structured by the boundaries of beginning, middle, and end.[62] If Priam's life cannot be judged until the end of the story, and that is our model, does it mean no human being can be counted happy as long as he lives? Is it always necessary, as Solon's wisdom's has it, to "look to the end" (1100a10–11)?[63]

Aristotle is alluding to the story Herodotus recounts of Solon, the Athenian wise man and legislator, on his visit to the court of the tyrant Croesus in Sardis.[64] Showing off his vast wealth to his visitor, Croesus asks him who among human beings is the happiest he had ever seen. Solon responds by expressing his admiration for the life of an Athenian citizen, a family man who died fighting for his city. Pressed by Croesus for a second best, Solon tells a story meant to illustrate the divine judgment that the best thing for any human being is to be dead. Croesus raises no questions about the meaning of this story. His only response is to express indignation at Solon's utter disregard for his own splendid life, and the wise man goes on to warn him of just how fragile it is. Croesus may be flourishing at the moment, but the wheel of fortune makes the future altogether uncertain; indeed, no two days, among the many thousands of a normal human life span, bring the same conditions. Great prosperity, in particular, is utterly insecure, since it is bound to arouse divine jealousy: if it is not a matter of chance but of divine punishment, a precipitous fall from the heights of success is inevitable. Solon can say nothing at the moment, then, about the happiness of Croesus; to judge his life, or any human life, one must "look to the end." Croesus gives no sign of even hearing Solon's message. It becomes meaningful to him only many years later, when he has indeed fallen from fortune: facing death by fire on a pyre set by the conqueror of his empire, he suddenly remembers, and is in fact saved by remembering, Solon's warning to "look to the end."

Solon wanted to convey to Croesus a complex lesson about what it means to be mortal. He begins by ranking two ways of life, which are encapsulated, it is true, in the different kinds of death that bring them to a close; but it is far from obvious if or how those lives illustrate the warning Solon goes on to convey, about just how much our happiness is determined by what is not in our control, so no life can be assessed until the closure that death provides. Aristotle calls our attention to the problem of the connection between the two elements of Solon's account by splitting them apart in his own treatment: Book X will allude in the end to Solon's ranking of human lives when it returns to the question of the best way of life, while Book I appeals now to Solon's teaching about the central importance of chance and the instability of happiness. Solon found the root of the volatility of fortune in divine jealousy, which is an explanation Aristotle would find incompatible with the idea of a divine being.[65] In presenting his teaching, moreover, Solon is led to a radical conclusion—the quality of a person's life is entirely determined by what befalls him—that Aristotle's own understanding of happiness and the human good must lead him to resist. And yet, as long as *eudaimonia* is admitted to rest on certain necessary conditions, which are not, or not fully, in our control, Aristotle finds it necessary to acknowledge some truth in the wise man's warning "to look to the end."

Of course, it is certainly strange, Aristotle grants, that one can call someone happy only when he is dead, above all if happiness is supposed to be the *energeia* of a living being. If what Solon meant is that a life can be judged blessed only when it is beyond the reach of misfortune, even that is problematic; for it is *thought* that some bad and good can affect the dead, just as a living person might be affected without being aware of it (1100a15–21). Aristotle soon raises doubts about the possibility of the dead being affected in any way (1103a34–b5); and when he later identifies the virtue of courage as a disposition in the face of the greatest fear, that is found to be fear of death, on the grounds that death is a limit (*peras*), for it is *thought* that no good or bad affects the dead (1115a26–27). Aristotle does not contradict himself in these claims but, rather, discloses a contradiction in ordinary opinion.

The notion, in any event, that the experiences of our descendants could affect us after we are dead would make no sense if *eudaimonia* were a feeling; but at this point, at least, *eudaimonia* is the quality of a life determined by certain objective conditions, independent of our awareness. We can imagine our children and loved ones living on after we are gone and undergoing changes of fortune of which we will never be aware but which could be understood nevertheless to affect the goodness of one's own life. Homer represents this experience as if it were not merely counterfactual when he portrays the journey of Odysseus to Hades, where Agamemnon and Achilles long for news of how their sons are faring.[66] But if it is intelligible at all to think of the fate of one's children affecting the quality of one's own life even after one is no longer alive, what about their children, and their children's children? The threat of the infinite first appeared in the possibility that every desire is for the sake of some other and there is no final end that would limit a meaningless chain of means; it seems to have been translated now into a temporal form that precludes any life from ever being finite, and thus able to constitute a whole. It is certainly strange, Aristotle admits, to think of the dead person revolving from happiness to misery and back again with every turn of the wheel of fortune over an unlimited time. And yet, Aristotle finally concedes, to deny any retrospective influence at all on the life of an individual by those who survive him appears friendless (*aphilon*, 1101a22–24): it is our ties to loved ones that make it impossible for death to provide the closure of a life that is complete because completed.

The acceptance of death as a final boundary, at any rate, would not solve the fundamental problem posed by Solon's warning. If it is possible to judge a life as blessed only when it is over, the whole time the individual is living it is impossible to predicate happiness of him. Aristotle reminds us, understandably, that if the happy person is characterized primarily by his engagement in activities in accordance with virtue, he enjoys as much stability as human life allows. And when an individual endures misfortune with patience, not out of insensitivity but out of greatness of soul, the beautiful shines forth

(1100b30–33); of course, the shining forth of the beautiful in misfortune is not happiness. However small a role fortune is granted, no present moment of well-being can assure us of the completeness that has been accepted as a condition for *eudaimonia*. The living subject will never stand at a vantage point from which he can definitively judge his own life. That is possible, if at all, only from a third-person perspective, when the subject to whom happiness can be attributed is no longer alive. *Eudaimonia* requires a life in *energeia* and an objective judgment on a complete whole, which look as though they can never be combined.

THE NONRATIONAL *PSYCHĒ*

Without having solved the problem of the "complete life" required for *eudaimonia*, Aristotle returns to what is supposed to be its core and sets the inquiry on the path ahead: "Since happiness is some kind of *energeia* of soul in accordance with complete or perfect excellence, excellence should be investigated; for perhaps it would also be better in this way that we contemplate happiness" (1102a5–7). We are to investigate virtue for the sake of contemplating happiness. But Aristotle immediately adds another motive: it seems that the true statesman has toiled most in this regard, since he wishes to make the citizens good and law-abiding. The practical aim of the statesman—to instill lawfulness in citizens—and our theoretical aim—to contemplate happiness—coincide in the common path of investigating human excellence. And that, Aristotle stipulates without any argument, means excellence of the soul (1102a16–17). The analysis adopts—or, one might say, it reflects the way ethical virtue adopts—an assumption about the independence of soul from body, which, according to Aristotle's theoretical investigation of soul, is one of the most difficult questions.[67] The overturning of the assumption assigning ethical virtue to the soul alone at the conclusion of the *Ethics* is a particularly vivid sign of the movement of its underlying argument (cf. 1178a14–22).

Aristotle exploits the assumed independence of soul and body to propose an analogy: just as a doctor who is to heal the eye must know the whole body, so the statesman must know the things concerning the soul (1102a18–20). The corporeal model combines a practical end, healing the eye, and a theoretical means to that end, knowing the whole body; but the psychic counterpart that spells out the analogy makes explicit only the corresponding theoretical means, knowing the soul. Left on our own to fill in the parallel practical end, we would reason that, just as the doctor's aim is to heal the eye, a part of the body, so the statesman's is to heal a part of the soul, perhaps more precisely the "eye of the soul." But if, as Aristotle had just considered, the aim of the true statesman is to make the citizens good and law-abiding, his theoretical subject should be the whole *polis,* of which the citizens are the essential parts.[68] By failing to put together the practical end and the theoretical means in characterizing the task of the *politikos,* Aristotle implicitly raises the question whether the "true statesman" is really the one who makes the citizens law-abiding or, rather, the doctor, whose aim is to heal the diseased soul[69]—an image that will reappear at crucial points as the argument of the *Ethics* unfolds.[70]

If the identity, and hence the purpose, of true statesmanship remains in question, so does the methodological advice Aristotle goes on to give the *politikos:* he must rely on an analysis of the soul sufficient for the things he is seeking, while anything more precise would be unnecessarily laborious (*ergodesteron,* 1102a25–26). The language recalls the argument about the human *ergon* and the questionable recommendation to be satisfied with a level of precision equivalent to the carpenter's in contrast with the geometer's (1098a26–32). Aristotle appears to be following that recommendation with the admittedly imprecise psychology he now introduces, based on "exoteric *logoi,*" which divides the nonrational from the rational part of the soul; yet he immediately sets to work qualifying it. One set of functions of the nonrational part—nutrition and growth—seems to be common to all living things, hence nothing distinctively human; but there seems to be another "nonrational nature of the soul," its desiring part, which nevertheless participates somehow in *logos.* The evidence comes from resistance to reason: in the individual who must exercise self-restraint—and even more obviously, in one who is unable to do so—there is something that strains against *logos,* like the limb of a paralyzed person that swerves in one direction when he chooses to move in the other. But the capacity to resist reason is at the same time a capacity to obey it. There appears, then, to be a nonrational part of the soul distinguished by its potential for obedience to *logos:* the *ergon* argument introduced this one sense of what it means to have *logos* (1098a4–5), with its reminder of Hesiod's second-ranking human type (1095b10–11).

Considering its potential obedience to reason, the desiring part of the soul, Aristotle remarks, could be understood alternatively as a subset of the rational, which would stand to the part having *logos* in itself like a child obedient to his parent.[71] This desiring part of the soul calls for our practices of admonition, rebuke, and exhortation—the tools for inculcating ethical virtue that are neither simply rational nor entirely divorced from reason. It is the assumed autonomy of this part of the soul that presents the obstacle to the Socratic position, which reduces virtue to knowledge.

The human soul ranges over the functions of nutrition and growth, sentience and desire, speech or rationality: it comprehends within itself the whole range that was distributed, in the *ergon* argument, over the spheres of plants, animals, and humans. That argument implied that the human is to be understood as part of a cosmological whole of the living; now, the human soul is itself the whole.[72] Each part of it, accordingly, could have a distinctive *ergon* by nature, which, if performed well, would allow the whole to be in *energeia;* but that would seem to preclude a distinctive *ergon* of the human being as a whole. When, however, Book VI opens with a revised psychology, it distinguishes within the rational part of the soul a particular practical function of reason, which sounds just like the human *ergon* as such—"the *praktikē* of that which has *logos*" (cf. 1098a3–4 and 1139a5–15). There seems, then, to be an *ergon* of one part of the human soul that represents the human as such. When this function is performed well, the whole soul should flourish. But this *ergon* cannot itself be the *energeia* of the soul in accordance with the most *teleia* excellence in any sense of the term: if the human *ergon* belongs only to a part—practical rationality—that stands in for the whole, its virtue—which turns out to be *phronēsis*—could not be complete human excellence, nor does it prove to be the most perfect human excellence.

It is in relation to this practical function of reason that the desiring part of the soul exercises its capacity for obedience to *logos,* and it is that relation, we eventually learn, that alone makes genuine ethical virtue possible. But the two functions have been assigned to separate parts of the soul, rational and nonrational, according to the "exoteric psychology" that has brought Book I to a close. And this psychology provides the *Ethics* the grounds for its fundamental division of virtue in two, ethical and intellectual, whose consequences will be exposed in the course of the argument that occupies Books II through VI.

PART II

The Beautiful and the Just

2

Excellence of Character

ATHENIAN STRANGER: Well, I say that the first infantile sensation in children is the sensation of pleasure and pain, and that
it is in these that virtue and vice first come into being in the
soul. . . . Pleasure and liking, pain and hatred, become correctly
arranged in the souls of those who are not yet able to reason,
and then, when the souls do become capable of reasoning,
these passions can in consonance with reason affirm that they
have been correctly habituated in the appropriate habits. This
consonance in its entirely is virtue; and that part of virtue which
consists in being correctly trained as regards pleasure and pains
so as to hate what one should hate from the very beginning until the end, and also to love what one should love—if you separate this off in speech and assert that this is education, you will,
in my view be making a correct assertion.

—Plato *Laws* II.653a–c, translated by Thomas Pangle

[ELEATIC] STRANGER: Let's divide it [the art of measure-
ment] into two parts, for they're needed for what we're now
striving for. . . . Isn't it your opinion that it's by nature that
the greater must be said to be greater than nothing other than
the less, and the less, in turn, to be less than the greater and
nothing else?
[YOUNG] SOCRATES: Yes, it is.
STRANGER: And what of this? That which exceeds the nature
of the mean and is exceeded by it, in speeches or maybe in
deeds—shall we not speak of it in turn as in its being a coming-
into-being, in which the bad and good ones among us have
their most particular differences?
SOCRATES: It appears so.
STRANGER: So, after all, it's these one must set down as the
twofold modes of being and judging of the big and the small,
and not only, as we just now said, must it be the mutually

relative measure, but rather as it has now been said, the mutually relative measure and the measure relative to the mean must
be said.

—Plato *Statesman* 283d–e, translated by Seth Benardete

A Non-Socratic Account

Having defined *eudaimonia* as "an activity of soul in accordance with complete or perfect virtue" and identified it as the first principle (*archē*), for the
sake of which everything else is done (1102a2–6), Book I seemed to promise
a movement of thought that would descend from that principle to deduce
what complete or perfect virtue is. Book II, however, in turning to the investigation of virtue, makes no explicit attempt to move from happiness as
the first principle. If, instead, it is meant to set in motion a path back to that
archē, that path is not a very direct one: though we are supposed to be taking
up the investigation of virtue in order to "contemplate" happiness (1102a7),
eudaimonia is never mentioned in the course of Book II, nor in relation to any
particular virtue of character discussed in Books III and IV.[1]

The investigation of human excellence that is supposed to lead back to
the question of happiness begins and ends with Socrates. On the basis of its
fundamental premise—the division of ethical from intellectual virtue—it
sets out in Book II to develop a conception of ethical virtue over against the
Socratic view, encapsulated in the formula "Virtue is knowledge";[2] it is the
acceptance, or partial acceptance, of the Socratic view that brings the discussion of intellectual virtue to a close at the end of Book VI. The acknowledgment of the truth in the Socratic position has the consequence of denying
the split between ethical and intellectual virtue that was the premise of the
whole account and, thus, appears to be an entirely new twist in the argument. Yet, as we recognize in retrospect, the Socratic position is in fact already lurking in the original definition of ethical virtue in Book II, which has
inserted at its core the prudent person, the *phronimos,* who would determine
the mean (1107a1–2); the account thus implicitly denies from the outset the
separation from intellectual virtue that was to guarantee the autonomy of
ethical virtue.

The understanding of ethical virtue as a disposition aiming at the mean
is introduced by recalling the foundational function argument of Book I,

which took human excellence to be a matter of performing the distinctive human *ergon* well. The good for a human being, according to that argument, lies in the exercise of this *ergon,* which was understood, however imprecisely, to be some kind of practice of rationality. While Book II is silent about happiness, the appeal to the human function links the account of virtue to the original question of the human good (cf. 1106a15–24 with 1097b24–28 and 1098a12–18). Had Book II attempted to spell out the derivation of human excellence from the human *ergon,* it would have moved immediately to the conclusion of Book VI and identified *phronēsis* as that which makes virtue a whole by looking to the good things as an end: it would have arrived directly at the Socratic understanding of *phronēsis* as that without which there is no genuine virtue at all (1144b14–17). The path of the argument from Book II through Book VI, then, must be the result of Aristotle's concerted effort to stave off as long as possible his acknowledgment of the Socratic position.

Without that deferral, it would not have been possible to bring to light the array of virtues and vices taken up for examination in Books III and IV. An important sign—perhaps the important sign—of the radical change that takes place in moving beyond the general account of ethical virtue in Book II to the particular virtues of Books III and IV appears in the discussion of the first of those dispositions: the courageous person, we will be told, endures his fears as he should—that much we have heard before—for the sake of the beautiful (*to kalon*), for that, Aristotle announces, is the *telos* of (the) virtue (1115b12–13). Book II says nothing about the beautiful—or anything else, for that matter—being the *telos* of virtue.[3] The beautiful proves to be, together with the just, the independent principles that show up in the manifold of particular virtues and withstand their absorption into *phronēsis:* the beautiful and the just supply the force of resistance against the Socratic move that would deny the autonomy of the sphere of ethical virtue.[4]

Aristotle's account of the "what it is" of ethical virtue, in Chapter 6 of Book II, may anticipate the Socratic unification of the virtues through *phronēsis,* but the preceding genetic account of how virtue comes to be is put forward against what is implied to be a Socratic understanding. The necessity of habituation—of constantly practicing the relevant actions in order to acquire a virtuous disposition—is a reality, Aristotle charges, that the many refuse to acknowledge; instead, they believe that they are philosophizing by "taking refuge in *logos*" and can become virtuous that way (1105b11–18).

Without yet mentioning Socrates by name, Aristotle borrows the language Plato's Socrates uses to describe his distinctive philosophical turn as a matter of "taking refuge in *logoi*" (*Phaedo* 99e). Socrates' formula for his characteristic way of inquiry becomes, in Aristotle's usage, a misguided and self-deceptive notion of how ethical virtue comes to be.[5]

Aristotle's treatment of ethical virtue thus unfolds by means of a twofold critique: implicitly, against the Socratic way of inquiry construed as a view about the coming to be of ethical virtue and, explicitly, against Socrates as the exponent of a certain view about what virtue is. The twofold target of critique has a common root—the Socratic overestimation of the action-guiding power of knowledge—but it is made of two distinct errors that call for two very different corrections. The supposedly Socratic misconception of how virtue is acquired is based, Aristotle implies, on a mistaken psychology, which denies the independence of a desiring part of the soul aiming at pleasure. To correct it requires recognition of the power of pleasure in human motivation, hence the necessity of channeling that drive through practice in order to form the right behavioral habits. In Socratic eyes, on the other hand, what habituation would produce looks as if it could only be "demotic virtue," control over behavior based on the calculation of how to maximize pleasure and minimize pain.[6]

The motivating role of pleasure may be decisive, as Aristotle sees it, in how virtue comes to be; it is something very different, however, that is missing from the misconception Aristotle ascribes to Socrates about what virtue is. The supposedly Socratic reduction of virtue to knowledge would amount to a failure to recognize the human orientation to the beautiful or noble, which elevates virtue in light of its intrinsic end.[7] The correction of the first error belongs to Aristotle's own analysis of how character is formed by the molding of pleasure and pain; the correction of the second error consists in his representation of the morally virtuous person as he understands himself. The two corrections are presented in opposition to a conception of virtue as nothing but knowledge; yet they look as incompatible with one other as each is with the Socratic view Aristotle represents as his target of critique. In the experience of the person devoted to it, the meaning of ethical virtue lies in its highest aspirations, the end at which it aims; an analysis of how pleasures and pains are channeled so as to form certain habits casts in advance a cold light on that self-understanding.

HABITUATION

Book II opens with an echo of Meno's question to Socrates: Is virtue acquired by teaching, or practice, or by nature, or in some other fashion?[8] Aristotle's immediate answer discloses a distinction that remained hidden in the formula for happiness as an *"energeia* of the soul in accordance with complete or perfect excellence": human excellence is twofold, and while intellectual virtue is mostly the product of teaching, which requires experience and time, ethical virtue (*ēthikē aretē*) is the product, as its name suggests, of habit (*ethos;* 1103a14–18). The separation of ethical virtue, which will prove to be so problematic, is inferred from the assumption that it comes to be by a process of habituation, not by teaching, whereas intellectual virtue is presented at the moment as all of a piece. Only when we turn to an examination of intellectual virtue in Book VI do we discover the importance of differentiating the virtue that can be taught from that which develops only with experience over time.[9]

Habituation presupposes that nature as given is not altogether determinative; if it were, that would make training both unnecessary and impossible. The evidence to which Aristotle appeals, however, comes not from an investigation of nature but from the intention of the legislator, which is to make the citizens good by habituation (1103b2–6). The law aims to produce a "second nature" by molding human character, while the tools it employs—praise and blame, reward and punishment—presuppose that the agent is responsible for what he does. The discussion of responsibility in Book III, which promises to be of service to the legislator, will argue for the greatest possible range of voluntary action; the account of habituation in Book II makes that problematic in advance by arguing that training from earliest childhood—before an individual could legitimately be held responsible—makes all the difference in the world (1103b23–25).

If it is true that our characters are developed out of repeated actions, for good or for bad, then the investigation must concern itself with actions and we are pursuing it, Aristotle maintains, not in order to know what virtue is, but to become good (1103b26–29; cf. 1095a4–11). Now, this is the purpose that had just been assigned to the legislator; the way in which the citizens become good through habituation in lawful practices, however, is obviously not the way we could become good by participation in this inquiry. What the two share is the impossibility of either purpose being accomplished by passive listening to speeches. But what is the distinctive deed by which the potential worth of the present speeches could be realized? Aristotle offers a suggestion when he admits that the question we are asking—How should one act?—has a simple answer: "in accordance with correct *logos.*" Yet that is only an "outline" (*tupos;* 1104a1–2; cf. 1098a20–24); filling it in looks like the deed through which we can become good—not as we would through moral education, but through an action of inquiry itself.

At the moment, Aristotle goes out of his way to emphasize the difficulty of grasping anything about human action through speech: if, in such matters, even a general theory can never be fixed, we should certainly expect no precision concerning particular cases, where what counts is the agent's on-the-spot perception of "the opportune" (*kairon*). Such discernment of the exactly right response in a given situation would in fact seem to represent the highest degree of precision.[10] What is under threat, however, is not the problem of getting the action right but the challenge of providing a theoretical account of what makes it right.[11] Faced with this danger, it is necessary "to come to the rescue of the *logos*" (1104a10–11). Aristotle speaks the words here of Plato's Socrates, who on the day of his death realizes the need to "come to the rescue of the *logos*" in the face of the threat of "misology"; his interlocutors, he recognizes, were on the brink of experiencing so deep a disappointment in his arguments for immortality, having expected too much from them, that it could have made them turn away from reason altogether (*Phaedo* 88e, 89d–e). Socrates' response was the proposal of a safer "second sailing," by "taking refuge in *logoi*" (99d–e); that is precisely the formula, however, by which Aristotle is about to describe the insufficiency of merely listening to speeches without performing the requisite deeds (1105b12–16). With this double allusion to the *Phaedo*, Aristotle alerts us to two polar dangers—either there can be no speech or argument about these matters, or there is nothing but speeches—that put into question the whole project of the *Ethics.*

The famous "doctrine of the mean" is now introduced with that twofold danger in mind. Aristotle recommends that we begin by "contemplating" an analogy:[12] just as bodily states of health or strength are naturally destroyed by need and excess but produced, increased, and preserved by the commensurate, the virtues of character, likewise, should be destroyed by deficiency and excess but preserved by the mean (1104a11–27). One who runs away from everything, Aristotle explains, becomes a coward, whereas one who encounters everything becomes rash—just as one who indulges in every pleasure becomes indulgent, while one who shuns them all in some sense becomes insensible. As reasonable as it may be to avoid these extremes of all or nothing, this initial description certainly leaves open an awfully wide range within which the mean could fall. It was the problem of "the opportune" that aroused our distrust in a *logos* of action; just how the appeal to the mean can overcome that distrust remains in question.[13]

The mean is introduced as the standard for the actions by which virtuous dispositions, like bodily states of health or strength, come to be; but since it is the same actions through which such a disposition is exercised, the immediate question we are compelled to address is what differentiates the established state from the process of its formation? Aristotle finds a sign of the difference in the pleasure that accompanies the action that flows from a formed disposition.[14] In the contest to the title of the human good, pleasure was immediately rejected as an end that would characterize a life more fit for cattle than human beings; now pleasure and pain, given their role in habituation, are admitted to be "the whole business for virtue and political science" (1105a11–12). Pleasure might still appear to play primarily a negative role—it, above all, causes us to do base actions, just as pain keeps us from doing beautiful ones; but this really means, Aristotle now explains, pursuing and avoiding the wrong pleasures and pains, or at the wrong time, or in the wrong manner. In fact, the other ends capable of motivating action, the beautiful and the advantageous, succeed just insofar as they appear pleasant to us. To habituate someone to take pleasure in seeking those ends, or pain in avoiding them, is thus the task of ethical education, and if pleasure and pain are to serve as such tools, they must be as malleable as they are deeply "engrained in the fabric of life" (1105a2–3). The molding of desire begins in early childhood by exploiting a natural inclination to find pleasure in being praised and pain in being blamed: Aristotle praises Plato for his understanding of this issue (1104b11–13).[15] To take pleasure in being praised or to feel pain in being blamed is a sign of our natural desire for the acceptance of others, beginning with our parents: habituation of character is thus made possible by the political nature of the human being before the rational nature is developed.

The problem of differentiating the genesis of a virtuous disposition from the exercise of it raises a broader question: if virtue is an inner state expressed through action, how can its presence be inferred from any external manifestation? Taking pleasure in performing the right action may be a sign of acting out of a virtuous disposition; it is not what it means to do so. To get at that, Aristotle first suggests a parallel to the arts: playing music in order to become a musician is different from playing as a musician. In the case of the arts, however, it is the performance or product that matters and the agent's state is not of concern, at least as long as he acts knowingly. The virtuous person too must act knowingly (*eidōs*), though Aristotle says nothing at the moment about what kind of knowledge is involved. He only contends that in contrast with the arts this is the least important measure for virtue and goes on to stipulate two presumably more weighty criteria: the virtuous person acts out of choice—choosing his action "because of itself"—and in a firm and unchangeable manner (1105a26–33). To defend the importance of these conditions over against the demand for knowledge, Aristotle adduces as evidence the development of a just or moderate character—the most plausible cases of a disposition acquired through repeated practice. We will be compelled to rethink this account when the argument eventually arrives at the conclusion that the necessary condition for genuine virtue is *phronēsis*, with the alternative being, not dispositions produced by habituation, but "natural virtues" (1144b14–17).

For the moment, the need for repeated practice overshadows the requirement for acting knowingly. And while it is not immediately evident how it is related to the requirement for acting out of choice, it is clearly decisive in forming a firm disposition. The individual who acts over time in an unchanging manner is admittedly different from someone who does the right thing on one occasion; his habitual behavior, however, hardly suffices to reveal the motivation behind it and that was the problem under consideration. The really crucial criterion, then, seems to be acting out of choice, though no explanation is given here about what it means to choose. When the issue is first taken up, early on in Book III, choice will be defined as the outcome of deliberation, a rational process of weighing alternatives as means to a given end—not necessarily a virtuous end.

It is, then, what appears to be only a remark in passing that most obviously, but also most problematically, addresses the question of motivation:

the virtuous person must choose his action "because of itself." This seems to mean "for the sake of itself," but Aristotle refrains from phrasing it in terms of a purpose, and thus avoids, or at least defers, a number of important questions. If the object of choice is strictly defined as the means to a given end, which is not itself chosen (1111b26-29), wouldn't the virtuous action necessarily be chosen for an end beyond itself? If a disposition of character is the result of having been trained to take pleasure in the right actions, how would one know that pleasure does not continue to be a, or the, motivation for acting properly? If, as Book I argued, the final end at which all human beings naturally aim is happiness, how could a virtuous action be chosen because of itself, unless it could be shown to be constitutive of happiness?

The schematic account of the requirements for possessing a virtuous disposition implicitly raises these questions about the inner state that virtuous behavior is supposed to express. But just when we would expect the discussion to take up these questions, it concludes instead by reiterating the necessity of repeatedly performing the appropriate actions in order to form a virtuous disposition. Yet the many, Aristotle charges, are like invalids who hope to become healthy by listening to what a doctor says without doing anything themselves to carry out his prescriptions (1105b14–16). This criticism of the many anticipates once more the problem of the akratic, which first appeared in Aristotle's description of his intended audience (1095a7–9) and then again in the psychology postulating the independence of the desiring part of the soul (1102b18–23). Lack of self-restraint is an inevitable consequence, Aristotle implies, of being taught what is right but failing to develop character by practice; such individuals "take refuge in *logos*" and believe they can, by philosophizing, become serious (1105b12–14).

The assumption ascribed to the many is the premise of all sophistry: there is nothing but speeches.[16] Aristotle has chosen a very odd way, though, to express his critique. Do the many really think of themselves as philosophizing? And why should their laziness be described through the formula for the Socratic turn—"taking refuge in *logoi*"? The many deceive themselves into being satisfied with acquiring a doctor's advice, whereas the Socratic error, one would think, is the belief that to become healthy one has to, and needs only to, become a doctor oneself.[17] Aristotle has, for the moment, brought them together on the common ground of a refusal to acknowledge the need for the hard work of habituation: the alliance of Socrates and the many stands against his own with Plato, whom he praised for recognizing the importance of molding pleasure and pain.[18]

ETHICAL VIRTUE AND THE MEASURE OF THE MEAN

Aiming at the Mean and the Mean as a Disposition of Character

In taking up first the problem of how virtue is acquired, Book II of the *Ethics* seems to repeat the problem Socrates expresses to Meno when he observes at the end of their conversation that their conclusion about how virtue comes to be present in human beings must remain doubtful since they have not yet attempted to investigate what it is in itself.[19] Of course, Socrates shows by his conduct of the argument, despite what he says in the end, how much one can learn about what virtue is from examining how it comes to be, and Aristotle's discussion of habituation does so no less. His account of how virtue is acquired may be insufficient to arrive at the definition of what it is, but it does, at least, provide the guidelines for determining the genus to which it belongs.

When the investigation of virtue turns finally to that question, in Chapter 5 of Book II, Aristotle seems to offer, in his familiar manner, a set of alternatives with no argument for their exhaustiveness. It is already clear, however, from the preceding discussion that we are seeking the perfection of the part of the soul that experiences feelings (*pathē*), and experiencing feelings entails having capacities for them (*dunameis*), as well as characteristic dispositions toward them (*hexeis*), so virtue must be one of these alternatives. The governing assumption for deciding among the alternatives is our ordinary practice of praise and blame: while we are simply moved by our feelings and possess by nature the capacities for them, that for which we could reasonably be praised or blamed, if anything, is the disposition to comport ourselves in a characteristic fashion in regard to our feelings. If our practices of praise and blame are justified, virtue and vice must be dispositions of the soul.

Of course, the obvious question now is, what distinguishes the virtuous disposition from the vicious one? To address that question, we return to the notion of the *ergon:* the proper excellence of the eye is that which makes the organ itself "serious" (*spoudaios*) and able to perform its *ergon* well (1106a17–19). Are these two effects simply identical and always the result of the same virtue? If not, this twofold effect might point to the tension between the single virtue of performing the human *ergon* well, which proves to be *phronēsis,* and the plurality of states of character that make a subject good. Of course, the "serious eye" is presumably nothing but one that sees well; twenty-twenty vision is its single excellence, and when it performs its function well, it is for the good of the body, or the animal, of which it is an organic part. The horse, however, which Aristotle adds as a further example,[20] is not an organic part of a larger whole, and the functions ascribed to it—running, carrying its rider, facing the enemy—serve different purposes, which we impose on the animal out of our own interests. Each of those functions would probably be best performed by a different sort of horse, and none in that case define the "serious horse" as such. If the *ergon* principle holds for all things, Aristotle reasons, without admitting any difference between the examples on which it is based, the excellence of a human being would be the disposition by which he becomes a good human being and able to perform his function well.[21] The human *ergon* was found to lie in our distinctive capacity as the living being that has *logos.* The excellence we are trying to define now, however, is not that of the human being as such but of the desiring part of the soul, which has been assigned to the nonrational side, though it is at least capable of listening to *logos.*

Inviting us "to contemplate what sort of nature" this excellence has (1106a24–26), Aristotle picks up the thread from the discussion of how virtue comes to be, when contemplation of the mean was called for in order to rescue the *logos* (1104a10–13).[22] The model for the measure of the mean is now furnished by the work of art, as a perfect whole from which nothing could be added or taken away without destroying what it is (1106b9–14). Whatever the equivalent to the artisan proves to be in the case of virtue, the work produced must be the state of character, or the expression of such a state in a given situation, and the continuum of a passion the matter upon which a form is imposed with a view to the mean. That measure, Aristotle explains, is not the arithmetic mean—defined by the extremes of the object— but the mean "relative to us." Its relativity indicates that it is not one and the same for everyone; its resistance to generalization, however, does not mean that it is not a precise and objective measure of what is good. Ten pounds of food may be a lot, and two very little, but six cannot be fixed in advance as the mean for everyone—for Milo the wrestler, it would fall far short. Yet the mean for him—apparently, a whole ox a day[23]—is a precise measure of what is objectively good for him, given his specific constitution and activities. Aristotle's example could perhaps be readily translated into psychic terms if the mean were nothing but a measure of intensity on the "divisible continuum" of a particular passion; the mean that is the aim of virtue, however, must also be the measure of the right time and place, relation to others, manner, and purpose (1106b18–23).[24] If Aristotle allows his reader to think of a mathematical standard in order to convince us that there is an objective measure of what is good for some individual in some situation, it must be finally in the service of dethroning mathematics as the sole claimant to the art of measure and the standard of precision.[25]

A measure as objective but as idiosyncratic as the right amount of food for Milo would require an expert to seek and choose it (1106b5–7): yet the virtuous person, we would have thought, has to choose his action himself, and the expert's knowledge would not be easily recognized by anyone who did not possess that expertise himself.[26] The original premise was that human excellence should make one able to perform the distinctive human *ergon* well. If, however, as Aristotle now infers from the model of trainer and athlete, every science (*epistēmē*) performs its function (*ergon*) well by looking to the mean and leading its works (*erga*) to that (1106b8–9), the *ergon* has apparently split, between a function, based on knowledge, and the work produced—more precisely, on the model of the athlete, a twofold set of *erga* produced. If the role of the trainer performing his *ergon* with a view to the mean were the model for the role of *phronēsis* in the process of habituation, the *erga* produced would be the bodily conditions of the athlete, analogous to the mean dispositions of character. The bodily conditions of the well-trained athlete, however, are only realized in the *erga* of the actions he performs; and the *ergon* that looks to the mean in determining those actions is, ideally, no longer supplied by the trainer but has been internalized by the athlete, analogous to the internalized *phronēsis* by which the virtuous person chooses his action (cf. 1106b36–1107a2).

From the model of the artisan and his work of art, Aristotle highlights one consequence in particular, albeit on the basis of a premise with no argument supplied in its support: if virtue is better and more precise than *technē*, and the good artisans look to the mean in fabricating their work, virtue should be a matter of aiming (*stochastikē*) at the mean (1106b13–16). Precisely when virtue is assigned a precision superior to art, its way of access to the mean is designated by a term that implies guesswork—a term Socrates uses, for example, to deny the artfulness of rhetoric.[27]

The mean in feelings and actions is a target, which there is one way to chance upon (*epituchein*) and infinite ways to miss (*apotuchein*). We are reminded of the image that originally stood for knowledge of the good (1094a23–24), but the question is not explicitly raised now about the end in light of which the mean is "just right." Instead, we are led to a definition of virtue by what seems to be a deliberately weak argument: since in feelings and actions excess and deficiency are errors, while the mean is praised and correct, and to be praised and correct are characteristics of virtue, so virtue, in aiming at a mean, must itself be some kind of mean state (1106b24–28).[28] Virtue, on this basis, can be defined as a disposition for choosing (*prohairetic hexis*), being in the mean in relation to us, determined by *logos*, as the prudent person (*phronimos*) would determine it (1106b36–1107a2).

The definition of ethical virtue is presented as if it were a conclusion whose elements are all drawn from the preceding discussion. The function, however, that was first ascribed to *epistēmē* and then to *technē* has now been reassigned to the *phronimos*, the person of prudence, who has never been officially introduced; and virtue, with that, has become a disposition of choosing (*prohairesis*), which has yet to become a subject of analysis.[29] What can be chosen, according to that analysis, is only the means to an end.[30] What, then, is the end to which the *phronimos* looks in choosing the mean?[31] That question returns at the beginning of Book VI, when Aristotle describes how the one with *logos* tightens and relaxes the strings—presumably, the intensity of the feelings—by looking to the target (*skopos*) (1138b21–25); but it is not until the end of Book VI that we realize how ambiguous that target is.

The formal definition of ethical virtue in Book II avoids that question, having replaced the mean in relation to feelings and actions, which the *phronimos* chooses, by the mean state between two extremes that constitutes a disposition of character. The mean of action and the mean of character, however, have altogether different ontological structures. The mean that is a target is that one right response, in feelings or actions, for a particular individual in a particular situation, among the infinite and indeterminate ways of missing the mark (1106b28–33). The mean that constitutes the disposition of character, on the other hand, is not a single point along an indeterminate range: it is one of three determinate states—courage over against cowardice and rashness, for example—that praise and blame have imposed as a tripartite division on the continuum of a passion.[32]

The mean that would be the right response in feelings and actions for a particular agent in a particular situation is a standard that will never be repeated; the judgment of it would require the greatest possible flexibility and could never be simply the product of a fixed disposition developed by habituation. While the mean in the form of the right response would be as infinitely varied as the situations in which it is sought, there would be only one virtue of being able to discover it, *phronēsis*. In sliding from that to the disposition of character that is a mean between two extremes, the virtues become many, individuated by the distinct spheres of feeling to which they are related. This development in the analysis of virtue as a mean was anticipated when the *ergon* argument moved from the single excellence of performing the human function well to a manifold of independent states (1098a14–18). Now, once again, we are left with the unanswered question how the one virtue of *phronēsis*, whose target is the mean in feelings and actions, is related to the mean dispositions that constitute the plurality of virtues of character.

A Second Sailing on the Way to the Mean

Having arrived at a general definition of ethical virtue, Aristotle pauses and reminds us that in matters such as these the truth always lies more in the particular; hence, the general account of ethical virtue, he recommends, should be tested by a survey of the distinct dispositions (1107a28–33). When the discussion of ethical virtue in general is resumed, in the last two chapters of Book II, the status of the mean is radically altered. Originally, the treatment of virtue as a mean state had little if anything to say about the contrary states that fall short of or exceed it; in the concluding chapters of Book II, the mean becomes nothing but a perspectivally shifting inference from the primary opposition between those states of excess and deficiency. The tripartite division of a mean state between two extremes, as it now becomes clear, could only be the object of a nonperspectival contemplation by an observer who did not himself stand somewhere along the line he contemplates. Once he is put into the picture, the mean necessarily appears in contrast with one extreme at a time by taking on, relative to it, the characterization of the contrary: the middle exceeds in relation to the deficient, while falling short in relation to the excessive (1108b15–19). This identification of the mean with one extreme is an appearance that shifts with change of perspective: a courageous person appears rash in contrast with a coward, cowardly in contrast with a rash person, just as a moderate person appears indulgent in contrast with someone insensitive, insensitive in contrast with someone indulgent. Anyone occupying one extreme pushes the mean off in the direction of the other: a coward calls a courageous person rash, a rash person calls him a coward (1108b23–26). There seems to be no standpoint from which the mean could be recognized as independent of either.

What began as a structure of three independent states thus becomes a dyadic relation between contraries. Each of the extremes can attach itself to the mean state and form a two-in-one, but not both at the same time, for the dyadic character of one is always in opposition to the other extreme, momentarily isolated.[33] While the mean, however, always comes to light collapsed with one extreme from the perspective of the other, it does not necessarily do so symmetrically; for one extreme may lie so much closer to the mean that only its contrary is commonly understood to be opposed to the mean. With this observation, Aristotle recalls the two respects in which he had at first identified the mean—in the thing itself or in relation to us—only now they designate a twofold cause of the asymmetry that makes one extreme alone appear contrary to the mean that constitutes the virtue (compare 1106a29–32 with 1109a5–19).[34]

The mean cannot appear as what it is in itself, since we—human beings generally as well as particular individuals—always stand at some position that affects our perception of it. It is, therefore, a task (*ergon*) to be serious, Aristotle concludes, since it is a task (*ergon*) to hit the mean (1109a24–26). To act or feel to the degree one should, in relation to the right person, at the right time, for the right purpose, or in the right way, is something rare, praiseworthy, and beautiful (1109a29–30): the idealization of hitting the mean brings with it one of Book II's rare references to the *kalon*.[35] It makes this unusual appearance, however, only to be abandoned almost immediately: given the great difficulty of hitting the mean directly, it is reasonable to resort to a "second sailing" (1109a34–35). Socrates, on the last day of his life, explains the "second sailing" on which he embarked when he turned from the self-blinding attempt to grasp the beings directly in the "eclipsed" light of the good and instead sought "refuge in *logoi*." In his insistence on the importance of practicing virtuous actions in order to develop a virtuous disposition, Aristotle had implicitly rejected that Socratic "second sailing" (cf. 1105b12–16); now he proposes the necessity of a second sailing on the way to virtue.[36]

This Aristotelian "second sailing" consists in abandoning the beautiful but daunting task of aiming directly at the mean, resorting instead to avoiding the worse of two extremes. Odysseus, Aristotle reminds us with a citation from the *Odyssey*, was warned that there would be no mean between the twin dangers of Scylla and Charybdis; knowing that he and his entire crew would be swallowed in the swirling waters of Charybdis, Odysseus was compelled to pull away from that threat and sail closer to Scylla, only to see six of his best men dangling from the monster's jaws, like fish, calling out to him in their last desperate words. This, Odysseus remarks, was the most terrible sight in all his journeys.[37] On this model, our options are all terrible, though not equally so, and the closest we can get to a mean is choosing the lesser evil.

Besides the unequal evil of the two extremes in themselves, there is the asymmetry resulting from our own inclination to one extreme rather than another. If we recognized that, we could compensate by dragging ourselves in the opposite direction, like carpenters who straighten warped timber.[38] The expert, like Milo's trainer, has disappeared; what has taken his place is a kind of self-knowledge, not, however, of one's own good, at least not directly, but of one's characteristic weakness. To acquire such insight, we must observe above all our inclinations to pleasure and react like the elders of Troy, who bid Helen begone just when, and precisely because, they admit her overwhelming beauty (*Iliad* III.156–160).

RESPONSIBILITY AND NATURE

The investigation of virtue was first recommended not only as a path toward the "contemplation of happiness" but also as a fitting task for the statesman; and the statesman was assigned a twofold function, one explicit—as the legislator who aims to make the citizens good and law-abiding—another by implication—as the psychic counterpart to the doctor who must study the whole body if he is to heal a part that is ill (1102a2–25). Book III opens with the articulation of a division between voluntary and involuntary action, which is said to be of importance for the legislator in his task of rewarding and punishing (1109b34–35); it puts off as long as possible any indication of the necessary conflict between the presuppositions of the legislator and those of the doctor of soul, whose concern is not with praise and blame but with knowledge of the causes of the psychic illnesses he seeks to cure.

The difference between those two horizons shows up vividly in the problem of dividing the class of voluntary action from involuntary. Restricting the category of the involuntary as narrowly as possible is in the interest of moral education and the law. That perspective is reflected in the opinion with which the analysis begins: it is *thought to be* the case that only those actions are involuntary that are done through compulsion, in which the agent has no causal control at all over what he does, or through ignorance, in which the agent is not and could not have been aware of the particular facts of the situation (1109b35–1110a4). Aristotle neither endorses nor rejects this opinion, but he begins immediately to uncover complications. For one thing, it is disputable whether to count as voluntary or involuntary actions that are in themselves unchoiceworthy but that are committed, nonetheless, through fear of a worse alternative or because of something noble. On this rare occasion, Aristotle calls on us to imagine a particular case: if a tyrant had in his power a man's parents and children and threatened to kill them unless he did something base, how would an act of compliance be evaluated? The act is admittedly not done under compulsion in the narrowest sense, since some kind of choice was made, but should it really be considered voluntary? And if so, would we be ready to blame someone for such an action? Aristotle offers an analysis on the basis of another case determined by circumstances: if someone in a storm at sea were to throw cargo overboard to save lives, such an action, which displays aspects of the voluntary and the involuntary, could be labeled "mixed"; but it resembles more closely the voluntary, Aristotle insists, for even if it could be considered involuntary in itself—something no one would choose, other things being equal—in this particular situation it was in fact chosen and not strictly compelled by outside forces.

The evaluation of any action, we now see, is complicated by the nexus of relations to which it belongs. To achieve something beautiful, it might be necessary to do something shameful, and we might praise someone who made that choice. Even if it were not praiseworthy, an action would deserve pardon if it were committed through fear of consequences that are greater than human nature can bear—a tyrant threatening to kill one's parents or children might fall under that description. But perhaps, Aristotle adds, there are some deeds that can never be excused by the claim that one was compelled to do them; of course, "perhaps" leaves open the possibility that there are none.[39] The acknowledgment, in any case, that there are situations in which one cannot do the right thing without doing something base or shameful has far-reaching consequences. It might seem to be a problem restricted to crisis situations—the situations tragedy represents—but it indicates more generally the limits of our freedom, already implied by the revised account of aiming at the mean, in the last chapters of Book II: we may often find ourselves having to choose the lesser of two evils, and the right thing to do may rarely be possible without some cost. Book I wrestled with the issue of the insufficiency of virtue alone to guarantee happiness, given all the factors beyond our control that affect the quality of our lives; now we are led to see the pressure of necessity on the sphere of choice itself, with the admission that there may be circumstances in which we have to choose something terrible to avoid something even worse.

Aristotle allows the reality of the problematic boundary between voluntary and involuntary action to appear, but only momentarily; in the horizon of the present discussion, which was to be of service to the legislator, that boundary must be maintained and the class of the involuntary confined to the narrowest possible territory. Actions done under compulsion, for which one cannot be held responsible, must be limited, accordingly, to those whose origin lies entirely outside the agent, and exculpatory ignorance must be similarly restricted. If the agent is unaware of some specific parameter of his situation, his action is nonvoluntary, but only an action that causes pain and regret upon discovery should count as involuntary, and not even all of those. If someone has gotten drunk, though he may act "in ignorance" of what he is doing, it is not "through or because of (*dia*) ignorance," that is, through a condition that would excuse his action (1110b24–27). Aristotle concedes the Socratic principle—every wicked person (*mochtheros*) acts in ignorance of what he should do and becomes bad through such error (*hamartia*)—but only to insist that this sort of ignorance does not make an action involuntary. It is ignorance of particular circumstances alone—and only particular ignorance one could not have avoided—that makes someone an unwilling victim, to be forgiven or pitied (1110b28–1111a2).[40]

From his examination of the causal and epistemic conditions thought to make an action involuntary, Aristotle draws a rather hesitant conclusion: voluntary actions *would seem to be* those in which the source of the action lies in the agent and he knows the particular circumstances in which he is acting. Perhaps, Aristotle continues in a qualified vein, actions committed out of anger (*thumos*) or desire (*epithumia*) are not beautifully spoken of as involuntary; these passions are at least *thought to be* as much a part of the human being as rationality (1111b1–2). Without simply rejecting the premise on which moral and legal practice relies, Aristotle slips in the qualifications that prepare for the radical view at which the *Ethics* finally arrives: each person really is, or is most of all, mind alone (1178a2–4), in which case actions done out of anger or desire would not be, strictly speaking, those of the agent himself.

As the argument moves beyond the assessment of actions to a consideration of character, it passes along the way through the topic of choice (*prohairesis*), which is the connecting bond of character and action (1111b4–6). In this context, choice serves the purpose of carving out, within the broad territory of the voluntary, a more restricted sphere of full responsibility: an action driven by anger or desire may be classified as voluntary, but it is not chosen. Choice is the end product of the process of deliberation, and we deliberate only about things that can go one way or another and over which we have some control. More specifically, what we deliberate about and finally choose is always the means to an end (1111b26–29); the end itself is the object not of choice but of wishing or wanting (*boulēsis*).[41] The doctor doesn't deliberate and choose whether to cure his patient—that end is given to him by his art—but how to go about curing. Of course, there are circumstances in which an individual would deliberate about whether an attempt should made to heal himself or another; but then healing would be one alternative among others to some further end, ultimately, happiness. Wishing has no constraints—we can wish for immortality—but we choose, after deliberation, what can be secured through our own actions. Choice can therefore be defined as "deliberate desire of things within our power"; with the reminder that such things are the means toward an end, this account of choice is completed "in outline" (1113a12–14). When it reappears, at the beginning of Book VI, it is no longer under the same restrictions (1139a31–b5): choice becomes something very different from a subset of the moral-legal category of the voluntary once the argument is no longer concerned with the ascription of responsibility but with understanding the relation between thought and desire in the human soul.

In contrast with the firm divisions of Book III's quasi-legalistic analysis of action, the concluding discussion of character, in Chapter 5, has almost the form of a debate, and it is not always clear on which side Aristotle stands. At issue is the implication of the Socratic principle: if one goes wrong only through ignorance of the right end, does that mean one can never be held responsible? According to proverbial wisdom, "No one is willingly wicked or unwillingly blessed" (1113b14–16). It seems to be half true, Aristotle grants—no one is unwilling to be blessed—but also half false—wickedness (*mochthēria*) is not involuntary.[42] Or else, he immediately adds, no human being can be said to be the source of his actions; but if it appears that we are such a source, they—presumably, the actions—are in our power. What Aristotle set out to determine, however, was whether our character states are in our power; and the extent to which those dispositions have sources outside the individual was the point of the whole preceding discussion of the need for habituation from earliest childhood.

Evidence for the premise of responsibility is supplied by the practice of legislators, who punish those who act wickedly—except those who acted wickedly under compulsion or through particular ignorance—and honor those who perform beautiful things, in order to repress the one and encourage the other, all on the assumption that such action is within one's power and that ignorance due to vice or negligence is no excuse. But Aristotle begins raising objections to the presuppositions of the legislator. Perhaps the individual who has strayed through a more general ignorance of right and wrong was simply not the sort of person to take the trouble to know; people are responsible for becoming careless, the rejoinder goes, through living that way. Of course, once a disposition is formed, Aristotle admits, one cannot stop being in that state merely by wishing it, any more than a sick man can get well that way; nevertheless, what is in our power at the outset should make what follows voluntary as well. Yet the discussion of habituation, once again, showed just how much the actions done in forming a disposition are imposed from without, before we are in a position to be held responsible.

Suppose, the determinist tries again, that everyone strives for that which appears good but no one has control over this *phantasia,* since it appears to each as determined by his character. Aristotle responds quite moderately: if each individual is *in a sense* the cause of his own disposition, he will be *in a sense* the cause of the way the good appears to him; otherwise, no one can be held responsible for doing anything bad, since the cause—as the Socratic would indeed argue—is his ignorance of the end. But Aristotle's determinist goes further than a Socratic appeal to ignorance, which would not necessarily have to be traced to some inborn defect: What if the good could appear to an individual in its true form only if he has this insight by nature? That is what it would mean to be wellborn *(euphuēs)* in the complete and true sense (1114b6–13). In responding to this claim, Aristotle brings the discussion back to its starting point, which does not exactly confirm the responsibility for our character that the argument was supposed to establish: even if the end is not fully in our control, we can be held accountable for the actions undertaken in pursuing it.

The implicit debate Aristotle has conducted on the issue of responsibility arrives at an almost shockingly qualified conclusion: *if, as it is said,* our virtues are voluntary and we ourselves are *in a sense co-causes* of our dispositions, and this is what makes us lay down the end of a certain sort, then our vices would also be voluntary (1114b21–24). Our virtues are assumed to be voluntary only on the basis of common opinion, and we recognize ourselves to be only, in a sense, "co-causes" of our dispositions. Even if one grants that character formation is not wholly determined by nature but under some human control as well, the whole discussion of habituation made clear how much that control lies in the hands of others—parents or teachers or whoever is responsible for rearing the young. Aristotle has responded to the determinist's case without really confronting it. The one firm point in the whole discussion is his repeated criticism of our hypocritical tendency to take credit for our strengths but not blame for our weaknesses.

❧ 3 ❧

Virtues and Vices

NICIAS: This, Laches, is what I say it [courage] is: the knowledge of terrible and of confidence-inspiring things, both in war
and in all other things. . . .
SOCRATES: And now, as it seems, according to your argument,
courage is not knowledge only of terrible and confidence-
inspiring things, but, as your argument now runs, courage
would be knowledge about pretty much all goods and evils and
in all conditions. . . . Therefore, Nicias, what you are now saying
would be not a portion of virtue but virtue entire.

—Plato *Laches* 195a, 199c–e, translated by James Nichols

[ELEATIC] STRANGER: I suspect that you believe that manliness (courage) is for us one part of virtue. . . . And that moderation is other than manliness, but, regardless of that, this too is a
proper part of that of which manliness is too. . . . Then we must
have the nerve to declare a somewhat amazing speech about
them. . . . That the pair of them is in a certain sense with a well-
founded enmity toward each other and admits of a sedition of
contraries in many of the things which are.
[YOUNG] SOCRATES: How do you mean that?
STRANGER: There are often many actions when we express our
admiration for the speed, intensity, and quickness of thought
and body, as well as of sound, in which we speak our praise of it
by using the single address of manliness. . . . And what of this?
Have we not often praised in turn in many actions the species of
quiet becoming? . . . Aren't we then saying the contrary of that
which we utter abut the former?

—Plato *Statesman* 306b–307b, translated by Seth Benardete

SOCRATES: And in truth justice was, as it seems, something of this
sort; however, not with respect to a man's minding his external

business, but with respect to what is within, with respect to what truly concerns him and his own. He doesn't let each part in him mind other people's business or the three classes in the soul meddle with each other, but really sets his own house in good order and rules himself.

—Plato *Republic* IV.443d–e, translated by Allan Bloom

The Beautiful as *Telos* of the Virtues

Fragmentation of the Virtues

If the excellence of the human being could be understood on the model of the excellence of the eye, there would be a single virtue that puts its possessor in good condition and enables him to perform his function well (1106a15–19). According to the *ergon* argument of Book I, the distinctive human function is "some practice (*praktikē*) of that which has *logos*" (1098a4), hence the virtue that enables one to perform it well should be *phronēsis*. But the *ergon* argument introduced the notion of a single human excellence derived from the human function only to reverse direction suddenly, so that performing well became a matter of doing so "in accordance with the proper excellence" (1098a15–16), and that shift in the argument opened up the possibility of a plurality of virtuous dispositions. The same movement was at work in Book II, when the original conception of virtue—as a disposition aiming at a mean determined by logos as the *phronimos* would determine it—was replaced by a plurality of virtues, each understood to constitute, in regard to some particular passion, a mean state between two extreme states, which count as vices. The manifold of passions, which together make up the desiring part of the soul, is the source of that manifold of virtues and vices that now furnishes the subject matter of Books III and IV.

"This part of the *Ethics*," it has been said, "presents a lively and often amusing account of the qualities admired or disliked by cultivated Greeks of Aristotle's time." Of course, one might then conclude: "Aristotle's moral ideas and moral ideals are, in some degree, the product of his time, and cannot be expected to be adequate in the world of today."[1] In Books III and IV of the *Ethics*, Aristotle is indeed holding up a mirror to his world, but that is not necessarily to endorse what figures on it. Once one simply notices the many statements that declare what is said or thought to be the case, one realizes how readily Aristotle manages to avoid speaking in his own voice. The territory of the dispositions under examination ranges widely—from the battlefield to the social gathering—and what is included is often as striking as what is left out: wittiness is a virtue; piety is not. The selection alone, then, is one sign of the distance at which Aristotle must stand from the conventions he is articulating.[2] Another sign is furnished on each occasion Aristotle pauses to note the limits of ordinary language in its identification of the virtues and vices, especially when this seemingly casual set of remarks turns out to indicate a pattern underlying the sequence as a whole.[3] Aristotle originally restricted the audience he considered appropriate for the inquiry through the warning that it would be accessible only to those already brought up to recognize "the that," and anyone satisfied with that starting point, he added, would have no need to seek "the why" (1095b5–8). The paradox of the strange invitation Aristotle extends to his intended audience—in which the familiar that makes participation in the inquiry possible also makes it unnecessary—is nowhere more evident than in Books III and IV. The dispositions are portrayed in a form recognizable enough to confirm, in part, why they are admired or reproved; but allowing ethical virtue to exhibit itself in this way is precisely what enables it to disclose its own contradictions and limits, which explains why, in the end, the life devoted to it is found to count only as "secondary happiness" (1178a9–10).

Although no explicit justification is offered for the selection and arrangement of the dispositions under examination—in keeping with the apparent presentation of ethical virtue simply in its own terms—an underlying order comes to light in a number of ways. The most obvious indication is the movement of the series as its sets out from courage and moderation, which are "thought to be the virtues of the nonrational parts" (1117b23–24), and finally reaches a set of social virtues culminating in wittiness, which lies at the farthest remove from the nonrational and looks as if it could just as easily be categorized an excellence of mind as of character. Yet the discussion does not conclude with that. Instead, it adds one more disposition—the sense of shame—which, though a mean between extremes, is denied at that point the status of a virtue.[4] The observation Aristotle makes—that shame causes us to blush just as fear makes us grow pale (1128b13–14)—seems to bring the sequence back in the end to where it began, with recognition of the bodily root of the passions of the soul. Shame is the counterpart, though, of fear, not of courage; it is itself a feeling and not a virtuous disposition.[5] The denial of its status as a virtue contradicts the claim put forward at the beginning of the discussion, when the true virtue of courage is separated from a set of states that are mere likenesses of it: "political courage" in that context is said to bear the closest resemblance insofar as it is motivated by a virtue, namely, shame (1116a28). That understanding of shame, we realize in the end, must reflect the perspective of the citizen soldier motivated by it; by the time we arrive at the conclusion of Book IV, the demotion of shame marks the culmination of the argument in its movement beyond that perspective.

The investigation of the plurality of virtues and vices in Books III and IV interrupts the continuity of the argument that began in Book II, by tying human excellence to the human function, and will conclude in Book VI, with the acknowledgment of the truth in the Socratic claim that *phronēsis* makes all the virtues a whole (1144b14–17). At two points along the way to that conclusion a particular virtue is singled out as one that somehow embodies the whole: greatness of soul seems to be, as it were, "some kind of cosmos" of the virtues (1124a1–2), and justice, in the sense of lawfulness, is "complete virtue," comprehending all the rest though exercised only in relation to others (1129b26–27). If these three particular virtues—greatness of soul, justice, and *phronēsis*—incorporate the same whole, each must do so in its own unique way. It is far from obvious, however, that the three different perspectives they represent necessarily complement each other in harmony. As the first two unfold in sequence, the relation between them uncovers certain tensions within the sphere of ethical virtue; and when *phronēsis* emerges as the third peak, it puts into question the boundary that assured the autonomy of ethical virtue as a self-enclosed sphere.

Phronēsis is identified by the end to which it looks, that is, something good for a human being (1140b20–21). At the moment ethical virtue is brought into connection with this end not only does the plurality of praiseworthy dispositions disappear, but also virtuous action, once subordinated to the self-interested pursuit of the good, can no longer be said to be chosen as an end in itself. If there were no resistance to that subordination, ethical virtue would not even provisionally appear to constitute an independent sphere of human excellence; no attempt could have been made, in that case, to understand the morally virtuous as they understand themselves. The resistance that makes such an understanding possible has its source in the principles instantiated by the two other virtues that bear a claim to incorporate the whole: the beautiful, embodied in the "cosmos" of greatness of soul, and the just, identified with the "completeness" of the lawful, govern the sphere of ethical virtue in their own distinctive, and possibly conflicting, ways. When he introduced these two principles as the subject matter of political science, Aristotle observed that they are so full of "wandering" it is debated whether everything just or beautiful is so only by convention and not by nature (1094b14–16). This question will be confronted for the first time in the discussion of political justice, where Aristotle tries to find a place—however obscure—for the just by nature (1134b18–19). No such claim is made about any virtue of character being beautiful by nature: the fourth book of the *Ethics* is the only one in which *"phusis"* or its cognates never appear.[6]

The analysis in Books III and IV of the *Ethics* offers a kind of phenomenology:[7] it presents the phenomena of ethical virtue—the opinions about what is beautiful and ugly, just and unjust—from the "inside," as experienced by those whose lives are defined by them.[8] It does so, however, only to an extent that coincides with the intention of subjecting those opinions to critical examination.[9] The representation of conversation in the Platonic dialogues displays Socrates' examination of his interlocutors' opinions, attempting to bring to light their inner contradictions and partial character, while at the same time indicating the germ of truth they may contain, often without the awareness of their spokesman; if the *Ethics* is attempting to accomplish some version of that task within the parameters of the treatise form, it must do so above all in its examination of virtues and vices in the course of Books III and IV.

Yet the treatment of each particular virtue of character, one might object, presents ordinary opinion in its narrowest possible construal, whereas Socrates' effort to grasp "the what it is" seems always to explode the boundaries that differentiate any specific virtue from the others. Any particular disposition ordinarily praised as virtue fails to count as human excellence, Socrates argues, unless it is based upon a true understanding of one's own good; but then it looks as if it can no longer be one particular virtue distinguished from others. This is the claim Aristotle sets out to debate, but finally comes to accept, in some form at least: the dispositions of character count as virtues and the actions that flow from them as virtuous only if guided by *phronēsis,* which makes human excellence, in the practical sphere, a unified whole.

The Socratic linkage of virtue with *phronēsis* is one consequence of the examination of opinion carried out in the Platonic dialogues, which Aristotle addresses explicitly. But that examination has another, more radical consequence. Whenever a particular disposition ordinarily praised for its excellence is found, under Socrates' analysis, to be giving itself a pretentious name, like "courage" or "moderation," while really consisting in a calculus aimed at maximizing pleasure and minimizing pain, it shows itself to be only "demotic virtue"; Socrates is led, on one occasion after another, to the conclusion that nothing but philosophy counts as true human excellence.[10] Now, it is one thing to argue that the virtues of character do not count as genuine human excellence unless guided by *phronēsis;* it goes further to imply that the truth of any particular virtue is philosophy.[11] One might accept, perhaps, that endurance of soul is beautiful and good only if guided by *phronēsis* without leaving behind altogether the ordinary understanding of what constitutes courageous action.[12] But what happens once the locus of true courage is found in the endurance of soul that allows someone, confronting an impasse in inquiry, to push ahead intrepidly into the unknown?[13] If the commitment to inquiry in the face of knowledge of ignorance is the primary form of courage, everything else is derivative or only a metaphoric extension, while the true virtue turns out to be one among other manifestations of philosophy as love of wisdom, which is to say, eros of the beautiful. If all the ethical virtues presented in *Ethics* III and IV pointed beyond themselves in this way, it would not be through their connection to the instrumental reasoning of *phronēsis* but, rather—as the discussion of moderation in particular will finally suggest—through their aiming at the *kalon.* This end arouses a paradoxically disinterested longing: it can take the form of a model for emulation, but it is not an object that can be possessed. If the beautiful so construed is a common principle that ethical virtue shares with love of wisdom, the noble, as *telos* of ethical virtue, is its particular instantiation.

Courage and Moderation

The seemingly casual selection of virtuous dispositions, which covers such a broad range in *Ethics* III and IV, stands out by contrast with the standard set of four virtues that typically appear in the Platonic dialogues. Yet, if ethical virtue is the excellence of the nonrational, desiring part of the soul, then courage and moderation, which are "thought to be the virtues of the nonrational parts" (1117b23–24), appear almost to exhaust the whole; in fact, they provide together a pattern that runs through the analysis of all the others.[14] Pleasure and pain have been found to be "the whole business of virtue and political science" (1105a10–12); but the pleasures relevant to moderation are in a sense the most basic ones, and the painful emotion that admittedly accompanies courage is a result of life itself being at stake. The other cases of explicitly paired virtues Aristotle examines—liberality and magnificence, greatness of soul and ambition—belong together as a matter of degree, whereas courage and moderation form a pair through their contrariety. Courage, or manliness (*andreia*), is tied by its very name to one gender, and *sōphrosunē*, as temperance, sobriety, or chastity, if not as sound-mindedness, looks just as partial. The same behavior praised with a view to *andreia* could be blamed with a view to *sōphrosunē*, or the other way around; and it would be most unusual to find an individual not inclined, by natural temperament or socialization, toward one of these dispositions while being, for just that reason, disinclined to the other.[15] The contrast of the two dispositions is manifest not only in the inclinations that are their roots but also in the specific ways each proves to be related to the end of ethical virtue.

In beginning with courage, the examination of the virtues starts with the one that displays itself most dramatically—with the greatest demand for self-sacrifice—and therefore, perhaps, most recognizably as an object of praise; but at the same time, it starts with the one that presents, for what may be a number of reasons, the most problematic case. It is hard not to assume that this is what Aristotle intends when he concludes the discussion with the surprising remark that courage is easy to grasp in "outline" (1117b21–22). In contrast with the general model—each virtue is a disposition between two extremes with regard to one specific passion—courage is analyzed as a virtue in relation to two passions—fear and confidence. In this one case alone, moreover, to understand what is praiseworthy in it requires working through a set of states that mimic it, and are mistaken for it, but cannot constitute the true virtue. It is in that context that we find, as representative of one of the mistaken understandings of the virtue, the first explicit invocation of Socrates. However the tension is to be understood, finally, between the Socratic position, as Aristotle portrays it, and the understanding of ethical virtue he is putting forward, courage is apparently the case most suited to bring that out.

Plato represents what is surely a familiar understanding of courage when he has the general, Laches, assure Socrates that anyone who is willing to stay at his post and face the enemy is courageous or manly (*Laches* 190e). Socrates, as we would expect, finds this description of a particular kind of action too narrow to count as a definition of courage: when he applies such a description to himself, in the course of his trial, he speaks of his conduct in war only as an image for staying at his post of philosophy and not running away out of fear of death.[16] What he is seeking with Laches, Socrates explains, is an understanding of courage that will cover the behavior not only of hoplites but also of cavalry and the whole warlike class, and, further, not just behavior in the face of the dangers of war but also of illness, or at sea, and, indeed, in an encounter with the dangers that lie in the attraction of pleasure (191a–191e). The account of courage in *Ethics* III eliminates one element of such an expansion after another until the proper sphere of the virtue appears to be sufficiently restricted. Courage involves not just resistance to the fear of death in general but of death in the "greatest and most beautiful danger"; and at least if we look to the honors bestowed in "cities and monarchies," this refers presumably to the dangers of war (1115a30–32). The city surely has reasons to honor those who are willing to sacrifice their lives for it, but that should in fact make us wonder if it is a sufficient guide to the proper ranking of the nobility of dangers. Facing death on the battlefield as illustrated by the Homeric warriors, in any case, turns out to be "political courage," which Aristotle will identify as only a shadow of the true virtue.

What distinguishes the truly courageous person is not fearlessness: if there were no passion that had to be brought under control, his disposition would hardly seem worthy of praise. If, on the other hand, there were a real conflict at work between a resistant passion and the attempt to overcome it, the condition would be one of self-mastery in the successful case or lack of self-mastery in the case of failure. The courageous person will experience fear, then, not just of terrors beyond what human nature can endure but even within those limits;[17] yet his disposition is worthy of praise because he experiences fear as he should and as *logos* determines. In providing the standard that measures what it means to fall short or exceed, *logos* determines the vices related to the virtue of courage: one who exceeds in fear—or one who is deficient in confidence, though this is less obvious—displays cowardice, while the contrary vice, rashness, is displayed by one who exceeds in confidence, or who is deficient in fear. This last condition, a kind of fearlessness, is too rare in human nature, Aristotle remarks, for ordinary language to have even assigned it a name.

The courageous person avoids cowardice or rashness by his disposition to experience fear just as he should, according to *logos;* but he must also do so for the sake of the beautiful; for the *kalon,* Aristotle suddenly announces for the first time, is the *telos* of virtue (or "of the virtue"; 1115b11–13). That the courageous person fears as *logos* dictates is a particular application of the original definition of ethical virtue in Book II; but that definition supplied no *telos* for ethical virtue and had nothing to say about the beautiful. When it is introduced now, it reflects the end of ethical virtue as the ethically virtuous person understands it. Aristotle will disclose his own understanding of the motivation at work in the ethically virtuous individual aiming at the *kalon* much later, in the discussion of friendship, where love of the beautiful is found to be a kind of self-love (cf. 1168b27–29, 1169a8–13).

Determination of a feeling by *logos* originally stood on its own as a characterization of the mean; the account of courage, however, as the first of the particular virtues, now confronts us with the question of how that standard is related to the beautiful as *telos.* While the mean provides the measure that differentiates the virtue of courage from its related vices, the beautiful as *telos* is a principle needed to differentiate the true virtue from those states that merely imitate it. The examination of those states provides the indirect path on which we come to understand something of what courage is—and perhaps, in that way, ethical virtue in general—by realizing what it is not.

The first of these shadows, which is most readily mistaken for the virtue because most like it, is the political courage of the citizen. To illustrate it, Aristotle cites Homer's representation of what is going on in Hector's mind as he stands outside the gates of Troy, caught in the grip of fear at the thought of Achilles' approach but resisting the desire to run as he imagines the shame it would incur. Aristotle quotes Hector's initial thought, "Polydamas will be the first to put a reproach upon me." Hector is looking back and thinking of his recklessness in refusing to heed the earlier warning by Polydamas to lead the Trojans inside the city. He now anticipates their future reproach: "Hector believed in his own strength and ruined his people."[18] The hero's concern with his own glory, Homer implies, can conflict not only with his own preservation but also with that of the city. Aristotle points to all the deficiencies of political courage by choosing Hector in this situation as its representative. Yet he highlights, instead, its likeness to courage itself: political courage is the closest approximation insofar as it comes to be through a virtue, that is, shame, and through desire for the beautiful, that is, honor (1116a2a–29). Aristotle's objective evaluation of this point of view will appear at the very end of the account of ethical virtue (1128b10); he must be speaking at the moment in the voice of the politically courageous individual himself, who identifies the *kalon* with honor and sees shame as a virtue. Within this horizon, acting out of shame and the desire for honor is a superior form of political courage, in contrast with that displayed by the troops, who may be motivated to abide the fear of death in battle but only by another fear— punishment at the hands of their commander. The contrast makes it all the harder to see how the higher-class political courage falls short of the true virtue.[19] To distinguish them, we would have to understand what the beautiful is, beyond honor, as the end that defines human excellence.

At an even further remove from the virtue of courage than the motivation of citizen soldiers is that of professional soldiers, whose skill in the use of arms makes them most efficient in avoiding perils and whose experience allows them to discern false alarms in battle and thus appear courageous to others. Now, being armed with the right skills or having familiarity with danger can stand in the path of unwarranted fear; but such a condition shows itself to be only an appearance of courage precisely when the threat does become great and the one who relied on his experience and professional skill is the first to flee. Aristotle introduces this misunderstanding of courage with his first explicit reference to Socrates.

To think of courage as a matter of experience and expertise is to miss entirely something like the strength of soul that makes us praise a disposition as virtue; that mistake, Aristotle suggests, lies at the heart of the Socratic belief that courage is knowledge (*epistēmē*; 1116b4–5).[20] If, however, Socrates did think of virtue as some kind of knowledge, what he must have meant, Aristotle is well aware, could not be the professional soldier's skill and experience.[21] When Socrates examines with two generals the question, what is courage? and they begin with Laches' conception of it as "some kind of endurance of soul" (*Laches* 190e), they are led to the proposal that it is a science (*epistēmē*) of what is frightening and confidence-inspiring (194e–195a), which proves to be a science of all good and bad things (199c). The definition of courage as an *epistēmē* is put forward, however, not by Socrates but by Nicias, whose understanding of it, and attraction to it, represents the distorted form in which an apparent Socratic principle shows up when it is filtered through a particular kind of soul.[22] The first explicit reference to Socrates in the *Ethics*, which is supposed to identify the Socratic understanding of virtue with professional expertise, brings the philosopher onstage in a kind of caricature.

The view Aristotle ascribes to Socrates does, however, raise a genuine problem: if there were some kind of knowledge of good and bad, it would presumably render superfluous all the particular, and apparently separable, virtues of character, which, according to the account in the *Ethics*, have to be instilled by training in a receptive nature.[23] If Aristotle intends to be the defender, in some way, of ethical virtue as ordinarily understood, he has good grounds for targeting Socrates, whose practice of examination brings to light the self-contradictions, or at least the limits, of the virtues as they show up in opinion. But the alternative that Socrates embodies is not a science of good and bad: it is the courage of the philosopher pursuing his quest for wisdom in the face of his knowledge of ignorance, or the moderation that accompanies his awareness of lacking the wisdom he desires. The ethical virtues of courage and moderation can always be in tension with one another; philosophical courage and philosophical moderation, as manifestations of the philosopher's desire for wisdom, amount to the same thing.

From the allegedly Socratic identification of courage as knowledge, Aristotle turns to the contrary pole, that passion of spiritedness, or *thumos*, which seems to be the most natural claimant to, or root of, courage (1117a4–5). The recognition of *thumos* in this context calls attention to the missing presence of this passion at several key moments at which it might have been expected.[24] When it is taken up for consideration now, Homeric citations return to illustrate a condition in which human beings can be likened to wild animals rushing upon an attacker.[25] The passion of *thumos* might inspire ferocious or intrepid action; but if it is like, or a matter of, fighting out of pain in anger or pleasure in revenge, it could not in itself be the exercise of a virtue, which must aim at the beautiful and result from choice determined by *logos*. *Thumos*, for that reason, is not sufficient for the virtue of courage;

but is it a necessary natural base of courageous action? If supplemented by choice and purpose, Aristotle allows, *thumos* seems like courage (1117a4–5); but is it possible to be driven by the passion of spiritedness and motivated at the same time by either *logos* or the beautiful?

The scale of dispositions resembling courage moves ever further from the true virtue as the analysis turns to the temperament of the confident—who would flee as soon as their expectation of safety was put into question—and yet another step beyond them, to the boldness of those who are simply acting out of ignorance of the dangers they face. The range of dispositions that only imitate courage may help explain why the virtue is analyzed in relation to two feelings, fear and confidence: in the more distant imitations, some kind of confidence takes the place of strength of soul in the face of fear,[26] whereas in the disposition most closely resembling the true virtue, some other fear—of disrepute or of punishment—overcomes the fear of death to motivate action that looks courageous.

In returning to courage itself after the discussion of the mere resemblances to it, Aristotle acknowledges the pain that accompanies the exercise of the true virtue, which violates the general principle—the exercise of every virtue should be pleasant. He tries to save that principle by considering that the end to be attained by courageous action might be pleasant, however obscured by the painful actions needed to reach it; but the suggestion of the hidden pleasure of the end drops out when Aristotle reiterates that the courageous person endures painful experiences because it is beautiful to do so, or shameful not to. What he emphasizes, finally, is how much more painful such experiences will be the more virtuous a person is, and the happier, for such an individual is aware that his life is worth most and he therefore stands to lose the most (1117b9–13). One is struck at this moment in particular with how mysterious true courage remains: its restriction to death on the battlefield was based, after all, on the evidence of how cities respond to such a deed. Aristotle spoke of true courage overcoming fear in the face of "the greatest and most beautiful dangers," but he did not tell us what he believes they are. Socrates, just before drinking the hemlock, finds it a "beautiful danger" to believe the tale he has just been telling his companions (*Phaedo* 114d), in facing the "terrible danger" of neglecting care for the soul (107c). Aristotle mentioned Socrates only to mock the thesis that courage is knowledge; but it is hard not to think of Socrates when Aristotle assigns true courage finally to the person who faces the end of a life he believes to be the most worth living, perhaps the only life worth living.

After all the complications of the analysis of courage, moderation (*sōphrosunē*) seems quite simple—at least in the starkly narrow form in which Aristotle manages to construe it. Every virtue, as it comes under examination in the Platonic dialogues, expands far beyond the bounds of its ordinary understanding; but *sōphrosunē* undergoes, in Plato's *Charmides*, an especially explosive expansion—from the first definition proposed, a quiet temperament (159b), to "the knowledge of itself and the other knowledges" (166e).[27] Aristotle's account appears to go as far as possible in the opposite direction, as he sets out to derive the boundaries of the domain from a consideration of the vice of indulgence: the pleasures of the body are separated, to begin with, from those of the soul. Then sight and hearing are eliminated as too refined, and even smell as only incidentally involved. Of the remaining pleasures of touch and taste, which are shared with all animals, taste in its function of discriminating has to be stripped away; indeed, even touch, the most universally shared of the senses, is said to involve too broad a sphere as long as it includes pleasures such as those of a massage or warm bath, for the enjoyment of which, even in excess, one is not blamed as indulgent or profligate. What remains are the pleasures of touch affecting only certain parts of the body: Aristotle refers to a certain gourmand, who wished that his throat might be longer than a crane's (1118a32–34). Over against the *sōphrosunē* that, under Socrates' examination, turns into an architectonic science, Aristotle reduces the virtue, finally, to a matter of controlling the appetites for food and drink and *ta aphrodisia,* as long as sexual desire can be understood simply on the model of desire for food and drink.

The moderate person enjoys such pleasures in accordance with the mean, and feels no pain, or only measurably, when they are absent. Nature, which appeared once in the discussion of courage to characterize *thumos,* is mentioned now to distinguish certain pleasures, the ones that are common to everyone and blameworthy only in excess, from others, those that are idiosyncratic and can cause one to go wrong in many ways. One who in any way exceeds the measure of the mean in his desire for pleasure, and thus displays the vice of indulgence, should be contrasted with one who falls short of the mean in that regard; but erring on the side of deficiency in this case is so rare that ordinary language once again—as in the case of fearlessness—

fails to supply a name and Aristotle must stand back from convention to correct it.

Given the boundaries to which moderation has been reduced, it is hardly surprising to find that the beautiful has disappeared almost entirely; once it came to light in the context of the virtue that requires the ultimate self-sacrifice, it is not at all obvious how it could manifest itself in the self-interested moderation of desire. Moderation seems to exemplify perfectly the general definition of ethical virtue in Book II—the moderate person cares for pleasures as correct *logos* dictates (1119a20)—without raising the question courage does when the beautiful is suddenly introduced as its defining *telos*. But while the density of appeals to the *kalon* throughout the discussion of courage stands in contrast with the virtual absence of the *kalon* from the discussion of moderation, it makes a rare but very important appearance at the end: in the moderate person desire harmonizes with *logos,* for the target of both (dual voice) is the beautiful (1119b15–16).[28] It is the virtue of courage, or the courageous action, which aims at the beautiful; it is not, on the other hand, the virtue of moderation but desire itself that is directed toward the beautiful when it is in harmony with *logos.*

If ethical virtue is a disposition that harmonizes desire with reason, moderation should be the paradigm case. Just before the conclusion of the discussion of moderation, however, desire is characterized as that which is in need of being chastised (*kolazein*), which is linked by a play on words with the vice of indulgence (*akolasia*): the virtue of moderation, accordingly, would be the state that results once the desiring part of the soul has been chastised and thereby brought into harmony with *logos.* Through punishment of some sort, two independent sources, desire and reason, are coordinated to aim jointly at the beautiful. This is the closest ethical virtue comes to the unity of "desiring reason" or "rational desire," which Aristotle will identify, at the beginning of Book VI, as the central principle of the human (1139b4–5). But the real possibility of reason that is itself motivated by desire, or desire that is itself rational, looks as if it is to be found above all, or perhaps only, in philosophical eros. The analysis of *sōphrosunē* began with an excessively restricted sphere; in the end, *sōphrosunē* discloses most clearly, perhaps, how the virtuous disposition of character produced by habituation could be understood as an adumbration of the natural condition of the erotic soul of the philosopher, and it accomplishes this through the *kalon.*[29] If the ultimate paradigm of *sōphrosunē* is the philosopher's desiring reason aiming at the beautiful, that is the product, as much as the philosopher's courage is, not of an *epistēmē* of good and bad but of the knowledge of ignorance that motivates the eros of wisdom.

Greatness of Soul

Pleasure, wealth, and honor, under examination in Book I as claimants to be the highest end of human life, all failed to meet that standard; but it is in relation to the passions generated by those ends that we develop our praiseworthy and blameworthy dispositions of character, which are taken up for examination in Books III and IV. Beginning with the fear that accompanies our attachment to life itself, which courage confronts, and the bodily pleasures and pains that constitute the territory of moderation, the sequence leads to the feelings we experience and character traits we develop with regard to wealth. The sphere of wealth—like that of honor, which follows—is divided on a scale of smaller and greater into two sets of dispositions, the virtues of liberality and magnificence, along with their related vices: their relation looks as if it could be understood on the model of the same word written in smaller or larger letters, which Socrates proposes as an image for justice in the individual and the city.[30]

Aristotle goes out of his way, once again, to avoid any metaphoric expansion of the meaning of the virtues whose proper sphere is that of money; only a few remarks hint at how Socrates could have found the paradigm of liberality in the philosopher's expansive soul and magnificence in his contemplation of all time and being.[31] However modest or private a form it is in which the liberal person gives, he does so not only correctly—to the right people, in the right amount, at the right time—but also for the sake of the beautiful (1120a24–26). Of course, the beautiful shows itself most vividly in the grand expenditures through which magnificence is displayed—a ship of war, the chorus for a performance of tragedy, temples or sacrifices to the gods; such projects express the greatness of the city but also that which transcends the city, through which it seeks to elevate itself. The "great and beautiful work" produced through the virtue of magnificence arouses "wondrous *theōria*" (1122b16–18): the grandeur of the *ergon* of magnificence brings our recognition of the gods, along with wonder and contemplation, into the political world. If the magnificent person can produce something on such a grand scale without being vulgar, it is because he is able to "contemplate the fitting" (1122a34–35); but, above all, he must spend for the sake of the *kalon*, for that is common to all the virtues (1122b6–7). It is in the discussion of magnificence, where the *kalon* is most naturally rendered "beautiful," [32] that it is, for the first time, explicitly announced as the common *telos* of all the virtues. Yet precisely at that moment, the beautiful ceases to be invoked as an end: no virtue after this point is said to be for the sake of the *kalon*.

This is what we would least expect in the very next case, when the grand scale of magnificence (*megaloprepeia*) is followed by greatness of soul (*megalopsuchia*), the virtue concerned with love of honor on the grand scale. If anyone could be said to stand in relation to the beautiful, it might seem to be the great-souled individual. Perhaps, however, he cannot be said to act for the sake of the beautiful, since that would mean aiming at a *telos* outside himself, while greatness of soul is itself "some kind of *cosmos*" (1124a1–2) and its possessor himself thus seemingly the subject in which the beautiful is incarnate. This is suggested by the analogy of greatness of soul to body: *megalopsuchia* involves magnitude just as corporeal beauty does, whereas a small person may be neat and well proportioned but never beautiful (1123b6–8). That the virtue whose name expresses "psychic grandeur" should be introduced on the model of the body indicates something from the outset of the ambiguity of *megalopsuchia* and what it signifies as the peak of the virtues of character.

As "some kind of *cosmos*" of the virtues, greatness of soul is either a crowning jewel above all the rest, or an ordered whole that comprehends all, or both. It is the virtue of character that stands above and adorns all the rest. Yet it might be thought at the same time to entail greatness in all the others (1123b30); at the least, the *megalopsuchos* cannot be imagined displaying any of the vices—fleeing in battle or acting unjustly—given his disdain for the ends that motivate others to fall into those vices. In its comprehensive status, *megalopsuchia* is the counterpart to justice as "complete virtue" (1130a8–10): the just person, in his obedience to law, would perform all the actions that otherwise flow from the inner disposition of a person possessing any of the particular virtues or, at least, would avoid all the vices. This general sense of the just, as the lawful, will be distinguished from its particular sense, as the equal; yet despite its distinct senses, the just manifests itself as one virtue, whereas the beautiful is fragmented into a plurality of virtues—and if *megalopsuchia* contains that plurality in itself, it must do so in a very different way than justice does. Greatness of soul looks like a *cosmos* of all the virtues of character in an individual elevated as distinctive and rare; the complete virtue represented by obedience to the law, on the other hand, is the lowest common denominator of human excellence and justice the virtue required of "everyman."[33] The two virtues express two independent principles—the just as a principle of equalization and the *kalon* as a principle of distinction— each of which, in its claim to represent the whole of ethical virtue, stands in potential conflict with the other. In fact, the beautiful instantiated by greatness of soul has a relation to the just, and the just to the beautiful, that proves to be a source of internal conflict within each.

Megalopsuchia and its related vices are dispositions concerned with what one claims for oneself relative to what one deserves: the great-souled individual is one who claims much and deserves much, and what he claims and deserves must be the greatest of external goods. That, Aristotle reasons, should be assumed to be what we offer to the gods, what is sought by the worthy, and what is given in recognition of the most beautiful things; that object is honor, which is in fact what the great do claim, as it appears "even without argument" (1123b17–24). But if it is honor that the great-souled individual deserves and demands, he is, at his very core, burdened with paradox: the honor that confirms what he is makes him dependent on others, which is the denial of what he is. For that reason, no honor would be adequate to what he deserves, yet there is no greater external good by which he could be rewarded. If it were to mean anything at all, the honor would have to come from someone he respects, but he cannot accept a superior, and perhaps not even an equal; whether he can have and be a friend in the fullest sense remains in question.[34] Greatness of soul appears in the ethical world as the beautiful incarnate; but at its core is a demand for justice—for the unequal honor that superior worth deserves—which cannot be satisfied.

In the self-defining, though self-defeating, demand for his just deserts, the great-souled individual seems to be moved by the passion of spiritedness, or *thumos*. That passion would fit uneasily, however, with his self-understanding as someone in whose eyes nothing is great (1124a17–20). In all his deportment he displays a sense of standing above the trivialities of life; and while he has no motive, therefore, to do anything shameful, neither is he inclined to feel admiration (1125a2–3). Now, someone who believes nothing worthy of admiration while expecting recognition of his worth on a grand scale embodies an insurmountable tension. The person for whom it might really be true that nothing is great would be one who recognized that the human being is not the highest thing in the world (cf. 1141a20–22, 1141a33–b2), but such an individual would stand outside the sphere of ethical virtue and all its concerns, not as its crowning jewel.

It is difficult to be great-souled in truth, Aristotle insists, since it is not possible without *kalokagathia* (1124a3–4). The term that, in its colloquial sense, designates the gentleman, a member of a certain social class, literally means the union of the beautiful and the good: the juxtaposition of these two senses captures the double vision of *megalopsuchia* and all the virtues of which it is the culmination.[35] While "in accordance with truth" only the good should be honored (1124a25), he who is deemed worthy of honor in the city must be visible in a way that goodness alone is not, and that visibility comes in large measure from the gifts of fortune—being highborn, wealthy, and powerful. His virtue may refer to the soul alone, but the *megalopsuchos* is marked by appearances—his dignified walk, his deep voice, his steady diction. He especially appreciates beautiful but useless possessions, which display his self-sufficiency (1125a11–12). If, as the *Ethics* will finally argue, it is theoretical activity pursued as an end in itself that has the greatest claim to self-sufficiency, the great-souled individual, who should be complete in himself, aims, however unwittingly, at something whose fulfillment necessarily lies beyond himself.

A man who feels no need of anyone and no lack of anything—beginning with the body and ending with the soul—is the image Socrates holds up as a mirror for Alcibiades on the occasion of their first conversation (*Alcibiades I* 103b–104c). Alcibiades believes himself most beautiful and biggest—which Socrates admits is visible to everyone; he knows he is born into one of the best families in the most important Greek city, with many powerful friends and connections, supported by great wealth, even if he takes the least pride in that. Thinking big of himself in all these ways, Socrates explains, Alcibiades is too much even for his big-thinking (*megalophronoi*) lovers, who have all run away from him, feeling themselves despised, leaving Socrates as the only one not to abandon him.

The big-thinking Alcibiades looks like the perfect representative of Aristotle's *megalopsuchos*.[36] But what makes him an especially illuminating exemplar of this figure is the inner uncertainty that haunts him at the same time, as he glimpses in himself the dilemma of honor as the measure of his worth. This is the Alcibiades that Plato portrays in the *Symposium*. The confident sense of his own superiority he experiences is threatened by one person only, someone who perplexes him so much he does not know if he is looking up to or down on him, if he is pursuing him as lover or pursued by him as beloved: that person is Socrates. Alcibiades expresses all his perplexity in his accusation against Socrates for his practice of *eironeia*, the deceptive self-deprecation that is really, Alcibiades suspects, an expression of disdain; he discerns, in Socrates' *eironeia*, the sign of a truly great-souled individual, who can cover up his greatness only because of his enviable freedom from the need for recognition.[37]

The virtue of *megalopsuchia* was originally distinguished not only from the excessive disposition of vanity but also from smallness of soul; and the person who might seem most small-souled of all was said to be one who claims less when he deserves recognition as great—just think what he would do, Aristotle notes, if he deserved less (1123b12–13). But if he were not in fact as great as he is, he would not need to make himself appear less. It is only the human being on a grand scale who would find it necessary to try to appear smaller in the eyes of those who look up to him:[38] the great-souled person, who cares more for the truth than opinion, always speaks and acts openly— except when he finds it necessary, before the many, to be ironic (1124b28–31). *Eironeia*, which consists in claiming less than one deserves of qualities held in esteem, is, according to Aristotle's tripartite schema, the vice of deficiency, over against the contrary vice of boastfulness, in relation to the mean of sincerity (1127a21–27). There is, then, among all the virtues in the *cosmos* of *megalopsuchia*, one alleged vice: *eironeia*. Yet this practice of self-belittling looks like the only way out of the deepest problem of greatness of soul, disarming from within the unsatisfiable demand for recognition in the form of honor.

Now, *eironeia* may indeed be a disposition that falls short of sincerity, which is supposed to be the virtuous mean.[39] Nevertheless, the subtle understatement of one's own merits can appear graceful or charming, as Aristotle admits at the end of his account of *eironeia*, and he calls upon Socrates to illustrate the point (1127b25–26). The essential object of Socratic self-deprecation is wisdom: the Socrates, according to all the other references in the *Ethics*, who believes virtue is knowledge comes to light at this one moment as the *eiron*, who claims only to know what he does not know. With the insertion of this characteristic Socratic trait into his portrait of the great-souled individual, Aristotle confirms all the ambiguity of that portrait. This ambiguity is not merely a rhetorical device; it is the reflection of the way a character like that of Alcibiades, as he himself divines, points beyond himself to Socrates, and ethical virtue, at its peak, to philosophy.

The Disappearance of the Beautiful

A certain grandeur—both of the city and of that which the city looks up to—casts its light on *megalopsuchia*, as it did on *megaloprepeia*, and, in doing so, seems to be responsible for bestowing on the particular virtue a name of its own; when the love of honor becomes private, it has no name. Of the eleven sets of dispositions in Books III and IV, the smaller-scale virtue in the sphere of honor is the central one.[40] It exhibits the most slippery of all boundaries separating the mean from the extremes and, partly for that reason, is the first of the virtues for which ordinary language has no name; it turns out to be the most radically anonymous of all, since Aristotle does not even coin his own term for it, as he does in other cases. Since this mean is utterly anonymous, love of honor (*philotimia*) and "nonlove of honor" (*aphilotimia*) each take turns invading its territory for praise and setting up the contrary for blame. The ambitious person is praised as manly and "lover of the beautiful," but the unambitious is praised no less for being measured and moderate: the disposition on the side of excess attaches itself to courage, that on the side of deficiency to moderation, when both vie for the claim to the praiseworthy mean. When it comes to blame, on the other hand, the ambitious person is reproached for loving honor more than he should according to correct *logos*, but the unambitious person is blamed just as much for not demanding honor even in regard to the beautiful things (1125b9–18). When measured by correct *logos*, love of honor looks excessive; when measured by the beautiful, lack of love of honor looks deficient. Ambition is blamed, in other words, for exceeding the due measure but praised for insisting on its due in regard to the beautiful things, lack of ambition praised and blamed for precisely the opposite reasons.

This unstable and indeterminate disposition exhibits most vividly the contrariety of the two measures that have been at work in the description of the virtues of character. On the one hand, each virtue is a mean—or a disposition to aim at the mean—in accordance with correct *logos*, which determines what should be done and when and how, by some person in some situation, to avoid excess and deficiency. This accords with the initial general definition of ethical virtue; but it leaves out the role of the beautiful, which was first introduced in the account of courage as the *telos* of virtue. After the central set of virtues concerned with honor, the beautiful fades from sight; it does not explicitly characterize the mean in regard to feelings of anger, for which Aristotle borrows the name "gentleness," nor any of the praiseworthy character states relevant to conversation and amusement and social pleasures. If *megalopsuchia* is a peak, these dispositions are all to be found on the path down from it, on the way toward justice, at which point the beautiful disappears entirely.

At the same time that the beautiful fades from sight, another development takes place: the virtues themselves become anonymous, at least in ordinary language. While every mean up to and including greatness of soul has a common name, after that point, none does, at least not until "wittiness" at the end. Anonymous dispositions had shown up prior to greatness of soul, it is true, but never in the case of a virtue: the extremes that Aristotle dubs "fearlessness" and "insensibility" were both said to be unnamed in ordinary language because they lie so far outside the common human range. After *megalopsuchia,* in contrast, it is the mean state itself that becomes anonymous, not because of its rarity but because of the infinite flexibility of the target at which it aims. The mean in regard to anger is as impossible to fix as the mean in regard to honor, which it follows: we often praise those deficient in anger and call them gentle, but we sometimes praise those who are harsh-tempered as courageous and capable of rule (1126a36–b2). It is only because we think the excessive extreme more opposed to the mean that the anonymous virtue takes on the name of the deficient extreme, "gentleness"; what constitutes that mean, however, which has no name of its own, can be determined only by a judgment in particular circumstances of those with whom, on account of what, and how one should be angry.

The first half of the list of virtues (ending with *megalopsuchia*) stands in relation to the second half (beginning with "love of honor") as the original account of ethical virtue—a disposition to aim at the mean (II.6)—stands in relation to a "second sailing"—avoidance of the worse extreme, which we recognize as our own inclination (II.8–9). The sliding virtue of "love of honor" exhibits precisely that point at which the mean ceases to appear as what it is but necessarily takes on the look of one contrary from the perspective of its opposite. It must have been the beautiful, then, that was responsible for picking out a mean disposition as something deserving linguistic recognition; when the beautiful is no longer an end, that mean disposition no longer has a name and cannot be distinguished in itself. The mean in feelings or actions is determined solely, once the beautiful disappears, by correct *logos;* and what correct *logos* picks out, as a result of deliberation, is a nameless point on a sliding scale, a nonmathematical measure of the mean, always needing to be contextually determined anew. If every praiseworthy state were identified only in relation to this measure, none would have a title of its own and, as Aristotle shows in this linguistic way, all the ethical virtues would be reduced to, or replaced by, *phronēsis.*

The dispositions in the closing set are those having to do with the pleasures of social interaction and conversation. A slight revision of the original list in Book II results in the sequence now ending with wittiness, which is not only a social virtue, on the way to justice, but one that seems to be on the way beyond ethical virtue altogether. With a pun Aristotle derives the name for the witty (*eutrapeloi*) from their characterization as full of "good turns" (*eutropoi*)—movements that *seem* or are *thought* to spring from character (1128a9–12). The tact, in any case, of the witty person, who says and listens to what is suitable to a decent and free person, is not independent of the conventions of a class; of course, one might wonder how Aristotle is evaluating that aspect of wittiness when he praises the decorum of modern comedy over the bawdiness of the older comic poets, presumably Aristophanes (1128a22–24). Insofar as comedy is a kind of abusive speech, perhaps, Aristotle admits, like some other kinds it should be regulated by law. He immediately responds with a claim that supports the greatest possible freedom from such constraints: the witty person who is charming and free is like a law unto himself (1128a31–32). With his charming or graceful style (*charieis*)—the same characteristic Aristotle attributed to Socrates in his practice of *eironeia* (1127b22–24)—the witty person brings the sequence of virtues to a close.

The account of dispositions we praise and blame, however, is not quite at its conclusion. It ends, strangely, with a mean that is said not to be a virtue. Shame (*aidōs*), Aristotle now insists, is not fittingly spoken of as a virtue since, in the first place, it seems to be more a feeling than a disposition (1128b10–11); as fear of disrepute, it is the counterpart of the fear of death, not of the virtuous disposition in regard to that fear. However unfitting it may be to speak of shame as a virtue, that is precisely how it was identified when it first appeared as the motivation behind the political courage of the Homeric heroes (1116a27–28); why that state falls short of the true virtue is brought to light, in part, only now with the denial that shame is a virtue. While Aristotle first spoke from "inside" the experience of ethical virtue, he now stands "outside" to disclose one, if not the, motivation of what looks like virtuous action while stripping away its claim to exemplify human excellence.

Shame, or a sense of respect (*aidōs*), is suitable to the young, who live by feelings and can therefore only be kept in check by them. It was for just this reason that the young person, or anyone guided only by feelings as opposed to *logos*, was originally excluded as an appropriate participant in this inquiry (1095a4–9). But if shame belongs to the process of habituation by which all the ethical virtues are inculcated, it is not clear that it can disappear altogether once those dispositions are internalized. To have a sense of shame is admittedly better than being shameless; and it could be considered decent "hypothetically," that is, one would be ashamed if one were to do anything base. In that case, a nonvirtuous element, operative counterfactually, would be responsible for holding one back from vice. But it is absurd, Aristotle insists, to praise a mature person for experiencing shame, or a sense of disgrace (*aischunē*), when he shouldn't do anything that would evoke that feeling; at least, the decent person (*ho epieikēs*) would not voluntarily do the base things that arouse shame (1128b26–29).[41]

When shame is defined in the *Rhetoric* as a kind of pain or uneasiness about past, present, or future actions that seem to bring disrepute, such things are admitted to be more shameful if the fault appears to be our own, but being voluntary is not a necessary condition: licentious actions are considered shameful even when done under compulsion, since the inability to resist is thought to be a sign of unmanliness.[42] In claiming now that the decent person is not susceptible to shame inasmuch as he does not voluntarily do base things, Aristotle seems to be speaking from the perspective of the *epieikēs* himself. This individual—whose designation connects him with equity (*epieikeia*), as the source of flexibility in justice—would never feel shame in the performance of deeds for which he could not justifiably be held responsible. He is saved from a tragic sense of moral deficiency by his refusal to accept responsibility for unintended deeds, whether understood as effects of the gods' manipulations or unconscious motivations. His point of contrast would be Oedipus, whose lack of responsibility for his deeds done in ignorance does not lessen the intensity of the shame that leads him to blind himself in anticipation of meeting up with his father and mother in Hades.[43] If the decent person is an unfit subject for tragedy, as Aristotle observes in the *Poetics,* it must be because of his immunity to shame of this sort, which keeps him from arousing our pity and fear.[44] The account of the virtues concludes by eliminating the tragic figure, in his central experience of shame, from the sphere of the ethically decent, just as the ethically decent individual is eliminated from the world of tragedy.

When the figure of the *epieikēs* reappears at the end of the book on justice, he displays what it means for equity to be the corrective for the generality of the law, which makes law unable to guarantee justice. The equitable person is someone who does not demand the utmost precision in carrying out the intention of the law but who is willing, even when the law is on his side, to be satisfied with less than his due (1137b34–1138a2). He has no expectation, perhaps not even hope, for the intervention of just and punitive gods who would guarantee a precise distribution of rewards and punishments. He would seem to be the character least vulnerable to righteous indignation, or *nemesis,* the feeling of pain at the sight of our neighbors' undeserved good fortune, which was the last of the dispositions, following shame, in the original outline of virtues and vices in Book II. It was introduced there, like shame, as a disposition that is not a virtue but a mean state of emotion praiseworthy in contrast with the related extremes: *nemesis* is the mean between envy, being pained by any good fortune of others, and schadenfreude, feeling pleasure in the bad fortune of others (1108a36–b6). It is the only disposition mentioned in that original survey that drops out entirely from the discussion of Books III and IV.

The passion of *nemesis* depends upon the belief that life is supposed to be perfectly just, and good fortune matched precisely to inner worth. It may be a natural human experience to wish or hope for a perfect correspondence between happiness and virtue. But the expectation for a moral order so precise that there can be no place for chance invites a dangerous disappointment. It is dependent on the hope for punitive gods who would make sure that good fortune never befell the undeserving, which is bound to lead to a bitter resentment. The *Ethics* began with a methodological constraint on the demand for precision in an inquiry about human actions and passions; such a demand might result in a disappointment that would tempt one to give up on such inquiry altogether. The phenomenon of righteous indignation exhibits the counterpart of that theoretical idealism in morality itself. If they shared a common root, it might not be possible to disarm the one without the other.[45] Whatever intention, if any, may lie behind the disappearance of *nemesis* from Book IV, the effect of its absence is powerful: had it not been eliminated, righteous indignation would have occupied the culminating position in the discussion of the virtues of character and cast the shadow of its underlying assumptions on the set as a whole. Instead, that discussion ends with a reference to the equitable person, anticipating the account of equity at the end of Book V; and that account occupies the culminating position in the discussion of ethical virtue as a whole, on its way to being absorbed into *phronēsis.*

Justice in the City and Justice in the Soul

Justice and Happiness

The investigation of justice and injustice in Book V begins with the invitation to proceed along the same path (*methodos*) as previously. But the question of what it means to be a just or unjust person, or even to act justly or unjustly, does not come up until the second half of the book, and then the assimilation of justice to the model of the virtues of character is admittedly strained. It is, for one thing, far from obvious how justice is to be understood as a disposition in relation to a passion: the proposed candidate, greed (*pleonexia*), would seem to refer, rather, to the vice of injustice and the single opposite of the virtue. One can't help but feel that Aristotle "doth protest too much" in the sequence of proposals he tries out for understanding justice as a mean, in the effort to demonstrate its consistency with the virtues of character.[46]

The analysis in Book V sets out to analyze the just, not as a disposition of character but as a principle, or set of principles, governing political, judicial, and economic structures. These principles are presented in mathematical form—despite the repeated warnings in the *Ethics* about the dangers of expecting the wrong standard of precision; the account abstracts as far as possible from the fierce passions and convictions involved in the actual appeal to such principles in political life. What the principles of justice aim to produce is an order of the community. If they motivate the individual, it is less through an internalized sense of shame than through fear of punishment: the support for justice comes primarily not from moral education but from the law with all its sanctions, which might be construed as an implicit admission of the limits of moral education.[47]

The turn to the investigation of virtue was defended at the end of Book I on two grounds: it should contribute to the contemplation of happiness, and it should be of concern to the true statesman, whose aim is to make the citizens good and law-abiding. The treatment of justice in Book V looks far more fitting for the latter purpose; in fact, it seems to belong to that branch of *politikē* whose proper subject is the city.[48] *Psychē* occurs only once, at the very end Book V, and then as a subject of "other speeches," which are being criticized.[49] Those are presumably the speeches of Plato's Socrates, whose analysis of the soul structure, analogous to the class structure of the city, uncovers the desire to punish at the core of the demand for justice.[50] The centrality of the spirited part of the soul and the desire to punish that moves it is almost nowhere to be seen in *Ethics* V: where Plato represents the moral and political idealism that springs from those roots, Aristotle gives us an account of justice altogether defanged.

In the midst of defending his own definition of happiness before the tribunal of common opinion, Aristotle referred to the inscription at Delos that declared justice most beautiful, health best, and the object of desire most pleasant. Aristotle insisted, in contrast, on the unity of happiness as best, most beautiful, and most pleasant (1099a24–29): his conspicuous omission of justice suggests that it does not belong, at least not in an immediate way, to the happiness of the individual. In order to illustrate the difference between the honor we show for the highest things and the praise we bestow on what is good for something else, Aristotle observes that no one praises happiness the way we do justice, because we consider happiness something more divine and better (1101b25–27). It comes as a surprise, therefore, to discover that, while *eudaimonia* never appears in the entire discussion of the virtues of character, it does come up, albeit only once, at the outset of the discussion of justice: the just things are said to be "productive and preservative of happiness and the proper parts of it in the political community" (1129b17–19). This statement is as important as it is obscure. Coming as it does immediately after the claim that the just in the form of the law aims either at the advantage in common *or at the advantage of the ruling power,* it might understandably arouse skepticism.[51] What exactly are the proper parts of happiness and what does it mean to speak of happiness in the political community? In the second book of the *Politics,* the last objection Aristotle raises to the city Socrates constructs in the *Republic* is that happiness is not something that can belong to the whole unless all or most of its parts, or at least some of them, have it. Happiness is not like an even number, whose defining character belongs only to what it is as a whole and not to each of its parts;[52] but the evenness of the even number looks like the fitting model for "happiness in the political community" as produced by justice.

Justice, in its most comprehensive sense, will be defined as "complete virtue," albeit in relation to others; but for that very reason, justice more than any other virtue is thought to be for the advantage of another (1129b25–1130a5).[53] To demonstrate that being just is in one's own interest is the challenge Socrates faces in the *Republic,* first posed by Thrasymachus, then renewed by Glaucon and Adeimantus (343c, 360c–d, 367b–e). To meet it, Socrates must radically reconstruct the meaning of justice: only if its primary application is to the proper order of the soul can he attempt to show that it is good for the possessor in itself and not merely in its consequences. The movement from the principle "one man, one job," as it governs the division of labor in the city, to the interpretation of it as a principle governing the order of the soul is an ascent, Socrates maintains, from a mere phantom image (*eidōlon*) of justice to the discovery of its truth (*Republic* 443b–d). And the radical implication Socrates draws is that the only measure of what is praiseworthy as just or beautiful in our actions relating to others should be the ability to preserve the desired internal order of the soul (*Republic* 443e–444a, 589e).

Socrates looks at justice in the city only as a model "writ large" in which to read the primary form of justice, in the individual soul. The *Ethics* turns this ranking upside down, after holding off as long as possible even considering the question. When, in the last chapter of Book V, an interpretation of justice is allowed that is applicable to relations among parts of the soul, it is only, Aristotle insists, as a metaphor, and even then, a metaphoric application of justice not in its primary sense—as a relation among free and equal subjects under law—but only in the derivative sense that can characterize the unequal relationships of the household (1138b5–8). If justice can be said to belong at all to the individual soul, it is only in this doubly displaced form. In the discussion of the virtues and vices in Books III–IV, it was the beautiful that put up resistance to the Socratic reduction of virtue to *phronēsis*, opening up an exploration of the plurality of dispositions we praise and blame in relation to the passions. The treatment of justice in Book V, in its resistance to the Socratic reconstruction of justice as the proper order of the soul, makes it possible to analyze the political, judicial, and economic structures that constitute justice in the city. Despite this analogy, the beautiful and the just are not exactly symmetrical. It is through the beautiful that the otherwise narrowly construed dispositions of character point beyond themselves, to raise the question, at least, whether the truth of human excellence is to be found only in philosophy. This seems to be precisely what Socrates discovers through his reconstruction of justice as an order of the soul; but when *Ethics* V ends with the acknowledgment of that Socratic move, Aristotle does not draw the same consequences from it. If he hinted at the possibility of philosophical courage or philosophical moderation, philosophical magnificence or philosophical greatness of soul, he seems unwilling to consider something like philosophical justice, in which the truth of justice in the ordinary sense is to be found. The horizon of the account of justice seems to be entirely encompassed by the *polis*. Just how much that is the case is indicated when suicide comes up in the end of Book V: it fails to supply evidence for the possibility of doing injustice to oneself, since the victim, Aristotle maintains, is not the individual who gives up his life but the city in the loss of its citizen.

The Mathematics of Justice

In the case of the virtues of character, two limiting vices, of excess and deficiency, were inferred from a primary account of the praiseworthy mean between them. The single vice of injustice, in contrast, provides the starting point from which the virtue must be inferred: we call "unjust" either one who breaks the law or one who tries to get more than his fair share, hence, Aristotle reasons, the just must have a comprehensive sense as the lawful and a particular sense as the equal. While the separation of the two senses will prove to be problematic, it makes possible at the outset a twofold abstraction, which allows, on the one hand, for an initial defense of the law of any political community in its claim to represent justice and, on the other, for a quasi-mathematical analysis of equality that implies an objective determination apart from any political opinions or passions of the soul.

While it may be true that we call a lawbreaker unjust,[54] identifying the just with the lawful looks like the potentially dangerous claim that obedience to the laws of one's own community, whatever they are, is sufficient to make one just and, if justice is complete virtue, a human being of full excellence. The movement of the argument in the course of Book V can be understood precisely as an effort to put this claim into question.[55] But Aristotle anticipates that movement from the start with his signature adverb of qualification: all the lawful things are *in a sense* (*pōs*) the just things (1129b12). The laws, after all, aim at the advantage of all in common—or, Aristotle immediately adds, at the advantage of the sovereign, either in accordance with virtue or on some other standard (1129b14–17). This is to admit in a casual aside the definition of justice—the advantage of the ruling power—that leads Thrasymachus to disdain it as something only the weak and foolish person would be willing to practice (*Republic* 338c–339a).

It is because the law commands actions in accordance with the virtues and forbids those in accordance with vices that such actions can be said to constitute "almost the majority of the lawful things" (1130b22–23); it is noteworthy that the point is illustrated only by prohibitions—not to desert one's post, not to throw away one's arms, not to commit adultery, not to speak badly (1129b19–24). Aristotle does not explicitly broach the question whether it is just to obey the law if its commandments and prohibitions do not coincide with virtue and vice independently determined. But he indicates that even when the behavior required does coincide, acting out of obedience to the law is altogether different from acting out of an internal disposition to aim at the mean, for the sake of the beautiful: obeying the law out of fear of punishment, Aristotle will eventually admit, should not count as acting justly in any essential sense at all (1137a9–14).

That there is a particular sense of justice apart from its comprehensive sense is inferred from recognition of a unique motive that differentiates injustice from the other vices, that is, seeking gain, or the pleasure of gain (1130b4–5). And if to be unjust is to get more than one's fair share, the just must be the equal—as it seems to everyone without any argument (1131a13–14). The simplicity of this universal, undefended agreement, for one thing, covers over the two forms that Aristotle is about to differentiate:

distributive justice, in its assignment of the limited goods available in the community, operates on the principle of geometric proportion, according to which equal shares are assigned to equal subjects and unequal shares to unequal subjects, while corrective justice rectifies violations of equality in individual transactions on the principle of arithmetic proportion, according to which the unjust loss to one party is compensated by taking away the unjust gain to the other without consideration of any difference in worth between the subjects involved (1130b30–1131a11).

In spelling out the mathematics of distributive justice, Aristotle makes it look as if all that is required is an application of geometric proportion such that equal subjects receive equal shares, unequal subjects unequal shares, in assets of the community such as political offices, honor, wealth, or security. But even if everyone agreed on this principle, the fundamental question would remain: equal or unequal in what? In the *Politics,* Aristotle identifies this as *the* problem that arouses "perplexity and political philosophy," and the discussion reflects the intense disagreement and hostility the problem can provoke.[56] In the account of distributive justice in the *Ethics,* it is admitted that the measure of equality will be different in democracy, oligarchy, or aristocracy; but the powerful political realities and human passions accompanying those differences, which the *Politics* represents, are covered over by the mathematical analysis in the *Ethics* of the formal principle of proportionate equality.

The covering over of such political realities and human passions by a mathematical analysis takes on another form in the *Ethics* in its account of corrective justice. Injustice, according to that account, is a violation of the equal in transactions between individuals, and all that is required to rectify the situation is to calculate the excessive gain by one party and transfer that amount to the party that has suffered the corresponding loss, thus restoring equality. While all such cases might call for corrective justice, Aristotle admits that the terms "loss" and "gain" must be extended from their ordinary territory in order to apply to involuntary transactions as well as voluntary ones (1132a11–14, 1132b11–20). It comes as a shock, however, to find that class of involuntary cases illustrated by actions like poisoning, murder, or robbery: the victim, after all, did not voluntarily give up his life or property! "Involuntary transactions," we suddenly realize, is the title of the class in which all crimes have been placed, although corrective justice deals with these violations by requiring nothing but compensation for loss. Compensation is rationally determined by calculation; but criminal deeds should call for punishment, and the passion that is the root of the desire for punishment is *thumos*, which is conspicuously absent here. Abstracting entirely from crime and punishment, Aristotle's analysis takes the sting out of justice.[57]

While all criminal deeds have been subsumed under "involuntary transactions," a cut is made in that set—between those performed furtively or in secret and those done violently or in the open—which doesn't seem to serve any purpose in distinguishing one form of corrective justice from another (1131a6–9). This is the division Plato's Athenian Stranger proposes in the *Laws* when faced with the problem of formulating a penal code, which is necessary for the city, while maintaining the Socratic premise that seems to make it impossible: if virtue is really a matter of knowledge and vice a matter of ignorance, the fitting response to erroneous action would be education, not punishment. How, then, can the legislator defend a code of punitive law, which should depend upon the differentiation of voluntary deeds or crimes from involuntary ones? The replacement the Stranger proposes for that distinction is the division between actions done furtively or in secret and those done violently or in the open, though his interlocutor is understandably baffled by how it solves the problem of justifying punishment only for voluntary action (*Laws* 864c).[58]

Adopting the distinction between furtive and open deeds, Aristotle divides involuntary transactions into two classes, over against the class of voluntary transactions. He runs through an apparently casual list of examples, but it is in fact systematic enough that each of the three classes is assigned seven examples. The case that lies at the exact center is "pandering" (*proagōgeia*):[59] according to Plato's Socrates, the fear of being accused of this practice leads midwives to conceal their true expertise in the art of matchmaking; and Socrates finds himself in the same position, as a midwife of young men's souls. This is the image of himself Socrates constructs as he reflects back on his life just before his trial and death.[60] One cannot help but wonder whether it is insignificant that it illustrates the furtive deed Aristotle places in the central position among involuntary transactions requiring corrective justice.

The categories of distributive and corrective justice were presented as if they were exhaustive forms of justice in the particular sense. Yet immediately after the analysis of the two is completed, another is introduced, the notion of requital, or reciprocity, which the Pythagoreans took to be the just simply (1132b21–23). The justice of Rhadamanthys—one must suffer what one has done—might sound like corrective justice; but it does not share in its principle of equality, according to which unfair gain is to be taken away and loss compensated with no consideration of the intention of the action or the status of the parties involved. Reciprocity, in contrast, requires treating a voluntary action differently from an involuntary one and taking into account the agent of the unjust action: a subject cannot requite a ruler by striking back at him, whereas a ruler should do more than simply strike back at a subject (1132b28–30). If, in any case, corrective justice only rectifies an unjust exchange, there must be a prior principle of what makes a just exchange, and that seems to be the role of reciprocity. Though it is not a matter of distributive justice, it shares in the principle of proportionate equality; and it is that principle, Aristotle adds, that holds the city together. The point will soon be illustrated by reference to the system of exchange based on a division of labor, but Aristotle first supports it on another basis: as long as people think they cannot requite harm with harm, they feel like slaves (1132b33–1133a2). Reciprocity might sound like a rational calculation—an eye for an eye—but the desire for revenge, which exemplifies it, is traced not to reason but to the spirited rejection of living like a slave.

This understanding of the bond of the political community shows up, however, only for a moment; it is quickly replaced by the interpretation of reciprocity as the principle of proportional equality operative in economic exchange.[61] The bond of the city, according to this interpretation, is the reality of natural need; but the vehicle, money, through which need can be expressed, is, as its name (*nomisma*) indicates, a product of convention. A product of convention makes possible what nature alone cannot—the commensurability of commodities—without which there could be no equality; without equality, no exchange; and without exchange, no community. Reciprocity in this form would be a sufficient bond if the *polis* were reduced to the prepolitical sphere of exchange. Aristotle hinted at its limitations when he began the discussion with an observation about the principle of reciprocity exhibited in the demand to punish, which is rooted in the need to feel free.

The Just by Nature

Right when the analysis of the principles of justice seems to have been completed, Aristotle suddenly reminds us that the thing being sought is "the just simply and the political just" (1134a24–26). The formula is ambiguous enough to make us wonder whether there are two subjects or one and, thus, whether the city is the locus of justice simply—a question that will prove important for understanding the relation of friendship and justice. The political just governs the relations of persons who are free and equal, either numerically or proportionately, leading a life in common for the sake of self-sufficiency under the law: it encompasses the general and the particular senses of the just, as the lawful and the equal.[62] Other human relations can be governed by standards of justice in a derivative sense—"despotic justice" between master and slave, "paternal justice" between parent and child, or "economic justice" between husband and wife; but the household is the sphere of one's own, and there is no possibility of injustice, nor therefore of justice in the primary sense, in respect to one's own, since no one chooses to harm himself (1134b9–13). This Socratic principle, Aristotle implies, far from compelling the identification of justice with the internal order of the soul actually requires the restriction of justice in the primary sense to the city, where independent subjects interact with each other.

It is only once the *polis* is established as the context in which justice primarily belongs that the problem arises whether there is anything just by nature or whether all the just things are only so by convention. Aristotle addresses this problem in one of the most notoriously cryptic and truncated discussions in the *Ethics*, with little if any help from explicit connections to the discussion that precedes or follows.[63] Of course, the whole inquiry has, in a sense, been conducted under the shadow of this question, ever since Aristotle's observation that our "wandering" opinions about the just and beautiful things raise doubts whether there is anything in them by nature (1094b14–16). That doubt was never explicitly addressed in regard to the beautiful; the question of what, if anything, is "by nature" arises above all, apparently, from the manifest variety of lawful things, together with the implicit claim by every community that its laws and customs instantiate the just.[64]

What is by nature is that which has the same power or capacity (*dunamis*) everywhere, whether it is thought to be the case or not.[65] The conventional, in contrast, is that which might have been determined in some other way at the outset, though once settled it is no longer indifferent: what is just by convention is so because it has in some sense been agreed upon (1134b18–21).

The examples Aristotle offers—a ransom of one mina for prisoners, a sacrifice of one goat or two sheep—illustrate, for one thing, the arbitrary element in any law due to the need to attach some number to it, however intelligible its principle may be in itself. But what is striking here is the sudden appearance of the sacred, which has been so absent from the *Ethics*. A law about sacrifice looks like an especially good example of something that has no reason for its specific provisions other than having been laid down the way it has been; in its particularity, it can require only obedience, though perhaps, for just that reason, it cannot help but raise a question about the utility of sacrifice in general and, with that, about the gods or god being worshipped.[66]

Some people think all the just things are by convention, Aristotle observes, on the assumption that what is by nature is unchangeable and has the same power everywhere—fire burns the same in Greece as in Persia— whereas the just things are manifestly changeable. "This is not so," Aristotle responds rather cryptically, "but it is in a sense": among us—whatever the case may be among the gods—all things are indeed changeable, and yet there is something by nature. Aristotle illustrates his claim by appealing to the phenomenon of the right hand being stronger by nature, though it is possible for anyone to become ambidextrous (1134b33–35). "Nature," in this illustration, is an innate capacity, the same everywhere, at least for the most part. Nature in this sense does not determine what is desirable, nor does it exclude transformation to bring about what is more desirable—like the natural capacities that can be turned into virtues by habituation.[67] Aristotle seems to be engaged in dialogue here with Plato's Athenian Stranger, who uses right-handed dominance to illustrate the problem of what is by nature. In the midst of investigating the question whether boys and girls should have the same education—particularly in preparation for the use of arms in war—he abruptly turns to issue a complaint about the current practice in the use of our hands: while by nature both hands are almost balanced in strength, like our legs, mothers and nurses make children "lame" by habituating them to use only the right hand, though anyone could be ambidextrous.[68] It is questionable whether Plato means to represent his Athenian Stranger as really believing we are all born almost ambidextrous. But if, the Stranger implies, ambidexterity—or the equality of men and women for which it stands in—is discerned to be the desirable condition, there is an especially effective justification for it in the appeal to what is given by nature as a standard. Aristotle apparently disagrees. Nature as the originally given state, he suggests, though it is not so inflexible as to preclude the development of what is discerned to be the desired condition, does not determine what that condition is, nor need it serve as the grounds of justification.[69]

The greater strength of the right hand illustrates what is by nature in one sense; but that is not the model Aristotle uses in the end when he holds up nature as a standard over against the things established as just merely by contract. These conventionally just things are not the same everywhere, because the regimes are not. The plurality of distinct sets of laws in different times and places reflects the partial understanding of justice animating the regime in which they are found. But there is one regime, Aristotle asserts in conclusion, that is everywhere in accordance with nature the best. It is possible, of course, that this "best" is and only could be a "paradigm in heaven," by which one might found a city in oneself.[70] If it is not the regime of any city in the ordinary sense, it would indicate the limits of the *polis* and its justice altogether.[71] The postulation of one regime best by nature would serve, in any case, to remind us that the laws of any actual city are relative to its regime, which might fall short of the best; in doing so, it would serve to moderate the original claim that obedience to the law is sufficient for justice. That claim belongs to "the that" of the decent person's upbringing. Aristotle's discussion of the just by nature, if nothing else, induces the perplexity that might make one dissatisfied with "the that" and aware of the need to search for "the why."

Injustice to Oneself

An account of the principles of justice does not tell us what it is, in the strict sense, to act justly or unjustly, let alone what it is to be a just or unjust person. Those questions introduce a classification in Chapter 8 of Book V, which recalls, with certain revisions, the classification of voluntary and involuntary action at the opening of Book III. For a violation of the principles of justice to count as acting unjustly, it must be voluntary, not performed under compulsion or in ignorance of the particular circumstances; and for that unjust action to count as the expression of an unjust character, it must not only be voluntary but also performed as a result of choice, rather than out of *thumos* or some other passion (1135b11–27).[72] Now, if justice is to be understood as a virtuous disposition of the individual, it should be a mean state between two extremes; yet while each virtue of character is a mean on a continuum between vices of excess and deficiency, acting justly is found to be a mean between doing injustice and suffering it (1133b30–32), and those contraries represent not the poles of a continuum but the relation between the agent of unjust action and the victim. Suffering injustice looks like an accidental experience that could not plausibly be considered blameworthy, but perhaps allowing oneself to be a victim of injustice might be (cf. 1138a28–32).

This question generates a set of perplexities, at the end of the fifth book, beginning with the puzzle whether it is possible to suffer injustice voluntarily.[73] The question brings to mind the argument Plato puts into the mouth of Callicles, who sets out to teach Socrates that doing injustice is bad only by convention, while suffering injustice is bad by nature (*Gorgias* 482d–483b). He is indignant at the violation of the just by nature when the inferior many use the chains of the law to bind the superior individual, who has the right to more than an equal share. It is especially infuriating when the great man appears willing to suffer such injustice: he should be blamed for failing, in effect, to be a *megalopsuchos* and claim the recognition he deserves. This is precisely Callicles' accusation against Socrates, and he holds philosophy responsible for the corruption of this powerful nature.[74]

Suffering injustice voluntarily might seem to be possible in the case of the person lacking self-restraint, who allows himself to be harmed. But Aristotle goes on to propose a qualification that would eliminate this possibility: if suffering injustice meant undergoing something against one's wish (*boulēsis*), no one would submit to it willingly, since no one, including the akratic, wants to be harmed (1136b1–9). The impossibility of suffering injustice voluntarily follows from the Socratic principle, with its assumption of a universal human inclination to want what one finds good for oneself. It should be just as impossible, in light of the Socratic principle, to do injustice to oneself. Now, that might seem to be exactly what the decent person (*ho epieikēs*) does when he takes less than his fair share. But such an individual, Aristotle objects, may be seeking more of something else, being greedy (*pleonektein*) for reputation or for the beautiful simply (1136b20–22): the one and only time that the *kalon* appears in Book V, it is as an object of greed, that is, injustice. In his apparent act of self-sacrifice, the decent person may in fact be acting unjustly, only not to himself but to the person from whom he is taking more than his fair share of nobility![75]

The decent person's paradoxical self-denial issues into a consideration of equity, which marks the peak of the account of justice.[76] Equity discloses the limits of the original identification of the just with the equal as well as with the lawful: it recognizes a common ground underlying the spirit of precision that would lead both to an insistence on getting exactly one's fair share and to a blind adherence to the law, which might apply a general rule to a particular case despite the inappropriate outcome it brings. Over against the just as the equal, equity corrects for a precision that falls short of justice; over against the just as the lawful, equity corrects for an imprecision that falls short of justice. Aristotle likens "the nature of the equitable" to the "Lesbian rule," which bends to fit what is being measured (1137b27–34). The equitable, in calling for a different measure, makes us rethink mathematics' claim to embody the precise as such.[77] As the last step in the whole analysis of ethical virtue, equity marks the point at which ethical virtue begins to overcome its own idealism. With the kind of judgment it calls for in response to the idiosyncratic parameters of a particular situation, equity looks like an ethical virtue that has turned into *phronēsis*. The question it asks, however, is not yet What is good for a human being? but, rather, What is the just? or, perhaps, What would the legislator have laid down if he had been present on the spot?

The consideration of equity, insofar as it seems to involve taking less than one's fair share, brings the argument back to the problem of doing injustice to oneself. Not only is that impossible, Aristotle determines, in the case of injustice as a violation of the equal—one cannot wrongly take from oneself what is already one's own—but even in the case of injustice as violation of the law. The test case is suicide. Socrates, on his last day, is called upon to defend himself against the charge of taking his own life: to do so, he responds, would be to violate the will of the gods, insofar as we are their property and compelled to remain alive—unless one finds oneself, as Socrates claims to at that moment, under "some divine necessity" (*Phaedo* 62b–c). To take one's own life, Aristotle allows, is an act of injustice, only not against the gods—he is silent about them—nor, since the harm suffered is voluntary, can it be an act of injustice against oneself. The victim, he concludes, is the city, as is indicated by the practice of casting dishonor on the corpse of the suicide.[78] As the locus of political justice, the city must be credited for providing the conditions for the autonomy of free and equal subjects under law; but it appears in the end to have swallowed up everything, including the life of the individual, which is not his own to take.

It is not possible to do injustice against oneself, Aristotle has argued, meaning to be as a whole the agent and, at the same time, the victim of an unjust action. But it is possible, he concedes at the last moment before Book V ends, to speak of a state of justice or injustice among parts of oneself, as in the case of "those *logoi*" that divide the part of the soul having *logos* from the nonrational (1138b8–9). "Those *logoi*" would seem to be the speeches of *Republic* IV, when Socrates discovers justice in the soul of the individual as the metaprinciple in accordance with which the calculative part of the soul reasons, while the spirited part, managed by it, commands and controls the desires. It is only by interpreting justice as a particular order of the soul that Socrates can identify the philosopher with the just person. But the soul whose structure is identified with justice in *Republic* IV cannot be that of the philosopher, whose reason is not simply instrumental and whose desires are not in need of being mastered by something else. The order of the soul Socrates describes, which may be the best possibility for the nonphilosopher, is really *enkrateia,* or self-mastery, its violation *akrasia,* or lack of self-mastery. This is precisely the conclusion at which the fifth book of the *Ethics* arrives: justice applied to the individual is only a metaphor, and only in relation to a derivative sense of justice, between unequal parties, in which a ruling subject must control the ruled (1138b5–13). The account of justice and, with that, of ethical virtue, ends in Book V by anticipating the divided self in Book VII. To get at the soul of the philosopher, it will be necessary to wait for the discussion of friendship, which involves in a different form the internalization of one's relation to another as a structure within the self.

PART III

The Return to the Good

4

Excellence of Thought

SOCRATES: Then, in sum, all the things undertaken and endured by the soul when directed by prudence come to end
in happiness, but when controlled by thoughtlessness in the
opposite?
MENO: It seems likely.
SOCRATES: If then virtue is something in the soul and is itself
necessarily beneficial, it must be prudence: since, indeed, all
things that pertain to the soul are, themselves in themselves
neither beneficial nor harmful, but when prudence or thoughtlessness is added to them, they become harmful or beneficial.
According to this argument, indeed, virtue being beneficial, it
must be some kind of prudence.
MENO: It seems so to me.

> —Plato *Meno* 88c–d, translated by George Anastaplo
> and Laurence Berns

SOCRATES: Just like Thales, Theodorus, while star gazing and
looking up he fell in a well, and some gracefully witty Thracian
servant girl is said to have made a jest at his expense—that in his
eagerness to know the things in heaven he was unaware of the
things in front of him and at his feet. The same jest suffices for all
those who engage in philosophy.

> —Plato *Theaetetus* 174a, translated by Seth Benardete

THE PIVOT OF THE ARGUMENT OF THE *ETHICS*

In turning from ethical to intellectual virtue, Book VI brings to completion
the investigation of virtue that began in Book II and, with that, returns in
the end to the question that initiated that investigation: What is human
happiness? Approaching this question through the lens of its account of

intellectual virtue, Book VI looks down on the insignificance of all things human; from that perspective, it finds happiness to consist in *sophia,* or theoretical wisdom, which has as its object the cosmos as a whole or the highest beings in it, while *phronēsis,* or practical wisdom, is found inferior precisely because of its concern with the human good. To reverse that ranking would be, as the last words of Book VI declare, as absurd as claiming that political science rules the gods because it issues orders about everything in the city (1145a10–11): the very reason offered in Book I in support of *politikē* as the sovereign and comprehensive science shows up at this point as a laughable basis for that elevated assessment.

The conception of wisdom now held up as the highest human perfection recalls the portrait Socrates paints in the *Theaetetus,* just before his trial and death: the theoretical man, in contrast with those who hang around the law-courts, lives a life in complete leisure and freedom from constraints, indifferent to ordinary human affairs, utterly ignorant of the way to the *agora,* not to mention the court or assembly. The teacher of mathematics to whom this portrait is presented sees in it the image of himself and Socrates in common;[1] but Socrates' own way of life in fact seems to have no place in either of the alternatives he portrays. His interlocutors believe they are conversing at leisure; but Socrates is engaged in the conversation on his way to collect the indictment for corrupting the youth, which will soon bring him to the Athenian court of law. The conversation represented in the dialogue, moreover, is based on a recounting of it that Socrates is said to have supplied to its future narrator—a recounting that occupied Socrates during the days after his trial while he awaited execution. Socrates' lifelong practice, which has brought him to these circumstances, hardly looks like that of the individual he describes, whose body alone dwells in the city while his mind is borne everywhere, beneath the earth, geometrizing on the surface, astronomizing aloft, discovering the nature of each of the beings of the whole without ever lowering itself to anything close at hand (173e–174a).

Book VI ends with such an image of the life that counts as human happiness. It looks as if an answer to the opening question of the *Ethics* has been reached and nothing would seem to be missing from the work if it came to a close at this point. Instead, the argument is called down from the heavens and compelled to embark upon a new beginning. If, setting out from that new beginning, the argument arrives in Book X at an account of happiness that looks the same as, or very like, the one at the conclusion of Book VI, it does so on different grounds, no longer based on an investigation of virtue. Book VI thus plays a pivotal role because it completes, not the argument of the *Ethics* as a whole, but what turns out to be only its first phase. And the figure who dominates this pivotal point—bringing the first stage of the argument to its end and motivating the need to start over again—is Socrates.[2]

The investigation of intellectual virtue in Book VI leads Aristotle, finally, to an agreement, or partial agreement, with the Socratic understanding of *phronēsis* as the core of genuine virtue. This critical moment in Aristotle's debate with Socrates, which was set in motion in Book II, transforms ethical virtue, with the result that it no longer constitutes an independent sphere. What was originally the duality of virtue of character and virtue of thought becomes the unity of practical virtue, or excellence of action. A new problem arises, however, in the wake of this transformation, which, in linking practical reason with ethical virtue, seems to open up a rift in the rational soul.

That problem is anticipated by the analysis of the soul with which Book VI begins. Just as the examination of ethical virtue was prepared for by the account at the end of Book I, which divided the nonrational soul in two, the examination of intellectual virtue in Book VI is prepared for by an account that divides the rational soul in two parts, theoretical and practical. The assignment of each to a territory of its own, perfected by a virtue of its own, puts into question the unity of the rational soul. That conclusion seems to be confirmed once *phronēsis,* as the perfection of practical reason, is fused with ethical virtue and, apparently, split off completely from theoretical reason. By the end of Book VI, however, *phronēsis* is assigned the role of operating in the service of *sophia,* as the perfection of theoretical reason. How, we are then compelled to ask, is the harnessing of *phronēsis* to ethical virtue compatible with its subordination to *sophia*? Can both these roles be fulfilled together?

Although Book VI sets *phronēsis,* finally, in the service of *sophia,* it says little explicitly about any effects of one upon the other. Instead, it highlights their separation by treating each as the perfection of a different way of life—the one exemplified by Pericles, the other by Thales or Anaxagoras. Setting the two in competition over the claim to the highest rank, the contest is settled in favor of the cosmological thinkers before Socrates finally appears on the scene as the proponent of the thesis that all the virtues are forms of *phronēsis,* or at least that there is no genuine virtue without *phronēsis* (1144b17–21). At that point, it looks as if Pericles can no longer serve as the adequate representative of *phronēsis;* at the same time, and for the same reason, the conception of *sophia* embodied by Thales and Anaxagoras as its representatives becomes just as questionable. Yet, while Socrates is the spokesman for a certain view about human excellence, he is not held up as an exemplar of it. Behind the dichotomy of political rule and disinterested contemplation of the cosmos lies the question, Who is Socrates? Or, more specifically, What is the relation between Socratic *phronēsis* and Socratic philosophy? If the pre-Socratic wise man exemplifies, in the words of the contemporary debate, an "exclusive" conception of the good life and its highest end, an "inclusive" conception looks as if it would have the impossible requirement of combining the life of Anaxagoras with that of Pericles.[3] But the doubleness—if that's what it is—of Socratic *phronēsis* and Socratic philosophy would make for a life that is neither exclusive in the way the contemplative life is portrayed nor inclusive in any merely additive way.

The Rational *Psychē*

It was said all along, the first words of Book VI recall, that it is necessary to choose the mean between excess and deficiency, which is determined by "correct *logos*," but that notion has yet to be examined (cf.1103b31–34). Looking to some target (*skopos*), Aristotle now explains, the person having *logos* tightens or loosens the passions, like adjusting the tension of a bowstring, and there is some boundary (*horos*) defining the mean state between excess and deficiency in accordance with correct *logos* (1138b21–25). Correct *logos* seems to have a double function: it determines the measure of the mean (*to meson*) chosen as the aim of action, and it sets the "boundary" of the mean state (*mesotēs*) that constitutes the virtuous disposition of character. It is itself determined in light of some target at which the rational individual looks; but that target, as we discover by the end of the sixth book, is understood in one way by the individual devoted to ethical virtue, who looks to the beautiful and the just, and in quite another by the person who looks to *sophia* as his guiding end.[4]

Aristotle recalls the decisive role of correct *logos* only to admit that advising someone to act in accordance with it is like advising a sick man to do whatever a physician would prescribe and expecting him to become wiser about what medicine to take. While the notion of correct *logos* binds the two halves of the *Ethics,* it can open up the discussion of intellectual virtue only by arousing dissatisfaction with the appeal to its authority in the account of ethical virtue. The issue is no longer that of the invalid who thinks he can become better simply by having a doctor's prescription without taking any action to implement it (1105b14–16); the problem now is finding a doctor to provide the prescription—or becoming a doctor oneself.

To address this problem, it is necessary to return to the psychology on which the investigation of virtue has been based. In Book I, that psychology was drawn from "exoteric *logoi,*" according to which the soul is divided into that which possesses *logos* and that which does not. That division proved too crude even to ground the division of ethical from intellectual virtue without first being qualified by an internal division of the nonrational, separating the biological functions, which have nothing to do with reason, from a desiring part of the soul, characterized by its capacity for obedience to *logos.* On those grounds, the psychology of Book I opened up the possibility that desire could be understood alternatively as a subset of the rational soul (1103a2–4). As Book VI opens with a psychology that focuses on the structure of the rational soul, we might expect it to take up that alternative. The structure it articulates, however, is no longer based on the political model of ruler and ruled, differentiating self-initiating reason from that which is merely obedient. Indeed, the function of desire or appetite is no longer explicitly involved at all; hence, the whole issue of the potential rationality of desire is covered over for now. Instead, Book VI divides the rational soul on the basis of an assumption about knowledge (*gnōsis*): what makes knowledge possible is the given likeness and kinship between the parts of the rational soul and the nature of the beings to which they are related.[5] The harmony of being and mind, which would seem to require a teleological cosmology for its support, is assumed without any argument: things governed by unchanging principles and those governed by principles subject to change must correspond to a division between the capacities by which we "contemplate" each,[6] which Aristotle now designates the calculative (*logistikon*) and the scientific (*epistēmonikon*) parts of the rational soul.

Aristotle continues to speak in Book VI, as he did in Book I, of three parts of the human soul, only now the central position, which was originally occupied by the higher part of the nonrational division, has been taken by the lower part of the rational division. Of course, the calculative faculty, whose function is that of deliberation, is certainly not just another label for the desiring function, nor can the peculiar excellence of each be the same. If they were, there could never be a conflict between desire and deliberation, which is just that experience of *akrasia* with which Aristotle has been concerned from the outset and which will compel the new beginning of Book VII. The rational part of the soul is subject to an internal division in Book VI, just as the nonrational was in Book I, but the two actions of dividing the soul occur in a sequence such that when either part of the soul is internally divided, the other remains unitary.[7] When one starts from the most basic level of the biological functions, the central part of the soul is the desiring function, and reason is an undivided third; when one takes one's bearings from the highest level, assigned to theoretical reason, the central part of the soul is the deliberative function, and the nonrational soul is an undivided third. Each account presents a tripartite division, with a single part of the soul central. But when the reader tries to put the two accounts together, the central function becomes dual. The problem posed in the process concerns the relation between desire and deliberation, or their respective perfections, the moral virtues and prudence.[8]

The psychology with which Book VI begins retains the separation postulated in Book I of the rational soul from the nonrational, under which desire was originally subsumed. That premise is put into question when Book VI proceeds, in its second chapter, to address the phenomenon of choice (*prohairesis*). The notion of choice played an important role when the discussion of ethical virtue led to the issue of responsibility, which introduced the question of what can be justifiably praised or blamed, rewarded or punished. In that context, choice was identified as the mark of a species of the genus of voluntary action: the agent who chooses acts voluntarily but, more specifically, on the basis of prior deliberation, not just from being moved by the passions of the moment. When Book VI returns to the notion of choice, it leaves behind the question of responsibility and the moral-legal horizon to which it belongs; the issue now has nothing to do with praise and blame but, rather, with understanding the psychology of action. *Prohairesis* was defined in Book III as "deliberate desire of things in our power" (1113a10–11), and that meant the means to a given end; it becomes, at this point, "deliberate desire" with no qualification (1139a23) and will soon be detached from deliberation in particular, which had precluded the possibility of its object being an end. In the role it now plays, choice becomes *the* origin, or principle (*archē*), of action. It is "serious" when the correctness of desire, manifest in pursuit or avoidance, corresponds to the truth of thought, manifest in affirmation or denial (1139a21–26). Choice as a source of action might thus appear to be a hybrid with its own double source—desire and "*logos* for the sake of something" (1139a31–33). But if *logos* itself is oriented toward an end, it no longer stands over against desire as an other; it can no longer be restricted, consequently, to instrumental deliberation, subordinated to nonrational ends given by an independent faculty of desire. The discussion of choice concludes, therefore, with a formula that cannot be understood as a hybrid of two independent subjects, desire and mind, but only as an inseparable unity in which each is indeterminately substance or modifier—desiring mind (*orektik nous*), or intellectual desire (*dianoetic orexis*); and it is this unitary source of action that is identified as the *archē* of the human being as such—or, perhaps one must say, the human being is such an *archē* (1139b4–5). Desiring mind, however, or intellectual desire, if it is not a synthesis of two independent sources, would seem to be possible above all, or perhaps only, in the lover of wisdom. The condition ethical virtue aims to produce, by habituating desire in accordance with correct opinion, is the natural condition of the philosopher moved by erotic rationality. If desiring mind or intellectual desire is the unitary principle of the human as such, it is exhibited paradigmatically by the soul of the philosopher.

INTELLECTUAL VIRTUES

Choice, as understood in the second chapter of Book VI, looks like the starting point from which a new understanding of the unity of the human soul will emerge. But the discussion proves to be only a first beginning, which comes to an abrupt end when the following chapter starts anew "from higher up" (1139b14). With that, the account of choice in Book VI issues into an analysis of distinct intellectual virtues, just as the account of choice in Book III ushered in an analysis of distinct ethical virtues. Construed as a union of desire and thought, choice should have bound the second half of the *Ethics* to the first by bringing to light an unanalyzed element at the core of ethical virtue—an element of rationality without which it would not be virtue at all. Instead, choice separates the second half of the *Ethics* from the first by introducing a set of virtues of thought as an independent sphere, separate from the virtues of character.

While the standard of choice was identified as a correspondence between the truth of thought and the correctness of desire, our attention is now restricted to the various ways the soul reaches truth (*alētheuei*) in affirmation or denial (1139b15–16). Let these ways be five, Aristotle stipulates without any argument: art (*technē*), knowledge (*epistēmē*), prudence (*phronēsis*), wisdom (*sophia*), and mind (*nous*). By the end of the analysis, all the others except *phronēsis* are reduced to or incorporated by *sophia*, with these two emerging as the respective perfections of the two parts of the rational soul. But just when the grounds seem to be prepared for an account of how the truth reached by the one might affect the other, the two are set in competition with each other in their separate claims to hold the highest rank of virtue and to determine what human happiness is. The philosophical life is not a contender. Philosophy, after all, is given no place in the set of intellectual virtues that are now being defined and evaluated:[9] philosophizing, apparently, is not the perfection of any particular cognitive faculty, at least not one that always reaches truth. Of course, the treatment of intellectual virtues in Book VI turns out to be as much an examination of opinion as the treatment of the ethical virtues was; and this examination of what it means to know brings to light, as much as the other did, all the questionable assumptions and inconsistencies lurking in opinion.

After dismissing "supposition" and "opinion," which are as capable of reaching falsehood as truth, Aristotle begins the analysis of the intellectual virtues with knowledge in the strict sense, observing that we all *suppose* what we know to be unchangeable and that, hence, the object of *epistēmē* must be necessary and eternal (1139b20–23).[10] Scientific knowledge is defined, then, on the basis of an ordinary supposition, immediately after supposition as such has been dismissed in light of its possible falsehood. All knowledge is *thought* to be teachable, but teaching, Aristotle reminds us, must begin with things previously known. To have scientific knowledge, then, one must have *trust*, and the principles on which such knowledge rests must be even more familiar (*gnōrimoi*) to the knower than the consequences derived from them: *epistēmē*, as a "demonstrative disposition," rests on a certain trust in the familiarity of principles that are not themselves subject to demonstration.

The territory of things that admit change, which has been excluded as a subject of *epistēmē,* includes all the objects of action and production (1140a1–3). Aristotle distinguishes between them only by appealing to *"trust in exoteric logoi,"* from which one can infer that the rational disposition involved in action (*praxis*) must be other than that involved in production (*poiēsis*), which results in some product beyond the process. If, as he implies, there is something questionable about the distinction between action and production, it would cast doubt on the important claim in Book II that the action flowing from ethical virtue is chosen as an end in itself (1105a32). A *technē,* like house building, brings something into being through a "disposition with *logos*"; but the definition is quickly restated in order to differentiate *technē,* as a "productive disposition with *true logos,*" from artlessness (*atechnia*), which is accompanied by false *logos* (1140a20–23). An artful mistake, accordingly, is a contradiction in terms; and a doctor who performs his task rationally but before a pertinent scientific discovery has been made could not be said to act with *technē.* With this replacement of expertise by perfection, Aristotle represents, one might say, a self-understanding of *technē,* which can mistake its aim of error-free practice for its very being.[11]

We have been asked to accept on trust the existence of a rational disposition concerned with action in contrast with production; rather than introduce *phronēsis* under that description, however, Aristotle recommends that we first *contemplate* the individuals said to be prudent (1140a24–25). What is especially *thought* to belong to such a person is the ability to deliberate beautifully about things good and advantageous for himself in regard not just to some partial good, like health, but to living well as a whole. But since no one deliberates about things that cannot change, *phronēsis* cannot be the same as *epistēmē.* Nor is it the same as *technē,* since production aims at an end beyond itself, whereas doing well (*eupraxia*) is its own end (1140b4–5): in contrast with *technē, praxis* has its end in itself; when contrasted with *theōria* at the end of Book X, it will be found to have an end beyond itself (1177b2–4). It remains, Aristotle concludes, that *phronēsis* is a true practical disposition with *logos* concerning things good and bad for the human being. To exercise such a disposition, which has become something more than deliberating beautifully about one's own advantage, would seem to require as its basis theoretical knowledge of human nature as such.

Aristotle does not exactly take up his own suggestion to contemplate those who are prudent; instead, he considers those *we believe* to be so, like

Pericles. The capacity to contemplate things good for themselves and for human beings is an ability that we believe belongs to the politician or his private counterpart, the household manager (1140b8–11). We contemplate those we think are practically wise and ascribe to them the ability to contemplate the good things for human beings generally. *Phronēsis* is therefore redefined—as a "true rational disposition about the human practical goods" (1140b20–21)—and the practical attribute originally characterizing the disposition itself thereby comes to modify only the goods with which it is concerned.

In contrast with *phronēsis* as well as *technē, epistēmē* is a *supposition,* Aristotle recalls, about that which is universal and necessary (1140b30–32). The analysis is compelled to return to the account of scientific knowledge because of the unsolved problem of how we know the first principles from which demonstration proceeds, which cannot themselves be objects of demonstration. Nor, in their presumed invariability, can they be objects of *technē,* or *phronēsis,* or of wisdom (*sophia*), since it is the task of the wise person, Aristotle adds rather cryptically, to have a demonstration about some thing (1140b33–1141a2)—but, presumably, not of the first principles of demonstration. It remains that such principles must be apprehended by mind (*nous*), Aristotle abruptly concludes, having offered no proof of the exhaustiveness of the set of alternatives or any account of how *nous* is supposed to function.

In *Metaphysics Gamma,* Aristotle confronts the challenge of defending the law of noncontradiction—the ultimate principle of all demonstration—which cannot be demonstrated without being put to use: his strategy is to turn the table on the skeptic, who in fact affirms the principle every time he tries to put it into question. Such a strategy of demonstration by refutation would not have been necessary, it seems, if this first principle of reasoning could have been declared the self-evident object of an intellectual intuition, and if it is not, nothing else would be a more likely candidate. There is another alternative for confronting the challenge of the indemonstrable principles of demonstration: for the sake of establishing one point, we have to begin with certain accepted premises, but those in turn can become an object of demonstration if we find further premises from which they follow, and so on. This is the hypothetical method of reasoning that Socrates proposes as a "second sailing," given the danger of trying to proceed directly by the light of the good (*Phaedo* 100a); but it amounts to admitting that complete wisdom is an asymptotic goal and we are always only along the way.

Aristotle acknowledges that his wishful appeal to *nous* is motivated by the common opinion that there really is such a thing as *sophia*, theoretical wisdom of the whole. In one common usage, *sophia* refers to the "most precise" of the arts. It slides beyond that on the grounds of the belief that there are people who are wise in general, from which it is inferred that *sophia* would be the most precise of the sciences (1141a16–17): from top-ranking technical excellence to an opinion about comprehensive knowledge, wisdom emerges finally as the peak of scientific precision.[12] The wise person, accordingly, would have to know not only the conclusions of demonstration but the truth of the principles from which they are derived. Hence *sophia* would be—the definition is conditional—*nous* together with *epistēmē: epistēmē* has been reduced to mere demonstration, with *nous* of first principles attached to it as something other—a "head," as it were. Only this combination makes *sophia* possible as knowledge of the most honorable things (1141a20)—we might wonder, of course, why the very human issue of honor has slipped into a description of the objects of knowledge that are supposed to transcend human concerns.

The positing of *sophia*, in its double form as comprehensive knowledge of all beings and precise knowledge of the highest beings, radically reorients the original premise of the *Ethics* and everything that followed from it: it is absurd, Aristotle now argues, to think that political science, which shares a common territory with *phronēsis*, is the most serious (*spoudaiotatos*), unless the human being is the highest being in the cosmos. The human good, which is the end for political science as well as *phronēsis*, must be lowered in rank along with them: since the good, like the healthy, is always relative to that for which it is advantageous, it means one thing for human beings and another for fish. Heraclitus got this right. Each kind of being describes as prudent and entrusts itself to one who theorizes well about its own good, Aristotle observes, as if imagining a judicious crane theorizing about the good for himself and his species.[13]

Even if the human is superior to the other animal species, Aristotle concedes, there are still things more divine in their nature than the human, the most manifest being the heavenly bodies. With the demotion of the human good, political science must subordinate itself to astronomy, or astral theology, directed toward "the most honorable things" in nature. Aristotle confirms the distinctly pre-Socratic perspective he has adopted by appealing to Anaxagoras and Thales, who are said to be wise but not prudent. Thales discovered the truth about reality as a whole while looking up at the stars in all his wisdom and falling into a well at his feet; and Anaxagoras, in his failure to explain how cosmic mind orders the universe with a view to the good, serves Socrates as a model for what must be avoided if he is to account for his own intentional action.[14] The knowledge these thinkers possess is admittedly rare, marvelous, difficult, and demonic but also, in its indifference to the human good, useless (1141b6–8).

Pre-Socratic *sophia* now stands in the sharpest possible contrast to *phronēsis* in its essential concern with the human things. The function most of all ascribed to the *phronimos* is being able to deliberate well; and deliberation, Aristotle recalls, is always about "things of which there is some end," which is a practical good. Nothing is said at the moment about how that end itself is recognized. The "good counselor simply" is someone skilled in aiming (*stochastikos*) in accordance with calculation (*logismos*) at the best of practical things for the human being (1141b13–14): whatever calculation may be involved in determining the means, his hitting upon the end itself depends, apparently, on the same kind of guessing (*stochastikē*) as that by which the ethical virtues were said to aim at the mean (cf. 1106b28).

Abstracting from the question of how the end is given, Aristotle spells out the kind of calculation involved by illustrating what he designates the practical syllogism. The illustration, which is the first in a sequence that ties the discussion of *phronēsis* in Book VI to the account of *akrasia* in Book VII, introduces a problem for the sequence as a whole.[15] Its explicit intention is to show that someone with particular knowledge based on experience is more likely to make the right choice than one who knows only the universal principle: a person who knows that chicken is good for health is more likely to eat the right thing than someone who knows only that light meat is digestible and therefore good for health, but not what kinds of meat are light (1141b16–21). These alternatives, however, split the theoretical from the practical in an unnecessarily exclusive way.[16] The best condition for acting well, with both security and flexibility, would be to know that chicken is good for health *because* it belongs to the class of light meats, which are digestible and for that reason beneficial. Experience may hit upon a particular case that works, but medical science provides knowledge of the characteristic of the class to which that particular belongs, which makes it possible to understand why it is desirable and, thus, to recognize justified exceptions or reasonable alternatives. If one possessed such knowledge and took for granted that health is the end to be sought, no doubts should plague the choice of what to eat. For the prudent person, however, it may be necessary to weigh whether in particular circumstances health itself should be sought, or how it should be ranked among other ends with which it might conflict, with an eye to living well in general. What seems to be required, at that point, is not only calculation of the means but also an understanding of the human good that is the final end.

If, as the *Ethics* originally postulated, the human good is split between that of the city and that of the individual, *phronēsis* must be split accordingly. Of that regarding the city, Aristotle now proposes, the legislative art is architectonic—there is, apparently, no architectonic form presiding over the individual and the city together—while the *phronēsis* involved in particular cases of action and deliberation gets the name *politikē,* which looks as if it comprehends the whole sphere of the city.[17] Yet *phronēsis* is thought most of all to be about oneself; hence, it is this concern that gets the name of the virtue as a whole (1141b24–31).[18] The senses of *sophia* had been extended from precision in the arts to an opinion about the possibility of comprehensive wisdom and, finally, to the most precise knowledge of the highest things. The ranking, however, of theoretical wisdom in that last form above practical wisdom was accepted before *phronēsis* too had been shown to have its own range of senses, which has now been extended from household management and Periclean political leadership to the wisdom involved in seeking one's own good.

The prudent person's deliberation is not merely a neutral skill but necessarily directed toward the good and must reach not only the right conclusion about the advantageous but on the right grounds and at the right time. The good counsel *(euboulia)* the prudent person displays is defined as "correctness of deliberation in regard to what is expedient toward the *telos,* of which *phronēsis* itself is a true supposition" (1142b32–33). *Phronēsis,* like *epistēmē,* has now been identified as a "supposition," but is it a supposition about the *telos* itself? Book VI is about to argue, on the one hand, that virtue furnishes recognition of the end and, on the other, that *sophia is* the true end. *Phronēsis,* in either case, if it is a supposition, would seem to be only about the means to the end—some kind of intuitive counterpart, apparently, to the correct reasoning of good counsel.

Whatever the object of its insight may be, *phronēsis* involves a commanding function that distinguishes it from understanding (*sunesis*), or good understanding (*eusunesia*), which is also concerned with objects of deliberation (1143a7–12). As that which judges or decides (*krinein*) what prudence commands, understanding seems to bring the borderline of the practical intellect into closest contact with the theoretical.[19] Correct decision (*krisis*) about the equitable in particular is the work of "so-called judgment" (*gnōmē*), which Aristotle ties by linguistic association to consideration (*eugnōmē*) and forgiveness (*suggnōmē*) (1143a19–24). Forgiveness, which now shows up as an intellectual virtue, is something different from the *pathos* of pity, which made no appearance in the discussion of the ethical virtues. Forgiveness involves the judgment that punishment is not called for, but, unlike pity, it does not rest on the assumption that life ought to reward the good; forgiveness recognizes the role of chance, while pity, like indignation, denies it. The linguistic ties that link judgment with consideration and forgiveness reflect their common bond in relation to the equitable: equity, which brought to a close the discussion of justice and, with that, of ethical virtue as a whole, now does the same for the discussion of the intellectual virtues, more specifically, those connected with *phronēsis*.

It is the same people who are thought to display all these qualities— consideration, understanding, *phronēsis*, and, Aristotle adds, perhaps surprisingly, *nous;*[20] hence, he advises, unproved opinions of the experienced and elderly or the prudent—as if they all belonged to the same class—deserve attention as much as that which can be demonstrated, for experience furnishes them with the eye to see correctly (1143b11–14). The "eye of the soul," we will be told in a moment, cannot acquire *phronēsis* without virtue (1144a29–31). The psychic eye would be an appropriate metaphor for *nous* in its role as a faculty of intellectual apprehension of first principles, which makes *sophia* possible.[21] By this point, however, "to have *nous*" has been so extended, or transformed into its idiomatic sense, that it means to be reasonable, to have the kind of good sense we expect from people of a certain maturity and experience.[22] The extension or drift in the meaning of *nous* in the course of Book VI, which has attached it to *phronēsis* no less than *sophia*, cannot help but make us wonder about the sharp cut between these two intellectual virtues that has been assumed in the argument.

PHRONĒSIS, SOPHIA, AND THE CLAIM TO HAPPINESS

Phronēsis and *sophia* have each been identified as the particular excellence of a proper part (*morion*) of the soul, yet that still leaves open the question of the usefulness of either one (1143b15–18). It is in addressing that question that Book VI brings us back for the first time to our original concern with understanding what human happiness is. Theoretical wisdom, Aristotle now reasons, since it does not theorize about the coming to be of anything, can have nothing to contribute to the question of what leads to happiness. And while *phronēsis* could be said to do just that, it seems superfluous; for if it is concerned with the just and beautiful and good things for the human being, these are what the good person already does (1143b21–24). When the question is raised once again, with a very slight modification—Can *phronēsis* help make people more able to do the beautiful and the just things? (1144a11–13)—the conspicuous omission of "the good things" invites us to fill in what *phronēsis* does, in fact, contribute: however well one may have been habituated to aim at the beautiful and just things, insight into and intelligent deliberation about what is truly good for oneself requires something more. Leaving that implication unstated, Aristotle grants for the moment that *phronēsis* could appear to be of no use to those who are already virtuous. It might be thought useful, then, only for those trying to become virtuous, but such individuals, Aristotle counters, could just as well take the advice of others: one who wants to be healthy does not have to study medicine in order to accomplish that purpose (1143b32–33). Of course, that analogy may be questionable: there is no need for the patient to be the doctor healing his own sick body, but true health of soul might be possible only for a doctor who heals himself—the best individual, according to Hesiod, who thinks out everything for himself, in contrast with one who listens to another speaking well (1095b10–11). Perhaps, then, *phronēsis* does after all contribute in some way to producing happiness; but it would do so, Aristotle reasons, through its role of ruling and commanding, and it would seem strange (*atopon*) if *phronēsis*, being inferior to *sophia*, were sovereign over it (1143b33–36).

The examination of these perplexities begins with the acknowledgment that *phronēsis* and *sophia*, each being the virtue of a proper part of the soul, would be desirable in themselves even if they did not "produce" anything; and yet, Aristotle insists, in fact they do. He invokes the medical metaphor once again to clarify the point, presumably about what both virtues produce, but in the middle of the statement only one is singled out: "not as medicine [produces] health, but as health [does], thusly *sophia eudaimonia*" (1144a4–5). *Sophia*, Aristotle explains, being a part of the whole of virtue, by being possessed and being in *energeia* produces happiness. This is a rather astounding claim, and it raises a number of questions. Why does Aristotle speak here of "producing" (*poiein*) happiness, and how are we to understand the model of health producing health? What does it mean to be in *energeia* having *sophia*? Is the possession of *sophia* a necessary condition for human happiness, and is it supposed to be as sufficient for happiness as health is for being healthy? Book VI has defined *sophia*, we should recall, as complete knowledge of the whole or knowledge of the highest beings in the whole, requiring intellectual intuition of the truth of the first principles from which its demonstrative knowledge would be deduced. Idealization, one might say, is always at home in the sphere of virtue, and the problematic completeness first associated with greatness of soul, then with justice, and soon with *phronēsis*, seems to show up in another form in the conception of *sophia* as the virtue that produces happiness. *Sophia* looks as asymptotic an end as perfect health—and human happiness with it, if it depends upon having *sophia*. Of course, if having *sophia* could mean having it precisely as such an asymptotic end, it would be the *energeia* of pursuing it that produces happiness.

In taking up the issue of the *energeia* that produces happiness, Book VI recalls the foundational argument of Book I, which defined the human good as a certain *energeia* of the soul. Only that argument distinguished the human good as an *energeia* from the "complete life" to which *eudaimonia* belongs (1098a16–20), whereas the present claim about *sophia* speaks no longer of the human good but only of *eudaimonia;* the question of what is good for a human being has, after all, been demoted as the "mere" concern of *phronēsis*, which is the very reason it has been assigned an inferior ranking to *sophia*, with its claim to be knowledge of the whole or the "most honorable" things in the whole (1141a1720, 1141b2–3). The argument of Book I inquired into the human good on the premise that for any subject with a distinctive *ergon*, its good lies in performing that *ergon* well. According to the models on which the argument was based—carpenter or shoemaker in the city, eye or hand in the body—when each part of a whole does its job well, the whole flourishes. The *ergon* unique to the human being was found to be some *"praktikē* of the being that has *logos,"* which sounds like a function of practical reason. Its exercise is itself an *energeia* of the soul, which would be performed well in accordance with *phronēsis;* but the human good, which is supposed to result from that exercise, was designated "an *energeia* of soul in accordance with the most complete or most perfect virtue" (1098a16–18). Book VI, with its claim about *sophia* and human happiness, seems to have arrived at a determination of that standard: although Aristotle has gone out of his way to remind us that *sophia* is only a part of the whole of virtue, even if the highest part—the perfection of the theoretical part of the rational soul—the *energeia* associated with it has been identified as that which produces happiness, or the flourishing of the human being as a whole.

The *ergon,* on the other hand, that must be performed well for the sake of that *energeia* is accomplished, we are told, in accordance with *phronēsis* and ethical virtue (1144a6–9): ethical virtue and *phronēsis* are each the excellence of a different psychic function, but the performance of the human *ergon* requires their cooperation. Virtue, Aristotle goes on to explain, makes the target correct, *phronēsis* the means to it (1144a7–9). We had just been told that *phronēsis* and *ethical* virtue accomplish the human *ergon* together; but when the issue of the end or the target arises, the qualification of virtue as "ethical" is dropped. We might naturally supply the missing qualification, and its absence would seem altogether accidental—if it were not the first step in what looks like a pattern in the concluding chapters of Book VI. Just a few lines later, we will be reminded that while some other faculty calculates the means to the end, "virtue makes the choice correct" (1144a20)—but what is that virtue? If the deliberating faculty were not in the service of a good end, it would not count as *phronēsis* but would be only a natural ability to calculate means for any aim. That neutral skill of practical reason, which Aristotle now labels "cleverness," is a necessary condition for *phronēsis,* but it is not sufficient: the "eye of the soul" cannot discern the good that is its end without virtue (1144a23–31). Once again, though, the virtue that makes the target visible to the "eye of the soul" is left unspecified. And that important indeterminacy is confirmed when Aristotle concludes that one cannot be *phronimos* without being good, with no further specification (1144a36–37).

If *sophia* is indeed the cause of human happiness in the way health is the cause of health, it should be the virtue to which *phronēsis* looks as the end; but the indeterminate references to "virtue" without qualification have preserved the linkage of *phronēsis* with ethical virtue in a way that has important implications both for practical reason and for character. Each is something different in its union with the other than when separated; hence, each requires an analogous internal division: cleverness in practical reason, when separated from virtue of character, has its counterpart in natural virtue (*phusikē aretē*) of character, when separated from *phronēsis,* and the two natural conditions both stand over against the unitary condition now designated as virtue in the sovereign sense (1144b1–4).[23] Our characters may be so determined, or at least so influenced by nature, that we could be not only moderate or courageous but even just, Aristotle now proposes, from birth. Yet in the absence of mind (*nous*), any natural disposition—even a moderate, courageous, or just one—can be a cause of harm; and just as a heavy person who becomes blind trips more dangerously, someone of good natural disposition may suffer the greatest harm.[24] If, however, such a person acquires *nous*—which has now become virtually synonymous with *phronēsis*—the disposition that was only a likeness becomes virtue in the sovereign sense.

Now, there is no reason that the possession of one particular natural virtue would involve any of the others. In fact, it is most improbable that someone who is naturally courageous is also naturally moderate, or someone naturally gentle also naturally ambitious. The naturally given temperaments do not necessarily belong together and might, indeed, conflict with one another. Genuine virtue, on the other hand, must be connected with *phronēsis;* and possession of the virtue of *phronēsis,* Aristotle now insists—in what might seem a rather unpersuasive claim—entails all the others at the same time.[25] Of course, if virtue were nothing but *phronēsis,* there would be no question about unity in the first place. The challenge arises with Aristotle's attempt to maintain some independent status for the various dispositions of character while insisting on their necessary unification through their connection to *phronēsis.* The passions and emotions in the *phronimos,* the argument seems to assume, must be so completely guided by a comprehensive awareness of his own good that the desiring part of the soul has no force as an independent source of motivation, with some particular disposition capable of being perfected separate from others. In that case, however, ethical virtues as a product of habituation seem to have almost disappeared, transformed by their connection with *phronēsis* into the unity of genuine virtue, set over against the independent and fragmented natural virtues as something other.

With this conclusion at the end of Book VI of the *Ethics*, we have reached the third peak in its investigation of human excellence. The great-souled person, in his disdain for the ends that lead others astray, was said to display all the rest of the virtues of character or, at least, to avoid the vices; and justice, in its universal sense as the lawful, was designated complete virtue, encompassing all the rest albeit in relation to others. While greatness of soul brings in its train the other virtues insofar as they look to the beautiful and while the just comprehends them through the law, *phronēsis* transforms them into an integral whole through its orientation to what is good for a human being. And if it is to carry out that task, Book VI has just proposed, the end to which it looks should be *sophia*.

The integral whole that has now been identified as genuine virtue leads back to Socrates, who, according to Aristotle, understood all the virtues to be forms of *phronēsis*. Although Socrates erred, Aristotle charges, in asserting this identity, he spoke beautifully in claiming that the virtues cannot exist apart from *phronēsis* (1144b17–21).[26] A sign of this, Aristotle observes, is the common definition of virtue as a disposition "in accordance with correct *logos*" (*kata ton orthon logon*), which means in accordance with *phronēsis*. But even that is not sufficient: a condition that just happens to coincide with correct reason, without being internally motivated by it, does not merit the title of virtue. Aristotle insists, consequently, on a slight correction of the common definition: virtue is a disposition "together with" or "by means of correct *logos*" (*meta tou orthou logou*), which is to say, together with or by means of *phronēsis* (1144b21–28).[27]

With this supposedly minimal refinement in its formula, virtue is required to have an internal relation to correct *logos*, which is more than mere consistency with it. At the same time, however, Aristotle is at pains to avoid the opposite pole, which would reduce virtue to *logos*. To illustrate that error, he reformulates the view of Socrates, who believed, we are now informed, that the virtues are *logoi*, inasmuch as they are *epistēmai* (1144b28–30). This is not precisely the claim put forward only a few lines before—that Socrates believed the virtues to be forms of *phronēsis* or not apart from *phronēsis*, which should mean, not apart from knowledge of one's own good.[28] Aristotle's last remark about Socrates in Book VI, which identifies the virtues as *epistēmai*, recalls his first explicit remark about Socrates in Book III, which identified courage as *epistēmē* (1116b4–5). This frame presents the Socratic position in its most dubious form, according to which virtue is scientific knowledge and nothing but *logos*. As Aristotle indicated by his original allusion to the Socratic turn (1105b12–18), this understanding of human excellence reduces states of character, and the strength of soul they might display, to mere speeches. In the course of his trial, it is true, Socrates sums up his lifelong activity as a matter of making speeches—about virtue and everything else—which he takes to be the greatest good for human beings (*Apology* 38a). But the virtues as *logoi* are the questions Socrates pursues through the deed of conversing (*dialegesthai*); and the passion that drives his pursuit—the pursuit that is itself the human good—is not a matter of mere speeches. Aristotle ascribes to Socrates the view that the virtues are *logoi* because they are *epistēmai;* the true understanding of human excellence hidden behind that formula is the practice of inquiry that constitutes Socratic philosophy.

Aristotle's reflections on the Socratic position lead him to the conclusion that it is not possible to be good in the sovereign sense without *phronēsis* any more than it is to be *phronimos* without ethical virtue (1144b30–32). Ethical virtue is confirmed as a necessary condition for the excellence of practical reasoning to be *phronēsis* and not merely the natural skill of cleverness; but nothing is said at this point about ethical virtue determining the end for *phronēsis*. When the issue of the end comes up one more time, as Book VI draws to a close, virtue is spoken of once again without qualification: choice will not be correct without *phronēsis* or without virtue, for "the one, the *telos*, the other makes us act on the things in regard to the *telos*" (1145a5–6). The absence of a verb in the first clause might lead one to assume "the one—that is, virtue—makes us aim at the *telos*"; but it is just as plausible, or more so, to read, "the one *is* the *telos*," and that, according to the argument of Book VI, is *sophia*.[29]

The person of ethical virtue has been habituated to choose his action "because of itself" (1105a32), which is to say, because that action embodies the beautiful or the just. Taking those aims as given, no less than health is for the doctor, on any particular occasion he must deliberate in order to choose the most effective means to achieve them. If he deliberates well, that would be the work of the virtue of *phronēsis*. In that role, *phronēsis* would be an instrument for the fulfillment of ethical virtue. *Phronēsis,* which is the virtue of one part of the rational soul as *sophia* is of the other, may have its highest manifestation in the practical wisdom of the statesman, or legislator; it is not itself the end of the political or active life, however—as *sophia* is the final end of the theoretical life—but serves in that life the ends of ethical virtue. Yet while ethical virtue understands its ends as ultimate, not as instrumental to the achievement of self-interest, *phronēsis* has been defined as a virtue of deliberation aiming at the good or advantageous things, for oneself or for human beings more generally. The *Ethics* began with the principle that the final end we all are seeking is happiness, and happiness has at this point been identified with *sophia.*

Phronēsis, then, must have a double face, turned in one direction toward the ends of ethical virtue and in another toward *sophia* as happiness. But can these two orientations be coherently combined in one life? The ends of ethical virtue, as the ethically virtuous person understands them, cannot be subordinated to anything beyond themselves, any more than *sophia,* as constitutive of happiness, can be subordinated to the ends of ethical virtue. Of course, actions resembling those that would be chosen from a disposition of ethical virtue might be a necessary condition for the person who looked to *sophia* as his end; and *phronēsis,* deliberating on the means to that end, would discern the desirable dispositions of character that make the pursuit of wisdom possible. Still, if practical reason does not count as the virtue of *phronēsis* unless linked with ethical virtue, and ethical virtue aims at ends chosen because of themselves, it looks as if the lover of wisdom, who pursues *sophia* as his end, could not be *phronimos* in the strict sense any more than he could be a person of ethical virtue in the strict sense. On the other hand, if *phronēsis* is by definition concerned with the good things for oneself or for human beings, and if the final end we all seek is happiness and that is produced by *sophia,* or the pursuit of *sophia,* then the philosopher would in fact be the true *phronimos,* and the ethically virtuous individual would be so only in a loose sense, which falls short of the standard.

The instrumental status of *phronēsis* in relation to *sophia,* however, generates a perplexity of its own, which Aristotle posed at the outset of the discussion when he noted how strange it would be if *phronēsis* were inferior to *sophia* when its capacity for ruling and giving commands should imply just the opposite (1143b33–35). At the very end of Book VI, the argument returns to address that perplexity: *phronēsis* is not sovereign over the "better part" any more than medicine is over health, for medicine issues commands not *to* health but *for the sake of* health. *Phronēsis,* by analogy, commands for the sake of *sophia.* Now, *sophia,* as a standard of perfection at which we aim but always fall short, looks as if it might have been more plausibly construed on the model of beauty in contrast with ugliness, rather than health in contrast with illness. If the standard is perfect health, however, that would mean invulnerability to death, and we would always be in a defective state, that is, to some degree ill;[30] *phronēsis,* as the equivalent of the art of medicine, would always be necessary. The concluding claim of Book VI—*phronēsis* commands for the sake of *sophia,* as medicine does for the sake of health—does not necessarily harbor any illusion about the possession of *sophia:* it seems to be a perfectly valid description of Socratic philosophy.

Book VII is about to set out on a new beginning, exploring the complex nature of the diseased human soul and the possibility of cure. If, as it assumes, *akrasia,* or psychic conflict, is disease of soul, health would appear to be the psychic harmony of self-restraint, which certainly looks different from *sophia.*[31] But the highest form of harmony—or, rather, unity—which was intimated by the account of choice at the opening of Book VI, is the fusion of desire and thought, and that seems to characterize most of all, or uniquely, the lover of wisdom. If the argument of the *Ethics* is compelled to continue because of the need to correct the understanding of health of soul that Book VI has presented, that correction requires looking beyond the imagined possession of *sophia* to the reality of love of *sophia.*

∾ 5 ∾
Pleasure and the Discovery of Nature

[SOCRATES TO PROTAGORAS]: The opinion of the many concerning knowledge is something like this, that it isn't a strong thing characterized by either leadership or rule. They don't think about it as though it were any such thing at all, but often when knowledge is present in a human being, they think that it is not the knowledge that rules him but something else—now spirited anger, now pleasure, now pain, sometimes erotic love, many times fear. They simply think about knowledge as they do about a slave, that it is dragged around by all else. So is your opinion about it something like this as well, or is it that knowledge is both noble and capable of ruling a human being, and that if in fact someone knows the good things and the bad, he won't be overpowered by anything so as to do anything other than what knowledge bids him to do, but rather prudence is competent to come to the person's aid?

—Plato *Protagoras* 352a–c, translated by Robert Bartlett

SOCRATES: So we shall actually be setting pleasure rightly, provided it is a genesis, if we set it into some different lot and portion than that of the good?
PROTARCHUS: Yes, yes, most rightly.
SOCRATES: Then we must be grateful, as I said at the beginning of the argument, to the one who laid information about pleasure, that it is a genesis, and there is not any being whatsoever to it; for it's obvious that he is laughing at those who assert that pleasure is good. . . . And this same fellow will laugh on each occasion as well at those people who gain their completion and end in becomings.

—Plato *Philebus* 54d–e, translated by Seth Benardete

A New Beginning: From the Bestial to the Divine

In the sixth book of the *Republic,* Socrates' discussion of the philosopher leads him finally to introduce the *idea* of the good as the *"telos* of the greatest study" (504d), though he is able and willing to present it only through the likeness of the sun, which presides over the visible cosmos just as the good presides over being as a whole. In the seventh book, Socrates withdraws from that cosmological horizon, with its potentially blinding highest principle, and turns in the opposite direction, to enter the shadow world in the darkness of the cave. The argument of the *Ethics* descends in a similar movement from the cosmic heights of *sophia,* as knowledge of "the most honorable things in nature" (1141b3), to the "new beginning" Book VII announces, which brings us back to the territory of human character. The descent seems to exemplify the second turnaround Socrates describes in his cave image, in which the one who has left that shadow world comes back, under some compulsion, to the place from which he set out, now seen in a new light.

The reconsideration of human character in Book VII of the *Ethics* takes the form of an exploration of the psychology of desire, and the perspective of the inquiry exhibits the effects of the path it has followed to reach this point. It seems to have left behind the gentleman as a member of its audience, along with the attempt to capture ethical virtue as the virtuous person understands it. The beautiful and just are no longer important concerns and the categories of praise and blame play almost no role.[1] Reproach and exhortation, which belong to the task of molding character, are now replaced by the aim of healing, which must rest upon an understanding of psychic illness: the *politikos* as legislator is replaced by the *politikos* as doctor of soul (cf. 1102a8–10, 1102a18–20). Having been freed, apparently, from seeing things through the lens of morality, the argument turns to a preoccupation with nature, signaled by the density of references to *phusis* and related terms;[2] more specifically, it is concerned with the natural attraction to pleasure and repulsion from pain that is evident throughout animal life, including human life.

While departing from the presuppositions of virtue and vice, the inquiry in Book VII brings to light a range of human character that extends beyond those alternatives. We are about to consider not only two complex states— self-restraint and the lack of it—that lie between the higher state of virtue and the lower state of vice but also two extreme states that lie outside those boundaries: once bestiality is acknowledged, as a condition lower than vice in its all-too-human form, it would at least "be fitting to claim" a contrary condition above the level of human virtue, which could be called heroic or divine virtue (1145a18–20). The inquiry of Book VII opens a window through which we glimpse the repellent bestiality of which human beings are capable. There is no illustration at all of divine virtue—at least not after it is introduced by a Homeric line at the beginning: "Hector seemed not to be the son of a mortal man but of a god" (*Iliad* XXIV.258).

The line is spoken by Priam, recalling Hector's behavior in the face of his impending death. Aristotle had chosen this situation, in Book III, as an illustration of political courage, more specifically, the motivation by shame that makes political courage fall short of the true virtue (1116a23). Aristotle quoted at that point a line from Hector's internal dialogue, as he stands outside the gates of Troy awaiting the approach of Achilles, tempted by fear to retreat but held in check by his sense of shame. His father and mother issue a poignant appeal to their son not to confront Achilles but to come inside the walls and save himself together with the Trojans. Their appeal fails (*Iliad* XXII.22–92). Priam seems to have forgotten that failed attempt to persuade his son when, in the passage Aristotle now cites, he is engaged in turning Hector into a legend. The notion of divine or heroic virtue was anticipated in a remark at the outset of the *Ethics* about how much more beautiful and divine it appears to be to achieve the good of the city over that of the individual (1094b9–10); but the fictional character who now represents heroic virtue is portrayed at the moment he subordinates the interest of the city to his own reputation, and his divine status is only a matter of seeming in the eyes of his father, who is holding him up as a standard by which to rebuke his brothers. Priam, at this moment, is preparing to leave on his mission to beg Achilles to give back the corpse of his son; in likening Hector to "the son of a god, not a mortal man," he speaks with a pitiful irony. Aristotle seems to have gone out of his way to furnish a particularly problematic illustration of divine virtue. Of course, postulating such a possibility may suffice to prevent the morally virtuous individual from conceiving of himself as the highest exemplar of human excellence, and that is an important preparation for the conclusion the *Ethics*.

As long as virtue and vice were thought of as two exhaustive alternatives, there was an implicit denial not only of any condition higher than virtue or lower than vice but also of any intermediary conditions between them. The human soul was assumed to be in state of internal unity, either positive or negative, resulting from the force of habit: in the virtuous character, desire is supposed to have been molded to harmonize with correct *logos*, while in the vicious character, an opinion about the good has been molded to serve desires contrary to reason. These two alternatives left no place for the possibility of a psychological condition analogous to lack of control over the body, in which a part of the soul could move on its own, contrary to the direction reason chooses. Although the psychology of Book I alerted us to the possibility of this experience of *akrasia*, or lack of self-restraint (1102b13–23),[3] only now has the argument prepared us to examine it.

The perplexity provoked by the attempt to explain this psychological experience is due almost entirely to Socrates, who denies its very possibility. Aristotle set the stage in Book II for his debate with Socrates when he interpreted the Socratic turn to *logoi* as a misunderstanding of ethical virtue. That misunderstanding was represented by the image of the invalid who believes his mere possession of the doctor's prescription is sufficient for becoming healthy (1105b12–15). To have the right "prescription" without the habits to carry it out in action is, Aristotle suggested, a situation especially vulnerable to *akrasia:* virtue, on the Socratic understanding, is essentially threatened by an experience the Socratic cannot explain. The debate with Socrates initiated by this image seemed to be brought to a close at the end of Book VI, with Aristotle's acknowledgment of *phronēsis* as the necessary condition for genuine virtue. Apparently, however, that acknowledgment is not sufficient: only a confrontation with the issue of *akrasia* can really put the Socratic position to the test. In the course of this confrontation, it looks as if Aristotle moves closer and closer to that Socratic position, which appears at first so counterintuitive, until by the end he is led to a recognition of its fundamental principle.

Aristotle's final confrontation with Socrates compels him to wrestle with all the puzzles involved in explaining the power of pleasure to lead us astray. It is not surprising, then, that the new stage of the argument, which follows on the completion of Aristotle's debate with Socrates, should begin with a theoretical analysis of the nature of pleasure. We are hardly prepared, though, for the discussion of *akrasia* to bring in its wake an argument for the goodness of pleasure as such or, more radically, for the possibility that pleasure, or some pleasure, might be *the* good![4] Opening itself up to this possibility, Book VII has come as far as possible from the attitude toward pleasure that marked its first appearance, in Book I, where it was indignantly rejected as the human good and seen as the mark of a life fit for cattle, not for human beings. Pleasure now comes to light as the natural end pursued, in some form or other, by humans no less than cattle. The hedonist thesis to which Book VII gives voice looks like the first consequence of a discovery of nature that emerges in the course of the argument; the first consequence, one should add, is not necessarily the most adequate development.[5]

Book VII begins by introducing divine or heroic virtue as the positive counterpart to bestiality, which will be analyzed in terms of the peculiar pleasures it involves; it ends by holding up not divine virtue but the enduring pleasure of god. That standard, however, as we shall see, issues into an assessment of human nature that strikes a surprisingly dark note, which seems to reverse entirely the argument for the natural goodness of pleasure that led up to this conclusion. Now, this is not the last word in the *Ethics* on the subject of pleasure: Book X will open with the puzzling recommendation that we should turn to a discussion of pleasure, which is too important a topic to be omitted. It is possible that the account in Book VII discloses a truth about pleasure that is subsequently suppressed; on the other hand, the final result of that account seems to suggest something problematic about its underlying assumptions, which must be corrected by reconsidering the topic of pleasure through a different lens. Perhaps there is something to both alternatives. The discovery of nature that takes place in Book VII does bring to light a truth about the universal role of pleasure and pain in animal life; but the understanding of nature it presupposes must be reexamined in light of the distinctive status of human nature if the argument is to assess the place of pleasure in the good life for a human being.

THE FACTION OF PASSION AND REASON

Laying Down the Phenomena and the Socratic Challenge

With his two references to Socrates at the conclusion of the sixth book, Aristotle appeared to concede far more than what he held back by his seemingly slight qualifications. According to the first formulation of his view,

Socrates reduced all the virtues to *phronēsis,* while Aristotle was willing to grant, at least, that *phronēsis* is necessary, if not sufficient, for any genuine virtue (1144b17–21). A second formulation ascribed to Socrates the view that all the virtues are *logoi,* inasmuch as they are *epistēmai,* while Aristotle was willing to grant, at least, that the virtues must be "together with" or "by means of *logos*" (1144b28–30). The seventh book returns to Socrates to confront his belief about how strange it would be if, when knowledge (*epistēmē*) was present in a person, something else prevailed and "dragged it around like a slave" (1145b23–24).[6] Aristotle explains, in a second formulation, that Socrates fought against the *logos* of *akrasia,* insisting that no one acts against his own best interest unless he is ignorant of it (1145b25–27). Such recognition of one's own good should be the work not of *epistēmē* but of *phronēsis.* The juxtaposition of two formulations of Socrates' stance against *akrasia*—one in terms of *epistēmē,* the other based on awareness of one's best interest—echoes the double reference at the end of Book VI to Socrates' understanding of virtue as knowledge. Without specifying which formulation he has in mind—or considering how one might be a distortion of the other—Aristotle issues his charge against the Socratic denial of *akrasia:* "This *logos* clearly disputes the phenomena" (1145b27–28).

The last mention of Socrates in Book VII—which is the last explicit reference to him in the *Ethics* as a whole—finds Aristotle abandoning his apparently confrontational stance: judging from the analysis of practical reasoning he has provided, "what Socrates sought seems to follow" (1147b14–15). The linguistic reason Aristotle gives, however, for deferring to Socrates at that point seems to mark no more of a fundamental agreement than the initial critique of Socrates indicates a fundamental disagreement.[7] If a genuine reconciliation had been achieved by this point, it should bring the discussion of *akrasia* to an end; instead, Aristotle's explicit concession to the Socratic view opens up a long and complex continuation of the discussion, addressing the question whether *akrasia* can be used in a qualified sense that would extend its sphere beyond the typical bodily pleasures to which most human beings are drawn. The conclusion of this discussion brings us back, in Chapter 10 of Book VII, to the original issue of the relation between *akrasia* and vice, but only to overturn the initial evaluation of these states and their ranking on the scale of human weakness. In the process, Aristotle expresses, without mentioning Socrates, his acceptance on the most fundamental basis of the

Socratic understanding of *phronēsis*. The Socrates to whom Aristotle has referred by name throughout the *Ethics* is typically identified as the exponent of a doctrine taken out of the context of the dialogue that is its source; only when Socrates is unnamed, it seems, does his view cease to sound like an exaggeration or distortion.

Aristotle's examination of the possibility of *akrasia* is introduced by methodological remarks more explicit than any time since the beginning of Book I. We are told that the inquiry is to be conducted in "the customary fashion," but if this way of proceeding has gone on before, it has never been described as it is now:

> One must, as in other cases, having laid down the *phainomena,* and first having become thoroughly perplexed, thus point out, in the best case, all of the common opinions (*ta endoxa*) about these experiences, but if not, as many as possible and the most sovereign; for if the difficulties are resolved and the common opinions left undisturbed, it would be pointed out sufficiently. (1145b2–7)

We are to proceed through an examination of opinions (*endoxa*), although now these are not opinions one has been brought up with, which serve to mold one's character, but, rather, theoretical attempts to explain the experience of *akrasia.* Examination of these opinions is to be preceded by a task of "positing the appearances" and becoming thoroughly perplexed. Our aim is to resolve the difficulties, which are presumably the perplexities we have encountered, while leaving the *endoxa* as little disturbed as possible—and the *endoxa,* we should keep in mind, can include the opinions of the wise as well as those of the many (cf. 1095a21–22, 1098b27–29). If the procedure were as conservative as this description makes it sound, one wonders why it must go through the path of thorough perplexity—an experience not encouraged since the discussion of the *idea* of the universal good in Book I (1096a11–12).

Aristotle's description of how the inquiry is to proceed might seem to suggest that the puzzles encountered arise from immediate observations about behavior; in fact, what the analysis goes on to posit is a set of common opinions and speeches. The *phainomena,* or "the things that appear," are the things we say and believe: the self-restrained person is one who abides by his calculation, the akratic one who abandons it; the former is thought to be praiseworthy, the latter blameworthy (1145b8–12).[8] Now, according to

Socrates, a person can act against his own good only if he is ignorant of it. If that opinion generates perplexity, it is by clashing not with uninterpreted experience but with another opinion or claim in speech—that it is possible through passion to do what one knows to be bad. One might anticipate that this clash would lead Aristotle to reject the Socratic claim; in fact, it prompts him only to call for an investigation as to what sort of ignorance Socrates must have had in mind (1145b28–29).[9] Aristotle responds immediately to the Socratic claim with the objection that the akratic, at least before coming under the influence of passion, is not ignorant of what he should be doing. If this means that he is ignorant at the time of acting, it almost concedes the issue to Socrates before the discussion begins.

What one would expect from the procedure recommended is an effort to "save the phenomenon" of *akrasia;* instead, the discussion sets out on a criticism of certain attempts at doing just that. According to one such attempt, it might be possible to act against one's better judgment if that were understood as merely a matter of opinion and not knowledge. This proposal will in fact turn out to be a feature of Aristotle's own account of *akrasia,* but at the moment he raises another objection: if opinion in all its weakness were overcome by desire in all its strength, that should make us more forgiving, whereas *akrasia* is thought to be something blameworthy.[10] The objection is supposed to motivate us to reject the explanation of *akrasia* as a matter of desire overcoming opinion; perhaps what we should reject, however, is the notion that someone should be blamed for a desire strong enough to overcome weak opinion. As the discussion unfolds, in any event, the model of disease takes over and talk of blame is abandoned in favor of concern with the possibility of cure.

If, within the horizon of opinion, we are committed to treating *akrasia* as an object of blame, it looks as if we need to conceive of something strong that is overcome by desire for pleasure, which would presumably make us less forgiving. That role would be assigned above all to *phronēsis;* but no one, Aristotle interjects immediately, would consider the prudent person capable of doing the most base things voluntarily (1146a5–7).[11] Once again, the Socratic view seems to have been conceded right from the start. If the prudent person shuns the base things, however, it is not insofar as they are base but insofar as they are bad or harmful, for it is quite specifically what is bad or harmful to oneself, according to Socrates, that no one does voluntarily.[12]

Aristotle eliminates from the outset the possibility of explaining *akrasia* as an overcoming of *phronēsis*, but he does so without explicitly developing the grounds of the Socratic view, which concerns what it means to know one's own good.

While Socrates denies the possibility of *akrasia,* the sophists exploit its paradoxes in order to display their own cleverness. Aristotle's debate with Socrates over the possibility of *akrasia* confronts us with the problem of distinguishing genuine philosophical perplexity from a sophistic game, which sets out to trap thinking by making it no more possible to stand still and accept a conclusion than to untie the knot in the argument and move forward. If, as such an argument has it, a foolish person is unrestrained, he would fare well; for in doing the opposite of what he believes, and believing good things to be bad, he would end up doing the good things (1146a21–31). One can, of course, respond immediately that the action of the foolish akratic, who succeeds by doing the opposite of what he thinks right, is a matter of mere chance and indicates nothing praiseworthy about the agent. To reject the sophistic paradox, it would be reasonable to argue that *akrasia* is essentially a matter of abandoning not just any opinion but only the true one. This is the response Aristotle eventually does offer (1151a29–b4). Yet he does not propose it now, for reasons exactly contrary to his preceding rejection of an appeal to the weakness of opinion to explain *akrasia:* since true opinion can be held with such certainty that its possessor takes it to be knowledge, it is no easier to account for the akratic's acting against opinion than his acting against knowledge (1146b24–30). Aristotle does not, for the moment, take up the possibility that true opinion about the right choice of action would mean a lack of understanding of the causes and consequences that make such a choice right and would, for just that reason, be vulnerable to conflicting temptations.

From the standpoint of the alleged Socratic view, which makes knowledge the only determining ground of action, the individual with a vicious disposition looks as if he could be cured simply by being persuaded to change his conviction about what is good. Trying to cure the akratic, on the other hand, who is already convinced that he is doing the wrong thing, is like trying to help someone who is choking on water by washing it down with water (1146a34–36). Aristotle's vivid metaphor captures what seems to be a genuine difficulty: if an individual already knows that what he is doing is wrong, what help could we possibly give him? But the opinion Aristotle voices about the curability of the vicious person does not acknowledge how much would be required for him to change into a virtuous individual: he would need first to adopt the principle that the akratic already has, and nothing would then prevent him from becoming akratic in his struggle toward virtue from that point forward. According to the initial survey of opinions, indulgence looks like a less recalcitrant disease than *akrasia;* the movement of the argument in Book VII is marked by the eventual reversal of that ranking (1150b29–35). The vicious person must come to light as least able to achieve what he truly wants—and what everyone truly wants, Aristotle seems to agree in the end with Socrates, is the good for himself.

Practical Reasoning and Its Failure

The preliminary rejection of various explanations for failing to act in accordance with what one knows to be best prepares for the attempt to locate the problem in what it means "to know." The obvious gap between merely possessing knowledge and actually exercising it provides a plausible starting point: if someone who is about to act knows his intended action is wrong but is not at the moment "contemplating" that fact, it should not be surprising if he acts against that merely latent recognition (1146b31–35). As plausible as it is, this first point says nothing about what sort of knowledge the akratic fails to exercise when he is not "contemplating" it and what prevents him from doing so. To address those questions, Aristotle turns to an analysis of the steps involved in practical reasoning, which is, presumably, not necessarily a conscious process on the spot but a reconstruction of the motivation for an action. Once the universal of a major premise is combined with the particular of a minor premise, "when one comes to be out of them," a certain action follows in practice, just as the affirmation of a conclusion would follow in theoretical reasoning (1147a25–28). Either the action follows immediately upon the end of the process of thought or, if the action is itself equivalent to the conclusion of a syllogism, there is a shadowy step before that end point when the two premises must be fused in the agent's thinking.

Like the discussion of *phronēsis* in Book VI, the account of practical reasoning in Book VII stresses the importance of knowledge of the particular: the possibility of acting against what one knows to be right is not problematic if that means the agent is exercising knowledge only of the universal premise in determining his action. And that holds, we are now told, not only in regard to the object but also to the agent. Turning once again to health as an illustration, Aristotle explains that in order to act properly, I must know not only that dry food is advantageous for human beings but also that food of a certain sort is dry and—though we might wonder how someone could be unaware of this—that I am a human being. If I am not exercising the knowledge that "this is such"—that the particular food before me is of the desirable sort for the kind of being I am—it would be perfectly understandable that I might act contrary to my general awareness of what is beneficial (1146b36–47a10). Book VI recognized the need to know that a certain sort of food is healthful (1141b14–22); nothing was mentioned then about the need to recognize either a particular instance as belonging to that kind or a particular individual as a member of the class that would be benefited. Recognition of oneself as human may be unproblematic when it comes to the question of the benefit of dry food for a human being; but what about "the unexamined life is not worth living for a human being"? That claim raises the most difficult and important questions about what it means to be human and to be aware of oneself as such. The argument of the *Ethics,* in any case, has assumed from early on a differentiation of sorts of persons for whom an action or passion might be beneficial or harmful; hence, the response called for in a particular situation would require recognizing oneself as the appropriate sort of person.[13] Someone who proceeded without such self-knowledge would not be described by a Socratic as truly knowing his own good yet acting contrary to it. Aristotle's appeal to practical reasoning has served, thus far, not so much to save the phenomenon of *akrasia* as to unpack the features of "knowing" that make Socrates declare it impossible.

Lack of self-restraint has been shown to result from a gap between knowledge of a general rule and recognition of its instantiation, but without any account of the role of passion as the cause of such a gap. That requires stretching even further what it can mean "to know": a person who, in a state of sexual desire or anger, acts against what he says is the right thing to do is really like someone who utters the right speeches while asleep, or in a state of madness, or when drunk. If the akratic knows the correct choice, it is only like an actor reciting lines on stage, whereas really knowing requires that the matter has "grown together naturally" with the knower (1147a21–22). The argument might look as if it were moving in a non-Socratic direction—

appealing to the capacity of sexual desire or anger to alter the state of the body and thus overcome the agent's judgment about his own good; but in its denial that real knowledge is at work in such a situation, it edges ever closer to the Socratic position.

This tension is encapsulated in Aristotle's proposal to investigate the cause of *akrasia* naturally, or physically (*phusikōs*)—typically contrasted with investigating logically, or linguistically (*logikōs*)—which is immediately followed by an attempt to reconstruct the reasoning process at work in the experience of psychic conflict. When, at the end of the account, desire is said to be responsible for "moving the parts" (1147a34–35), it is not clear whether it is the members of the body or the steps in the process of reasoning to which this refers, and that ambiguity is the very heart of the problem. The syllogism that stands in for physiology implicitly raises the question thematic in *De anima:* anger, as the desire for revenge, involves the blood boiling around the heart, but how can the physiologist's account of the affections of body be put together with the dialectician's account of the experience of soul? [14]

To bring the role of desire into the analysis of practical reasoning, Aristotle offers a new example: someone who held the major premise "All sweet things should be tasted" and the minor premise "This thing before me is sweet" would be compelled, if he were able, to taste it (1147a29–31). This process of reasoning exemplifies the motivation of the indulgent person. In the case of the akratic, on the other hand, there is one universal premise, forbidding the tasting of such things, present alongside another, identifying all sweet things as pleasant, while the minor premise "This thing is sweet" is active (in *energeia*). Whereas the correct *logos* is a bare prohibition, which expresses no understanding of the positive good in light of which the tempting thing is harmful, desire has translated itself into an opposing *logos* with a reason—sweets are pleasant. Hence, Aristotle concludes, the akratic is in a sense—the famous Aristotelian "in a sense"—motivated by *logos* and opinion: beasts could never be akratic (1147b1–5). The individual lacking self-restraint knows the correct *logos* forbidding the action he is considering. But desire, having clothed itself in the form of a contrary universal rule, becomes a major premise in his reasoning, which, when it combines with a minor premise about the particular situation, is able "to move the parts" (1147a35): it sets in motion the parts of the syllogism in the mind of the akratic no less than the parts of his body as he reaches out for the sweet thing that promises pleasure.

The person lacking self-restraint is aware of the correct *logos* only in the way someone drunk or asleep would be; if he can be said to follow the wrong rule in some state of ignorance, then once the immediate situation is past, his ignorance should be dissipated and his knowledge recovered. For an explanation of how that happens, Aristotle advises, one must turn to the physiologist: there must be a physiological explanation as well, then, for how the knowledge in the mind of the akratic was occluded in the first place. What it would mean to carry on the investigation *physikōs* is indicated only at this moment, by what appears to be a momentary digression in the midst of the analysis of the syllogism. That digression asks the question, What bodily condition led the akratic to be in the state he is in when he acts? The analysis it interrupts asks a different question, What is going on in his mind once he is in that state?

Whatever the physiologist might explain, we must return to the analysis of the syllogism to determine exactly what step in the akratic's reasoning has been clouded by the effects of his passion. The belief he once had, we might expect to hear, which has now been suppressed by the competing *logos* of desire, is the correct *logos*—"Sweets are forbidden." Aristotle refers instead to "the final premise" (*he teleutaia protasis*), which the akratic in his passion does not possess, or possesses only in the way someone drunk might recite lines of poetry (1147b9–12). This explanation has long disturbed commentators. The "final premise" is described as an opinion about an object present to the senses, which is "sovereign in actions." One might think it referred to the minor premise "This is sweet"; but that premise, we have been told, is in *energeia*, and if it were not, there would be no motivation for the akratic's action. Perhaps in this kind of situation, then, where the desire for pleasure clashes with an internalized prohibition, there is no possibility of registering a neutral judgment of fact not already colored by one opinion or another about the crucial property of the object as choiceworthy or not.[15] The "final premise," in that case, would be a judgment of the particular that incorporates one universal predicate or the other—either "This is a sweet, one of those things that should not be tasted" or "This is a sweet, one of those things that is pleasant."[16] The person in whom a struggle is going on might move from one perception of the situation to the other or even hold both together; eventually, recognition of the character of the object as forbidden would have to prevail for self-restraint, or *enkrateia*, whereas the akratic, if he expresses that recognition at all, is doing nothing but making sounds. The attraction of pleasure shows up the weakness of the correct *logos,* which Aristotle has carefully formulated as a bare prohibition—a rule that would not have the motivating power of an understanding of one's own good.

At this point, however, Aristotle does not address the question of what such an understanding involves. Instead, he calls attention to the universal premise, which is *thought* to be the object of *epistēmē* in the sovereign sense, and finds that it is not this knowledge but only "the aesthetic" that has been dragged around by *pathos* like a slave; hence the consequence Socrates drew—that knowledge can never be overcome—seems to follow (1147b13–17). This concession is as unsatisfying as the analysis on which it is based. For one thing, the universal premise "Sweets are forbidden" does indeed appear to be overcome, even if only through the overcoming of the particular judgment that would have instantiated it if it were guiding the action. Knowledge of such a universal, in any case, is not what Socrates would consider sovereign over action. If he found some sort of knowledge necessarily stronger than the allurements of pleasure, it would not be on account of its universality; it would be the recognition of one's good in its concrete instantiation, on the premise that all human beings desire the good for themselves.

The discernment of a particular situation as belonging to a certain sort that is beneficial for oneself, or for human beings in general, is the work of *phronēsis,* not *epistēmē.* The Socratic position had originally been represented by two formulations (1145b23–28). Aristotle has now conceded to the first— it would be strange if *epistēmē* could be dragged around like a slave; he has not confronted the other—no one acts against what he supposes to be best. Aristotle's akratic fails to see the sweet thing before him as something forbidden to taste, although he possesses an opinion expressing that general prohibition. He would be a counterexample to the Socratic thesis only if he acted with full recognition that the action is bad for his health and without thinking there was some other benefit outweighing its harm; such recognition would require an understanding of what the good life consists in and what role health plays in it relative to all other goods. Aristotle has not provided any such counterexample.

Socrates was introduced as the proponent of a thesis that was supposed to be obviously preposterous, yet the possibility was left open from the start that some form of ignorance is always responsible for an action performed contrary to one's own good. Aristotle made an effort to pinpoint that moment of ignorance by reconstructing the thought processes of an agent involved in such an action; he proposed along the way, however, a deeper cause of that ignorance in the physiological effect of the state of passion, which temporarily clouds the akratic's perception of his situation.[17] Has he, then, while making a concession to Socrates on the basis of an analysis of the agent's reasoning, in fact undermined it by his recognition of the physiological effect of passion? Even if one were to grant that anti-Socratic aspect of Aristotle's analysis, it would still be possible ask, What makes the akratic vulnerable to this experience of overwhelming passion in the first place? That question, which the Socratic would have to raise, has not yet been addressed. One might expect, then, that the concession Aristotle claims to have made to the Socratic view, though it is his last explicit reference to Socrates in the *Ethics*, is not sufficient to bring the discussion of *akrasia* to an end.

Akrasia Extended: Beyond the Pleasures of Indulgence

Aristotle has managed, somehow, to give credit to the Socratic position while recognizing that the desire for pleasure can conflict with and prevail over some kind of knowledge. His supposed agreement with Socrates has been accomplished on the basis of an analysis of what it is to know, without inquiring at all into the nature of pleasure, which would explain its power over human action. Aristotle begins to approach that task by returning to one of the questions raised at the outset of the discussion: in relation to what kinds of pleasures can lack of self-restraint be displayed? On the basis of ordinary usage, it was agreed that "*akrasia* simply" refers to lack of self-restraint in regard to a core set of pleasures, the same as those in which indulgence can be shown—food, drink, and the *aphrodisia;* yet people are admittedly said to be unrestrained in anger, for example, or in the pursuit of honor or gain (1145b19–20). The question resumed now, whether *akrasia* can be spoken of in a qualified sense, appears to be a merely linguistic issue; in fact, however, the discussion it sets in motion issues into a whole new depiction of human nature.

Our understanding of pleasure was taken for granted as long as it was assumed to fall within the familiar sphere of indulgence; it becomes an issue with the admission of pleasures and desires above and below that sphere. In taking our understanding of pleasure for granted, we took the nature of the human being for granted; correcting for that at this point leads us into the realm of abnormal psychology. We discover, on the one hand, the possibility of such intense devotion to something otherwise admirable or decent that it produces behavior more disturbing than ordinary human vices. At what is supposed to be the opposite pole, we encounter the kind of bestiality or madness that seems so out of place in the civilized world it can only be assigned to the most remote corners of the earth, if not to fantasy. Here, alone, the *Ethics* provides evidence for the dark observation made in the first book of Aristotle's *Politics:* while the human is the best of animals when perfected, apart from law and justice the human is the worst—the most unholy and savage particularly in regard to sex and food (1253a32–37), which seems to mean, given a previous reference to the Cyclopes (1252b23–24), incest and cannibalism as a sign of what the uncivilized human would be.

The expanded range of pleasures, including the cyclopean ones, unfolds in Book VII of the *Ethics* through a series of classifications that is puzzling in many ways.[18] These analyses are developed, in the first place, before even raising the question, What is pleasure? Perhaps, however, that ontological inquiry would never arise if it were not provoked by facing the bizarre assortment of activities in which human beings can apparently find pleasure. When, in any case, the question, What is pleasure? is raised and addressed, in the last chapters of Book VII, it provides the basis for a new analysis of kinds of pleasure: what is essentially pleasant is distinguished from what is only accidentally so, depending on whether it accompanies the activity of an organism in its fulfilled natural condition or only on the way to restoring that condition. It is far from obvious how that analysis, which should apply to any organism, fits into the preceding series of classifications, which is concerned primarily with pleasures sought by human beings and, more specifically, with demarcating among such pleasures the boundary between those that are recognizably human and those that are not.

This series of classifications begins with a division between necessary and nonnecessary pleasures (1147a23–35):[19] that division presupposes that nature determines certain activities necessary for the survival of the individual organism and the species, and it is the basic bodily pleasures attached to those activities that make up the objects of *akrasia* proper. The nonnecessary pleasures human beings might seek, like those of victory or honor or gain, belong to desires that are presumably of a higher rank than bodily ones; but since they are capable of being pursued in excess, against one's best judgment, they can be objects of *akrasia* in a qualified sense. This division would be sufficient if our only purpose were to clarify an extended use of the term "*akrasia*"; carrying out that task, however, brings to light a vastly expanded realm of human behavior, which emerges through the introduction of nature as a standard.

The pleasures previously designated "nonnecessary" are relabeled, accordingly, as pleasures "choiceworthy by nature" and set over against a contrary class, while necessary pleasures become an intermediary class between the two extremes (1148a22–25). The nature that can be a standard for choiceworthy pleasures must be that which defines a particular kind of being; what is now said to meet that standard for a human being are the "beautiful and serious" things, which seems to mean any pleasures beyond bodily ones, like those one might take in money or gain, victory or honor. But however beautiful and serious they may be, such things can be the object of an unbounded dedication that exceeds what is natural to—that is, what is ordinarily sought by—a human being. Aristotle evokes the figure of Niobe, who, in her immoderate love of or pride in her children, boasted about them in competition with the goddess Leto and was punished by the death of her children at the hands of the gods. This kind of passion is a theme of tragic poetry, which has been largely absent from the concerns of the *Ethics;* it lies on the horizon now, with the recognition that what is in itself choiceworthy by nature could be pursued to such an unnatural extreme that it begins to look indistinguishable from what is supposed to be its opposite, the pursuit of pleasure contrary to nature.[20]

Turning to that class of pleasures unimaginable to most of us, Aristotle traces them to the abnormal dispositions in which they are rooted—bestial ones, like cannibalism, or diseaselike conditions and madness, like that of a slave who ate his fellow slave's liver, or a man who made a sacrifice of his mother and partook of it himself (1148b24–27).[21] Such perversions, Aristotle reasons, could result from being impaired, or from habit, as in cases of childhood abuse, or they could be due to a "wicked nature" (1148b17–18): *phusis*, which serves as the standard that makes these pleasures contrary to nature for a human being, provides an explanation at the same time for deviation from that standard in the case of particular individuals. And the appeal to nature as a cause brings with it, quite surprisingly, moral blame: that which thwarts what is pleasant by nature must be something wicked in our nature. Now, what is pleasant by nature for a human being is what one should enjoy; ultimately, this would be the pleasure that accompanies the activity by which one would fulfill one's highest potential as a human being. Within the realm of bodily pleasures and desires, however, nature as a standard represents a boundary beneath which behavior ceases to be recognizably human. But, finally, nature itself—as the inborn constitution of an individual—can be the cause of the failure to meet even that minimum standard; thus, *phusis* in a natural being, at least in a human being, can be torn between these senses. The ambiguity of *phusis* expresses the discovery in Book VII that nature is as much a source of recalcitrance to the realization of what is good for a human being as it is a guide to the determination of that good.

The descent of the inquiry below the limits that circumscribe the domain of the human as such makes it necessary to rethink vice along with lack of self-restraint. Behavior of extraordinary indulgence, or folly and other vices, can be carried to such extremes that it too lies below the lower boundary of the human. Book VII initially proposed a spectrum of states of character from subhuman to superhuman in which bestiality looked like an independent realm of human aberration, lower than vice, which is in turn lower than lack of self-restraint.[22] What we have discovered is bestiality as a potential within the sphere of vice as well as that of *akrasia:* vice and *akrasia* are fundamentally distinct conditions defined by the relation of desire and reason, with each having as its content a "human and natural" range and, below that, one of greater depravity. The bestial desires and pleasures, Aristotle observes, are more terrifying than vice in its human range but not as bad (1150a2)—not as bad in the sense that they are so repulsive and so alien they escape our judgment of blame. We cannot recognize in one who seeks them a human being to condemn. If reason, in the unrestrained person, is too weak to control bad desires, while reason in the vicious person has been corrupted by bad desires, in the bestial person, it seems to be absent altogether (1150a3–8).[23]

The extension of *"akrasia"* beyond the core of bodily pleasures that constitute the sphere of indulgence has led to the acknowledgment of bestial, mad, and morbid desires, by which human beings violate their humanity. But that extension allows for the possibility, at the same time, of *akrasia* in regard to the passion of *thumos,* spiritedness or anger, which is now identified as a more elevated form of lack of self-restraint than the desire for bodily pleasure (1149a25–26). The argument of the *Ethics* has attempted from the beginning, it seems, to diminish or suppress the role of *thumos:* it was left out of the analysis of the soul in Book I, which provided a basis for the investigation of virtue and vice; the spirited passion of righteous indignation (*nemesis*), which concluded the list of virtues and vices in Book II, disappeared from the discussion of those dispositions in Book IV; and when the account of corrective justice in Book V reduced criminality to unfair gain in "involuntary transactions," the requirement of compensation displaced altogether the spirited demand for punishment. It looks, then, as if it is particularly in relation to justice that *thumos* has been suppressed. It was recognized, after all, as the passion that bears a resemblance to courage and seems to provide the natural roots of that virtue. And it finds a place now, in an inquiry that is exploring the complexities of human psychology in an effort to understand the conflict of passion with reason.

In a poetic figure, which stands out in the *Ethics, thumos* is likened to a hasty servant who hurries away before hearing everything the master is saying (1149a26–29).[24] Desire, which is aroused whenever *logos* or perception declares something pleasant, is contrasted with "hot *thumos*," which rushes off to take revenge as soon as *logos* or imagination (*phantasia*) registers an insult, as if having reasoned (*hōsper sullogisamenos*) that it is necessary to go to war immediately. The *logos* or perception that announces to desire the promise of pleasure may be less deceptive than the imagination that elicits *thumos;* but whether provoked by imagination or *logos,* the tendency of *thumos* to proceed "as if" following a syllogism is enough, apparently, to consider it "in a sense" guided by *logos* and, hence, less shameful to yield to than desire. The impulse of anger is more natural, the argument continues, than the desire for pleasures—at least those that are in excess and not necessary: the desire for pleasure can extend beyond a natural core, in a way that anger does not.[25] In contrast with the wiliness of desire, moreover, anger is frankly or openly expressed, which makes yielding to *thumos* less unjust. To confirm the greater injustice of desire, Aristotle refers to the pleasure of fulfilling it, in contrast with the painfulness of acting in anger (1149b14–18); but what about the pleasure that comes with the satisfaction of anger?[26]

The comparison of various forms of *akrasia* with one another, or of *akrasia* relative to other defective human conditions, was to be based on the standard of curability (cf.1146a31–34). In this argument, however, yielding to anger has been ranked higher than yielding to pleasure by the criteria of shamefulness and injustice. This evaluation looks as if it comes to light through the eyes of spiritedness itself. *Thumos* must be assigned a higher rank if it is to play its role in the psychological mechanism of mastering desire;[27] even when anger itself is the passion to be mastered, reason can perhaps accomplish that task only by eliciting the commanding power of spiritedness on its side, and that passion is motivated by the assumption of the injustice or shamefulness it aims to defeat. However natural a passion *thumos* may be, the account that assigns it a higher rank as less shameful and less unjust than *akrasia* in pleasure is not a naturalistic one. It reflects the perspective of *thumos* itself—which seems to have slipped into play when the failure to fulfill the standard of nature was blamed on a "wicked nature" (1148b18; cf. 1154b28–31). The *Ethics* allows *thumos* to reveal its own nature by the way it has brought back the moral categories apparently left behind when the account of psychic conflict adopted as its model the medical art, in its sole concern with understanding disease and trying to cure it.

A Socratic Conclusion

The initial survey of opinions in Book VII ranked vice superior to lack of self-restraint, on the grounds that it is more curable; when the argument returns to that issue, after the long digression on the extended senses of *akrasia,* that opinion is overturned (cf. 1146a31–1146b2 and 1150b29–36, 1151a20–26).[28] The initial opinion assumes an exaggerated interpretation of the Socratic position, reducing virtue to knowledge: the indulgent person only needs to be taught the right principle in order to be cured, whereas no further information would suffice to change the behavior of the akratic, who already knows what he should be doing. The vice of the indulgent person, according to the initial opinion, is nothing but a lack of information that can be readily corrected. Since, moreover, his vice is supposed to represent an inner consistency of desire and conviction, we might be tempted to imagine him, however immoral, as strong and in control, while the akratic, who betrays his convictions, might be thought less immoral but weak and out of control. The condition of the indulgent person, however, as someone without regrets for his actions is finally admitted to be worse, like a chronic disease in contrast with the intermittent one of *akrasia.* The indulgent person, we are led to see in the end, is no different from the akratic in possessing the sort of character to yield to excessive bodily pleasure; he is just so far gone that his very opinion about what is right has been molded by that character. Passion is always in control when one acts against correct *logos;* but it is so much so in the case of the vicious person, in contrast with the akratic, that he has come to be unaware of it and only deceives himself if he believes he is self-determining in his vice.

Among the perplexities about *akrasia* first considered was that raised by the sophists, who play with the consequences of the assumption that self-restraint is standing by any opinion one holds, true or false, and lack of self-restraint abandoning it. But an action turning out beneficial or harmful, in that case, would be purely accidental, whereas self-restraint should be essentially beneficial and lack of self-restraint essentially harmful. What the self-restrained person stands by, then, as Aristotle confirms in the end, is true *logos* and correct choice, and that is what the unrestrained person abandons; the desirable condition is distinguished from the undesirable one by the ability to preserve not any opinion indifferently but true opinion (cf. 1146a17–21 and 1151a29–1151b4). Originally, Aristotle rejected the explanation of *akrasia* as the overcoming of true opinion rather than knowledge, on the grounds that one can produce just as strong a subjective conviction as the other (1146b24–30); but true opinion has now shown itself to be the form correct *logos* takes in the divided soul of the self-restrained person as well as one who lacks self-restraint. There is some standard of knowledge beyond true opinion, this suggests, that not only stands in the way of *akrasia* but also makes self-restraint unnecessary.

That standard was lurking in the initial survey of opinions, which included the view that the prudent person is incapable of *akrasia;* but that was countered by another, seemingly contrary, opinion—that the prudent and clever person can be akratic (1145b17–19). Aristotle now clarifies the error: cleverness, as a neutral skill of calculating means to any end, is certainly compatible with *akrasia,* but *phronēsis,* being inseparable from "serious character" and a matter not of simply knowing what is right but of doing it, precludes lack of self-restraint (1152a6–14). The akratic, Aristotle recalls, could be said to have knowledge and act against it only in the way someone who is asleep or drunk has knowledge, since the proper discernment of his situation is clouded over by the physiological effects of the passion he is undergoing. But what makes someone susceptible to that condition in the first place, the argument now recognizes, is the absence of *phronēsis,* that is, a lack of real understanding of his own good. It is at this point, not at the end of the third chapter, that Aristotle should concede: "What Socrates sought seems to follow."

Aristotle began his debate with Socrates, even before mentioning his name, by criticizing the many for "taking refuge in *logos*," as if Socratic philosophy were the product of a naive belief in the omnipotence of speech, which would deny any need for habituation and, thus, bound to promote *akrasia*. In completing his debate with Socrates, after the last mention of his name, Aristotle arrives at the contrary understanding: what makes one vulnerable to *akrasia* is precisely reliance on virtue acquired solely through habituation, which takes the form in our mental landscape of mere opinion and is insufficiently powerful to meet the strength of a conflicting desire for pleasure. The power required would belong only to an awareness of one's own good, based on an understanding of the human good. To achieve such an understanding is, in fact, the aim governing the turn to *logos*, beyond any habituation, that constitutes the inquiry of the *Ethics* itself. In arriving at a Socratic understanding of human motivation without, in speech, crediting Socrates for it, Aristotle has managed to achieve what he set out to do at the outset of the investigation of lack of self-restraint: while leaving common opinion as undisturbed as possible, he has refuted the objections—only the refuted objections turn out to be those leveled against the Socratic view!

Book VI brought the investigation of virtue to an end with an acknowledgment of the Socratic principle that there is no genuine virtue without *phronēsis*, while introducing, at the same time, the possibility of "natural virtues" that fall short of that standard. The discussion of lack of self-restraint reaches its conclusion in Book VII by noting the contrast between being akratic by nature and becoming akratic as a result of habit. The character state developed by habituation may be easier to cure, but even habit, Aristotle adds, is hard to change, precisely because it is so like nature; in the words of the poet Evenus, "Habit over a long time becomes in the end nature for a human being" (1152a32–33). Nature at this point seems to stand for the intractable, and if habit differs at all, it is only a matter of degree. Aristotle makes no effort to disagree with this rather sober assessment of the possibility of change. The instability of the diseased soul shows up in the tendency to act against one's best judgment, moved by passion, and then to turn around and regret it; but that tendency can be as firmly rooted, or nearly so, once it has developed out of habit as it would be if its source were nature. The investigation of pleasure and pain that follows aims, in part, to discover the grounds for this condition.

PLEASURE BY NATURE AND THE GOOD

Book VII turns from the discussion of psychic conflict to the investigation of pleasure and pain with a remarkable statement of intention:

> It is the task of the political philosopher [the one philosophizing in the political manner] to contemplate pleasure and pain; for such a one is the architect of the *telos* looking toward which we speak of one thing as simply bad, another good. (1152b1–3)

The "political philosopher" makes his appearance here for the first and only time in the *Ethics*, not accidentally, it would seem, just after Aristotle has come to his most complete acceptance of the Socratic understanding of human motivation.[29] Political philosophy now takes over the architectonic role assigned in the first book to *politikē*—political practice, or the science of politics—insofar as it is directed to the human good as its end. But the *telos* at this point seems to be something the political philosopher designs, which becomes in turn the standard for what is regarded as good or bad. If he is to carry out the task assigned to him as architect of the end—the contemplation of pleasure and pain—he must stand at some distance from the opinions of the city and conventional morality in its concern with praise and blame. The account in Book VII moves so far in that direction that it ends up treating human life as just one form of life among others, all inclined by nature toward the pursuit of pleasure and the avoidance of pain.[30] The assignment of this naturalistic account to the political philosopher almost sounds ironic: if this moment marks a new stage in the movement of the argument of the *Ethics*, the turn to nature in Book VII and the treatment of pleasure that comes with it must be nothing more than a necessary beginning for the path political philosophy must pursue.

Indeed, following that path leads finally to revisiting the topic of pleasure at the outset of Book X. According to some commentators, the accounts in Books VII and X are too overlapping, according to others, too distinct, to have been intended as parts of one work.[31] The treatment of pleasure as it develops throughout the *Ethics* with all its twists and turns, culminating in this double account, seems more than anything else to have furnished scholars with evidence for the fragmentary character of the work. If there is, on the contrary, an argument that makes the *Ethics* a whole, those same twists and turns in the treatment of pleasure would have to be understood as signs of the movement of that argument. That movement is indicated, to begin with, simply by the way the late accounts, in both the seventh and the tenth book, raise the question, What is pleasure? Other matters in the *Ethics* elicit the Socratic *ti esti* question, What is it?[32] No other discussion, however, requires or allows the kind of theoretical analysis we are led to in asking, *Ti esti* pleasure? In wrestling with that question, the discussion must deploy categories of ontology and psychology that cast doubt on the status of the *Ethics* as an autonomous political science with a restricted territory and way of proceeding.

The distance traversed since the initial rejection of pleasure as the human good in Book I is manifest not only in the way Books VII and X raise the question of what pleasure is but, even more directly, in their evaluation of it, although that evaluation is worked out in different ways by the two accounts and with subtly different results. One influential analysis assures us that "the difference in the introductions [to the two accounts] does not seem significant for our purposes."[33] But those introductory comments shed light on the distinctive context of each treatment of pleasure and, thus, on the role each plays in the argument of the whole. The tenth book will turn to pleasure as a concern of the utmost importance in forming character; while willing to admit the goodness of pleasure in itself, it sets out to differentiate beautiful pleasures from shameful ones and looks to the "serious man" as a standard. When the seventh book, in contrast, takes up the task of "contemplating pleasure and pain," the standard it holds up is nature, and its primary concern is the question of what constitutes pleasure according to nature.

Book VII has been devoted so far to an investigation of the experience of being led astray from right reasoning by pleasure. The thematic examination of pleasure thus begins, understandably, by taking up three negative opinions: (1) no pleasure is good at all; (2) even if some pleasures are good, most are base; (3) pleasure could not be the good (1152b8–12). Aristotle focuses on the first and last, but—much to our surprise—only to demonstrate how inadequate the arguments are in support of these opinions.

The most extreme view—that no pleasure is good at all—rests on the most obviously weak arguments. Its advocate points to children and animals as the agents who pursue pleasure, whereas the moderate person avoids pleasure and the prudent one pursues what is painless. Of course, Aristotle is willing to grant, certain pleasures get in the way of certain activities—no one can think while enjoying the pleasures of the *aphrodisia,* but any activity is enhanced by its own proper pleasures (1153a20–24). An appeal to particular undesirable pleasures can be eliminated, then, as a sufficient basis for the claim that pleasure as such is not good. But if that view is to be fundamentally undermined, it is necessary to take up the ontological assumptions on which it is based.

The claim that no pleasure is good—and even more clearly, that pleasure cannot be *the* good—is based on the assumption that pleasure is a coming to be (*genesis*): pleasure is identified as the path of return toward the natural state of the organism—eating when hungry or drinking when thirsty—while it is presupposed that whatever is good, and certainly *the* good, must be a *telos,* not a *genesis.*[34] The process, Aristotle counters, through which an organism is restored to its natural disposition may be pleasant, but it is only incidentally so; what is actually being experienced is the removal of a painful state. That which is essentially pleasant, on the other hand, is the activity of a disposition already in the natural state.[35] Pleasure, Aristotle concludes, should be defined not as a "perceptible *genesis*" but, rather, as "the unimpeded *energeia* of a disposition in accordance with nature" (1153a13–15). What is pleasant simply does not depend on any deficiency of the natural state and, thus, does not involve pain or desire at all—the desire, at least, to overcome a deficiency. Aristotle mentions only one case: the *energeia* of contemplation (1152b35–1153a2). One might, of course, be motivated over time to pursue this activity by coming to be aware of one's ignorance and seeking knowledge in the hope of overcoming it. But there is a pleasure in the *energeia* of *theōria* itself—however rarely human beings might experience it—that is not due to the satisfaction of need; and even if the awareness of ignorance were admitted to be painful, this pleasure cannot be reduced to the overcoming of that pain.

On the definition of pleasure as an unimpeded *energeia,* nothing precludes it from being good, or even *the* good. Even if certain pleasures may be base—as the second opinion under examination has it—some particular kind of pleasure could turn out to be the highest good. Perhaps, Aristotle proposes rather unexpectedly, this is actually necessary: if each disposition has its unimpeded activity, that one activity, or more than one, in which happiness consists must be, when unimpeded, the most desirable thing, and that *is* pleasure; so the highest good would be some kind of pleasure. It makes sense, then, that people think of the happy life as pleasant and "weave" pleasure into happiness (1153b10–16), but perhaps they don't go far enough. While acknowledging the possibility that some particular pleasure is the good, Aristotle has set in motion an argument that does not stop with that possibility, and he is prepared to follow out its consequences.

Looking around and seeing pleasure pursued not only by all human beings but by all other animals too, some thinkers are led to the conclusion that pleasure is something bad; Aristotle, on the contrary, now finds it a sign that pleasure is somehow the best thing (1153b25–26).[36] He offers in support a passage from Hesiod: "Talk to which many people give voice never entirely dies" (*Works and Days* 763). In the context, the poet is advising his brother not to do anything that would make him an object of gossip, which acquires a life of its own. Aristotle has inserted the citation in such a way that "talk to which many people give a voice" stands in for "pleasure sought by all living beings": they must be on to something in their universal pursuit of the same end, just as there must be something to a rumor that everyone reports. If there is indeed some one end that all living beings seek, how could that help but be good—or, rather, *the* good?

Aristotle has borrowed the verse from Hesiod, it seems, to support the thesis of hedonism. But the ambiguity and complexity of his intention come to light if we turn to Hesiod and notice the next line, which Aristotle has conspicuously omitted:[37] "Talk to which many people give voice never entirely dies. / Even talk is some kind of god." Now this line would appear to have a critical import: in treating all the different pleasures that living beings pursue as some one thing, namely, pleasure itself, we are guilty of a misleading reification—or, more precisely, deification. We turn pleasure into a god, or what amounts to the same, an empty *idea*. Aristotle appears to confirm this critical point when he goes on to note that since it is not the same nature and not the same disposition that is or seems best for all, it is not the same pleasure all pursue. But he proceeds immediately to make an astounding proposal: perhaps, however, what all pursue is not the pleasures they believe they do or would say they do but, indeed, the very same pleasure, for "all have by nature something divine" (1153b29–32).

The single pleasure all are seeking, even if they are not aware of it, is a mark of the divine. Readers have understandably identified this single pleasure as the pleasure of contemplation.[38] The *energeia* of *theōria* had been singled out, it is true, as *the* example of pleasure not dependent on prior pain (1153a1–2); and it will be described at the conclusion of the *Ethics* as the activity human beings participate in, to the extent that we do, by virtue of something divine in us (1177b26–28). The present passage began, however, by considering the pursuit of pleasure by all living beings, humans and beasts; and while it is only humans, presumably, who could be pursuing a pleasure other than what they *believe* or would *say*, the passage ends by identifying that single pleasure as the sign of something divine in all living things.[39] The divine manifests itself in the pursuit of pleasure across all animal life, even if, or precisely because, every other source of pleasure in some way emulates but falls short of the most pure form, which has been located in the *energeia* of *theōria*.

The turn to nature in Book VII seems to have reached a peak here. The argument at this moment, more than any other in the *Ethics*, brings us back to the original aim the inquiry set for itself, as a search for *the* good, before turning to the human good. All living things, in this comprehensive vision, must be understood in relation to the highest form of life, which exhibits the highest level of awareness. According to *Metaphysics* Λ, that form of life, which we call "god," must be pure *energeia*, and that *energeia is* pleasure.[40] Aristotle leads us to ponder this idea by the truncated passage from Hesiod he cites in *Ethics* VII: perhaps pleasure too really is some kind of god!

The analysis of Book VII has refuted, rather convincingly, the arguments put forward in support of the thesis that no pleasure is good and, more surprisingly, that pleasure cannot be the highest good. The thesis left suspended maintains that while some pleasures might be choiceworthy, others are not; its truth might seem to be clearly supported by consideration of bodily pleasures, those in particular relevant to the vice of indulgence. Yet even this seemingly moderate view is put into question: if these pleasures are not good, why are the pains contrary to them bad? Since, however, the best support for a true opinion is to explain the reasons for a conflicting false one, it would be useful, Aristotle urges, to consider why bodily pleasures appear so choiceworthy. People seek excessive pleasure to drive out excessive pain, and bodily pleasures serve just that purpose, as a cure; their intensity comes from the juxtaposition with the pains from which they provide relief. Then there are some individuals—like youth generally or people with a "melancholic nature"—whose natural condition is such that they experience a neutral state as a painful one, which they are driven to overcome. According to the physiologists, toil or strain is the general condition of animal life—even seeing or hearing is said to be painful, though we have supposedly become inured to it. What morality would blame as vice can be explained by the causality of purely natural processes.

Curative pleasures have the power they do for an organism in a state of illness. Pleasures, on the other hand, that do not accompany the restoration of the organism to a balanced state are not dependent on prior pains; the one example we have been given is the pleasure of contemplation. Why, the question arises in the end, if there is pleasure accompanying the activity of an organism in its natural state, is it impossible for anything to continue to give us pleasure always? If "god" represents a being with a simple nature, such a being would enjoy continuously a single pleasure. But that is a foil against which to recognize the reality of human beings, who are not all of a piece; hence, for us "change in all things is most sweet" (1154b28–29). Aristotle is citing here the words of Euripides' Orestes. Lying down in his demented state, he begs his sister to help him stand up; when one is sick, he observes, any change to a neutral state has the appearance of the positive state of health.[41]

Aristotle's Euripidean citation suggests that we are fundamentally in a state of illness, from which any momentary release is experienced as pleasure. Book VII ends with this explanation of that condition: the pleasure we take in change itself is due to some wickedness (*ponēria*), for just as a changeable human being is wicked, so is a nature that needs change, being neither simple or decent (1154b29–31). The reproach against a wicked nature, which first showed up as one possible cause of the rare attraction to pleasures contrary to nature (1148b18), is now generalized to the human condition. The turn to nature in Book VII looked as if it were meant to provide the enlightened understanding that is possible only after one is freed from the constraints of conventional morality. The experiment with a purely naturalistic account, however, which has allowed the hedonist thesis to be given a hearing, has taken a strange turn in the end:[42] an understanding of nature that culminates in the possibility of pleasure being the good concludes with resentment against our "wicked" nature, which sets so many obstacles to our enjoyment of the pleasure that comes with the single eternal activity of a god.

6

Friendship and the Discovery of the Self

SOCRATES: But in my opinion, they mean that those who are
good are alike and are friends to each other, while those who
are bad—as is in fact said about them—are never alike, not even
themselves to themselves, but are impulsive and unsteady. And
what is unlike and at variance with itself would hardly become
like or a friend to anything else. . . . This then, my companion,
is in my opinion what they are hinting at when they say that
what is like is a friend to its like, namely that he who is good is
a friend to the good—he alone to him alone—while he who is
bad never enters into true friendship either with good or with
bad. . . . And yet I'm uneasy about something in it.

—Plato *Lysis* 214c–d, translated by David Bolotin

RATIONAL AND POLITICAL NATURE

Friendship made its first appearance in the *Ethics* in what seemed to be a
rather incidental manner. As a friend of "the men who imported the forms,"
Aristotle felt compelled to apologize in advance for his critical examination
of the *idea* of the good; but it is sometimes necessary, he reminded himself,
for the sake of the truth to sacrifice the things of one's own, especially on the
part of the philosopher, for whom both are dear (or friends), though it is holy
to honor the truth more (1096a11–17).[1] Attachment to a friend thus shows up
first in its apparent conflict with devotion to the truth—since that requires
standing back from what is "one's own," which appears to mean loyalty to
one's friends. "The things of one's own," however, could mean, even more
plausibly, one's own opinions—and the need to sacrifice them in the search
for the truth might come to be recognized only through dialogue with another, which proves to be the defining activity of friendship (1170b10–12).

The relation to one's own, which is supposedly an obstacle to the objectivity of the truth, may in fact be, when it takes the form of philosophical friendship, the only realistic path in pursuit of the truth.[2]

Aristotle's comments in Book I about examining the *idea* of the good, which seem to express a conflict between allegiance to a friend and the quest for the truth, contain a model in miniature for the apparent tension that runs through the *Ethics* as a whole between the political nature and the rational nature of the human being. But if those comments actually point to the role friendship plays in the quest for the truth, they would imply an inseparability of our political and our rational nature that makes each dependent on the other for its own fruition. That inseparability comes to light through a transformation in the understanding of the highest form friendship can take. The argument begins in Book VIII with a model of "perfect friendship" as a relationship between those who are alike in virtue and drawn together by recognition in the other of the sense of completeness each experiences in himself. The argument concludes, at the end of Book IX, with the paradigm of philosophical friends, who recognize in each other the awareness each has of what he lacks and hence of the need for dialogue with the other.

A remarkable occurrence takes place in the course of this movement from one pole of the discussion of friendship to the other. The human good, which the *Ethics* set out to discover, was identified in Aristotle's initial "outline" as an *energeia* of the *soul* in accordance with complete or perfect virtue for a human being (1098a16–18), and human virtue was simply declared to be excellence of the soul (1102a16–17). This sounds so familiar, perhaps, that we do not ask why human virtue is not virtue of the human being, or the human good an activity of the human being; we do not look for any argument to justify the abstraction of "soul" as the subject. In fact, we do not realize how much has been taken for granted until Book IX designates the friend as "another self" (*allos autos*; 1166a31–32) and, with that, leads for the first time to the recognition of the human being not as soul but as self. That it has taken so long to arrive at this conception of the self comes as a surprise. Even more surprising is the claim about how it is to be understood: the self, we will be told, is, or is most of all, mind (1166a16–17, 22–23; cf. 1168b34–35). When the *Ethics* at last introduces the notion of the self and we expect an acknowledgment of the human being as an inseparable union of body and soul, the self is identified with mind—the only thing conceivably separable from the composite being.[3] The principle of identity that should, presumably, belong to the individual in all his particularity is instead assigned to that which can be understood as the most impersonal and anonymous aspect of the human being.[4]

This is quite naturally the understanding of the self that will provide the basis for an answer, at the end of the tenth book, to the question of the activity that constitutes happiness. But why should it first emerge in the context of friendship? The contemplative life is affirmed, in the tenth book, as one that exhibits to a greater extent than any other human life "so-called self-sufficiency," that is, independence from others (1177a27–28). But when self-sufficiency (*autarkeia*) was first introduced as a characteristic believed to belong to happiness, Aristotle insisted that it could not mean a solitary life: since the human being is by nature political, the good life must be one with family and friends and fellow citizens (1097b8–13).[5] The self of the tenth book, for whom the good lies in the most single-minded devotion to the activity of contemplation, instantiates, supposedly, the rational nature of the human at its highest level, and the transcendence, apparently, of our political nature. The subject who can enter into the relation with a friend—what we might call the dialogic self—instantiates together the rational and the political nature of the human in a way that compels us to rethink the meaning of each in its separation from the other.

PERFECT FRIENDSHIP AND OTHER SPECIES

Friendship is so desirable that no one would choose to have all other goods if it meant living without friends (1156a5–6). No such claim is made in the *Ethics* about any other aspect of human life. The claim is defended, initially, by acknowledging the necessity of friendship in all of life's varied circumstances: good fortune and prosperity are enhanced when shared with friends, while in the face of poverty or misfortune friends are believed to be our only resource. The young need friends to keep them from going wrong, the older need the care that friends can give, and those in their prime need friends with a view to accomplishing beautiful actions. Aristotle cites the *Iliad* in support—"When two go together, they are more able to conceive a plan and to act" (1155a14–16): "beautiful actions," we notice, has dropped out. The line Aristotle invokes, after all, is spoken by Diomedes, seeking a partner to share with him a bloody night raid on the sleeping Trojans—a strange choice if one wanted to pick out a single instance to illustrate as clearly as possible how companionship necessarily fosters noble deeds![6]

If friendship is a necessity throughout our lives, nature seems to have co-operated fully with this need: unlike the virtues, which have to be produced by training, friendship is more directly rooted in our natural inclinations. This is evident, at least, in the affection parents feel for their own offspring, which looks like something common to all animals. The natural root of friendship shows itself in the attraction of any member of a species to its fellows but, especially, in the case of our own species, as we can see from relationships that spring up among those traveling abroad, who find some kinship simply as human beings (1155a16–22). At the same time, friendship *seems* to be the bond that holds the city together, and legislators *seem* more serious about friendship than justice, since they strive to avoid faction and promote concord, which *seems* to be some kind of *philia* (1155a22–26). But concord among citizens, we later learn, *appears* to be political friendship (1167b2–3), which is not friendship proper; and legislators are, or should be, concerned with friendship precisely because of the threat to concord posed by personal relations between friends, in all their intensity and exclusivity.[7]

Elaborating on the political importance of friendship, Aristotle expresses the opinion that those who are friends have no need of justice, whereas those who are just still need friendship (1155a26–28). That friendship, with all its pleasures and rewards, has some claim to a superior role over justice, with all its rules and obligations, finds support as the exploration of friendship unfolds; it goes quite a bit further to suppose that friendship dispenses altogether with the need for justice. In fact, various forms of friendship bring their own demands for justice, and the discussion eventually becomes absorbed in weighing such claims and assessing their priorities.[8] The opening chapter of Book VIII, however, reveals no trace in friendship of a connection with its contrary, strife. Friendship is understood to be not only a necessity in human life but something noble or beautiful as well; having many friends, in any case, is *thought* to be beautiful (1155a30)—an opinion that will be explicitly rejected in the discussion that follows.[9] The statement about the nobility of friendship, applied in particular to having many friends, expresses, like most of those that make up this initial survey, what is thought or said to be the case. As the starting point of the analysis, Aristotle holds up a mirror to ordinary opinion about friendship, and what appears on it will show itself to be, in many respects, an idealized image.

Like the general agreement about happiness as a final end, which only served to open up a debate about what it is, the general agreement Aristotle has discovered, or constructed, about the desirability of friendship opens up the disputed issue of what it is. At the core of the dispute is the question whether friendship is primarily a relationship between subjects that are like or subjects that are unlike. The attraction of likes or unlikes, while spoken of in the language of human experience, lends itself readily by metaphor— as Euripides no less than Heraclitus and Empedocles testify—to serve as a cosmological principle (1155b1–7).[10] Making a Socratic turn, Aristotle dismisses such speculations about the whole of nature and sets out to analyze friendship as a strictly human phenomenon: we are to inquire not about the general principle of the attraction of likes or opposites in the natural universe but about whether friendship has more than one form and whether all people can be friends or only the good.

The two questions prove to be integrally connected: a division of kinds (*eidē*) allows friendship to be construed so broadly as to encompass relationships between individuals who are not good, however paradigmatic friendship between the good may be. Friendship apparently calls for just the opposite of the strategy Aristotle pursued in treating the virtues of character, each of which was construed as narrowly as possible, with only passing hints as to how it points beyond the confines in which it was cast.[11] Aristotle finds the principles for a classification of friendship in the motives of our attraction to others: however messy a mixture all our actual relationships may be, the difference between liking someone because we find him good, or pleasant, or useful yields a tripartite division of pure types of friendship (1155b17–19). This expansion of *philia* is in part guided by ordinary language: we call people "friends" who like each other for all these reasons (1157a25–30). But beyond ordinary language, the analysis captures some kind of generosity of nature: we are allowed, or compelled, by our political nature, even if we are not simply good, to participate, however defectively, in this most desirable experience.

Distinguishing the motives of our attraction to others establishes a division of kinds without yet determining what friendship as such is. The starting point for addressing that question lies in the common assumption that an inanimate object cannot be a friend. We do not wish for the well-being of such an object, unless it is with our own interest in mind; but *they say*— Aristotle does not confirm the claim—that one should wish the good of a friend for his own sake (1155b31). Goodwill, however, is not enough; it must be reciprocated if it is to count as friendship, and even that is not sufficient, unless both persons are aware of each other's regard. An inanimate object, of course, cannot return our affection or even have any awareness of it. The *philo-sophos*, however drawn he is to becoming wise, cannot be, in the precise sense, a *friend* of wisdom. Strictly speaking, he is a "lover of wisdom," in whom *sophia* arouses eros, though it is itself indifferent to the one who seeks it.[12] Eros, which is directed toward an object beyond the lover, which has no need for the lover, highlights by contrast what it means for friendship to be, essentially, a mutual relationship between two individuals.

Friendship, more specifically, is a relationship of two individuals bound by a reciprocal, jointly acknowledged affection and genuine goodwill for each other. This is a comprehensive conception that is supposed to encompass three species: we can wish the good for a friend, Aristotle proposes, "on account of" any one of the qualities—goodness, pleasantness, or usefulness—that has attracted us to him (1156a6–10). But liking someone for the utility or pleasure he supplies to us, or wishing him well with regard to that pleasure or utility, is admittedly not really liking him and wishing him well for himself. A friendship motivated by pleasure or utility seems incapable, in that case, of living up to what friendship aims to be, as expressed in its supposedly comprehensive definition. Such a relationship is, for one thing, bound to be precarious: an association motivated by usefulness dissolves as soon as one party ceases to provide the benefit the other seeks from him, while one motivated by pleasure is as unstable as the taste that initiated it. Of course, even character, Aristotle eventually admits, can change in ways that might make the preservation of a friendship impossible (1165b13–31)— perhaps the most somber reminder of how little, if any, permanence there is in human life.

The instability of friendship, however, is nowhere more evident than in the volatile relationships of the young, who are, Aristotle explains, particularly erotic; looking to friendship only for pleasure, they end their attachments as quickly and passionately as they fall into them, sometimes changing in the course of the day (1156b1–4). The erotic relationship makes its first appearance here to illustrate the inevitable precariousness of an association guided by feeling and motivated by pleasure. And yet such relationships, which are typical of youth, bear a closer resemblance to the highest form of friendship than relationships motivated by profit, which are typical of old age. Older people, or those who are sick or bad-tempered, may genuinely wish each other well, but they don't necessarily take pleasure in each other's company and therefore do not want to spend their time together, whereas young people find pleasure in "living together" (*suzēn*), and it is living together that makes the potential of friendship an actuality (1156b4–6). Pleasure is the instrument through which nature drives us toward the actualization of friendship. Friendships based on pleasure are closer to the primary form for another reason: such relationships are more likely to obtain between individuals who are alike, whereas relationships based on utility are almost by definition between unlike individuals, insofar as each seeks in the other what he but not the other lacks and needs. When each partner in such a relationship is engaged in calculating the profit to be gained from the other, the very claim to be friends invites deception, or self-deception, about the grounds for their association. Friendships based on utility, consequently, provide an especially fertile ground for complaints and recriminations.[13] But such difficulties are bound to plague as well a relationship motivated by pleasure when the two parties seek pleasure from one another in diverse and potentially conflicting ways: Aristotle calls upon the erotic relationship once again as a model (1157a6–14).

Feeling affection for the friend himself and wishing him well for his own sake looks as if it characterizes only the highest kind of friendship, that of the good, who are alike in virtue (1156b7–17). Their relationship is distinguished from the inferior forms of *philia* because their aim is not to get pleasure or profit from each other; yet their association is in fact both beneficial and pleasant not just in their own eyes, as all friendships are, but simply so. The friendship of the good is a standard, therefore, not just as the highest type but as comprehensive: it is *teleia philia*, and the ambiguity of this characterization—complete or perfect—is essential to its status.[14] It is *philia* in the primary sense (1157a30–31) not just because it is best, but because it encompasses all the grounds for friendship: only for that reason can relationships aiming at pleasure or utility bear a likeness to the primary form that allows them to count as types of *philia* at all.[15] The internal structure ascribed to friendship, which incorporates a set of *eidē* that fall short of the perfect or complete standard (*teleia philia*), prepares for the conclusion of the *Ethics,* which distinguishes a perfect standard (*teleia eudaimonia*) from that which falls short while nonetheless counting as happiness (1177b24, 1178a9–10).

The friendship of the good, however, which constitutes the standard of *philia,* has been presented in an abstract form, which we fill in largely by recognizing, from the more concrete account of the inferior forms of friendship, what it is not. Who are "the good" involved in such a friendship, and what is the virtue they possess alike? The *Ethics* has rarely referred to "the good" simply, and they are not identified now as the decent or the serious, the prudent or the wise; the virtue they have in common remains unnamed. Would two individuals, each of whom is supposed to be good in himself and, in essential respects, like the other, have any need for one another, and, if not, is friendship still a realistic possibility for them? [16] They certainly would not be driven by an awareness of their own deficiency to try to complete themselves through union with each other, as if they were two halves of one whole.[17]

JUSTICE IN FRIENDSHIP

As the discussion develops, *philia* comes to cover a range of relationships—familial, economic, social, political, erotic—that extends far beyond those we would ordinarily speak of as "friendship." This extension leads, understandably, to the claim that *philia* seems to be coextensive with justice (1159b25–27), which had been defined as complete virtue, albeit in relation to others. Particularly in the face of this extension, it is rather shocking to realize that the whole discussion in Books VIII and IX is conducted without ever defining the friend over against what it means to be an enemy: enmity seems to be as deliberately excluded from the examination of friendship as punishment was from the analysis of justice or righteous indignation from the investigation of the virtues.[18]

The eventual recognition of justice as an issue in all our relations to others raises a question about the claim put forward at the outset of Book VIII, that friendship is so superior it dispenses with the need for justice altogether. That friendship does in some sense lie on a higher plane than justice is an idea that seems to be supported by the movement of the argument of the

Ethics itself: the place justice occupies in the first stage, which concludes the investigation of ethical virtue, is replaced by friendship in the second.[19] Friendship, like justice, is an expression of our political nature as beings who find their fulfillment in living together with others; friendship, however, is a natural response to that fundamental human need, and it is, or should be, experienced as a pleasure, whereas justice is experienced as an obligation, one that imposes a set of requirements on our actions in relation to others independent of any feelings we may have for them. Justice may require some sacrifice of our immediate self-interest or perceived self-interest, while friendship is supposed to involve a natural coincidence between our self-interest and that of our friend. Friendship provides a source of comfort in misfortune and enhancement of good fortune that cannot be sought in justice. The function of justice in ordering relations in the political community may provide a necessary condition for the realization of the good for the individual; it is not an integral element of that good, as friendship is. Justice may preserve "the parts of happiness in the political community" (1129b17–19), whatever that means exactly, but it does not contribute directly to the happiness of the individual as friendship admittedly does.

These differences are reflected in the opposite directions in which the argument moves in the two discussions. Book V insisted on the status of justice as primarily a relation among independent individuals or, rather, among citizens in the *polis,* under the law; the notion that one could be unjust to oneself was rejected. More precisely, the possibility of justice as an order of the soul was admitted, but only at the very end of the analysis, as a metaphor, and even then only as an extended meaning of justice in a derivative sense, applied to unequal relations. "Justice in the soul," as the proper mastery by the ruling part of the soul over the ruled, turned out to be self-restraint. In the treatment of friendship, on the contrary, the relationship with another is found to be derivative from a certain order within the individual and the friend has finally to be understood as an "other self."

Ordinary opinion, in its ranking of friendship over justice, captures a profound truth about the nature of human things; it does not follow, as opinion has it, that friendship makes it possible to dispense with justice entirely.[20] The particular and exclusive relationships of friendship could never furnish the bond that holds all citizens together in the city. If such a bond could be provided by *philia* at all, it would be only in the diluted sense according to which like-mindedness (*homonoia*) can be called "political friendship" (1167b2–3; cf. 1155a24–26). Now, however desirable citizen concord might be in its likeness to friendship, it would be a dangerous enterprise to depend on it as a substitute for the law, in its claim to instantiate the principles of distributive and corrective justice.[21] Not only is friendship incapable of taking the place of justice in the city as a whole, but within personal relationships the demand for justice does not simply disappear. Indeed, the question of what expectations and obligations belong to various relationships appears, Aristotle eventually concludes, to be nothing other than a question of justice in some sense (1162a29–31); and the closer the relation of *philia,* the stronger the demand for justice (1159b35–1160a8).[22]

Friendship and justice cover the same territory, Aristotle reasons, insofar as every partnership or community (*koinōnia*) *seems* to involve some element of justice as well as friendship; but since, as *they say,* the political community aims at the advantage in common, all other associations, which aim at some particular advantage, *seem* to be parts of the political community (1160a9–11). A number of examples are offered—sailors or soldiers, members of a tribe, societies for sacrifices or festivals—all of which, Aristotle repeats, *seem* to be parts of the political community (1160a21); when the discussion concludes with yet another repetition—all limited communities *appear* to be parts of the political community (1160a28–29)—Aristotle's refusal to confirm this appearance should make us doubt his endorsement of it. The *koinōnia* of an army may be part of the political community and subordinate to it, but what about the family or the friendship of two individuals? Of what political community is the relationship of Plato and Aristotle a proper part? It is only from the perspective of the city and its end, as Book I had already suggested, that every human association is a subordinate part of the political whole. If justice does play a role in all personal relationships, it does not belong simply to the city and its laws. The discussion of friendship compels us not only to move beyond but to reconsider the analysis of justice in Book V—in particular, the question of whether "the political just" is "the just simply" (1134a24–26).

The idea that justice should be superfluous among friends has its strongest evidence in the ideal friendship of the good; the further one gets from that ideal, the more the demand for justice imposes itself. What begins as a beautified portrait of two individuals alike in virtue, each attracted to the goodness of the other, descends finally to a consideration of the disappointments within and conflicts among our roles as children, parents, citizens, business partners, comrades, lovers. Questions of justice may not be too intrusive as long as the relationships concerned embody the proverbial standard of friendship as equality (*philotēs isotēs*; 1157b36); but they flood in with the admission of an "other *eidos*" of friendship, found in relationships between superior and inferior subjects (1158b11–14).

To expose the threat that inequality poses for friendship, Aristotle turns our attention to the extreme case: a human being could never be friends with a god (1158b35–1159a5). Friendship is supposed to be characterized by wishing one's friend the best for his own sake, but one can do so only as long as he remains himself, and that means, ultimately, a human being. The extreme case thus reveals a general tension—between goodwill and equality— that lurks at the heart of friendship as such.[23] There is, presumably, some boundary, particular to every relationship, beyond which inequality cannot increase without destroying friendship. Within that boundary, a friendship between superior and inferior can be maintained, Aristotle proposes, as long as each partner feels affection for the other in proportion to worth (1158b23–28). This is an application of the principle of distributive justice, which provides the primary standard for fair treatment of citizens in the political community, who make unequal contributions and deserve unequal rewards; in the case of friendship, it can be only a second best, always falling short of the ideal of strict equality between two individuals who do not need to compensate for a difference in worth.

Even as second best, however, is it really possible for affection to be governed by the standard of rendering to each his due? The lover, in any case, who complains about his love not being returned, would hardly be satisfied with requital proportionate to the beloved's assessment of his worth (1164a3–4). Sometimes, Aristotle admits, it is not possible to give back what is due—children can never give to their parents what they deserve, or human beings to the gods (1163b15–18). At the beginning of the ninth book, Aristotle makes a rather surprising addition to these examples: one can never pay back what is due, but only as much as one is capable of, to fellow "participants in philosophy" (1164b2–6). Aristotle could pay his debt to the "men who imported the forms" only by subjecting their views to examination in the service of searching for the truth (1096a11–17). The problem of paying back what one owes calls attention to the status of "joint participants in philosophy," teacher and student, presumably, as an exemplary relationship between unequals, on a par with child and parent, or human and god.[24] Philosophical friendship, in this respect, stands in contrast to the friendship of the good, which is supposed to obtain between partners who are alike and equal.

Aristotle locates the inequality of partners as an essential feature in two spheres of life in particular—political relationships between ruler and ruled, on the one hand, and domestic relationships between members of the family, on the other (1158b12–14). An elaborate analogy between the two assigns to three *eidē* of regimes and their corresponding deviations "likenesses and paradigms, as it were" among relationships in the household (1160b23–24).[25] As "likenesses," family relationships would appear to be reflections of structures whose primary form is political; but the household, with its diverse relationships of husband and wife, parent and child, siblings, master and slave, contains in one whole the archetypes for all the distinct forms of regime, only one of which would be found at any particular time in a particular political community. The one case, in any event, in which the family seems to be the original and the political structure the likeness is the paternal relationship as paradigm for kingship: Homer calls Zeus "father" because "kingship wants to be paternal rule" (1160b25–28).[26] If kingship is derived from the parental relationship, it is only because it treats the political community like a large family and does not recognize the essentially distinctive nature of the *polis*.

The language of the political relationship between ruler and ruled may be borrowed to describe unequal relationships within the family; but the household, Aristotle argues, is more primary and necessary than the city, because the human being is by nature more of a "pairing" being than a political one—that is suggested, at least, by the animal kingdom as a whole (1162a16–19). The first book of the *Politics*, in contrast, sets out to establish that the city is prior by nature to the household and to the individual, as a whole is prior to a part (1253a19–29). Of course, this contrast would not be a contradiction if the household and the city are each "prior" in a different sense. Still, there is a different perspective at work in each analysis, and that difference shows up in the distance at which each stands from the conventions of the city: while the *Ethics* speaks of human virtue, the *Politics* speaks of the virtue of woman or child or slave—the excellence, that is, defined by a particular role in the order of the *polis* and the household as subordinate to it.[27] The difference in the horizon of the two treatises is indicated by their claims about friendship with a slave: while the *Politics* allows the possibility of friendship between master and slave only when both are fit by nature for their particular roles (1255b13–15), the *Ethics* maintains that a master cannot be the friend of a slave as a slave but only to the extent the slave transcends, as a human being, his slavish role (1161b2–8). As the *Ethics* discloses above all in its discussion of friendship, we may have a political nature, but the human being cannot be understood simply as a political being, at least not if that means being defined exclusively by one's distinctive role in the *polis* or household.

The multiform (*polueidēs*) sphere of associations in the household may be articulated by analogy with the division of political regimes; but all family relationships are derived, ultimately, from a single source most firmly rooted in nature—parents' love for their children (1161b16–19).[28] While a child feels, or should feel, indebted to his parents for the great good they have conferred on him in giving him life and nurture, the love a parent feels for his child has a more natural, and more powerful source: in their children, parents see "other selves, as it were, separated from themselves" (1161b28–29). The account of parental *philia* provides the first sign of a new principle of friendship that goes deeper than the useful, the pleasant, or even the good. The source of parental love is a projection by the individual of himself onto another. But it is precisely this self-projection by the parent—Aristotle speaks, in particular, of the mother—that allows her to wish and act for the good of the child without any calculation of expected returns: the root of the most selfless of all human relationships is the attachment to one's own being.[29] This particular paradoxical relationship anticipates a crucial turn that brings us to the fundamental ground of friendship as Aristotle understands it.

THE FRIEND AS AN OTHER SELF

Internal Harmony and the Possibility of the Self

The discussion of friendship seems to be completed once it has descended from the perfect friendship of the good to an analysis of all the conflicts and disillusionments that make our real relationships so precarious; yet it starts all over again, in the fourth chapter of Book IX, with the introduction of the "other self" as the right way to understand the friend. From the whole preceding discussion, Aristotle culls the features thought to be definitive of friendship in order to demonstrate that they characterize primarily an inner state of the individual (1166a1–2). In the best friendship between two individuals, one wants for one's friend the good, or apparently good things, for his sake, and one acts to procure them; one wishes, on the most basic level, for the very being and life of one's friend, for his sake. For two people to be friends, though, it is not enough only to want what is good for one another; friends must enjoy spending time with each other, they choose the same things as each other, and they experience sorrow and joy together with one another. If this kind of harmony is thought to pertain to the relationship between two individuals who are friends, it is, Aristotle now argues, because it is to be found above all within the decent person (*ho epieikēs*) as an individual. In fact, he adds in passing, such internal harmony belongs to all who consider themselves decent, although, he reminds us, the serious person seems to be the measure (1166a11–13). While holding onto the authority of the *spoudaios*—who momentarily replaces the *epiekēs* for this purpose— Aristotle is apparently willing to extend to all who have some modicum of "self-esteem" the possibility of a self not torn apart by faction.[30]

The individual who possesses within himself the marks of friendship with another is someone who desires the same things with his whole soul (1166a13–14).[31] He wishes the good, or apparently good things, for himself and acts on them for his own sake because he does so for the sake of the intellectual part (*to dianoētikos*), which seems to be just what each individual is. He wishes to live and be preserved himself, but most of all he wishes for the life and preservation of that by which he exercises prudence (*phronein*). In wanting life, he, like everyone, wants something good for himself; but it is, in this case, truly for himself, because the life he wants preserved most of all is that of the thinking part (*to nooun*), which would seem to be what each individual is, or is most of all. A person like this wants to spend time with himself and does so with pleasure, having fond memories and good hopes and an intellect (*dianoia*) well stored with objects of contemplation (*theorēmata*). Like two friends who experience pain and pleasure in sympathy with one another, he does so in relation to himself, inasmuch as he does not find something pleasant at the moment and then regret it a moment later.

Only such an individual, precisely because he alone can be said to have, or to be, a self, can be related toward a friend as he is toward himself, for the friend is another self (*allos autos;* 1166a29–32). Friendship with another is the extension of an inner harmony, which has been traced, in turn, to the identification of mind as the self, or most of all the self. Mind, it is true, has been assigned a whole array of functions—that with which one thinks things through, reasons practically, or has insight.[32] But this set of functions is no longer attributed to distinct parts of the soul: the logic of whole and parts, which underlies the analysis of the soul, has been replaced by the logic of essence, which makes mind, whatever its variety of functions, the unifying principle of identity that constitutes a self.[33]

In contrast with the inner harmony of the decent person—or all those, Aristotle granted, who suppose themselves decent—the base person is precisely that individual whose soul is filled with faction (1166b5–10). Always desiring one thing and wanting another, unable to experience consistently his own joys and pains, such a person cannot be said to have, or to be, a self at all. We recognize, certainly, the condition Aristotle is describing here, but defining the base person in this way entails a radical alteration of the premise underlying the whole investigation of ethical virtue: suddenly there is no difference between vice and *akrasia,* or lack of self-restraint. Only two alternatives are now admitted—either the integrity of the self or the failure to achieve that.[34] The one is made possible by the inner harmony ascribed to the decent; the other results from the inner faction ascribed to the base. The language is that of morality, but it has been grafted onto a new psychology.[35] The original figure of the vicious person—whose recognition of his own good has been so destroyed that his bad desires can be in harmony with wrong judgment—no longer appears as a real possibility; everyone, it is now presupposed, has some inkling of the good and some awareness of its absence.[36] And the inevitable consequence of not desiring with one's whole soul the good one perceives, however dimly, is the internal dissension that, in turn, makes friendship with another difficult or impossible.[37]

The standard is set by the decent person, who seems to be standing in for the ethically virtuous individual more generally, in whom the desires, which belong to the nonrational part of the soul, have been brought into harmony with practical reason through habituation (cf. 1128b21–25). According to the present account, however, the inner harmony of such an individual is the consequence of the role of mind as the principle of the identity of the self, which was never proposed, and could not have been, in the account of ethical virtue. The psychic harmony produced by habituation appears, in this new light, to be some kind of simulacrum of the primary unity of the self as mind. This unity of the self was anticipated at one earlier moment in the *Ethics*—in the revised account of choice (*prohairesis*) that appeared in the second chapter of Book VI, which identified the single source of human action as "desiring mind" or "intellectual desire" (1139b4–5). That fusion of mind and desire, which is supposed to be the unifying human principle, would seem to characterize above all, if not only, the soul of the philosopher moved by eros for wisdom. After its fleeting appearance in Book VI, it does not resurface until we are reminded of it here in Book IX by the account of the self as mind in the individual who desires the same things with his whole soul.

A Friend of Oneself

Although the features ascribed to friendship with another have been traced to a condition of internal harmony, Aristotle leaves open the question whether it is intelligible to speak of being a friend with oneself (1166a33–34). That possibility seems to be taken for granted when the question is raised, later in Book IX, whether one should be a friend most of all to oneself or to another (1168a28–29). The problem arises from the speeches of morality and the conception of the self they presuppose. "Self-lover" (*philautos*) in ordinary language is a term of reproach, on the assumption that the base person acts only for his own sake, while the decent person acts because of the beautiful and for his friend's sake, disregarding his own; but the deeds, Aristotle observes, do not harmonize with such speeches. *They say*, in any case, that one should like one's best friend most, and the best friend is one who wishes someone well for his own sake, even if he will never know of it; yet this is the case above all, Aristotle reasons, in the relation of an individual to himself.[38]

To support the idea that the individual's relation to himself is the standard to which friendship with another approximates Aristotle appeals to the proverbial wisdom of a formula like "one soul" (1168b6–7). Calling to mind Euripides' *Orestes,* in which this formula appears, Aristotle advances the portrait of human motivation that began with a citation from the *Orestes* about the neediness on which pleasure depends (1154b28–29) and that will culminate with a line from the same drama about the neediness on which friendship depends (1169b7–8). In the context to which Aristotle now alludes,

Orestes has just returned to Electra to report his failure at persuading the assembly to commute the sentence of death they are facing, having managed only to replace the threat of public stoning by a pledge of their joint suicide. Electra begs her brother to take her life, but when he refuses, she promises to put the sword to herself, seeking only one last embrace: "Oh dearest one, having a body longed for and most pleasant to your sister, and one soul." Orestes yields, ready to throw off all shame: "This is all we two will have of marriage bed and children" (1045–1051). If one's best friend is always oneself, Aristotle's Euripidean allusion suggests, friendship with another should find its most perfect realization in incest.

While Aristotle has appealed to proverbial wisdom to support the notion that one is—or in the best case should be—most of all a friend to oneself, his justification for the idea turns on the meaning of *"philautos."* In its ordinary use as a term of reproach, it refers to one who distributes to himself more than he should of money or honors or bodily pleasures, gratifying the desires and the irrational part of the soul, which is assumed to be the only form of self-love. If someone were serious, however, about doing the just or moderate things and, in general, striving to procure the beautiful for himself, no one would blame him (1168b25–28). What exactly one would get in "procuring the beautiful for oneself"—when orientation to the beautiful should be, almost by definition, entirely disinterested—is a question Aristotle does not explicitly raise.[39] At the moment, he is prepared to conclude that someone who assigns the best and most beautiful things to himself should most of all be called a "lover of self." The decent person (*ho epieikēs*), Aristotle elaborates, is most fully a *philautos* because he gratifies the most sovereign part of himself: he is obedient to mind, and mind chooses the best for itself (1169a16–18). Of course, it is far from obvious that obeying mind as the sovereign part of oneself is identical with aiming to procure the beautiful for oneself, such that both these forms of praiseworthy self-love would be the same.

It is, in particular, the striving for the *kalon* that exhibits the paradoxical character of a self-love that manifests itself in self-sacrifice. Precisely in aiming at the beautiful for himself, the serious person (*ho spoudaios*) will do many things, including laying down his life, for the sake of his friends and fatherland (*patris;* 1169a18–20): the term, which appears only here in the *Ethics,* lends a fitting tone to the description of the hero, who prefers one intense moment of glory to a long period of mild contentment. He is prepared to give up money, honors, or the other goods people fight over, choosing instead the great and beautiful thing for himself; but that is itself something one individual achieves at the expense of another, and thus an object of competition in its own right. The noble self-lover, in his eagerness to distribute more of the *kalon* to himself, violates the principle of equality and, thus, points to the potential conflict of the beautiful with the just.[40] In his greed for the most selfless action, he is prepared not only to give up his life, if necessary, but even to relinquish the performance of such a beautiful deed if he finds it more beautiful to be the cause of his friend performing it! The image of the noble self-lover stepping aside so his friend can have the glory of sacrificing himself is one of the more comic moments in the *Ethics* or, perhaps, tragicomic ones. Through this portrait of the self-sacrificing self-lover striving for the *kalon,* Aristotle uncovers a root of ethical virtue as such, which could not have been disclosed in the discussion of the virtues as experienced by the ethically virtuous individual. Action for the sake of the beautiful, looked at from the outside, is a powerful means of serving one's self-interest; but that objective consequence cannot be the motivation of the agent, in his own self-understanding, without destroying its own possibility.[41]

Self-love, Aristotle has tried to establish, is not blameworthy in itself; it depends on the identity of the self being gratified. The common term of reproach recognizes only the lowest form of self-indulgence, much as the common reproach of pleasure recognizes it only in its lowest forms. To demonstrate this point has, presumably, been the primary concern of the argument. The demonstration has been accomplished, however, through an ambiguous portrait of the acceptable self-lover, who looks like a single type only relative to his contrary. When considered more closely, the individual who is ambitious for the beautiful and universally praised for his deeds hardly seems to be one and the same as the individual who is a self-lover because of the way he gratifies the mind. Any apparent unity of the class in fact conceals a double species: behind the figure of the self-sacrificing self-lover devoted to the beautiful stands the philosopher, who is a lover of self as mind.

Reciprocal Self-Awareness

The discussion that began at the outset of Book VIII with the view of friendship as something no one would choose to live without is driven, by the end, to question that assumption. If the friend is an other self (*heteros autos*), who makes up for one's own deficiencies, then the blessed person, *they say,* being self-sufficient, has no such need (1169b4–7). Enlisting Euripides once more to cast a shadow over a sunlit portrait, Aristotle cites the bitter words of Orestes: "When fortune favors us, what need of friends?"[42] Without immediately rejecting the dark view implied by that question, Aristotle admits how strange it would be to attribute all good things to the happy person but leave out friends, who are thought to be the greatest of external goods (1169b9–11). When that title was assigned, in the discussion of the great-souled individual, to honor (1123b17–20), it reflected the self-understanding of such a person, while exposing, at the same time, the internal contradictions that stand in the way of gaining satisfaction from honor.[43] Friendship may bring satisfactions that honor cannot—as the great-souled individual himself seems to suspect—and would thus be of higher worth (1125a1). But the present claim is that friendship is *thought to be* the greatest external good, and if the friend is really an other self, perhaps the benefit friendship brings should not be understood as an "external" good at all.

If there is any truth to the claim that none of us would choose to have all other goods and yet live without friends, that is because the human being is by nature political and meant to live together with others and surely, being together with friends is preferable to life with strangers. The obvious need for friends, which seems to have been settled immediately, could have been questioned, Aristotle reasons, only by someone who recognized that the blessed person does not need friends for the sake of utility or for pleasure—or only a few friends for that purpose, since his life is intrinsically pleasant—but who then drew the inference that he has no need for friends at all; and that conclusion, Aristotle counters quite moderately, is *perhaps* not true. The issue, then, is not sufficiently settled. We have affirmed the political nature of the human being, which requires friendship for its fulfillment; but what that claim really means remains to be clarified by the series of arguments that follow.

The first argument takes us back to the starting point of the *Ethics,* with its identification of happiness as some kind of *energeia.*

(1) If to be happy lies in living and being in *energeia,*

(2) and the *energeia* of the good person is serious and pleasant in itself, as it was said to be at the beginning,

(3) and that which is one's own is also among the pleasant things,

(4) but we are more able to contemplate our neighbors than ourselves and their actions than our own,

(5) for good people, the actions of the serious who are their friends are pleasant, for they have both things pleasant by nature;

(6) the blessed person, therefore, will need such friends, if he chooses to contemplate actions that are decent and his own;

(7) and such are the actions of the good person who is a friend. (1169b31–1170a4)

The problem that creates our most fundamental need for friends seems to be the difficulty—though perhaps not impossibility—of being immersed in action and at the same time, standing at a distance to contemplate oneself. Book I struggled with the issue of how happiness could be attributed to one's life as whole when that would require the perspective of the spectator who "looks to the end," at which point there would be no subject to experience the *energeia* of happiness. Imagining Hades, where the existence of the individual would continue after death, only gave rise to further difficulties, introducing a whole set of questions about the limits that determine a complete life. Contemplation of the actions of one's friend looks as if it is meant to provide a solution: the serious person, while himself a subject in action, is at the same time an object through which his friend can contemplate his own decency, if he chooses to do so. No claim is made that this contemplation is necessary because it is itself the *energeia* in which happiness consists.

At the core of this first argument is the pleasure, at least for the good person, in a certain oblique contemplation of himself. Another way in which friends contribute to the pleasure that should belong to the life of a happy person was prepared for by the analysis in Book VII of pleasure as unimpeded activity: since it is much easier to maintain an activity continuously when it is practiced with other people rather than alone, the blessed person, who should enjoy the pleasure of such continuous activity, cannot live a solitary life (1170a5–8).[44] And sharing activities with friends, we assume, is more desirable than with strangers. Our limited capacity to enjoy continuous pleasure was blamed, in Book VII, on our "wicked nature" (1154b28–31), while it will be explained, in Book X, as a result of fatigue (1175a3–10); the best possibility of overcoming those limits, the present argument suggests, lies in the greater continuity made possible by sharing an activity with friends.

If participating in an activity with one's friend increases its continuity and enhances its pleasure, living together with the good would be, as Aristotle credits Theognis with observing, a kind of practice in virtue (1170a11–13). The poet will be cited in the last words of Book IX—"Noble things from the noble"—to express the way the decent seem to become better through their friendship with one another, each taking the impress from the other of the features that please him; of course, the base, it will be admitted at that point, just as naturally assimilate themselves to one another and thus become increasingly wicked through their association (1172a8–14).

For the moment, the question of friendship's contribution to virtue is left aside in favor of examining "more natural" grounds for the desirability of friends (1170a13–14). Aristotle had offered a "more natural" argument earlier when he addressed the surprising fact that the benefactor seems to care more for his beneficiary than the other way around; while admitting that it might be due to the expectation of a return, Aristotle found it more natural to explain the greater affection of the one who bestows the benefit by recognizing the status of the beneficiary as the actualization of the benefactor's own being.[45] The more natural argument now introduced—probably the longest single argument in the *Ethics*—is no longer concerned with friendship as guidance for the young, support for the old, or companionship for those in their prime; it has nothing to say about the natural impulse out of which marriage and family arise or about the development of character through association with a friend who is decent. The argument turns, rather, simply on the awareness of being alive as something good in itself. It is perhaps surprising, with that in mind, to hear that the aim of this naturalistic argument is to show why "a serious friend seems to be choiceworthy by nature for a serious person." If the argument does not simply rely on an appeal to the authority of the *spoudaios*,[46] its claim about what is good for him must be an inference from what is found on independent grounds to be good by nature.

Aristotle provides such grounds when he sets this argument in motion with a premise, or set of premises, about what it means to be alive for human beings as such.

(1) To be alive is defined for animals by the capacity of perception, and for humans by that of perception and thinking;

(2) but since a capacity is to be understood from the *energeia,* and the sovereign sense is in the *energeia,* to be alive seems to be in the sovereign sense to perceive and to think.⁴⁷

One further premise is introduced before the argument is spelled out:

(3) To be alive is one of the things good and pleasant in themselves; for it is determinate, and the determinate is of the nature of the good, but what is good by nature is also so for the decent, wherefore it seems pleasant to all. One should not take one's bearings from a wicked and corrupt life or a painful one, for such a life is indeterminate, as are the things belonging to it.

Aristotle does not go on to elaborate what it means to be determinate and why that is a mark of what is naturally good;⁴⁸ instead, the argument proceeds on the basis of a different sort of evidence for life being good and pleasant.

(4) If to be alive is itself good and pleasant, as it seems to be from the fact that all desire it, the decent and blessed most of all,

(5) and if one who sees perceives that he sees, one who hears perceives that he hears, one who walks that he walks, and there is always something perceiving that we are in *energeia*

(6) so that when we perceive, we are aware that we are perceiving; and when we think, that we are thinking,

(7) and to be aware that we are perceiving or thinking is to be aware that we exist, for to be was found to be perceiving or thinking

(8) and if to perceive that one lives is one of the pleasant things by itself, for life is good by nature, and to perceive that the good is one's own is pleasant,

(9) and if being alive is choiceworthy, especially for the good, because to be is good for them and pleasant, for they are pleased by perceiving that which is good in itself

(10) and if the serious person feels toward his friend as he does toward himself, for the friend is an "other self" (*heteros autos*),

(11) then, just as his own being is choiceworthy to himself, so is that of his friend, or nearly so.

(12) But to be was found to be choiceworthy because of perceiving it as something good, and such a perception is pleasant in itself;

(13) therefore, one should perceive together (*sunaisthanesthai*) with one's friend that one exists,

(14) but this would come to be through living together and sharing speeches and thoughts, for that would seem to be what living together means for human beings, not, as for cattle, feeding together.

(15) Then if to be is choiceworthy in itself for the blessed person, being good by nature and pleasant, and the being of his friend nearly so, the friend would also be one of the choiceworthy things.

(16) But that which is choiceworthy for him must belong to him, or he will suffer a lack.

(17) Therefore, one who is to be happy needs serious friends. (1170a13–1170b19)

The *Ethics* has been working out, from the beginning, the objective conditions of what makes a human life good, but the present argument discloses, for the first time, that no set of objective conditions is sufficient; life can count as choiceworthy only with awareness of being alive and of the goodness of being alive.[49] What is to be demonstrated, we might have expected, is that such awareness can be acquired only through awareness of one's friend's life and its goodness. But what we are given, it seems, is, rather, a claim about a primary awareness of oneself that can spill over to an awareness of the life of the friend.[50] The perception of the desirability of one's friend's life, then, could only enrich what must already be perceived as a desirable life of one's own. If it is in any sense necessary, it is apparently because a life without that enriched perception would be missing something desirable and, therefore, would not be the life of a blessed person.[51]

This would be the rather minimal conclusion of the argument, in any case, if it stopped with the assertion that the being of the friend is nearly as choiceworthy as one's own being.[52] But one further step adds a new point—one should "perceive together" (*sunaisthanesthai*) with one's friend that he is—and the argument's concluding remarks bring to light just what this "perceiving together" means.[53] The status of the friend as an other self makes it possible for the awareness of one's own life and the pleasure accompanying that awareness to be extended to another. But that is not possible as long as the other is merely the passive object of my apprehension; I must apprehend him as another subject, undergoing or capable of undergoing the same experience of awareness I have of myself. "Perceiving together" is thus accomplished, as the argument concludes, by sharing speeches and thoughts, that is, through dialogue.

Originally, appreciation of the decency of our own actions was found to be more available through the relationship to a friend, whose decent actions, in their likeness to our own, could be the object of our contemplation. According to the "more natural" argument we have just been given, the friend is not merely an object but a co-perceiver of the desirability of his own life and of his friend's. Contemplation of action presupposes a distance between the self as subject and the friend as object; sharing speeches and thoughts is a form of being together. Yet in the contemplation of action, the friend seems to be nothing more than a mirror for the self; only in speaking together is it possible to discover the differences that individuate us. The friend was first designated "another self" (*allos autos*; 1166a32), suggesting the replication of oneself in another individual; as a partner in dialogue, he becomes an "other self" (*heteros autos*), forming a pair with oneself precisely because of the difference that makes him genuinely other. Participation, through dialogue, in what might be thought the nonpersonal or anonymous activity of mind, looks like the way to discover what is uniquely one's own.

The question of the need for friends was settled at the outset by an appeal to the political nature of the human being; what we have discovered since then is that the realization of our political nature takes place through dialogue. But sharing speeches and thoughts is at the same time the realization of our rational nature. This defining activity of friendship explains how it can be that the self, which emerges together with the recognition of the friend as an other self, is mind, or mind most of all. Friendship as the medium of the joint realization of our rational nature and our political nature is essentially dialogic, and the subject of friendship so conceived is the dialogic self. Dialogue allows and requires movement in two directions—not only an extension from self to other but also the ongoing constituting of the self through the relation to the other. The dialogic self is not fully given as a necessary condition for friendship but comes to be what it is in part through friendship. Sharing speeches and thoughts is motivated by and at the same time produces an awareness of one's partial perspective or incompleteness; it introduces into friendship the possibility of some kind of longing, which the friendship of the good as originally conceived seemed to preclude. This possibility emerges along with a transformation in the understanding of eros and its relation to *philia,* which brings the discussion of friendship in the *Ethics* to a close.

FRIENDSHIP, EROS, AND PHILOSOPHY

The "natural argument" of the ninth chapter is resumed and completed, after a brief digression, in the last chapter of Book IX. We return with those concluding reflections to the question of how friends acquire together awareness of themselves and of each other, only now this essential characterization of friendship is introduced by way of contrast with eros:

> Just as seeing is most welcome for lovers, and they choose this sense over the rest, as that in accordance with which eros most of all is and comes to be, isn't it thusly for friends living together that is most choiceworthy? For friendship is *koinōnia,* and as one stands in relation to himself, thus he is also toward his friend; and just as the perception about himself, that he is, is choiceworthy, so it is in regard to his friend; but the *energeia* of this comes to be in living together (*suzēn*), so friends quite reasonably aim at this. (1171b29–1172a1)

What seeing is for lovers, living together is for friends. This rare appearance of eros in the *Ethics* makes us suddenly aware of how absent the issue has been from Aristotle's account of human life, in the sharpest contrast with the Platonic dialogues, in which no theme seems to be more central and ubiquitous.[54] Plato has Socrates praise with the greatest eloquence the divine *mania* of eros, which inspires the mad lover to worship the beloved like a god, while the beloved may not even be aware of the lover's existence; friendship, according to Aristotle, is a necessarily reciprocal relationship between two human beings who must realize their limits as humans (cf. 1159a3–11). The awareness of and longing for what one lacks, which lies at the core of eros for Plato, seems to have no place in the relationship to which Aristotle assigns the highest rank, the friendship of two adults equal in virtue. Precisely as a longing for what one lacks, eros has its paradigm in the love of wisdom; friendship resists any such reconstruction. Here, if anywhere, Platonic madness appears to be altogether replaced by Aristotelian sobriety.

When the last chapter of *Ethics* IX opens with its seemingly casual reference to eros, it looks like one more in a series of intermittent appearances in the course of the long discussion of friendship; closer inspection discloses a development in the sequence, which suggests that the role of eros may not be as peripheral as it first appears.[55] Plato's *Phaedrus* furnishes a model for that development, in the sequence of three speeches presented in the first half of the dialogue, through which eros undergoes a radical alteration as it passes from an object of blame to one of the highest praise. The initial condemnation of eros, in the written speech ascribed to the rhetorician Lysias, is expressed in the voice of a "nonlover," who is then exposed, in Socrates' revised version of the speech, as a lover in disguise, seeking to win for himself the favors of the beloved. Halfway through his speech Socrates stops, uncovers his head, which he had covered in shame, and prepares to leave but is held back by his *daimonion;* afraid, as he claims, of being punished by the god Eros and ashamed at having presented such a vulgar view of lover and beloved, Socrates sets out to purify himself by offering a "palinode" that will hold up the divine madness of eros as the source of our greatest blessings.

The sequence of references to eros in Books VIII and IX of the *Ethics,* echoing this model, unfolds in two stages, in the course of which friendship no less than eros undergoes a transformation that fundamentally alters the relation between them.[56] What appears in the first stage is a nonlover's perspective on eros as a source of inevitable disappointment, which would evoke distrust in any reasonable person. The erotic relationship is set in opposition to the satisfaction of perfect or complete *philia,* which is to be found between two partners, each aware of his own completeness mirrored in the other. A turning point in the discussion leads in the end to a very different paradigm of friendship, rooted in an awareness of incompleteness each has in himself. This development brings along with it a new understanding of eros, which becomes no longer a frustrating alternative but the defining core of *philia* in its highest form.

The erotic relationship is first introduced in Book VIII as one that is natural to youth: guided by feeling and motivated by pleasure, it is an association of those who fall quickly and passionately into attachments and end them just as quickly (1156b1–4). But it is not just the fleeting nature of the erotic relationship that makes it so problematic; as originally depicted, it is almost defined by the very different aims each partner seeks to satisfy through association with the other, in a way that is bound to invite deception, or self-deception, on the part of one or both. The disparate and potentially, or almost inevitably, conflicting aims of lover and beloved make their relationship a foil for the perfect friendship of the good, with its dual subject, each directed toward the other, supposedly, in just the same way.

Even a friendship based on pleasure or utility has the potential to exhibit something like the strength and stability of perfect friendship as long as each partner receives the same or similar benefit from the other—at least this would be the case, Aristotle proposes, when it is pleasure from the same source that the two friends offer each other, as in a friendship between two witty people. In an erotic relationship, by contrast, the lover's pleasure comes from gazing at the beloved, but the beloved's from receiving the attentions of the lover; when the bloom fades, the former lover no longer finds pleasure in the sight of the individual who was once his favorite, and he in turn no longer receives the lover's attentions.[57] It is possible, Aristotle grants, that in some cases the two remain friends if they have come in the course of time to appreciate each other's character, but that does not belong to the essential nature of the erotic relationship (1157a3–12).[58] Aristotle speaks the language of the nonlover portrayed by Lysias, who tries to seduce a beautiful boy by persuading him of how much more advantageous and enduring a relationship he offers, with each partner looking to his self-interest, than any association with the lover, who is, by his own admission, out of control. The lover, as Socrates argues in his revision of the speech of Lysias, even in a state of passion is harmful to his favorite in every way and most unpleasant; he is bound to be false to his former promises once his passion ceases, and mind and moderation take over from eros and madness.[59]

This depiction of the erotic relationship continues with its last appearance in Book VIII (1159b16–19). The essential nature of friendship, as proverbial wisdom has it, is "equality and similarity" (*philotēs* is *isotēs* and *homiotēs*); but this is most perfectly instantiated by those who are alike in virtue, whereas relationships based on utility are likely to hold between opposites, since each turns to the other seeking something he lacks. One might "drag" into this class, Aristotle remarks, the relationship between lover and beloved, or between a beautiful and an ugly person. Lovers, consequently, appear ridiculous when they demand to be loved: if they were worthy of it, that would make sense; but what if there is nothing lovable about them? If eros is subject to the requirement of justice, it must be on the distributive principle;

and the lover can expect to be loved only to the degree of his worth. This is, once again, the argument of the nonlover, who tries to dissuade the beloved from feeling obligated to requite the lover's feelings just because the lover happens to be filled for the moment with those feelings. If the beloved were to look to his self-interest, he would realize he should grant his favors not to those who beg for them but to those who are able and willing to repay him; and the nonlover, who has never neglected his own advantage and has no regrets, should be in just such a position.[60]

Eros seen through the eyes of the nonlover makes one more appearance, in the first chapter of Book IX (1164a2–12). At this point—in the midst of an extended examination of the complaints and conflicts that plague relationships of diverse sorts—friendship as "equality and similarity" looks like a distant ideal, and the question now concerns the possibility of friendship between unequal partners. For such a friendship to be established and maintained, the inferior party must bestow fondness relative to the worth of his superior; affection would have to be measured and controlled in accordance with the principle of distributive justice, which would be only some kind of imitation of the relationship between two individuals who are simply equals. Aristotle calls upon the erotic relationship, once again, to illustrate the problem. In economic associations, money provides a common measure that makes exchange possible, but lover and beloved have nothing analogous: each is trying to enter into an exchange that will serve his individual interests without any common measure to render their offers commensurate. The lover complains that his love is not requited—however unlovable he may be—and the beloved that the lover fulfills none of his promises.[61] The one is seeking pleasure, the other utility, and neither loves the other person in himself. The erotic relationship thus exhibits the defectiveness of the two inferior forms of friendship together, and it looks, thus far, as if there is no higher standard in the case of eros equivalent to the perfect friendship of the good.

When eros next appears, however, after the introduction of the friend as another self, it has undergone a decisive turnaround. Once the erotic relationship ceases to be defined by contrast with the friendship of the good, it is no longer construed as an association between unlike partners with conflicting ends; in fact, the beloved as an active subject drops out and the only feature that remains from the original portrait is the emphasis on vision. The context in which this new understanding is introduced (in Chapter 5 of Book IX) is an analysis of goodwill (*eunoia*): since it is possible to feel goodwill for another without feeling the affection or developing the intimacy of friendship, goodwill seems to be the starting point, but only the starting point, of friendship, in the same way, Aristotle proposes, as the pleasure of sight is the *archē* of loving. No one loves without first being pleased by the looks (*idea*), but one may enjoy the form (*eidos*) without necessarily loving; only when one longs for what is absent and desires its presence can one be said to love (1167a3–7). From its starting point in the lover's gazing at the beloved, eros necessarily turns into longing; inspired by an *idea* and *eidos* through the sight of the beloved, eros is essentially an experience of distance, absence, and incompleteness. Friendship, in contrast, as it develops out of goodwill into being together, is an experience of union, presence, and fulfillment.

Book IX returns to this contrast when it concludes its account of what it means for friends to want to live together by an analogy with the lover's desire for sight (1171b29–32). The conjunction of seeing and being together is a Platonic one: despite the distance required by the one and the union aimed at by the other, these two seemingly incompatible elements somehow belong together in eros.[62] Aristotle, it seems, has split them apart and assigned contemplation to lovers, being together to friends. Sight, in fact, which was originally only the starting point of eros, is now said to be not only that from which eros comes to be but that in which its being lies. The vision that is so desirable to lovers is not only an initial experience that arouses longing but the very object of that longing. It is not simply, then, the contingent absence of a particular individual that evokes such desire nor his presence that would fulfill it; the beloved, on whom the lover fixes his gaze, must essentially point beyond himself to something else that is at a distance and necessarily remains so. The lover takes pleasure, Aristotle observed, in the sight of the looks and form of his beloved—the *idea* and the *eidos* (1167a4–6): eros, however mysteriously, elevates the vision of the beloved into the sought-for object of *theōria*.[63]

The lover, who is defined by his longing for the vision of what is absent, cannot be completed by union with the beloved; friends, on the other hand, are what they are by the *koinōnia* of living together. The discussion of friendship concludes with a description of the forms their living together might take: some friends drink together; some play dice together; others practice gymnastics together and hunt together or philosophize together (1172a1–6). We are given a small, apparently arbitrary sampling of activities for which friends might happen to have a common taste; yet the list is introduced to illustrate the claim that each individual wants to pass his time with his friend in the activity that expresses whatever it is for him to be, for the sake of which he chooses to live. In his final juxtaposition of "philosophizing together" (*sumphilosophousin*) and "hunting together" (*sugkunēgousin*), Aristotle completes his account of friendship with an intimation of *the* mystery, one might say, of Socratic philosophy, which is captured in the favored metaphor of hunting, where the hunting of the beings is inextricably bound up with the hunting of beautiful youths.[64] Looking back from that concluding example, one is tempted to recall how the other activities mentioned so casually—drinking together (*sumpinousin*), playing dice together (*sugkubeuousin*), practicing gymnastics together (*suggumnazontai*)—all serve in the Platonic dialogues as the context, or the image, for philosophy in its various aspects.[65] If sharing speeches and thoughts is what it means for human beings to live together, philosophizing together cannot just be one activity among others in which friends participate with one another: all other activities, which only accidentally require sharing speeches, are in this regard infinitely many ways of aspiring to philosophy, which would alone fulfill what friendship aims to be.[66]

Hunting—the lover's hunting of the beloved or the philosopher's hunting of the beings, or the two together—begins with the recognition of what one lacks and the desire to attain it, even while recognizing its propensity to escape from one's grasp. The longing for what is absent was supposed to differentiate eros from *philia;* it now seems to have become that which friends of a certain sort might share as the basis for being together with each other. The initial standard of *philia,* the perfect friendship of the good, was supposed to obtain between two partners, alike in virtue, who each see mirrored in the other his own sense of completeness. Its place has been taken in the end by the friendship of those "philosophizing together" who each recognize in the other desire based on an awareness of his own incompleteness. *Philia* in this form is defined by the incorporation in itself of eros—though not, apparently, the eros of each for the other, as lover and beloved; without turning the relationship of philosophical friends into that of lover and beloved, Aristotle recognizes the joint eros each has in common with the other for that which lies beyond them both.[67] It is this eros that motivates their desire to be together as friends. In every other form of friendship, the fulfillment of being together stands at odds with the longing of eros; only in philosophy do friendship and eros belong together, and necessarily so.

This relationship exhibits paradigmatically the way friends live together by sharing speeches and thoughts—that is what *sumphilosophein* must mean. But sharing speeches and thoughts is supposed to define the distinctive mode of living together for human beings as such, which makes it the realization of our political nature at the same time that it expresses our rational nature. This joint fulfillment of our double nature, which is the essence of friendship and something no one would choose to live without, looks like the peak in the *Ethics* of the search for the human good and the good life for a human being.

❧ 7 ❧

Happiness

SOCRATES: And he [the philosopher] doesn't even know that he does not know all these things, for he's not abstaining from them for the sake of good repute, but in truth his body alone is situated in the city and resides there, but his thought, convinced that all these things are small and nothing, dishonors them in every way and flies, as Pindar puts it, "deep down under the earth" and geometricizes the planes, "and above heaven" star gazing, and in exploring everywhere every nature of each whole of the things which are and letting itself down to not one of the things nearby.

—Plato, *Theaetetus* 173e–174a, translated by Seth Benardete

PLEASURE REVISITED

Speeches and Deeds

Book IX ended with a description of friends pursuing together the activities in which they each take pleasure; friendship, as it develops through such common pursuits, was found to be necessary for happiness above all insofar as it makes possible a self-awareness without which one would not recognize the goodness of being alive. Book X opens with an account of how pleasure graces an activity through which such awareness is achieved. Of course, it is admittedly puzzling that the *Ethics* returns to the topic of pleasure, after the thematic analysis in Book VII, with the remark that such an issue should not be omitted. Aristotle could, it seems, have justified the renewal of the investigation in light of the particular concern that motivates it: we should turn our attention to pleasure and pain because those are the rudders by which we steer the course of the young, and learning to enjoy or dislike what one should is thought to be of the greatest importance with regard to virtue of character (1172a19–23). Now, that point was acknowledged at the beginning of the discussion of ethical virtue in Book II; but the aim of the argument then was to emphasize the need for habituation because of the way pleasure causes us to do base actions and pain to abstain from beautiful ones (1104b8–11), whereas now the issue of the role of pleasure and pain in the formation of character opens up the problem, What is pleasure? In contrast with Book VII, however, the current account approaches that problem with a view to the question of whether there is a distinctively human pleasure or pleasures—pleasure that comes with an awareness that belongs to us as human. Book X does not abandon the standard of nature introduced in Book VII; but it makes a Socratic turn, prepared for by the intervening discussion of friendship, that compels us to rethink that standard with a view to the place of pleasure in human life.

The debate about the status of pleasure is renewed at this point in its sharpest form: according to some thinkers, pleasure is the good; according to others, it is something altogether base (*phaulon;* 1172a27–28)—no one argues that pleasure is bad. In contrast with the seventh book, the critical examination of these conflicting opinions in the tenth book is clearly demarcated from the analysis that follows of what pleasure is. The task of the opening examination is not simply to judge the truth of the opinions under consideration but also to evaluate their persuasiveness: which speech is "protreptic" and able to turn its audience to live in accordance with it? That concern runs through the tenth book as a whole, in the way it finally takes up the question of happiness no less than its opening examination of pleasure.[1]

In approaching, first, the negative opinion about pleasure, Book X creates a frame for the argument of the *Ethics* as a whole with an implicit reminder of the first appearance of the topic: when pleasure was put forward as a candidate for the human good, it was immediately rejected as a view of the vulgar many, without any analysis of what pleasure is or what forms it can take. That kind of unqualified rejection of the goodness of pleasure, Aristotle now warns, is inevitably ineffectual and possibly harmful; for in matters like these, he recalls from the beginning of the inquiry, speeches are less trustworthy than deeds (1172a34–35; cf.1095a4–11). Someone who undertakes the task of moral education, if he sees most people enslaved to pleasure, might think it a salutary teaching to turn them completely in the opposite direction; but that strategy is bound to backfire. The person who speaks of all pleasure as bad is sure to be attracted at some time to pleasure in one form or another, and since most people are not very discriminating judges, they will take his apparently hypocritical behavior as a proof of the complete falsehood of his speeches and not recognize any germ of truth in them. Speeches are persuasive, Aristotle reiterates, only when they harmonize with deeds, which is a sufficient basis, in the context, for rejecting the antihedonist thesis. Turning to its contrary—that pleasure is *the* good—Aristotle speculates that the real cause of it being taken seriously is the character of its spokesman, Eudoxus, who did not live the life of a lover of pleasure in the ordinary construal of what that means. In this case, his deeds contradict his speeches, but it is precisely that disharmony that makes the speeches seem true because they are not merely self-serving.

The chief evidence Eudoxus supplied for his thesis is the observation that all animals, rational no less than nonrational, pursue pleasure; if each being seeks its own good, he reasoned, what is good for all must be *the* good.[2] Aristotle responds impatiently not to Eudoxus but to any objectors: to deny that what all seek is good is simply nonsense—"What seems to all, that we say is"—and someone who tries to take away our trust in what all believe cannot be very persuasive himself (1173a1–2). If we saw only the nonrational animals striving for pleasure, we might wonder, but rational animals seek pleasure just as much. And perhaps even in the lower animals, Aristotle proposes, "there is something natural, superior to what they are in themselves, striving for their proper good" (1173a2–5). This idea recalls Book VII's claim about the divine dimension in all living things, which pointed to pleasure as the best thing (1153b32); only now, Aristotle finds in the striving of all animal life the indication that pleasure is good, while quietly dropping the question of *the* good.

Eudoxus finds further support for his thesis that pleasure is the good in the argument that anything good is made even better by the addition of pleasure. Plato used just such an argument, Aristotle reminds us, to refute the view that pleasure is the good; for pleasure is better in combination with *phronēsis* than alone, but anything that can be made better by the addition of another good does not meet the measure of the sufficient (1172b28–34). This was a principle Aristotle held up in Book I as a standard for happiness; it serves now to put into question the radical claim that pleasure is *the* good, but only while establishing, once again, that pleasure is good.[3]

The hedonist thesis, which identifies pleasure as *the* good, looks, in this discussion at any rate, like a reaction, equally overstated, to the denunciation of pleasure as altogether base. What leads to that denunciation is the belief that there are shameful pleasures, which are taken as paradigmatic. Aristotle proposes a variety of possible responses. One could deny that such experiences are pleasures—at least to any who are not diseased. One could admit that, simply as pleasures, they are desirable, though perhaps not worth the price of engaging in the activities from which they arise. Or one could argue that pleasures differ in form (*eidos*) and that only a certain sort of person enjoys a certain kind of pleasure. There are very different assumptions behind each of these responses, but for the moment, any one of them is sufficient to avoid the conclusion that pleasure, as such, is bad. In its effort to reject the antihedonist thesis, the discussion has pointed to, without explicitly raising, the question, Can pleasure be differentiated into kinds? It has examined the debate between two opposing teachings about the goodness of pleasure without raising the fundamental question, What is pleasure? To approach those questions we must, Aristotle announces, start over again from the beginning (1174a13–14).

What Is Pleasure?

The investigation of pleasure itself, "what it is and what sort," turns on the concept of *energeia* and its contrast with *kinēsis* and *genesis*. With its appeal to ontological categories explicitly developed in the *Metaphysics*, the analysis carries us once again, as it did in Book VII, beyond the territory and the *methodos* that the *Ethics* set for itself. A motion (*kinēsis*), like building a house, is not complete at any moment as it unfolds but only once its product is achieved, when it is no longer in process; an *energeia*, on the other hand, like seeing, has no beginning, middle, and end but is complete at any moment. Pleasure, Book X sets out to establish, is just such an *energeia*, and those thinkers who deny that pleasure is good, or *the* good, because it is a *kinēsis* or *genesis* have simply misunderstood its nature. Pleasure does not have the temporal structure of coming to be; it is "a whole in the now" (1174b9).[4]

Pleasure may be an *energeia*, as opposed to a motion or a becoming, but it is not one that stands on its own; it is attached in some way to a primary activity, more specifically, to an *energeia* of being aware, and that means being alive. The importance of such awareness for human beings came to light in the description of friends, who each become aware in conjunction with the other of being alive and of the goodness of being alive (1170b8–12). In other animals, to be aware is to perceive; in the human being, it is to perceive and to think. The account of pleasure in Book X assumes the analysis of cognition worked out in *De anima,* which takes perception as the model for thinking: just as the sense faculty, say, of sight, is at work simultaneously with its object, the visible thing, so the faculty of thinking is at work simultaneously with its noetic object.[5] When that faculty is in the best condition and directed toward the "most beautiful" of its objects, the *energeia* in which both are actualized together is thought to be complete or perfect (*teleia*), and that is most pleasant (1174b14–20).

Each *energeia* has a pleasure that completes or perfects it, but—and this is the problem—not in the same way the *energeia* is already completed by the faculty of perceiving or thinking and its object.[6] Pleasure, as Aristotle puts it at one point, does not complete or perfect as an "indwelling disposition" would but as some kind of "supervening *telos,*" like the bloom of youth (*hōra;* 1174b31–33). If that indwelling disposition belonged to the joint actualization of the faculty of perceiving and its perceptible object, or the faculty of thinking and its noetic object, pleasure would come in its wake as an experience resulting from the activity. If, however, the indwelling disposition characterized separately each member of the pair—the faculty of perceiving or thinking, on the one hand; its perceptible or noetic object, on the other—perhaps the pleasure that accompanies the activity of perceiving or thinking could be understood itself as the *energeia* of their joint actualization: the "*hōra*" to which pleasure is likened is either the bloom on the cheek of youth or the season of life itself.[7]

As long as both members of the pair involved in the *energeia*—the faculty of perceiving or thinking and the object of perception or thought—remain in the same condition, the *energeia* should endure, and pleasure with it. Why, then, the question arises, does no one feel pleasure continuously? When this question came up at the close of Book VII, the continuous pleasure of the god was held up as a standard and our inevitable experience of falling short blamed on some wickedness of our nature (1154b28–31). Book X now offers a different explanation of the impediment to continuous pleasure: when we get fatigued and the intensity of our attention fades, pleasure fades with it (1175a3–10). From what appeared to be a purely naturalistic perspective,

Book VII looked at what is common to all living beings and found pleasure to be a universal end, whereas the account in Book X considers pleasure in connection with distinct activities, appropriate for different living beings and not assumed to be of equal worth; yet it was the account in the seventh book that ended, unexpectedly, with an expression of moral indignation at our own defective nature, which is only now replaced by an appeal to the natural limitations of our capacities.

However limited our capacities may be for unimpeded activity and, hence, for continuous pleasure, everyone understandably reaches out for pleasure, Aristotle reasons, inasmuch as all long to be alive, which must mean, minimally, all who are alive long to preserve their life or, beyond that, all long to actualize their capacities as a particular kind of living being. To be alive in the fullest sense is to be aware, through whatever *energeia* a living being is capable of being aware, and pleasure is the grace note on such an *energeia*. Life itself is some kind of *energeia* (1175a12)—a corpse shows by contrast what this might mean—and every individual actualizes his capacities for being alive through the activities he enjoys; pleasure completes or perfects those activities and, thus, completes or perfects life, which is desirable. Do we choose to live, then, because of pleasure, or do we choose pleasure because of living (1175a18–19)?[8] The question about "choosing to live," if that means more than just rejecting suicide, must be about the end for a living being—whether it is to be as fully alive as possible or to experience the pleasure that accompanies that. Aristotle raises the question but refrains from answering it.[9] He finds it sufficient for the moment to recognize that pleasure and life appear to be yoked together in an inseparable way: either pleasure is the end, or it is at least the means we choose—or nature "chooses"—in the service of life itself as the end. Now, this presumably holds for all living beings; but each kind of living being is at work being alive in a different way, so if there is likewise a differentiation of kinds of pleasure, there would be no one thing, pleasure as such, that could count as the end for all, any more than life as such could.

The discussion of pleasure in Book X ends with this issue—or, more precisely, with the question why pleasures *seem* to differ in form or kind (*eidos*). We believe that things different in kind, such as natural organisms or artifacts, must be completed or perfected in different ways, and activities likewise. Since, then, the activity of thinking is different in kind from those of the senses, as are the activities of one sense in comparison with another, it should follow that the pleasures completing or perfecting those activities are themselves different (1175a21–28). It may well be true that any activity in which we take pleasure is intensified, while it declines when we are distracted by other pleasures, and an activity we find painful to engage in is impeded by that experience. But this observation shows only that different individuals are pleased by different activities, which are in turn enhanced by the pleasure taken in them; it hardly settles the question whether pleasure itself is divisible into kinds, yet only on that assumption would it follow that, just as activities are distinguished as decent or base, so are the pleasures akin to them (1175b24–27). Still, pleasures might be thought more inseparable from the activities they complete than the desires motivating those activities, and even those desires are praised or blamed. Indeed, pleasure is so inseparable from the activity that some thinkers identify them—precisely the position Book VII seemed to adopt (1153a14–15); but it would be strange, Aristotle now reflects, if pleasure were itself a matter of sensing or thinking (1175b34–35). If, however, the pleasure is not identical with the activity, does it necessarily absorb, as its own characterization, the shameful or decent quality of the activity to which it is attached? [10]

Now, it might seem that pleasure is as divisible into kinds as species are, since every animal that has a peculiar *ergon* is *thought* to have a distinctive pleasure in actualizing that *ergon* (1176a3–5). The human being, then, should have a species-defining pleasure, but Aristotle immediately acknowledges the vast variety of sources of pleasure among members of the human species. Of course, the example he offers of the relativity of pleasure implies a standard: what tastes sweet to a feverish person is not the same as to a healthy one. In all such cases, Aristotle announces, things are as they appear to the serious person (*ho spoudaios*); and *if* that is beautifully said, as it is *thought* to be, the pleasant would be whatever appears pleasant to the person who is such a measure (1176a15–19). The standard that Book VII sought in pleasure according to nature, Book X finds in the *spoudaios;* but Aristotle expresses this conclusion with striking hesitancy. At the beginning of the *Ethics,* Aristotle characterized the multiple layers of his audience by citing Hesiod: "He is the best of all who thinks out everything for himself, / while he too is worthy who is persuaded by another speaking well" (1095b10–11). His appeal now to the authority of the *spoudaios* as the standard of human pleasure sounds like a claim meant for one who listens to another speaking well; it would hardly be satisfactory to one who thinks through everything for himself, though perhaps he would be the one who needs it least.

The standard of the serious person serves, in any case, only to dismiss pleasures thought to be shameful; it does not answer the question which pleasures, if any, among those thought to be decent belong to the highest or most complete fulfillment of the human being. If, Aristotle reasons, there is an activity characteristic of the "perfect and blessed person," the pleasure perfecting it would be the primary human pleasure, the rest secondary or lower (1176a26–29). With its ranking of kinds of pleasure, based on the activities to which the pleasures are attached, Book X seems to retreat from the radical position Book VII entertained when its treatment of all life as homogeneous implied the status of pleasure as the single end; it discloses, at the same time, the element of truth in the gentleman's view, represented in Book I, that dismissed pleasure as the end only of a life fit for cattle. Pleasure, Book X has argued, is the added grace that accompanies the activity of a living being when it is at its best, and different forms of life are actualized in different activities. If we are searching for the human good, it must be found in an activity that actualizes the potential of the human being as such; and if pleasures are different in kind, there is a unique sort that graces that activity and enhances it.

If the argument of Book X has moved beyond the understanding of nature that dominated Book VII, it seems to be by means of an eidetic division of pleasure corresponding to the heterogeneity of kinds of living beings or of individual human beings. Yet, what Aristotle has actually been trying to explain is why it is *thought* that each species has a pleasure as distinct in kind as its defining *ergon*, or why we *believe* more generally that pleasure falls into kinds; he has not endorsed that opinion in his own voice. It remains, then, an unconfirmed premise for the separation of decent from shameful pleasures, based on the authority of the serious person, followed by the internal ranking of decent pleasures as primary and secondary, based on the standard of the perfect and blessed person. Of course, the differentiation of human beings, determined by the different activities that define their lives, does not depend upon a division of the kinds of pleasures they enjoy. That eidetic division of pleasure itself remains unsettled; but however problematic its assumptions, the ranking of primary and secondary forms of human pleasure prepares us for the ranking of primary and secondary forms of happiness, with which the argument of the *Ethics* is about to conclude.

THE THEORETICAL LIFE

After its long and circuitous journey, the argument of the *Ethics* is finally prepared to address the question of happiness—in outline (*en tupō;* 1176a30–32). When the human good was deduced from the *ergon* argument in Book I, it was only an outline, to be filled in over time (1098a20–24): if we are still seeking only an outline, either the hope of filling it in is not to be satisfied, or not in the speeches of the *Ethics,* but perhaps in the only way possible, which was indicated at the beginning by the requirement for some kind of action that would make these speeches meaningful (1095a3–6, 1103b26–31). Book X, in any event, speaks no longer of the human good, which was the object of the search undertaken in Book I, but only of *eudaimonia;*[11] and that subject reintroduces the necessity of a complete life, which proves as problematic at this point as it did in the first book (cf. 1177b24–26 and 1098a18).

Having determined that happiness is not a disposition—a state one could be in while sleeping through a whole lifetime—it should be posited, Aristotle urges, as some kind of *energeia* (1176a35–b2): now that it is no longer distinguished from the human good, *eudaimonia* must take on the role of an *energeia* while still characterizing a complete life. *Eudaimonia* must be an *energeia,* moreover, that is desirable in itself. Activities in accordance with virtue are *thought to be* such; but, it is now admitted, so are the pleasures of playful activities. They are thought to be productive of happiness because the powerful spend their leisure in such pastimes, though perhaps, Aristotle considers with surprising hesitancy, we should not take our bearings from such individuals (1176b4–18). We should assume, rather, that happiness does not lie in play, for the honorable and pleasant things are those that appear so to the *spoudaios:* the authority of the serious person is to settle the question of the inferiority of playfulness.[12] It would be strange, Aristotle reasons, if play were the end, when it seems to be a matter of rest and we rest for the sake of going on with work; but what if there is a form of play that is not simply instrumental? This first stage in the final discussion of happiness has elicited conventional respect for the serious over against disdain for the playful without examining the assumptions on which that division has been based. It never asks one question in particular: Does the philosopher belong, or solely belong, on the side of the serious?[13] The next and last appearance of "philosophy" in the *Ethics* is in connection with the marvelous pleasures it produces.

On the basis of the promissory *ergon* argument in Book I, the human good was found to be "an *energeia* of soul in accordance with the best and most *teleia* virtue." Prepared now to pin down that admittedly imprecise formula, Aristotle finds it reasonable to suppose that happiness is an activity in accordance with "the strongest (*kratistē*) [virtue]," which would be that of the best thing in us, though he is remarkably tentative about identifying what that is: whether it is mind (*nous*) or whatever is thought to rule and lead in accordance with nature and to have insight into beautiful and divine things, whether it is itself divine or the most divine thing in us, its distinctive activity would be complete or perfect *eudaimonia*. And that, Aristotle announces, was said before to be theoretical activity (1177a12–18). The identification of *theōrētikē* as complete or perfect *eudaimonia* presumably refers most directly to Book I, where the *theōrētikos bios* was introduced as a candidate for the title of human happiness, though its evaluation was at that point deferred for further consideration (1096a4–5). Now, at this decisive moment when the question we have been pursuing throughout ten long books is finally to be resolved, Aristotle tells us that it has already been answered![14]

In any case, Aristotle assures his reader, the thesis about perfect happiness might seem to agree not only with the things said before but with the truth. To defend that claim, however, it is necessary to speak as if everything just stated conditionally had been demonstrated: *theōria* is the strongest *energeia* because *nous* is the highest thing in us and its objects the most knowable (1177a18–21). For further support, Aristotle turns to our belief that happiness must be mixed with pleasure. Of all activities in accordance with virtue, that in accordance with *sophia* is agreed to be most pleasant; this is an inference, at least, drawn from the wondrous pleasures thought to belong to philosophy, on the questionable grounds that there must be more pleasure in possessing something than only seeking it (1177a22–27).

If the final teaching of the *Ethics* were to satisfy the original criteria for happiness, it would have to offer an account of a complete life determined by an end that is a distinctively human activity, one that is able to meet the criteria of finality and self-sufficiency. Those terms are echoed in Book X just closely enough to be mistaken for the same meaning they originally expressed.[15] In the first book, happiness was supposed to be *teleia* as the final end for the sake of which all other ends are chosen; in Book X, *teleia eudaimonia* refers to a certain kind or degree—primary happiness—in contrast with that which falls short. The title is awarded to contemplation because it is the only thing never chosen for the sake of something else, not because everything else is chosen for its sake; if the gods provide a fitting model, it is not because they do everything in life for the sake of contemplation, but because they should not be imagined to do anything else at all (1178b7–28).

The finality of happiness was supposed to entail its self-sufficiency, defined in Book I as the quality of that which on its own makes life choiceworthy and lacking nothing (1097b14–16). This is the criterion, above all, that makes the thesis of Book X so questionable: how could contemplation by itself possibly fulfill that demand? But no such claim is, in fact, made at this point. What is now said to belong most of all to theoretical activity is "so-called self-sufficiency" (1177a27–28), which no longer means the capacity by itself to make life complete but only the capacity to be carried on, as far as possible, independently of necessary conditions. Theoretical activity, in its claim to finality and independence, stands in relation to practical activity, it is argued, as leisure does to business; but leisure, of course, depends on someone attending to business. It is the self-sufficiency of the city, with its division of labor, that makes possible the relative freedom from necessity the contemplative life enjoys.

In arguing for the superiority of the theoretical life, Book X returns to the ordinary meaning of self-sufficiency, as independence from others, which had been set aside in Book I with the claim that the human being is by nature political (1097b8–11). While the wise person, like all human beings, requires certain necessary conditions in life, including relationships to others, his defining activity of contemplation does not depend on such relationships, as that of the just person does, or the courageous, or even the moderate one—at least in certain situations calling for moderation. The wiser someone is, the more he should be capable of carrying on contemplation alone, although, Aristotle concedes for a moment, perhaps he would do better with "co-workers" (1177a28–b1): they would be indispensable for those who did not claim to be wise but only in search of wisdom. Such individuals— the friends who "philosophize together" (1172a5)—would share, in their non-self-sufficiency, needs but also pleasures unknown to one who is wise or thinks himself so. The "wondrous" (*thaumastas*) pleasures of philosophy, from which the pleasure of wisdom was inferred, cannot help but make us think of the experience of wonder, which, according to Aristotle, is the

beginning of philosophy and would no longer exist if philosophy were sup-
planted by wisdom.[16]

An activity pursued for its own sake and accompanied by its own proper
pleasure, most self-sufficient and leisured, as capable of continuity and as
free from fatigue as is possible for human beings should constitute perfect
happiness—*if* it occupied a complete length of life (1177b25). The same
translation of an activity into a lifetime with which the *ergon* argument concluded now reappears, bringing in its wake an acknowledgment of the limits of human capacity: such a life would be higher than human, and if mind
is divine, the life in accordance with mind would be divine in comparison
with human life. And yet, Aristotle insists, we should not listen to those who
warn that mortals should think mortal thoughts; we should strive, rather, as
far as possible to "immortalize" (*athanatizein*) ourselves. Nature sets certain
necessary limits on human capacity, but those limits are not the product of a
willful prohibition and the attempt to overstep them is no crime.[17] No jeal-
ous gods hold us back from emulation of the divine, which is somehow part
of us; in fact, "it might even be thought that this is what each individual is,
being the sovereign and better." What it is to be human must be understood,
however paradoxically, in light of an aspiration that points beyond the human as such.[18] On that measure, the life in accordance with mind would be
best by nature, most pleasant, and happiest, since that is the life most truly
one's own (1178a2–8).[19]

The final teaching of the *Ethics,* identifying happiness with *theōria,* looks
like what contemporary debate has labeled an "exclusive" conception of human happiness; it appears to many, or most, readers to be a startling conclusion for the argument of the *Ethics* as a whole.[20] Almost as soon as this
conclusion is stated, however, the range of *eudaimonia* is extended, along
with the understanding of what it is to be human: the life in accordance
with "the other excellence" has a happiness of its own, albeit of a secondary
rank, because its activities are the human, all-too-human (*anthrōpikai*) ones
(1178a9–10).[21] The ethical virtues belong to the human as a composite being, since they are products of training the passions and the passions are
integrally tied to the body; even prudence, insofar as it takes its end from
the ethical virtues, shares indirectly in this tie to the body. This moment
marks a radical turnaround in the argument of the *Ethics.* Ethical virtue and
prudence have been treated all along as the perfections of two parts of the

soul. The *ergon* argument in Book I spoke of the human good as an *energeia* of the soul without asking anything about its relation to body. The psychology that prepared for the investigation of ethical virtue, in its appropriate imprecision (1102a16–26), made it possible, or necessary, to dispense with what proves to be a fundamental question for the theoretical inquiry into the nature of the *psychē*—in what way, if any, soul is separable from body (*De anima* 403a3–b15). If the assumption of the independence of soul is appropriate to the inquiry of the *Ethics,* it is because of the way it illuminates the perspective of ethical virtue itself: someone who looks to the beautiful as his end and chooses his action because of itself does not understand his character formation as a molding of passions tied to the body. At this moment in Book X, Aristotle stands outside that perspective and indicates his agreement with the Socratic understanding of the extent to which the "so-called virtues of soul" are not much more than habits of the body (*Republic* 518d).

Ethical virtue has been granted the title of second-place happiness; but this does not mean that ethical virtue, strictly understood, could be ordered under the higher end of primary happiness, at least not in the life of any individual.[22] If the best life is one devoted to *theōria* as its final end, prudence, in looking to that end, might indeed determine the need for behavior that coincides with that of ethical virtue; but that would not be the action that flows from a virtuous disposition, which must be chosen "because of itself" (1105a31–32).[23] With that requirement, Aristotle captured the conviction of the ethically virtuous person; but now that theoretical activity has been granted the privileged status of being the only thing desired for its own sake, every practical end is said to be for the sake of something else (1177b2–4).[24] This admission is another mark of the turnaround in the argument of the *Ethics:* the self-understanding of ethical virtue—as a condition belonging to the soul independent of the body and directed at an end that cannot be subordinated to any other—has at this point been disclosed as a misunderstanding.

While the reconsideration of ethical virtue puts into question the independence of soul from body, the conception of *theōria* as perfect happiness postulates the "separated" life of mind; a more precise account is simply deferred for another occasion (1178a22–3).[25] The theoretical life as lived by a concrete human being, at any rate, is not entirely freed from necessity, even if it needs less "equipment" than other ways of life do. A liberal person, or a just one, needs wealth—as Socrates is taught by Cephalus (*Republic* 330d–331b)—just as a courageous person requires strength, or a moderate one opportunities for indulgence; but all of those conditions might be impediments for one devoted to *theōria*. Of course, an individual living the contemplative life, to whatever extent he does associate with others, will choose, we assume, to act in accordance with virtue—which is not the same as acting out of a virtuous disposition; thus, he too will need external goods to live as a human being (*anthrōpeuesthai;* 1178b5–7). To picture the theoretical life in its purity, we must think of the gods: it is ridiculous to imagine them paying back debts they have incurred or acting moderately in the face of bad desires. If the gods are living, though, as they are thought to be—not asleep like Endymion—they must be engaged in some activity; and after anything practical, let alone productive, is eliminated, the only thing fitting for god is contemplation (1178b8–21). Banished from the world of the *Ethics* all along, the gods appear onstage at the end, first to remind us how much the ethical virtues are tied to human needs, then—with a sudden replacement of the plural by the singular *theos*—to support the possibility of a life exclusively devoted to the supremely blessed activity of *theōria*. The human activity most akin, Aristotle concludes, would constitute the greatest happiness.

Having identified the theoretical activity of the god as the standard for human happiness, Aristotle turns for support in the opposite direction and calls upon the evidence of the nonhuman animals: having no theoretical capacity, they do not partake at all of happiness (1178b24–25). *Eudaimonia* has a range that extends in its application only to beings capable of *theōria*, and to the degree they have that capacity. Locating the best possibility for a human being between god and beast thus leads to a qualified conclusion—happiness would be some kind of contemplation (*theōria tis*); and as this qualification might suggest, our nature—the first reference to *phusis* in this context—is not self-sufficient with regard to contemplating (1178b33–34). The point seems to be twofold: our intermittent participation in this activity must be traced to something in us more than human, but also, this activity of *theōria* alone is not all a human being needs.

A "blessed life" for a human being, at least, depends upon certain necessary conditions and external goods—though not a great quantity, as Aristotle calls upon both Solon and Anaxagoras to attest. In Book VI, the prudent person was sharply contrasted with the wise;[26] now the representatives of the political life and of the theoretical life speak in one voice, at least in their agreement on a commonplace that almost everyone would accept, or profess to accept.[27] Perhaps, Aristotle reflects, Solon spoke beautifully when he declared those happy who, measurably equipped with external goods, did the most beautiful things, as he believed, and lived moderately; for it is possible, Aristotle agrees, with measurable possessions to do what one must (1179a9–13)—of course, doing what one must is not quite the same as doing what is most beautiful.

The whole argument of the *Ethics* is framed by this allusion now, together with that in Book I, to the story Herodotus tells of the visit by Solon to Croesus, the tyrant of Lydia.[28] Solon's claim about the sufficiency of moderate wealth and power comes in his response to the question Crosesus poses to him about the happiest human being he had ever seen. That, Solon boldly replies, would be Tellus, an Athenian citizen who lived in sufficient prosperity, enjoyed children and grandchildren, and finally died in battle, for which he was honored by his city. Amazed at Solon's audacity in holding up such a model above his own life of wealth and power, Croesus asks for the second-best, and is given a response that must have been even more unintelligible to him. Solon tells the story of Cleobus and Biton, two brothers of Argos, athletes, devoted sons, who offered their bodily strength in the service of filial duty and, ultimately, the sacred. When their mother was once to be taken to a festival of Hera and no oxen were available to pull her cart, the brothers harnessed themselves to the yoke and made their way to the temple; upon arrival, with everyone rejoicing and praising them, their mother prayed to the goddess to grant the greatest blessing a human being could have, and the brothers lay down, never to rise again.

Upon hearing Solon's ranking of the two best human lives, Croesus demands to know how so little could be made of his own magnificent happiness. Solon responds by issuing a warning about the volatility and vulnerability of every human life, and above all one that reaches the heights, which inevitably arouses divine jealousy. To judge the goodness of any life, therefore, especially in conditions like those Croesus enjoys, one must "look to the end." This is the teaching to which Aristotle referred in Book I (1100a10–11), opening up an array of problems raised by the requirement for happiness to extend through a "complete life." Book X continues to hold up that measure (1177b25); concerned now, however, with the question of the best human life, it is no longer preoccupied with the role of fortune and re-calls, instead, Solon's ranking of two alternative lives. While the meaning of each life is encapsulated in the death that completes it, only the second best is essentially defined by death. Solon's first choice locates happiness, from a human, all-too-human perspective, in the active life defined by attachment to family and city. The life Solon assigned second place, on the other hand, is nothing but an emblem of the judgment, from a god's point of view, that a human being is always better off dead—which makes good fortune look like an overstepping of the human condition, hence a provocation of divine jealousy.[29] Aristotle, in contrast, has just rejected any notion of divine limits on human aspiration (1177b30–34), and that is reflected in Book X's ranking of human lives: it assigns to the moderate life Solon judged best some claim to human happiness, though only of a secondary rank, while it is silent about Solon's next best, which denies the goodness of human life as such.

In place of that tragic vision, Aristotle supports his own proposal about the best human life by invoking the testimony of the theoretical man, whose representative is the pre-Socratic cosmologist Anaxagoras. When asked about the happiest human being, Solon does not point to himself;[30] Anaxagoras does. Or so Aristotle infers from the statement attributed to him: he would not wonder if he appeared strange to the many, since they judge only by externals. What he meant, Aristotle explains, is that most people judge happiness in terms of wealth or power, and the theoretical life surely has no claim to preeminence on those standards (1179a13–16). But if the philoso-pher's happiness is always invisible to the nonphilosopher, any image of the philosophical life projected for those who do not live it—including the one Aristotle is offering at this very moment—can be judged only by "externals."

What Book X in fact holds up as the highest possibility for a human being is the theoretical life as perceived from the outside—unwearied, indepen-dent, without any use; the pure life of contemplation is at home only on the Isles of the Blessed (cf. *Republic* 519c). Its exemplar is Thales, the first philoso-pher, who, lost in contemplation of the heavenly bodies, missed what was right at his feet, fell into a well, and discovered the nature of reality. Thales furnished an object of ridicule in the eyes of a servant girl;[31] a philosopher whose thought was, or was believed, to clash more directly with the conven-tions of the city would have to worry about more than being laughed at for his uselessness.[32] He might, upon reflection, find it worthwhile for himself and for the city if he could make the unthreatening life of falling into wells with one's eyes on the stars an object not of ridicule but of admiration. He would have to convey, to those whose "secondary happiness" is merely human, that the *polis* can ennoble itself by making a place—even supplying the conditions—for the divine within it. Now, it would surely be a challenge to elicit such recognition for the philosopher, who only looks toward wisdom as his end while progressing in knowledge of ignorance; even if anyone believed someone's claim to live this way—Socrates' profession of knowledge of ignorance earned him the charge of being ironic—no one looking at it from the outside would find it a mark of the life best for a human being. If the philosopher's self-projection is to generate admiration from the nonphilosopher, it may have to be something like Book X's image of the godlike possessor of wisdom.

Aristotle finds his own speeches in harmony with the opinions of the wise—who should not need mere opinions; but the real test in such matters, he reminds us, must lie in "deeds and life" (1179a17–20). The emptiness of speeches detached from deeds has been the problem haunting the inquiry ever since the consideration of its fitting audience in Book I (1095a2–11). It led, at the beginning of Book X, to a criticism of the moralist who teaches that pleasure is altogether bad only because he considers it morally salutary, while his inevitably conflicting deeds would make his speeches objects of contempt (1172a34–b7). With the reminder of that warning, Aristotle now introduces the deed that is to support the decisive speech identifying happiness with *theōria:*

> One who is active in accordance with mind, who cares for this and is best disposed toward it, also seems to be the most dear to god. For if some care for human things comes to be from the gods, as it is believed, it would be reasonable that they rejoice in that which is best and most akin, and this would be *nous,* and that they reward those who welcome and honor this most, as caring for the things dear to them, and acting correctly and beautifully. That all these things belong most of all to the wise one is not unclear. Therefore he is dear to god. And the same one is most likely the happiest. (1179a22–32)

The promised deed is nothing but a common opinion—one rejected just a few lines earlier, when Aristotle considered how ridiculous it would be to imagine the gods engaged in ethical actions since they would never, as divine beings, have the problems and the needs that require such a response. A piety based on the hope of divine rewards, which has been almost entirely absent from the *Ethics,* is suddenly assigned a prominent place, in support of its final teaching on human happiness. Is Aristotle, then, like the dour moralist he criticized, guilty of presenting what he regards as a salutary teaching without being committed to its truth? There is one crucial difference: Aristotle calls our attention to what he is doing in the process of doing it. Having substituted an opinion about the gods' rewards for any deeds, he warns us what we must still be seeking if these *logoi* are to be something more than mere speeches.

THE LEGISLATIVE ART

The internal articulation of happiness into primary and secondary rank, which seems to bring the argument of the *Ethics* to an end, recalls the two classes of his intended audience that Aristotle first described in the words of Hesiod—those who think through everything for themselves and those who listen to another speaking well. In an unexpected coda, the *Ethics* expresses its concern with the third of Hesiod's human types—he who neither thinks for himself nor listens to another speaking well (1095b10–13). This expansion is one last mark of the movement of the argument of the *Ethics.* After reaching, at the conclusion of Book VI, the heights of the cosmic perspective from which *sophia* is found to constitute human happiness, it descended to embark on a new beginning in Book VII; now, after a second ascent has led to the recognition of the theoretical life as perfect happiness, the argument is called down from the heavens one more time and dragged into the homes and the cities.[33] The last chapter of the *Ethics,* which accomplishes this descent, provides, as is commonly recognized, a transition to Aristotle's *Politics;* but at the same time, in casting a certain light backward, it transforms the status of the preceding inquiry, which is no longer a whole in itself but becomes part of a larger whole.

If, Aristotle begins, we have spoken sufficiently, in outline, about "these things"—happiness in its double form?—and the virtues, friendships, and pleasures, should we believe that the choice (*prohairesis*) has a *telos* (1179a33–35)? The question, on the surface, concerns the completeness of the selection of topics. But the language suggests that the inquiry itself, or our participation in it, constitutes a choice; and its *telos,* as in all practical matters, Aristotle reminds us, is not to theorize and to know but to act.[34] It is necessary, therefore, not just to know about virtue but to have and use it—unless, Aristotle adds at this late point, there is some other way we become good (1179a35–b4). If action is necessary to overcome the incompleteness of the speeches of the *Ethics,* it can take two forms: we are about to hear about the action of the legislator who puts his knowledge of virtue to use in the political world, but there is also, as the entire inquiry implies, the action of the reader who thinks through everything for himself.[35] The one presupposes the independent categories of *theōria* and *praxis,* or speech and deed, the other their inseparability in one activity.

The problem of the weakness of speeches set in motion Aristotle's long debate with Socrates, which began when he borrowed the formula for Socratic philosophy—"taking refuge in *logoi*"—to criticize the many, who believe speeches are sufficient for acquiring virtue (1105b12–14). That charge is now turned, as it should have been all along, against those who claim to teach an all-powerful art of speaking. But the division between philosopher and sophist, or between demonstrative argument and persuasive rhetoric, is bracketed for the moment, while our attention is fixed on the crucial division between reliance on mere speeches in any form over against recognition of the need for force. The former may be fine for Hesiod's first two classes in common; the latter is needed by the third.

Overestimating the power of speeches, Aristotle indicates, results from a failure to understand the psychology of the many. One who is not a lover of the beautiful cannot be moved by mere speeches to gentlemanship, more literally, beauty and goodness (*kalokagathia,* 1179b7–10).[36] But even in the case of one who will listen to speeches, "the soil must be tilled": the soul of the listener must have been habituated from early on to enjoy the beautiful and dislike the ugly, and that, Aristotle insists at this point, is difficult except under the right laws.[37] Living with moderation and endurance, it can now be admitted, is not pleasant to the many, especially to the young, and the burden is mitigated only if it becomes habitual, which requires the regulation of the law. Not just youth, however, but the whole of life must be under the law, at least for those more responsive to the threat of punishment than shame.

Anyone moved more by necessity than by *logos* or the beautiful must be controlled from without by "some kind of mind and correct order having force" (1180a17–18): *nous,* which just played its sublime role as the separate subject engaged in the activity of *theōria,* is now replaced by *nous* joined with compulsion to constitute law. The problematic conjunction of mind and force, however, opens up a debate about the strengths and weaknesses of law as a means of fostering human excellence. The debate unfolds in a restless movement from one side to another, which this question is apt to provoke;[38] and each step along the way brings a slight alteration in the issue at stake—the need for compulsion and its most effective source, the difference between common and private care, the education of many in contrast with one, written and unwritten law, treatment of the individual and universal knowledge, experience and expertise.

Law is necessary, the argument begins, because it compels obedience, while paternal authority, operating within the household, is not powerful enough for that, nor is any single individual—unless he is a king or something like that, whose rule turns the political sphere into a virtual household. Of course, paternal authority, it will soon be granted, involves natural ties of affection, which provide a source of strength legal enactments could never have. Individuals are resented, nevertheless, if they are perceived as willfully thwarting our inclinations, whereas the law, in its impersonality, can make constraint look like necessity. Yet most cities are apparently unaware of this, leaving their citizens to live in cyclopean fashion, each one as he wishes "laying down the law for children and spouse" (1180a26–29). Aristotle states what appears to be a moderate point about private authority with an appeal to Homer's cannibalistic monster:[39] the seemingly innocuous prerogative of households and families to arrange their affairs becomes, through this allusion, the sign of an uncivilized core in the hearts of citizens, which requires for its control law devoted to "correct common care." But since that is so often neglected in the cities, Aristotle admits, it would seem fitting for the individual to try to make the best contribution he can to the upbringing of his own children or those close to him. Yet on the basis of all the prior arguments, Aristotle adds, the individual would seem most able to do so if he became *nomothetikos* (1180a32–34): the art of legislation, in some form or other, looks like the necessary bulwark against the cyclopean potential in human beings.

Forms of "common care"—in the household as well as in the city?—cannot come to be, the argument has established, without laws and, if they are to be decent, serious laws; but if the arts of music and gymnastics furnish the model, it should make no difference whether the law is written or unwritten, designed for the education of one or many. The art of medicine, on the other hand, reveals how individual treatment can be precise in a way that the law, in its necessary generality, never could be (1180a34–b10). If all healthy bodies are similar enough for the gymnast to train as a group, each diseased body is unique, and the doctor who sets out to heal must target the particular individual he treats; of course, even then, he bases that treatment on his knowledge of the art, which is concerned with universals.[40] Now, a nonexpert could admittedly treat someone well if his experience involved precise observation of particular cases; in fact, some people seem to be their own best doctors (1180b16–20)—the only option, the *Ethics* has implied, for the philosopher as doctor of the soul. But if the universal is more knowable, the argument concludes once again, anyone who wants to contribute to the upbringing of many or few must try to acquire the art of legislation. *Nomothetikē*, which was originally identified as the architectonic part of *phronēsis* with regard to the city (1141b24–25), has now been extended to encompass the private sphere: it is an indispensable condition for anyone who wants to make another better—*if*, Aristotle adds with some hesitation, it is through laws that we become good (1180b23–25).

However desirable the art of legislation may be for acting in private and in public, the question remains whether there is anyone from whom it can be learned. In the case of *politikē*, the politicians who practice it based on experience show no ability to transmit their skills, at least not to their own children, while the Sophists who profess to teach it do not practice it.[41] They display their ignorance of politics by reducing it to rhetoric, confirming the essential mark of sophistry in the naive or self-serving assumption that only speeches count.[42] Aristotle implies his own answer to the question of who teaches the legislative art while preparing for the move from the *Ethics* to the *Politics* with a very surprising claim: since legislation (*nomothesia*) has been left unexamined by our predecessors, perhaps it would be better for us to investigate it (1181b12–14). If there is any way to teach potential legislators, it should lie in the investigation now to be undertaken in the *Politics*. Of course, in introducing that project as one with no predecessors, it looks as if Aristotle is playfully ignoring Plato's *Laws,* whose echoes have been so audible, especially in this last chapter of the *Ethics*—or perhaps, one might say, Aristotle's silence about the *Laws* implicitly raises the question whether or in what way the dialogue is really about legislation.[43]

The *Ethics* ends with the recommendation to proceed with an investigation of legislation and regimes in general in order that "philosophy concerning the human things may be completed as far as possible" (1181b14–15).[44] The project that began as "some kind of political science" (*politikē tis*) was assigned an architectonic role, on the grounds that such a science governs the use of all the others in the city (1094b4–7); it was dethroned when Book VI arrived at the conclusion that the city is not *the* whole and the human being not the highest being in the whole (1141a20–22, 1145a10–11). Once the new beginning of Book VII led to the conclusion of Aristotle's debate with Socrates, the project of the *Ethics* turned into "political philosophy" (1152b1–2). Now, as the *Ethics* issues into the *Politics*—just when we might expect it to be labeled "political science" simply—it acquires a new designation that does not speak of any relation to the *polis:* if there is a dyadic whole that joins the *Ethics* to the *Politics,* it must be construed as "human philosophy."

The defining *telos* of this dyadic whole was identified, at the beginning of the *Ethics,* as the human good, which appeared to be the same for the individual and the city, even if greater and more complete in the case of the city (1094b7–10). That issue is not taken up for explicit examination until the opening chapters of Book VII of the *Politics,* when the argument turns to the question of the best regime: in working out a political analogue to the best life for the individual, it supposedly confirms the opening claim of the *Ethics.* Or so one would conclude if one were satisfied with a kind of metaphor, according to which a city with no neighbors threatening it—an isolated island-city, or a world empire?—is equivalent to the theoretical life of the individual.[45] If a claim to the identity of the good for the individual and the good for the city were indeed established, it might seem to indicate that the human being is fully determined by his life as a citizen in the *polis;* it might be thought to imply that what it is to be a human being is exhausted by what it is to be a political animal.[46] The replacement of *politikē* by "human philosophy" at the end of the *Ethics* serves to put that understanding into question.[47]

A SOCRATIC ANSWER TO A SOCRATIC QUESTION?

The *Ethics* does not end at its apparent peak, identifying perfect happiness with the life devoted to *theōria;* instead, it goes on to introduce the need for a study of legislation, on the grounds that it is not sufficient only to know about virtue, but one should try to put that knowledge to use. The peak the inquiry seemed to reach with its recognition of a pursuit of knowledge desirable for its own sake requires, as a supplement, recognition of the usefulness of knowledge in the political world. But that external supplement is not the only corrective in the *Ethics* for its final teaching about the perfect happiness of the theoretical life; the presentation of that teaching already contains within itself a demand for reconsideration, with Aristotle's reminder of the need to interpret speeches in light of deeds. This reminder should have alerted us to something paradoxical about a thesis that responds to a question of the greatest practical importance, What is the good life for a human being? with the answer, "pure *theōria.*"

What is the good life for a human being? is the Socratic question that the *Ethics* set out to address. Is it, we should now ask, a Socratic "answer" at which the inquiry arrives in the end? Plato's Socrates comes closest to making his own answer thematic at his public trial, in the context of explaining why he would not accept it if the penalty imposed on him were only the demand to remain quiet and live in silence. His reason—though he doubts the jury will be persuaded by it—is the conviction that the unexamined life is not worth living for a human being (*Apology* 38a). Taken literally, Socrates' claim, however playful, is shockingly radical: all his fellow citizens—whom he had just likened to a sleeping horse, annoyed at the gadfly who awakens them—might as well be dead. Aristotle, who is perhaps less playful, appears more generous: "happiness" can be expanded to include a life governed by ethical virtue, albeit only as a secondary form relative to the perfect happiness of the theoretical life.[48]

Of course, when primary or perfect happiness is referred to as "happiness" simply (1178b28–32), it might seem to imply that the secondary form is not, strictly speaking, happiness at all. What is supposed to make the best life superior, if not the only exemplar of happiness, is, as its very designation indicates, a single-minded devotion to *theōria* as the highest end; and that activity is construed in some kind of purified form that looks alien to the life lived by Plato's Socrates, which he identifies as the one life worth living for a human being. *Theōria,* according to the argument of Book X, is the highest human activity because it is the only one desirable solely for its own sake. It is, for just that reason, granted the title of *teleia eudaimonia,* as the most perfect fulfillment of what it is to be human; but looked at in that light, it is in fact of the greatest use and necessity.[49] And yet, one could not deliberately pursue this activity for the sake of the fulfillment it brings without instrumentalizing it in a way that appears inconsistent with its being for its own sake.

This apparent inconsistency characterizes, in particular, the situation of the pre-Socratic philosopher—at least the figure constructed in the *Ethics*—who seeks or claims to possess *sophia* as knowledge of the whole, which is desirable solely for its own sake, while utterly ignoring his own interests and the question of the human good more generally; his knowledge was admitted to be "unusual, wondrous, difficult, and demonic," but completely useless (1141b3–8). In his selfless pursuit of *sophia,* which has now been established as the most fulfilling human activity, his situation exhibits the same incongruous structure as that of the noble self-lover in his self-sacrificing devotion to the *kalon,* which is, in fact, in the service of his self-interest, though he could not in principle pursue his end on that understanding of it.[50] Viewed from the outside, the pre-Socratic philosopher's disinterested activity of *theōria* shows itself to be in the service of his own good; but in his indifference to the question of the human good, he cannot recognize it as such.

Now, the Socratic does not set out to philosophize, any more than does the pre-Socratic, by calculating the benefit he will achieve through this means; he is naturally drawn by a passion to an activity desirable in itself, which just happens to be in his greatest self-interest. But the Socratic philosopher, who is characterized by his central concern with the question of what is good for a human being, is fully aware, and must be aware, of the paradoxical self-fulfillment that comes with his disinterested practice: he recognizes that the activity he engages in as an end in itself, because not in the service of any higher end, is in fact the good that makes human life worth living. He understands his own activity to be the paradigmatic expression of a natural desire, in all human beings, for possession of the good and knowledge of the good, which must be of the greatest use, if without it everything else we possess and everything else we know is useless (cf. *Republic* 505a–e). Driven by a selfless and uncalculating eros of the beautiful, he discovers and embraces his own good in that very pursuit.[51]

It is the theoretical life as represented by the pre-Socratic cosmologist that Book X of the *Ethics* holds up as the model of perfect happiness. That life, which looks to *sophia* as its end, is completely other than its competitor, the practical life determined by the ends of ethical virtue, which is found to fall short of perfect happiness. This dichotomy of mutually exclusive and jointly exhaustive alternatives seems to exclude the very possibility of a life devoted to theoretical reflection on the question of the human good; it has no place for philosophy understood in such a way that political philosophy is its "eccentric core."[52] Aristotle had warned that the final teaching the *Ethics* offers about happiness might be a matter of mere speeches; the deed he furnished in its support, however, was nothing but an opinion about the gods' rewards for the favored human life. Aristotle pointed to a very different deed, though, when he first characterized his intended audience through the words of Hesiod, who described the best individual as one who thinks through everything for himself. For those engaged in that deed, Aristotle's warning, at the conclusion of the *Ethics,* is a reminder that the end we are seeking is what we have been doing.[53] The *energeia* of *theōria* in which we have participated is not solitary or disinterested contemplation of the cosmic whole. Its subject matter is the human things—which means, above all, those conceptions of the just, the beautiful, and the good that play a determinative role in political life—and its way of proceeding, in the absence of perfect wisdom, is an ascent from opinion through the examination of opinion.[54] This is an *energeia* of *theōria* that takes place through the activity of sharing speeches and thoughts, which is, as the discussion of friendship established, what living together means for human beings; it is in that way a realization at once of our political and our rational nature, which the dichotomy of political action and contemplation hold apart.

The way the deed of the *Ethics* undercuts the exhaustive alternatives offered by its speeches about human happiness maps onto another discrepancy between speeches and deed. The concluding distinction between two lives each with its own claim to happiness is anticipated early on with the division of human excellence into the two supposedly independent spheres of ethical and intellectual virtue, based on the psychology that divides desire from reason in the human soul. Aristotle argues for that division by means of an extended critique of the thesis he attributes to Socrates—the identification of virtue with knowledge, which denies any autonomous sphere of excellence of character. He excludes from that debate with Socrates, conducted in the course of Books II–VII, any references to Plato. In this way, Aristotle constructs the figure of Socrates the "intellectualist," while separating off Plato as a different thinker with views of his own—despite the barrier to such a separation that Plato imposed by the use of the dialogue form itself. And yet, in the treatment of almost every topic covered in the course of the *Ethics,* one can hear the echo of a discussion in the Platonic dialogues—as numerous references throughout this study and the citations at the beginning of each chapter are meant to indicate. The speeches of the *Ethics* create a separation of Socrates from Plato; but the action of the *Ethics* involves Aristotle's ongoing, if implicit, dialogue with an imagined interlocutor who is indistinguishably the Platonic Socrates or the Socratic Plato.[55] The sharing of speeches and thoughts, through that dialogue in deed, is the activity in which Aristotle has from the start invited his reader's participation.

APPENDICES

Socrates, Plato, Philosophy
in the Nicomachean Ethics

Plato (I.4.1095a32–34): For Plato was well perplexed and sought whether the path is from the principles or to the principles, as in the race course from the judges to the finish line or back again.

Philosophy (I.6.1096a11–17): Perhaps it is better to examine the universal and be thoroughly perplexed about how it is spoken of, yet such an inquiry becomes troublesome on account of being friends with the men who introduced the forms. But perhaps it might be thought better, and necessary for saving the truth to give up the things of one's own, in other ways too but especially being philosophers; for while both are dear, it is holy to honor the truth in preference.

Philosophy (I.6.1096b30–31): But perhaps these matters [the ways in which things are called good] should be dismissed for now; for to be precise about them would be more akin to another philosophy.

Philosophy (I.8.1098b16–18): So it would be beautifully said [that happiness lies in actions and activities of the soul], being in accordance with this old opinion and agreed on by those philosophizing.

Plato (II.3.1104b11–13): Hence one ought be habituated somehow directly from youth, as Plato says, so as to enjoy and be pained in the things in which one ought; for this is correct education.

Philosophy (II.4.1105b12–15): But the many do not do these things [become habituated by practice], but taking refuge in *logos* they believe they philosophize and will in this way be serious, like invalids who listen carefully to physicians but do nothing to follow the things prescribed.

Philosophy (II.4.1105b16–18): Just as those will not be in a good condition of the body, being taken care of in that way, neither will these in regard to the soul philosophizing in this way.

Socrates (III.8.1116b3–5): And experience about particulars is thought to be courage; whence Socrates believed courage is *epistēmē*.

Socrates (IV.7.1127b22–26): The ironic, speaking in understatement, appear to be more charming in character, for they seem not to speak for the sake of profit, but avoiding the pompous, they mostly disown things held in esteem, as Socrates used to do.

Socrates (VI.13.1144b17–21): Hence some say all the virtues are forms of *phronēsis*, and Socrates in one way sought correctly, in another he erred; for in believing that all the virtues are forms of *phronēsis* he erred, but that they are not without *phronēsis*, he spoke beautifully.

Socrates (VI.13.1144b28–30): Socrates believed, then, that the virtues are *logoi*, for they are all *epistēmai*, whereas we believe they are together with *logos*.

Socrates (VII.2.1145b23–24): For it would be terrible, as Socrates believed, with *epistēmē* being within, for something else to rule and drag it around like a slave.

Socrates (VI.2.1145b25–27): For Socrates used to fight against the *logos* completely, as if there were no such thing as *akrasia;* for no one acts against what he supposes best except through ignorance.

Socrates (VII.3.1147b13–17): And since the last term is not the universal or thought to be scientific knowledge like the universal, what Socrates sought seems to follow; for it is not when what is thought to be knowledge in the sovereign sense is present that the pathos comes to be, nor that [knowledge] that is dragged around because of the pathos, but the sensible.

Philosophy (VII.11.1152b1–2): To theorize about pleasure and pain belongs to one philosophizing in the political manner.

Philosophy (IX.1.1164b2–6): It seems to be in this manner also for those who have shared in philosophy; for the worth is not measured by money, and honor would not come to be equally matched, but perhaps it is sufficient, as in relation to gods and parents, [to pay back] what is possible.

Philosophy (IX.12.1172a1–6): Whatever it is for each to be and for the sake of which they choose to live, in this they want to spend their time with friends; hence some drink together, some play dice together, others practice gymnastics together and hunt together or philosophize together, everyone spending the days together in that which most of all they cherish in life.

Plato (X.2.1172b28–32): By such an argument Plato denies that pleasure is the good; for the pleasant life is more choiceworthy together with *phronēsis* than apart from it, but if the mixed is superior, pleasure is not the good; for the good does not become more choiceworthy with anything added to it.

Philosophy (X.7.1177a22–27): We believe that pleasure ought to be mixed in with happiness, but the most pleasant of activities in accordance with virtue is agreed to be that in accordance with *sophia;* at least philosophy seems to have pleasures wondrous in purity and firmness, and it is reasonable that the pastime be more pleasant for those who know than for those who seek.

Philosophy (X.9.1181b12–15): The issue of legislation being left undiscovered by our predecessors, perhaps it would be better for us to examine it, and generally about the regime, in order that as far as possible human philosophy might be completed.

APPENDIX 2

Virtues and Vices (Nicomachean Ethics *III and IV*)

COWARDICE	COURAGE	ANONYMOUS
(excessive fear) (deficient confidence)	(The courageous person will fear as he should and as *logos* dictates, and for the sake of the beautiful.)	("fearlessness") (excessive confidence = rashness)

ANONYMOUS	MODERATION	INDULGENCE
("insensibility")	(The moderate person desires what he should, as he should, when he should, and as *logos* commands. . . . The desiring part harmonizes with *logos*, for the beautiful is the aim of both.)	

STINGINESS	LIBERALITY	PRODIGALITY
	(The liberal person gives for the sake of the beautiful and correctly, to whom he should, and how much, and at the right time.)	

MEANNESS	MAGNIFICENCE	VULGARITY
	(The magnificent person spends for the sake of the beautiful, for this is common to the virtues; *theōria* of a great and beautiful deed is wondrous.)	

SMALLNESS OF SOUL	GREATNESS OF SOUL	VANITY
	(*Megalopsuchia* is in magnitude, just as beauty is in a large body. . . . The great-souled person claims and deserves the reward for the most beautiful things, and such is honor.)	

LACK OF LOVE OF HONOR	ANONYMOUS	LOVE OF HONOR
(praised as measured and moderate; blamed for not demanding honor even in regard to the beautiful things)		(praised as manly and as loving the beautiful; blamed for loving honor more than he should or from the wrong source)

ANONYMOUS	ANONYMOUS ("GENTLENESS")	IRASCIBILITY
("inirascibility") (praised as gentle)	(The gentle person feels anger in regard to what he should, as he should, when he should, and for as long as he should.)	(praised as manly, able to rule)
SURLINESS	ANONYMOUS ("FRIENDLINESS")	OBSEQUIOUSNESS
	(The friendly person approves of what he should and as he should and disapproves of pleasures that are not beautiful or that are harmful.)	
EIRŌNEIA	ANONYMOUS ("SINCERITY")	BOASTFULNESS
(Socrates as exemplar)	(This case should lead us to trust that the mean is in every case a virtue.)	
BOORISHNESS	WITTINESS	BUFFOONERY
	(The witty person is a law unto himself.)	
BASHFULNESS	SHAME	SHAMELESSNESS
	(a mean but not a virtue)	
[SCHADENFREUDE]	[NEMESIS]	[ENVY]
	(last mentioned case in Book II, missing in Book IV)	

APPENDIX 3

Categories of Justice (Nicomachean Ethics *V*)

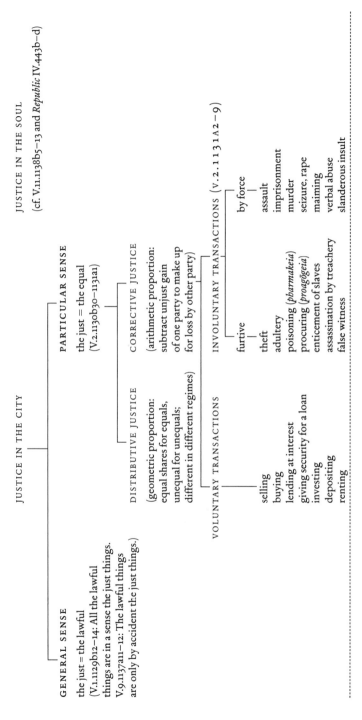

GENERAL SENSE

the just = the lawful
(V.1.1129b12–14: All the lawful
things are in a sense the just things.
V.9.1137a11–12: The lawful things
are only by accident the just things.)

JUSTICE IN THE CITY

PARTICULAR SENSE

the just = the equal
(V.2.1130b30–1131a1)

DISTRIBUTIVE JUSTICE

(geometric proportion:
equal shares for equals,
unequal for unequals;
different in different regimes)

CORRECTIVE JUSTICE

(arithmetic proportion:
subtract unjust gain
of one party to make up
for loss by other party)

VOLUNTARY TRANSACTIONS

selling
buying
lending at interest
giving security for a loan
investing
depositing
renting

INVOLUNTARY TRANSACTIONS (V.2.1131A2–9)

furtive

theft
adultery
poisoning (*pharmakeia*)
procuring (*proagōgeia*)
enticement of slaves
assassination by treachery
false witness

by force

assault
imprisonment
murder
seizure, rape
maiming
verbal abuse
slanderous insult

JUSTICE IN THE SOUL

(cf. V.11.1138b5–13 and *Republic* IV.443b–d)

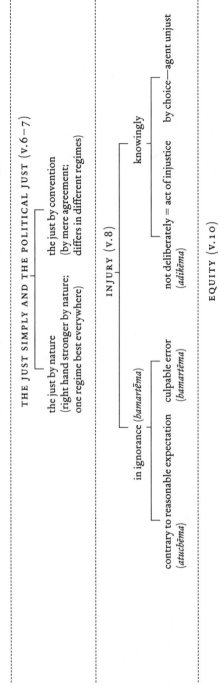

RECIPROCITY (V.5)

simple equality
("an eye for an eye")

proportionate equality
(economic exchange)

THE JUST SIMPLY AND THE POLITICAL JUST (V.6–7)

the just by nature
(right hand stronger by nature;
one regime best everywhere)

the just by convention
(by mere agreement;
differs in different regimes)

INJURY (V.8)

in ignorance (*hamartēma*)

contrary to reasonable expectation
(*atuchēma*)

culpable error
(*hamartēma*)

knowingly

not deliberately = act of injustice
(*adikēma*)

by choice—agent unjust

EQUITY (V.10)

(the nature of the equitable = correction of defect of law because of universality)

APPENDIX 4

Classifications of Pleasure (Nicomachean Ethics VII)

(VII.4,1147b23–35) things productive of pleasure

- necessary, connected with body; same sphere as moderation and indulgence (e.g., nutrition and the *aphrodisia*) *akrasia* unqualified
- not necessary, but choiceworthy in themselves (e.g., victory, honor, wealth) *akrasia* in regard to something

(VII.4,1148a22–b14) desires and pleasures

- of beautiful and serious things, choiceworthy by nature (e.g., money, gain, victory, honor, loving parents or children) admit of excess, but no wickedness or *akrasia* simply
- intermediate, necessary, only excess blamed
- the opposite of choiceworthy by nature

(VII.5,1148b15–1149a7) pleasant things

- by nature
  - simply: in accordance with genus of animals and humans
- not by nature pleasant but become so by:
  - being impaired
  - habit
  - a wicked nature
  - related dispositions
    - bestial (e.g., cannibalism)
    - through diseases
    - sometimes madness
  - disease-like states (e.g., plucking out hair, biting nails, eating cinders and dirt, homosexuality)
    - by nature — not akratic
    - from habit (e.g., childhood abuse) — not akratic

Excessive states of folly, cowardice, indulgence, ill-temper: beyond vice, either bestial (e.g., some remote barbarians living only by sensation) or disease-like (e.g., epilepsy or madness)

(VII.6.1149b26–1150a3) bodily desires and pleasures (vs. *thumos*, 1149a25–b25)

human and natural—
in genus and magnitude,
sphere of moderation and indulgence

some bestial (less evil than vice but more terrifying),
others through being maimed and diseases

(VII.7.1150a15–18) pleasures (also desires and pains)

necessary within certain limits,
excess not necessary

not necessary

(VII.12.1152b33–1153a7) pleasures

restoration to natural state—
only accidentally pleasant

activity in natural state—
pleasant simply

(VII.14.1154a11–19, 1154b15–17) bodily pleasures

necessary pleasures—good up to a point
(e.g., food, wine, the *aphrodisia*)

pleasures unaccompanied by pain,
by nature pleasant, not accidentally

NOTES

INTRODUCTION

1. Alfarabi, "The Philosophy of Aristotle," i and xix, in *The Philosophy of Plato and Aristotle*, pp. 59 and 130. On problems raised by the translation of the second passage, which is from the conclusion of "The Philosophy of Aristotle," see chap. 7, n. 51, below. On Aristotle's own way of proceeding toward the Platonic understanding of human perfection, see Muhsin Mahdi's discussion in "On Aristotle's Starting Point," in *Alfarabi and the Foundation of Islamic Political Philosophy*, pp. 196–207.

2. In defining the Socratic way by its subject matter, Aristotle departs from Plato's Socrates, who on the last day of his life describes his distinctive turn not by its subject but by its way of proceeding—turning away from direct investigation of the beings to "take refuge in *logoi*," in which the truth of the beings might be examined (*Phaedo* 99e). In the *Apology*, Socrates denies the accusation against him for investigating things above or below the earth—at least no one present ever heard him doing so; but while that denial might find support, Gerald Mara observes, in Xenophon's or Aristotle's Socrates, it is clearly problematic in the case of the Platonic Socrates (*Socrates' Discursive Democracy*, p. 37).

3. Rather surprisingly, there are only a handful of explicit references to Socrates' *eironeia* in the Platonic corpus (see my analysis in "Socratic *Eironeia*"). One of these is the accusation Thrasymachus levels against Socrates for his ironic claim to knowledge of ignorance (*Republic* 337a), which captures the frustrating experience Plato represents in so many of Socrates' interlocutors.

4. Perhaps the most striking case is the discrepancy, in the *Republic*, between the "best city in speech" and the city in deed of Socrates and his interlocutors, or what Seth Benardete dubs the "dialogic city" (see *Socrates' Second Sailing: On Plato's "Republic,"* esp. p. 140). Another example, which proves to be especially important for Aristotle's *Ethics*, is the discrepancy in the *Theaetetus* between Socrates' description of the philosopher, who is so removed from the city that he does not even know his way to the *agora* or the lawcourt (*Theaetetus* 173c–175e), and Socrates' own situation, indicated by the dramatic setting of the conversation, which occurs, as we find out at the very end (210d), just before Socrates receives the indictment for corrupting the youth and which he then reports to the narrator during his days in prison awaiting execution (142c–143a).

5. This is the story Socrates tells at his trial (*Apology* 22d–e).

6. Aristotle's identification of the Socratic turn by its restricted territory is mirrored in his own corpus, which links the *Ethics* with the *Politics* and treats the pair as a particular discipline whose distinctive subject matter calls for a distinctive mode of proceeding.

7. *Charmides* 166e. This development represents a distorted mirror of Socratic philosophy as it has taken hold of the soul of Socrates' interlocutor, who has his own reasons for his adaptation of the Socratic teaching (see chap. 3, nn. 22 and 27, below).

8. Leo Strauss, *The City and Man*, p. 27; the following discussion is drawn from pp. 25–29. Strauss's account begins to take a turn when he considers the possible effects the philosopher's examination may have on those who are addressed by it, which suggests that, after all, "the moral-political sphere is then not unqualifiedly closed to theoretical science" (p. 28). "Considerations like these," Strauss concludes from his discussion of Aristotle, "induced Socrates and Plato to assert that virtue is knowledge and that quest for prudence is philosophy" (p. 29)—a conclusion haunted by its silence about Aristotle. My study of the *Ethics* aims to address the questions raised by that silence.

9. On this translation of *ta kala*, see chap. 1, n. 2, below.

10. In *Reading Aristotle's "Ethics": Virtue, Rhetoric, and Political Philosophy*, Aristide Tessitore develops an account of the argument of the *Ethics* as a coherent whole, in part by paying attention to the complexity of its intended audience, which he describes, in an introductory remark, as one "characterized less by a desire for theoretical knowledge and more by an attraction to goodness. Hence, those who are beneficiaries of a decent upbringing, have some experience of life, and have attained a certain level of maturity, are in a position to derive the greatest benefit from Aristotle's book and, as such, are its primary, though not necessarily exclusive, addressees" (p. 17). Differences between Tessitore's reading of the *Ethics* and the one developed in this study arise in part from a different understanding of Aristotle's primary audience.

11. Moses Maimonides addresses his *Guide of the Perplexed* to someone for whom "the validity of our Law has become established in his soul" but who has also "studied the sciences of the philosophers and come to know what they signify. The human intellect having drawn him on and led him to dwell within its province, he must have felt distressed by the externals of the Law.... Hence he would remain in a state of perplexity and confusion as to whether he should follow his intellect ... and ... consider that he has renounced the foundations of the Law" or turn his back on the intellect and be left with "imaginary beliefs to which he owes his fear and difficulty" ("Introduction to the First Part," in *The Guide of the Perplexed* 3a–b; 1:5–6).

12. The aporetic character of Aristotle's writing, Arlene Saxonhouse notes, is not what we would be led to expect by the tradition (*Athenian Democracy, Modern Mythmakers, and Ancient Theorists*, pp. 116–17). In *The Harmonization of the Two*

Opinions of the Two Sages: Plato the Divine and Aristotle, Alfarabi describes the apparent difference between Plato's more hidden and Aristotle's more open manner of writing and then adds: "But the modes of abstruseness, obscurity, and complexity in Aristotle's procedure, despite his apparent intention to explain and elucidate, will not be concealed from anyone who carefully investigates his scientific teachings, studies his books, and perseveres with them" (p. 131). See, however, the discussion by Charles Butterworth, the work's translator and annotator, of the status of Alfarabi's attempted "harmonization" (pp. 119–24).

13. See Appendix ("Socrates, Plato, and Philosophy") and chap. 3, n. 20. Richard Cox analyzes the pattern in which all explicit references to "philosophy" in the *Ethics* lie outside the frame of the sequence of speeches on Socrates: those speeches reflect, Cox argues, the "rhetoric which proves, on reflection, to derive from and to be an expression of Aristotle's public presentation of his 'political science': *hē politikē*" ("Aristotle's Treatment of Socrates in the *Nicomachean Ethics*: A Proem," p. 123). In "Aristotle's Political Presentation of Socrates in the *Nicomachean Ethics*," Aristide Tessitore examines the explicit references to Socrates in the *Nichomachean Ethics* under four thematic treatments—courage, truthfulness and irony, prudence, and incontinence—and shows, in the process, how "Aristotle attempts to bring readers to some positive, if critical, appreciation for Socrates' life and teaching" ("Socrates in Aristotle's 'Philosophy of Human Affairs,'" p. 204). This is especially well illustrated by the discussion of incontinence (pp. 212–14).

14. The general Nicias proposes the definition of courage as an *epistēmē* of fearful and confidence-inspiring things, which turns out to be knowledge of good and bad things in general (*Laches* 194e–195a, 199c; cf. chap. 3, n. 22, below). Aristotle provides us with another playful puzzle when he speaks of Plato's *Laws,* the only dialogue in which Socrates makes no appearance whatsoever, as "Socratic speeches" (*Politics* 1265a3–4; cf. chap. 7, n. 43, below).

15. "The impact of Plato on Aristotle's philosophy can hardly be exaggerated": Robert Heinaman introduces with this statement a collection of articles based on a colloquium devoted to examining how Aristotle reacted to and was influenced by Plato's ethical views (*Plato and Aristotle's "Ethics,"* p. ix). As those essays make clear, dialogue between such thinkers does not necessarily mean agreement, though disagreement emerges out of a deep common ground.

16. As Cox notes, "The sudden ending of the speeches on Socrates is all the more perplexing since the rest of the *Ethics* treats themes which the Platonic Socrates had himself treated, themes such as the nature of pleasure, friendship, and not least, in Book X, the "theoretical" aspect of the life of the philosophic man" ("Aristotle's Treatment of Socrates in the *Nicomachean Ethics,*" p. 136).

17. On the reference to the "political philosopher," see chap. 5, n. 29, below.

18. Aristotle's understanding of the human being involves, as Michael Davis shows in his study of the *Poetics,* three interrelated determinations—as the rational animal, and as the political animal, but also as the imitative animal (see *The Poetry of Philosophy,* esp. p. 4).

19. Cf. Chap. 10 of Aristotle's *Poetics*.

20. The *Ethics* would illustrate, then, despite its form as a treatise, the essential relation Seth Benardete suggests when he observes: "Irony is incompatible with science; it is at home in political philosophy. . . . Socrates the master ironist and Socrates the first political philosopher seem to be the same. And if they are the same, political philosophy would have to be double—with one face turned toward and the other away from the city" ("Leo Strauss' *The City and Man*," p. 5).

CHAPTER 1

1. The *Nicomachean Ethics* itself, as "some kind of *politikē*," or political art, is defined at the outset as a distinctive *methodos* (1094b11) whose speeches are of worth only in connection with some kind of *praxis* (1095a5–11), while it is finally designated a *prohairesis* whose *telos* is not "merely theoretical" (1179a33–35).

2. The apparently casual adverb *kalōs* in the opening statement of the *Ethics* introduces a subject that will be central to the inquiry, beginning with the identification of its subject matter—the just things and *ta kala* (1094b14–16). The translation of *to kalon* is as problematic as it is important if it is true that "Athens seems to have been as passionately devoted to the beautiful as Jerusalem to the just" (Seth Benardete, *The Being of the Beautiful*, p. xv). "Noble"—the traditional translation— might seem to be especially appropriate for the concern in the *Ethics* with the *kalon* as the *telos* of the ethical virtues (e.g., 1115b12–13): the noble, one might say, is the particular way the beautiful shows up in the sphere of morality. If, however, the ethical virtues point to something beyond themselves—beyond what they are as dispositions of character produced by habituation—it is through aiming at "the beautiful" as their *telos* (cf. chap. 2, n. 3, and chap. 3, n. 28, below).

3. The question, "What is being?"—which is the subject of the sought-for science of Aristotle's *Metaphysics* (983a22)—was not just in the past but is now and will always be sought for and perplexing (1028b3–4).

4. See, especially, the ninth book of the *Metaphysics*. According to that account, a motion (*kinēsis*)—like dieting, learning, walking, or building—is incomplete until its product is completed, at which point it ceases to exist; it is contrasted with an *energeia*—like seeing, living, thinking, or being happy—which has no external product and is itself complete at every moment. In this context, an action (*praxis*), or at least a complete *praxis*, unlike a motion, does have its end in itself (1048b19–28). *Energeia* is connected to *ergon* through the example of two subjects defined by their relationship: the *ergon* of the teacher (transmitting knowledge to the student) is the *telos* of his practice, but it is the *energeia* of the student that displays this *ergon*—and, Aristotle adds, "nature is like this" (1050a17–23).

5. The initial statement about *ergon* and *energeia* becomes all the more puzzling when we are told, just at this point as the first chapter comes to an end, that it is of no consequence whether "the ends of the actions are the *energeiai* themselves or something else apart from them" (1094a16–19). An *energeia* exercised as an end in itself, though, would seem to resist integration into a larger hierarchy, unlike the

ergon that is the product of an activity. If it is the city, then, as Aristotle will soon indicate, that turns the plurality of arts into an ordered whole, perhaps it can do so only by treating each as productive of an *ergon*. The opening statement of the *Ethics* about *energeia* and *ergon*, as Michael Davis puts it, "reproduces a motion in which activities originally understood as for their own sakes are subsequently understood as instrumental" ("Father of the *Logos:* The Question of the Soul in Aristotle's *Nicomachean Ethics*," pp. 176–77).

6. Aristotle speaks carefully here, preparing the grounds for the explicit distinction between wishing (*boulēsis*) for an end and choosing (*probairesis*) the means (cf. 1111b26–27).

7. This is the first step in an extended pun—(cf. 1095a3–5, and n. 17 below; 1096b20, and 1097b12–13)—borrowed from Plato's *Philebus*, in which the infinite (*apeiron*) multitude of individuals and the infinite within each is said to make one indefinite (*apeiron*) in thinking (17e4; cf. Seth Benardete, *The Tragedy and Comedy of Life: Plato's "Philebus*," p. 94). The link Aristotle makes between the infinite chain of ends and desire being in vain recalls the same link in the *Philebus:* Socrates' playful cosmology, in supporting the ancient claim that mind orders the universe by setting limits on the unlimited, is not in vain (30d6).

8. Aristotle will soon attack the defenders of the *idea* of the good for just this assumption (1097a1–4). In speaking of the decisive thing in life, Aristotle uses the formula, *rhopē biou*, by which Oedipus refers to the approach of his death (Sophocles *Oedipus at Colonus* 1508): Aristotle anticipates, perhaps, the slide in the course of Book I from the *telos* as the purpose of life to the *telos* as the termination of life.

9. At the end of the long argument of the *Philebus*, Socrates admits they must try to grasp clearly the good—or some outline (*tupos*) of it (61a)!

10. See *Apology* 22d–e; *Republic* 433a–b; and *Charmides* 171d–172a.

11. Alfarabi traces such a movement when, after describing the divine inquiry into the ultimate causes of the beings, he turns to the science of man and political science, through which one "will come to see in what are included in the totality constituted by the city and the nations the likenesses of what are included in the total world" ("The Attainment of Happiness" i.20, in *The Philosophy of Plato and Aristotle*, p. 24). See n. 72 below.

12. The argument that begins here is not resumed, explicitly, until the first three chapters of Book VII of Aristotle's *Politics*, in which such a metaphor is developed and applied to a single city in isolation (1325b24–33; cf. chap. 7, n. 45, below).

13. On the disagreement about the kind of equality relevant to distributive justice, see *Politics* 1282b14–1283a23. On different burial customs, see, e.g., Plato *Minos* 315c–d. To illustrate the attachment of a people to their own sacred things and customs, Herodotus tells a story of Darius inquiring about burial practices. When he once asked a group of Greeks what he would have to give them to eat the bodies of their fathers after they had died, they replied that there was no price. He then asked certain Indians, whose custom is to eat their dead fathers, what it would take for them to burn the bodies of their dead fathers and they shouted aloud,

commanding him to be silent. Herodotus draws the conclusion that Pindar was right: "Custom is the king of all" (*Histories* III.38). But he shows at the same time, as Seth Benardete observes, that all customs are not equally preferable: the Indians, in their practice of cannibalism, have closed their mind to any other custom, while the Greeks listen in silence to the thought of a different way, even if they don't change their own (*Herodotean Inquiries,* pp. 79–80).

14. While many, Socrates claims, "would do, possess, and enjoy the reputation for things that are opined to be just and beautiful, even if they aren't," when it comes to good things, "no one is satisfied with what is opined to be so, but each seeks the things that are, and from here on out everyone despises the opinion" (*Republic* 505d).

15. It is out of just such a concern that Socrates issues his warning against the threat of "misology" and the need for a way of proceeding that is safe from that threat (see *Phaedo* 89c–90c). Cf. my discussion in *The "Phaedo": A Platonic Labyrinth,* pp. xii–xiii, 115–19.

16. The Athenian Stranger in Plato's *Laws* appeals to that "most beautiful" of Dorian laws, which prohibits only the young from inquiring into the laws, in an attempt to free his elderly companions for their investigation; but he then faces the challenge of infusing them with the youthful spirit of questioning that would motivate such an examination in the first place (634d–636a). Maimonides seems to be facing the same problem when he discusses those who could benefit from study of the "divine science." Explaining why "the teaching of this science to the young is disapproved of," he observes that "the flame of growth" in the young gives rise to perplexity and, consequently, one can engage in this study without harm only when that flame is extinguished (*The Guide of the Perplexed* I.34; 1:77); but isn't that precisely when a "guide of the perplexed" would be unnecessary?

17. Aristotle links the subject of the inquiry with its audience by the pun he had already introduced: in place of the infinite (*apeiros*) chain of choices in the absence of a final good, which would make all desire in vain (*mataian*) (1094a20–21), we now have the inexperienced (*apeiros*) character of the young, who, in being determined by feelings, would listen to these speeches in vain (*mataian*) (1095a3–5). The role of the good as the final end that would make desire meaningful is now assigned to the relation between speeches and deeds that would give this project its significance. In his search for the sophist, Plato's Eleatic Stranger introduces the problem of whether and how the "spoken images" of one's youth can be corrected by the "deeds in actions" one encounters over time (*Sophist* 234c–e).

18. This is the first of the three references in the *Ethics* to Plato (see appendix 1). Socrates offers an account of the difference between ascending to the *archē* and descending from it in his description of what is supposed to be the highest segment of the "divided line" (*Republic* 511b–c).

19. Cf. Aristotle's description in *Metaphysics Z* of the attempt to advance toward what is more knowable by nature starting from what is more knowable to us, "by means of those very things" (1029b3–14). Following the same principle, his inquiry in the *Physics* sets out from the understanding that all natural things appear to have

within themselves a principle of motion and of rest; the demand to prove the existence of such things before proceeding would be like someone born blind trying to reason about colors (184a16–22, 193a2–9).

20. Churchill, we are told, was once given a copy of the *Ethics* by an enthusiastic admirer of Aristotle. After reading it, "Churchill returned it with an expression of his delight, adding simply, 'But it is extraordinary how much of it I had already thought out for myself'" (C. E. Bechhofer Roberts, *Winston Churchill*, p. 102).

21. Alfarabi indicates his understanding of such a project when he concludes "The Attainment of Happiness" by reflecting on the philosophy handed down by Plato and Aristotle: "Both have given us an account of philosophy, but not without giving us also an account of the ways to it and of the ways to re-establish it when it becomes confused or extinct" ("The Attainment of Happiness" 63, in *The Philosophy of Plato and Aristotle*, p. 50).

22. Given Aristotle's account of who could and would benefit from this inquiry, "there seems to be no need," Marc Guerra concludes, "for a book like the *Ethics*. Why then Aristotle would write a lengthy treatise on moral and political science and who this work is written for are something of a puzzle" ("Aristotle on Pleasure and Political Philosophy: A Study in Book VII of the *Nicomachean Ethics*," p. 171).

23. Aristotle would be looking, in that case, for an audience not unlike Glaucon and Adeimantus, who want Socrates to show them the real good of practicing the justice praised by convention (see *Republic* 358b–376e.)

24. The *Ethics*, as C. D. C. Reeve sees it, is addressed to people who have reliable *endoxa*, but conflicts among their opinions lead to *aporiai*, which Aristotle aims to resolve by means of dialectic (*The Practices of Reason: Aristotle's "Nicomachean Ethics*," p. 189). There is a difference, of course, between those who are aware of and disturbed by the *aporiai* to which the conflicting *endoxa* give rise and those who are not; if the *Ethics* is addressing both, it is presumably not addressing them in the same way.

Thomas Smith sees the *Ethics*, more specifically, as a "course of teaching that means to explore the question of the best life as it appears from the perspective of one particular horizon—that inhabited by ambitious young men of the ancient Greek city-state." Aristotle's "dialectical pedagogy," as Smith understands it, "moves from the reputable opinions his audience holds about the good life to a consideration of those opinions in order to see where and how they break down on their own terms" (*Revaluing Ethics: Aristotle's Dialectical Pedagogy*, p. 6).

25. Hesiod *Works and Days* 293–97. The citation turns out to be even more thematically appropriate for Aristotle's purposes if one takes into consideration the one line omitted from the middle of Hesiod's verse—"He is the best man of all who thinks out everything for himself, seeing which of his courses will turn out better at last"—a line whose echo will be heard in the proverbial wisdom of Solon's "Look to the end" (cf. *Ethics* 1100a10–11).

Machiavelli recalls Hesiod's class division in a discussion under the title "Of Those Whom Princes Have as Secretaries": "There are three kinds of brains: one that understands by itself, another that discerns what others understand, the third that understands neither by itself nor through others; the first is most excellent, the second excellent, and the third useless" (*The Prince,* chap. 22, p. 92).

26. When asked to explain what he meant in calling himself a "philosopher," Pythagoras distinguished three ways of life by analogy to a festival, to which some go to compete, some to make a profit, and others just to contemplate (Cicero *Tusculan Disputations* V.3.8–9). The problem of what it means to speak of a "life of something" is central to the *Philebus,* in which the question of whether the good is pleasure or some activity of mind gets translated into a contest between the life of pleasure and the life of mind (see n. 40 below).

27. On various proposals about this reference in Book X, see chap. 7, n. 14, below.

28. It is the questionable hypothesis of the parallel structure of the city and the individual that allows Socrates to treat the appetitive part of the soul as analogous to the moneymaking class in the city (see *Republic* 431b–d, 434c, 436a–b, 441a).

29. See, e.g., 1152b35–1153a2. The argument for the noninstrumental status of pleasure is developed in Book X in preparation for resuming the original question of happiness (1176b8–11).

30. See, e.g., *Sophist* 250e4, where the Eleatic Stranger announces their arrival at "thorough perplexity" once being has shown itself to be as problematic as non-being. In *Metaphysics B,* Aristotle argues for the need to start the inquiry by being "thoroughly perplexed beautifully" (995a23–33). It is striking that the one point in the *Ethics* at which Aristotle engages in what might be thought a criticism of Plato, in contrast with Socrates, he does not mention his name.

31. See appendix 1.

32. Aristotle introduces his critique of the Platonic account in almost the same words through which Socrates expresses his critique of Homer in the last book of the *Republic:* precisely because he has been so powerfully affected by Homer's magic, Socrates warns, "It would not be holy to betray what seems to be true" (607c). In both cases, the apparent critique proves to be an acknowledgment of the greatest debt, which Aristotle has apparently learned from Plato how to express quite beautifully.

33. Plato avoids, for example, as Strauss observes, presenting a conversation between Socrates and the Eleatic Stranger or Timaeus. Instead, the Platonic dialogue always represents the main speaker adapting his teaching to interlocutors who are not on the same level of understanding and, thus, leads the reader to consider how that teaching would have to be reconstructed apart from the particular context in which it has been embedded (Strauss, *The City and Man,* pp. 54–55).

34. This reasoning is illustrated by the regress argument Socrates presents in the *Lysis:* if each "friend" is loved for the sake of something else until arriving at "the first friend," that final end would be the only true friend (*Lysis* 219c–220b). See Michael Davis's discussion in *The Autobiography of Philosophy,* p. 77.

35. On the "eye of the soul," see 1096b29, along with 1102a18–21, 1143b13–14, and 1144a29–31.

36. The inclusion of the weaver here might make one think of Plato's image for the statesman (*politikos*) and his architectonic art (see *Statesman* 279b–280a, 311b–c).

37. Aristotle's criticism of the idea of the good as a guide has a parallel in his criticism in the *Politics* of the *Republic*'s best regime as a model for political practice; but that criticism is in fact "in agreement rather than disagreement, with Plato," Harry Jaffa observes. "The disagreement lies deeper and concerns whether a model which transcends practice and can never be imitated in practice reveals the nature of practice more truly than a model which lies within the range of what is possible in practice" ("Aristotle," pp. 81–82). On the connection between Aristotle's criticism in the *Ethics* of the Platonic idea of the good and his criticism in the *Politics* of Socrates' proposal for a communistic city, see also Mary Nichols, *Socrates and the Political Community*, pp. 163–64.

38. Noting that the *Nicomachean Ethics* begins with the good for man, the *Eudemian Ethics* with *eudaimonia*, T. H. Irwin remarks that Aristotle does not consider it a tautology to claim that "the good for man is *eudaimonia*" ("The Metaphysical and Psychological Basis of Aristotle's *Ethics*," p. 51 n. 1).

39. Aristotle's *Politics* puts forward the claim that only the "complete community" of the *polis*, in contrast with the household or the village, can be said to achieve "the limit of self-sufficiency, *so to speak*" (1252b28–30; my emphasis).

40. Plato used such an argument to refute the view that pleasure is the good, Aristotle later recalls (1172b28–34). He is alluding, presumably, to the thought experiment Socrates conducts in the *Philebus:* turning the experience of pleasure and the activity of thinking into "the life of pleasure" and "the life of mind," and imagining each entirely separate from the other, leads to the conclusion that any addition of one to the other would make either better, hence, neither alone could have the sufficiency of the good (see *Philebus* 20c–22b and 60c–61a).

41. W. F. R. Hardie, *Aristotle's Ethical Theory*, p. 23. While a comprehensive plan of life is compatible with the paramount place that might be given to one kind of activity, Aristotle fails, Hardie charges, to make that distinction explicit. Hardie speaks elsewhere of Aristotle "fumbling for the idea of an inclusive end" while arguing for happiness as a dominant end ("The Final Good in Aristotle's *Ethics*," p. 300). If the alternative to a comprehensive whole of ends is the exclusive identification of happiness with a single activity, it is misleading, Fred Miller notes, to speak of a "dominant" end, which is not strictly a contrary of "inclusive" (review of *Reason and Human Good in Aristotle*, p. 112). The tension between an inclusive and an exclusive conception appears not just in Aristotle's account of *eudaimonia* but in various forms throughout his thought (see chap. 7, n, 18, below)—whenever a comprehensive understanding of a whole is insufficient without an understanding of its most perfect part, or a comprehensive understanding of a class without an understanding of its most perfect member, even if, or precisely because, the two accounts are at odds with one another.

42. *Eudaimonia* cannot be desired for the sake of something else, as J. L. Ackrill puts it, because it is "the life that contains all intrinsically worthwhile activities." *Eudaimonia* is able to make life lacking in nothing only because of its all-inclusive character ("Aristotle on *Eudaimonia*," p. 21). The argument in Book I does acknowledge the possibility that a plurality of ends would jointly constitute "the practical

good," but with the implication that it would be an impasse in the search for the final end (1097b22–23).

43. On the exclusive conception of happiness put forward in Book X, see chap. 7, nn. 20–24, below.

44. According to the "dictionary" of Aristotle's *Metaphysics, teleios* can mean "complete," a whole from which no part is missing, or "perfect," the highest exemplar of a kind (1021b31–1022a1). That Aristotle would refrain from clarifying this ambiguity in his criterion for *eudaimonia* or the human good when, as the *Metaphysics* indicates, he is perfectly capable of doing so, is difficult to explain except by assuming he has reasons for proceeding as he does.

45. After providing a helpful survey of the positions taken in the contemporary debate, Tessitore presents the case for Aristotle's deliberate ambiguity, shaped by specific apologetic concerns, given that the work is "not primarily addressed to 'philosophers' but to the better sort of persons referred to in classical literature as 'gentlemen'" (*Reading Aristotle's Ethics*, p. 17).

46. What satisfies this longing for something "more manifest" (*enargesteron*) turns out to be the human function (*ergon*), which shows that the human being is not by nature idle (*argon*): could this play on words be meant to suggest that if there is a human function, it is exhibited by our deed of trying to make it more manifest?

47. Socrates proposes such an argument in his final attempt to persuade Thrasymachus that being just is for one's own good (cf. Dominic Scott, "Aristotle and Thrasymachus"). Socrates establishes that the *ergon* of a thing is that which it alone can perform, or that which it can perform better than anything else, and that that specific work or function entails a specific virtue; inquiring then whether the soul has such an *ergon,* one it could not accomplish well if deprived of its own virtue, he arrives at the conclusion that "a bad soul will govern and manage things badly while the good soul will in all these things do well" and that "he who lives well is blessed and happy, and he who does not the contrary" (*Republic* 353a–354a). The argument, which was supposed to demonstrate the worth of being just, seems in fact to indicate that the distinctive human virtue, by which the soul manages things well, would be prudence.

48. Aristotle does succeed, Kathleen Wilkes argues, in linking the notion of "the life of a good man" and "the life good for a man" in a single concept of *eudaimonia.* What is to be rejected, she maintains, is the identification of it with the theoretical life, when he should have maintained that the better a man is at practical reasoning, the better a life he will lead ("The Good Man and the Good for Man in Aristotle's *Ethics,*" p. 354). But practical reason is only instrumental, and the evaluation of the life it orders depends on the end toward which that life is directed.

49. The artisan gets the satisfaction of his interest, or the means of satisfying his interests, by being paid for his service (cf. *Republic* 346c–e).

50. In the intellectual autobiography Socrates presents on the last day of his life, the final stage he describes, before turning to his own way of inquiry, was his discovery of the failure of Anaxagoras—or any other thinker, including himself—

to explain the cosmic order as a product of mind looking to the good (*Phaedo* 97b–98b).

51. These functions of the human soul only *appear* to be held in common with plants and animals, if, as the analyses of *De anima* lead us to think, once parts of soul (like the nutritive, sensitive, appetitive, or imaginative) are integrated into a larger whole, they are no longer exactly what they are on their own. When Maimonides, in his work *Eight Chapters,* begins a discussion of health and disease of soul with an account of the parts of the human soul, he is at pains to insist that the soul belonging to each species is unique: "Man's nutritive part, for example, is not the same as the nutritive part belonging to a donkey or a horse," and individuals of different species "are said to be 'nourished' solely due to the equivocal character of the word" (Chapter I; pp. 61–62).

52. Moral virtue counts as an activity in accordance with reason, Edward Halper argues, in two ways: virtuous actions are in accord with what reason dictates (the correct *logos* that determines the mean) and they contribute to the further exercise of reason—ultimately, to the activity of contemplation (*Form and Reason: Essays in Metaphysics,* p. 63). Practical reason may be at work in morally virtuous action and the life devoted to it as much as in a life devoted to *theōria,* but practical reason looks to an end beyond itself—and, in the case of moral virtue, that end is not itself the exercise of reason. Virtuous action could serve the end of contemplation, as Halper argues, only if it could be performed both for its own sake and for the sake of some end beyond itself (p. 68); but are those two different intentions capable of operating at the same time in the same action (see chap. 7, n. 23, below)?

53. Translations do not always bring out sufficiently the hypothetical character of the argument. T. H. Irwin does not translate "if" until the clause numbered sixth above (see Irwin, trans., *Aristotle: Nicomachean Ethics,* p. 17). J. E. C. Welldon introduces it in the second half of the argument, after doing without it for the first half (see Welldon, trans., *Aristotle: The Nicomachean Ethics,* p. 24).

54. What is at stake here is really only brought to light at the end of Book X, where ethical virtue along with the passions, and *phronēsis* insofar as it serves ethical virtue, are assigned to the composite being (see 1178a14–23).

55. Timothy Roche argues for an "inclusive end" reading of the *ergon* argument, appealing, for one thing, to Aristotle's acknowledgment that having reason includes not just the exercise of one's own reason but also the capacity for obedience to reason in another, which is assigned to the desiring part of the soul; hence, he concludes, morally virtuous activity must be part of the function and end of man ("*Ergon* and *Eudaimonia* in *Nicomachean Ethics* I: Reconsidering the Intellectualist Interpretation," p. 182). But however broadly human rationality may be characterized, that does not settle the interpretation of the standard implied when the human good is identified as an activity of soul in accordance with the "*teleiotatē* virtue," the most complete or the most perfect virtue.

56. See, esp., 1144a3–9, where the ranking of *phronēsis* as inferior to *sophia* leads to a distinction between *ergon* and *energeia* (cf. 1145a6–11 and 1178a9–23).

57. Distinguishing *eudaimonia* as a way of living (*zoē*), i.e. the exercise of a certain capacity of soul, from a person's "total life," Robert Heinaman argues that *eudaimonia* in accordance with "the most *teleion* virtue" must mean in accordance with the most perfect, not the most comprehensive virtue ("*Eudaimonia* and Self-Sufficiency in the *Nicomachean Ethics*," pp. 32–38); but that leaves open how *teleios bios* is to be understood. Cf. David Keyt's discussion of *teleios bios* and *teleia eudaimonia* ("Intellectualism in Aristotle," p. 377; and see chap. 7, n. 24, below).

58. See *Metaphysics* 1048b22–27.

59. When Aristotle excuses the admittedly crude psychology he introduces at the end of Book I as sufficient for the purpose of investigating virtue (1102a24–27), he implies its contrast with a theoretical inquiry into the nature of soul, which according to *De anima* is among the most precise of sciences (402a1–5).

60. The role of the *ergon* argument in the *Republic* as Benardete describes it would be equally applicable to Aristotle's *Ethics:* the argument "seems to be a promissory note that, we are led to believe, the rest of the *Republic*, once it has supplied the conditions and determined the obstacles, will pay in full. It presents schematically the terms and relations on which the *Republic* must make good" (*Socrates' Second Sailing*, p. 30).

61. See *Meno* 70a and 100b.

62. See *Poetics* 1450b21–34.

63. On the echoes of Solon's "look to the end" in the Greek tragedies, see T. H. Irwin, "Permanent Happiness: Aristotle and Solon," pp. 2–4. Cf. Martha Nussbaum's discussion, in *The Fragility of Goodness: Luck and Ethics in Greek Tragedy and Philosophy*, esp., pp. 327–36.

64. See Herodotus *Histories* I.30–32, 86–87; see also chap. 7, nn. 28–30, below. Solon's account of the instability of fortune, which turns out to express a distinctively "Greek" interpretation of divine jealousy, leads to the conclusion, in Benardete's words, "that man in his entirety is nothing but circumstance and luck," though that does not seem to be the conclusion one would draw from Solon's stories about the best way of life for a human being ("Second Thoughts," in *Herodotean Inquiries*, pp. 215–16).

65. See *Metaphysics* 982b29–983a5; see also chap. 7, n. 17, below.

66. See *Odyssey* XI.457–464 and 512–540.

67. See *De anima* 403a3–b19.

68. See *Politics* 1274b39–75a2.

69. The problem of the correspondence of city and soul, out of which the whole *Republic* is constructed, is contained in miniature in the gaps of Aristotle's analogy:

	practical end	theoretical means
doctor	to heal the eye	must study the whole body
politikos	[to heal part of the soul?]	must study the things concerning the soul
	to make the citizens good and law-abiding	[must study the whole *polis*?]

In the *Gorgias,* the task of making the citizens good and law-abiding is the political analogue to gymnastics, whereas healing the soul, as the analogue to medicine, is assigned to justice, understood in the context as punishment (*Gorgias* 464b–465d). The medicine of punitive justice is required only when the gymnastics of legislation fails. By the end of the *Gorgias,* Socrates characterizes himself as one of the few Athenians, if not the only one, to try to practice the political art truly (521d).

70. See, esp., 1105b14–18, 1138b29–32, 1145a6–9, 1150b32–35, 1152a27–29. Aristotle introduces the doctor of soul in the psychology at the end of Book I that provides the basis for the investigation of virtue, but he does not allow the medical model, with its abstraction from issues of responsibility, praise, and blame, to take over until Book VII of the *Ethics.* That movement of the argument becomes conspicuous by comparison with Maimonides' *Eight Chapters,* which begins treating virtue and vice as health and disease of soul as soon as it opens, with an Aristotelian analogy: "The doctor who cures bodies needs first to know, in its entirety, the body he is curing and what the parts of the body are, I mean the body of man. And he needs to know what things make it sick so that they may be avoided and what things make it healthy so that they may be pursued. Similarly, the one who treats the soul and wishes to purify moral habits needs to know the soul in its entirety and its parts, as well as what makes it sick and what makes it healthy" (Chapter I; p. 61). The question implicitly raised in the *Ethics* about the identity of the "true statesman" arises in *Eight Chapters* when Maimonides identifies the physicians of the soul as the "wise men" (Chapter III; p. 66), departing from Alfarabi's model: "The physician who cures bodies needs to be cognizant of the body in its entirety and of the parts of the body. . . . Likewise, the statesman and the king who cure souls need to be cognizant of the soul in its entirety and of its parts" (*Selected Aphorisms* v, in *Alfarabi: The Political Writings,* p. 13).

71. When the argument comes around to an analysis of the rational part of the soul, in the first chapter of Book VI, this suggestion seems to be forgotten (see "Psychology Revisited: The Rational *Psychē*" in chap. 4 below, esp. n. 7).

72. The soul is "somehow all things" (*De anima* 431b20–21). It is one thing to argue that the soul of the individual is an integral whole, with its distinct powers in a hierarchical order, as the psychology at the end of Book I establishes, quite another to make such a claim, as the *ergon* argument seemed to imply, about the cosmos as a whole. Joshua Parens argues that Alfarabi's Aristotle presents a persuasive case for "a hierarchy of powers within the individual soul" but discovers the limits of our knowledge when it comes to the cosmic whole (*An Islamic Philosophy of Virtuous Religions,* p. 115).

CHAPTER 2

1. The rare appearance of *eudaimonia* (or related terms) from the end of Book I until the end of Book VI begins with the statement in Book III that we want to be happy but do not choose it (1111b28–29). One reference that does associate virtue with happiness serves only to bring out the problematic character of the

one particular virtue, courage, that is a source of pain (1117b10–11). The only other connection with dispositions of character is the claim that boasters pretend to qualities that are deemed to make one happy (*eudaimonismos*, 1127b17–18). The single reference to *eudaimonia* in Book V occurs in the puzzling description of justice as that which produces and preserves "happiness and its parts in the political community" (1129b17–19; cf. "Justice and Happiness" in chap. 3).

2. The understanding of virtue as some kind of knowledge and vice as some kind of ignorance is a corollary of the principle that everyone desires the good: if he is in fact guilty of corrupting the young, Socrates argues at his trial, it could only be out of ignorance, since he is aware that corrupting his associates would ultimately bring harm to himself and no one wishes to harm himself (*Apology* 25c–26a). In the *Meno* Socrates develops an argument identifying virtue with knowledge but only by sliding from *epistēmē* to *phronēsis* (see n. 9 below). Socrates reveals more about his interlocutor than himself when he gets Gorgias to agree—though it lands him in a self-contradiction—that anyone who learns justice is necessarily just (*Gorgias* 460b–c).

3. The beautiful or the noble as the *telos* of ethical virtue belongs to the horizon of the particular dispositions taken up in Book III, where Aristotle gives voice to the self-understanding of the ethically virtuous person. Book II, instead, focuses on the mean as the standard that differentiates the virtuous disposition over against the dispositions of excess or deficiency, and the mean is determined by the prudent person with a view to what is good. Quite apart from the role of the *kalon* as *telos*, however, there is an aesthetic dimension of a condition determined by the measure of the mean. Socrates suggests it when he remarks in the *Philebus* on how everything beautiful comes to be for us through the measure of the mean as a limit on the unlimited (26a–b).

The mean is first introduced in Book II of the *Ethics* as that which produces and preserves *ta summetra* (1104a15–18), which is an aspect of the beautiful (see *Metaphysics* 1078a31). When Book II goes on to discuss the mean as a measure of virtuous action, it supports the point by analogy with the mean as the measure of a well-made work of art, which is destroyed by any excess or deficiency (1106b9–14). Aristotle's use of this analogy is one among other reasons Joe Sachs offers for translating *kalon* as "beautiful" (see his introductory essay to *Aristotle Nicomachean Ethics*, pp. xxi–xxv). Kelly Rogers notes the features of underlying order and propriety that belong to the *kalon* ("Aristotle's Conception of *To Kalon*," pp. 355–358). Gabriel Richardson Lear finds three central elements—"effective teleological order, visibility, and pleasantness"—to be marks of the fine or beautiful ("Aristotle on Moral Virtue and the Fine," p. 117).

4. It is, accordingly, in the discussion of courage, where the beautiful is introduced as the *telos* of virtue, that Socrates makes his first explicit appearance in the *Ethics*, targeted for his mistaken understanding of virtue as knowledge (1116b4–5).

5. Socrates expresses his assessment of the status of virtue produced by habituation in the myth of Er, with which the *Republic* concludes: the person drawing

the first lot to choose his next life, who recklessly makes the choice of a tyranny without realizing the misery it will bring, was one of those, Socrates explains, who came down from heaven after living a life in a well-ordered city, practicing virtue by habituation without philosophy (619c–d).

6. As Socrates explains to his companions on the last day of his life, all those who are said to be courageous or moderate except the philosopher are willing to face death only for fear of greater evils, just as they refrain from pleasure for fear of being deprived of other pleasures—purchasing virtue by exchanging pleasures for pleasures or pains for pains, when true virtue is possible only with *phronēsis* (*Phaedo* 68d–69b). Playfully speculating on the fate of souls after death determined by their way of life, Socrates imagines those individuals who practiced "demotic virtue" out of habits and without philosophy becoming some "political and tame genus," like bees or wasps or ants (*Phaedo* 82a–b).

7. In Plato's eyes, as Strauss puts it, "What Aristotle calls moral virtue is a kind of halfway house between political or vulgar virtue which is in the service of bodily well-being (of self-preservation or peace) and genuine virtue which, to say the least animates only the philosophers as philosophers" (*The City and Man*, p. 27). If Aristotelian moral virtue is such a "halfway house," it would seem to be because of the end at which it aims, the *kalon*, in contrast with the process of habituation through which it comes to be.

8. The question had been raised about happiness in Book I (1099b9–11). Meno opens his conversation with Socrates by immediately posing this apparently disinterested question (*Meno* 70a) and indicates what motivates his asking it only in the end, when he reports that Gorgias, whom he is presumably paying well, restricts himself to teaching an art of speaking without making any claim to transmit human excellence (95c).

9. The conflation of teaching and experience in the statement about intellectual virtue at the beginning of Book II recalls Socrates' argument in the *Meno* about virtue as knowledge, which begins with the claim that virtue should be teachable if it proves to be *epistēmē* and ends by demonstrating that if virtue is profitable, it must be *phronēsis*, or guided by *phronēsis* (cf. 87c and 88c–d).

10. Plato's Eleatic Stranger holds up the standard of "the precise itself," which is determined not just by the arithmetic measure but by the measure of the mean (*Statesman* 284b–d; cf. n. 25 below).

11. Aristotle tries to deflate expectations for precision in his own account when he characterizes it as being "in outline" only (e.g., 1098a20–24, 1103b34–1104a4). Otfried Höffe finds the ground of that methodological restriction in the tension between the particularity of any intended action and the generality of philosophical expression ("Ethik als praktische Philosophie-Methodische Überlegungen," p. 37).

12. The model for the inquiry was supposed to be the carpenter, who studies the right angle sufficiently for his purpose, not the geometer, who is a "contemplator of the truth" (1098a29–32); but the mean will be introduced twice in the course of Book II as an object of *theōria* (1104a11 and 1106a24–26).

13. The opportune, according to the Eleatic Stranger, belongs with the measured, the fitting, the needful, and other such standards in the class of "the measure of the mean," which can never be reduced to mathematical determinacy (*Statesman* 284e).

14. Aristotle indicates the extent to which such pleasure must be learned and what its limits are by illustrating it with the most paradoxical case—only a moderate man takes pleasure in abstaining from pleasures—and then admitting the most obvious exception—a courageous person can be expected to face danger without pain, but perhaps not with pleasure (1104b4–8).

15. See appendix 1. Plato's Athenian Stranger, after defining education in just this way, encapsulates its import in his image of the human being as a puppet, jerked around by the cords of pleasure and pain, unless controlled by the forceful cord of the law (see *Laws* 644b–d and 653a–c).

16. This point becomes explicit in the last chapter of the *Ethics*, in a discussion of the limit of the power of speeches and the need for the compulsion of the law (1179b4–18).

17. Plato's Athenian Stranger, having presented the slave doctor who treats slaves as a model for all existing legislation, imagines such a doctor coming upon "a free doctor conversing with a free patient and almost philosophizing in using *logoi*": he would break into laughter and say, "You fool, you are not healing the sick one, but almost educating, as if he needed to become not healthy but a doctor" (*Laws* 857c–d).

18. See appendix 1. The single reference to Plato in the first book of the *Ethics* praised him for his perplexity about whether inquiry should proceed from the principles or to the principles (1095a32–33); the single reference to Plato in the second book praises him for recognizing the importance of molding pleasure and pain through habituation (1104b12–13), which is one way certain sorts of first principles can be acquired (1098b3–4).

19. The conclusion Socrates is putting into question here is that virtue appears to come to be by "divine fate" (*Meno* 100b).

20. The eye and the horse are two of the three examples Socrates employs in the *ergon* argument of *Republic* I, which is supposed to establish that justice renders the subject in whom it comes to be present able to accomplish his proper *ergon* and that, for this reason, the just are happier than the unjust (352d–354a). The other example Socrates offers is an artifact, the pruning hook, which is not the only thing that can accomplish the function it performs but the best thing for it (see Benardete's discussion in *Socrates' Second Sailing*, pp. 30–32). This would imply that there is a function the human being, or the soul, is "designed" to do best. The question of why Plato includes such an example is, perhaps, more difficult than the question of why Aristotle does not.

21. We expect to hear of the "serious man"—analogous to the "serious eye" and the "serious horse"—but the *spoudaios*, who will be called upon when the argument needs to rely on an appeal to authority, is replaced at this moment by the "*agathos anthropos*."

22. In discussing the difference between the role of the mean in the formation of a virtuous disposition and its role as a measure of actions that spring from a virtuous disposition, Sarah Broadie suggests that this double role indicates the "Janus-quality" of Aristotle's conception of moral virtue: excellence of character is, on the one hand, a reflection in the individual of the community in which he was reared; on the other, it is the source of the mature individual's own response to a particular situation. Broadie finds it uncertain whether Aristotle himself is aware of shifting between the mean applied to quality of character and the mean applied to a particular response in feelings or actions (*Ethics with Aristotle*, pp. 95–96). There seem to be two separate, though related issues here: first, the mean as a state of character versus the mean as a measure of action and, second, the distinction in the latter case between actions guided by others in order to develop the proper disposition and actions chosen by the individual out of a formed disposition.

23. This is the report of Athenaeus (X.412–13), cited by W. F. R. Hardie in "Aristotle's Doctrine That Virtue Is a 'Mean,'" p. 36.

24. Such requirements lead to Rosalind Hursthouse's objections (in "A False Doctrine of the Mean," pp. 108–9) against J. O. Urmson's attempt to defend Aristotle's teaching that being disposed to exhibit a particular emotion "to the right amount" is a reasonable way to understand excellence of character ("Aristotle's Doctrine of the Mean," p. 163).

25. Socrates pursues a similar strategy when he holds up to the Sophist Protagoras the promise of a hedonistic calculus (*Protagoras* 356c–357e) without acknowledging the measure of the mean, even though he had introduced it as a standard for the proper length of their speeches (338b). Only if we can establish the measure of the mean as something other than the mathematical measure, the Eleatic Stranger realizes, will we be able to identify the statesman as "a scientific knower of matters of action" (*Statesman* 284c).

26. Consider the statesman who, if he ruled by knowledge of the mean, might have to purge the city for its own good, but against the law, by killing or banishing citizens (*Statesman* 294c–e; cf. Benardete, "Plato's *Statesman*," in *The Being of the Beautiful*, pt. 3, pp. 129–30).

27. See *Gorgias* 463a, 464c, 465a, where Socrates links *stochazomai* with aiming at pleasure and not the good or the best; at 502e, he criticizes contemporary rhetoricians for not speaking with a view to the best, not *stochazomenoi* at that end. Cf. Socrates' description of the role of "guesswork," in contrast with mathematical measure, in music, at *Philebus* 55e–56a, 62c. On virtue's access to the mean as a matter of improvising and conjecturing, see Nancy Sherman, *The Fabric of Character: Aristotle's Theory of Virtue*, p. 25.

28. Urmson thinks it "perfectly plain, in fact, that for Aristotle what is primarily in a mean is a settled state of character" ("Aristotle's Doctrine of the Mean," p. 161). But the argument has derived that characterization, on rather questionable grounds, from the very different notion of the mean as a target in feelings and action.

29. Both choice and the *phronimos*, Francis Sparshott observes, seem to come out of nowhere (*Taking Life Seriously: A Study of the Argument of the "Nicomachean Ethics,"* pp. 98–99).

30. The restriction of choice to the means and never the end is the way it looks, at least, within the discussion of responsibility (1111b26–27); by Book VI the argument will look at choice from a very different perspective (cf. 1139a32–b5).

31. The discovery of the mean by "the practically insightful person," in Deborah Achtenberg's description, means that "the virtuous individual would look at the situation he or she is in, in all its complex particularity and, through perception, deliberation, deliberative imagination, and practical insight, determine what is good and then, as a result, desire it, and, as a result of the desire do it" (*Cognition of Value in Aristotle's Ethic: Promise of Enrichment, Threat of Destructions*, p. 122).

32. The mean of action is to be understood on the basis of Pythagorean principles, as Aristotle indicates, in which a limit is imposed on the single continuum of the unlimited (1106b27–35): it is like considering the unlimited range of hotter and colder and picking out the limit not simply as a mathematical measure but as the point that is "just right" for someone in some circumstances (cf. *Philebus* 25e–26b). The mean of character, in contrast, divides the indeterminate continuum of a passion into the triad of *eidē* made up of one virtue and two vices: character, unlike action, can be subject to something like the process by which Theuth produced, out of the indefinite continuum of sound, an alphabet of discrete elements, classified into distinct kinds (see *Philebus* 18a–d, and Benardete's analysis in *The Tragedy and Comedy of Life*, pp. 121–26).

33. This dynamic structure can be found in Socrates' analysis of the soul in Book IV of the *Republic*, where *thumos*, or the spirited part of the soul, is first assumed to be one with the calculating part of the soul over against desire, then allied with desire over against calculation (439e–441c; cf. chap. 4, n. 7, below).

34. It is not entirely clear why Aristotle distinguishes courage and moderation in this regard: while a disproportion "in the thing itself" makes us think that rashness is more like courage and, hence, we lay down cowardice to be the real contrary of courage, a disproportion "in us" makes the desire for pleasure, to which we are more inclined by nature, appear more contrary to the mean and, so, we speak only of indulgence as the contrary to moderation (1109a8–8–12, 1109a14–19).

35. There are three other references to the *kalon* in Book II, all in the third chapter, on the role of pleasure and pain in habituation and their possible conflict with the noble or beautiful (1104b10–11, 1104b30–31, 1105a1).

36. Socrates offers this image of his "second sailing": in their direct approach to the beings, his predecessors risked blinding their soul, just as one would blind his eyes trying to look directly at the sun in an eclipse; Socrates sought to protect himself from that danger by turning to the examination of opinions in *logoi*, just as one would protect one's eyes by looking at the eclipsed sun indirectly, through an image (*Phaedo* 99d–100a). The "second sailing" Aristotle now proposes, which is supposed to replace the direct route to the mean, will be reflected in a pattern

behind the apparently unsystematic discussion of the virtues and vices in Books III and IV (see "The Disappearance of the Beautiful" in chap. 3 below, and appendix 2, "Virtues and Vices").

37. Cf. *Ethics* 1109a30–32, and *Odyssey* XII.219. The line Aristotle cites is from the speech Odysseus makes to the pilot of his ship. Odysseus himself has been warned of the twofold danger they face and the need to calculate which of the alternative evils is worse, but he tells his companions, as he admits in narrating the event, only of the path they must avoid, while he is silent about the threat of the terrible fate that awaits them in the other direction (cf. XII.55–126 with XII.201–259); he realizes, apparently, that they might not proceed at all if they knew what awaited them. It is Circe who provides Odysseus with this warning, though Aristotle, oddly, refers to Calypso. Is it possible that he means to evoke the connotation of that name, "the hidden," just when the hiddenness—or absence—of the mean is being acknowledged? An even more playful thought: is there a wordplay on "*Kalupso*" and "*kalon*," which in the previous line characterizes the hidden mean and the difficulty of hitting it directly?

38. Children who don't obey the admonitions of their elders are like bent wood, in the image of Plato's Protagoras, and must be straightened out with threats and blows (*Protagoras* 325d).

39. Harry Jaffa is alerted to the importance of this "perhaps" by Aquinas' omission of it. It is noteworthy, Jaffa observes, that there is no qualification in Aristotle's statement about cases of actions deserving pardon, but only about the possibility of actions that could never be pardoned (*Thomism and Aristotelianism*, pp. 104–109). In support of that possibility Aristotle chooses a fictional example (from a play of Euripides now lost): there is something ridiculous in the plea of Alcmaeon to excuse his deed of matricide because of the threat that motivated it— apparently a curse of childlessness and famine (1110a26–29). This certainly looks like an unacceptable appeal to compulsion; but it does not rule out the possibility of some situation in which even matricide would be pardonable.

40. Aristotle lists, as possible cases of particular ignorance, the agent, the action, that which is affected by the action, the instrument, the effect, or the manner of the action (1111a3–6). The first case, in particular, suggests that the natural home of involuntary action done through ignorance is tragic drama, which paradigmatically portrays the agent who does not know who he is. David Daube discusses how and why Aristotle includes under actions done through ignorance cases both of error and accident, though neither, he argues, carves out a place for a special status of negligence. What might otherwise be considered negligence, as a lesser degree of guilt than voluntary crime, is rather, as Daube puts it, "the soil in which the latter grows. It is the sloth, the reprehensible lack of moral fibre, which results in, and grounds your responsibility for, evil actions . . ." (*Roman Law: Linguistic, Social and Philosophical Aspects*, p. 139). Cf. chap. 3, n. 72, below.

41. The question naturally arises whether the end of *boulēsis* is the good or the apparent good: if the former, no one "wants" what he mistakenly takes to be good;

if the latter, one must admit that there is nothing "wanted by nature." Aristotle proposes that while each person wants that which appears good to him, the end that is truly and simply wanted is the good; but that can be identified, for the moment, only by appeal to the authority of the serious person (*ho spoudaios*), "as if he were a canon and a measure" (1113a22–33).

42. Susan Sauvé Meyer calls attention to Aristotle's concern with rejecting the "Platonic asymmetry thesis," according to which our good actions are voluntary, while our bad ones are not. But when it comes to the issue of responsibility for character, "Aristotle is keenly aware," Meyer notes, "as Plato was before him, that only someone who has been raised in optimal conditions will have correct views about what is fine and shameful," and he insists at the end of the *Ethics*, accordingly, on the need to be raised under correct laws (see "Aristotle on the Voluntary," pp. 151–56).

CHAPTER 3

1. The first statement is by W. D. Ross (*Aristotle*, p. 197); the second, by W. F. R. Hardie (*Aristotle's Ethical Theory*, p. 20).

2. The political philosopher, Leo Strauss observes, starts from the prephilosophic understanding of the attitudes or actions generally praised, but in raising the question, What is virtue? is led to move beyond that dimension, as Aristotle's selection and arrangement of the virtues illustrates (see "On Classical Political Philosophy," in *The Rebirth of Classical Political Rationalism: An Introduction to the Thought of Leo Strauss*, p. 62).

3. See appendix 2, "Virtues and Vices."

4. The original list in Book II ended with two such dispositions—shame and righteous indignation (*nemesis;* 1108a30–1108b6). On the disappearance of that final disposition from the discussion in Book IV, see "The Disappearance of the Beautiful" in this chapter, and n. 45 below.

5. "The blush of shame and the paleness of fear," Seth Benardete writes, "comprehend the moral virtues" ("On Greek Tragedy," in *The Argument of the Action*, p. 140). A more radical disclosure will come at the end of the *Ethics*, when the bodily root of the passions is extended to the virtuous dispositions themselves (1178a14–16).

6. Equally striking is the absence—with one telling exception—of any reference to the *kalon* in Book V (see the discussion of 1136b17–22 in the last section of this chapter and in n. 75 below). "*Phusis*" and related terms come up repeatedly in Book III's discussion of the voluntary and involuntary (1110a25, 1112a25–32, 1113a21, 1114a24–26, 1114b14–18)—most importantly, concerning the question of responsibility for one's character. After that, "*physis*" comes up in Book III not in reference to courage or moderation but only about *thumos* as a passion that can be mistaken for courage (1117a4), and about certain desires (1118b9–19) or about pain as destructive of the nature of an animal (1119a22–24).

7. As Jaffa shows, by way of a critical assessment of Aquinas's commentary, although Aristotle recognizes "the ultimate dependence of morality upon a transmoral good," he sets out to treat "the whole of morality, and even the various lev-

els of morality, as having a kind of independent existence, which must be grasped primarily (but not ultimately) from the point of view of those who actually live on these various levels" (*Thomism and Aristotelianism*, pp. 143−44).

8. Yet in comparison with the *Politics* (at least the first book), the level of the inquiry in the *Ethics* seems to stand at a far greater distance from convention: while the *Ethics* assumes from the start that its subject is human virtue, or virtues of the human being as such, the *Politics* speaks of activities or virtues proper to man versus woman, Greek versus barbarian, free man versus slave. That the first book of the *Politics* does, in fact, lead to the recognition of human virtue and human nature is an argument Evanthia Speliotis works out in "Women and Slaves in Aristotle's *Politics* I," p. 83.

9. For just this reason, one might say of the description of moral phenomena in *Ethics* III−IV what David Bolotin says of Aristotle's *Physics:* though it is a masterful description of natural phenomena, it cannot be understood as a phenomenology (*An Approach to Aristotle's "Physics": With Particular Attention to the Role of His Manner of Writing*, pp. 2−4).

10. On Socrates' account of "demotic virtue" as a hedonistic calculus and his playful description of those whose virtue is not grounded in philosophy, see *Phaedo* 68c−69c; 82a−b; see also chap. 2, n. 6, above. Reflecting on the experience of the turnaround of the soul in his cave image, Socrates speaks of the dispositions produced by habits and practice as "so-called virtues of the soul," which are really closer to virtues of the body (*Republic* 518d−e; cf. 500d). In the *Charmides*, according to Alfarabi, Plato investigated the moderation generally accepted in cities and what the moderation is that is true moderation; in the *Laches*, he investigated what the multitude believes to be courage and what true courage is ("The Philosophy of Plato" 23, in *The Philosophy of Aristotle and Plato*, p. 60).

11. Distinguishing these two points might help clarify the debate Victor Gourevitch and Hilail Gildin conduct about Leo Strauss's understanding of the divide between genuine and vulgar virtue (see Gildin, "Leo Strauss and the Crisis of Liberal Democracy," p. 102 n. 6.) According to Gourevitch, Strauss understands genuine virtue, which is only philosophical virtue, and vulgar virtue, which includes all political excellence, to be mutually exclusive; there is no in-between, no "halfway house," possible (see Gourevitch, "Philosophy and Politics, I−II," esp. p. 305). But to deny the possibility of any genuine "intellectual virtue" in the political sphere, Gildin objects, would mean there is no basis for discerning any difference in merit between the gentleman and the great ruler or founder. Of course, the intellectual virtue that distinguishes the political leader or founder is not philosophy but *phronēsis*.

12. *Laches* is led to an inconsistency, Christopher Bruell explains, when he proposes the definition of courage as a certain endurance of soul, which would be most impressive in the greatest dangers, while believing at the same time that a virtue could not be harmful; for endurance, in that case, if it is to count as courage, would have to be governed by prudence, though prudence aims at minimizing the dan-

ger and risk that make endurance impressive to Laches. To bring out this problem, Bruell notes, Socrates employs a narrow, seemingly "un-Aristotelian" interpretation of prudence; but "to follow the path sketched by Aristotle," he goes on to suggest, "would be to postpone the surfacing of a difficulty rather than to remove it" (*On the Socratic Education: An Introduction to the Shorter Platonic Dialogues*, pp. 57–58).

13. See *Laches* 193a and 194a, where Socrates points to their own conduct in pursuit of the question, What is courage? as the key to understanding courage. Benardete finds a counterpart in the *Charmides*, where the search for what *sōphrosunē* is leads to the suggestion of a "hermeneutical *sōphrosunē*," which consists in "questioning the wisdom of the authority to which one defers" ("On Interpreting Plato's *Charmides*," in *The Argument of the Action*, p. 243; cf. "Plato's *Laches*: A Question of Definition," in *The Argument of the Action*, p. 273).

14. See the discussion later in this chapter, in "The Disappearance of the Beautiful," of the way courage and moderation operate as opposing principles in determining the most anonymous of the virtues, love of honor (1125b9–26).

15. The Eleatic Stranger in Plato's *Statesman* thus illustrates the possibility of variance within virtue by courage and moderation, whose roots lie in the natural inclination of individuals to be either slow and cautious and patient or quick and bold and impetuous (306a–308b).

16. See *Apology* 28e–29a. Socrates first criticizes Laches' proposal for its failing to meet the demand for a universal definition (*Laches* 191e); in the end, he criticizes Nicias's proposal—courage is knowledge of fearful and confidence-inspiring things in war and everything else—for comprehending the whole of virtue and not capturing specifically the part being sought (199e).

17. The mean for which the courageous person would be praised is the measure of the stance toward fear within human limits, while the cowardly or rash would be blamed for falling short of or exceeding it. Aristotle's silence about how the courageous person would act in regard to terrors beyond human limits should be connected, Jaffa remarks, with Book III's statement about actions that are pardonable because done under pressures no human being could withstand (see *Thomism and Aristotelianism*, pp. 98–109; and chap. 2, n. 39, above).

18. *Iliad* XXII.100, 107. Priam's allusion to Hector's conduct at this same moment will provide Aristotle's only illustration of "divine or heroic" virtue in Book VII of the *Ethics* (1145a18–22; see "A New Beginning: From Bestial to Divine" in chap. 5). Although Hector is moved by shame and the desire for honor to stand and fight, as soon as Achilles comes into view, he is filled with fear and begins to run. After circling the walls of the city three times in flight, he finally takes a stand only because Athena comes in the guise of his brother and deceives him into thinking he is not alone. The deficiency of political courage, in its motivation by shame, is confirmed by the one other case cited in *Ethics* III—Diomedes' unwillingness to flee from Hector as he imagines Hector's future boast before the Trojans (*Iliad* VIII.139–156). Nestor, who has recognized a sign from Zeus, rightly urges Diomedes to flee and responds to his worry about Hector's reproach by assuring him that it would never

be convincing to the Trojans, who have all experienced the effects of his power as a warrior; Diomedes, unlike Hector, is persuaded to overcome his sense of shame and act prudently.

19. The opening discussion of courage leads, in what is almost a dialogue form, to the conclusion that the virtue shows itself, above all, in facing the noble danger of death in battle. Courage, as Laurence Berns observes, "first comes to sight in its most elementary and most conspicuous form, in the perspective of the citizen soldier." But once political courage is introduced as a mere likeness of the true virtue, "the hero of the introductory dialogue on courage now has first place among the likenesses" ("Spiritedness in Ethics and Politics: A Study in Aristotelian Psychology," pp. 343–44). Cf. Lee Ward, on the role that honor plays in political courage and its relation to the noble (in "Nobility and Necessity: The Problem of Courage in Aristotle's *Nicomachean Ethics*," pp. 80–82).

20. See appendix 1, and introduction, n. 13, above. Cox calls attention to Aristotle speaking here of "*ho Sokratēs*," indicating the Socrates of the Platonic dialogues, in contrast with the historical individual ("Aristotle's Treatment of Socrates in the *Nicomachean Ethics*," p. 141). Cox cites in this regard Alexander Grant (*The "Ethics" of Aristotle*, 2: 188), who in turn refers to Bishop Fitzgerald. Roger Crisp mentions this source on "the Socrates" as a literary character (W. Fitzgerald, *Selections from the "Nicomachean Ethics" of Aristotle*, p. 163) in "Socrates and Aristotle on Happiness and Virtue," p. 55. While the significance of "*ho Sokratēs*" as a reference to the Platonic character is convincing, it is not obvious why it should appear only in the first of the seven references to Socrates in the *Ethics*.

21. This is confirmed in the *Eudemian Ethics*, which begins on the same note: "Socrates the older believed the *telos* is to know virtue, reasonably, since he believed all the virtues to be forms of *epistēmē*" (1216b2). Later in the work, however, Aristotle explicitly distinguishes the kind of skill or experience that gives the experts confidence, which is their knowledge of means of rescue from dangers, from what Socrates must be thinking of, which is knowledge of the things truly fearful (1229a15–16, 1230a6).

In the *Protagoras*, Socrates at first appeals to the knowledge of the expert—illustrated by divers who dive into wells boldly because of the skill they possess—in his attempt to get the Sophist to admit that courage belongs to the whole of virtue through its association with knowledge (349e–350a); but as the argument unfolds it arrives finally at the understanding of courage as *sophia* concerning the things that are frightening and those that are not (360d; cf. note 23 below). See Gerald Mara's discussion of the "intellectualism" Aristotle ascribes to Socrates: while it might be an accurate representation of some things Socrates says, it seems "dramatically at variance with much of what he does, for Socratic practice"—as Mara goes on to demonstrate—"is frequently incongruous with a strong intellectualist foundation for virtue" (*Socrates' Discursive Democracy*, pp. 62–82).

22. The conversation in the *Laches* begins with two fathers seeking advice about whether it is worthwhile to have their sons take lessons from the latest teacher

of hoplite fighting; while Laches finds the worth of such training questionable, Nicias encourages it, on the grounds that such an *epistēmē* can make an individual "bolder and more courageous than himself" (*Laches* 182c). Nicias—as Thucydides' portrait of him in the Sicilian expedition shows so vividly (*The Peloponnesian War Books* VI–VII)—is a man driven by fear and superstition, who would welcome an *epistēmē* that could take the place of what Laches calls "endurance of soul." The distorted form of the Socratic teaching that appears in the definition of courage proposed by Nicias in the *Laches* has a striking counterpart in the *Charmides*, regarding the question, what is *sōphrosunē*? (see n. 27 below).

23. Of all the virtues of character, courage seems to be the most recalcitrant to this absorption into knowledge, and its unification with the other virtues, perhaps, the most challenging task. Plato's Protagoras, at least, after granting to Socrates the unity of four of the virtues—wisdom, moderation, justice and holiness—holds out for the independence of courage (*Protagoras* 349d); in the end, however, he has no way to avoid Socrates' conclusion that courage must be linked with the other virtues if it amounts to wisdom concerning what is frightening and what is not (360d).

24. *Thumos* is missing, to begin with, from the two analyses of the human soul in *Ethics* I.13 and VI.1 (see chap. 4, n. 7, below). Spiritedness finds a powerful expression in *nemesis*, or righteous indignation at the undeserved good fortune of others; but that experience, which concludes the list of virtues in Book II, disappears entirely from the discussion of virtues in Book IV, and *thumos* with it. One might most expect to hear of *thumos* in a discussion of crime and punishment; but the account in Book V of corrective justice speaks only of compensation for loss, while ignoring the thumotic demand for punishment. *Thumos* does make an appearance in Book VII (in Chapter 6), when Aristotle's exploration of the psychology of the divided soul is extended from bodily desires to the passion of spiritedness.

25. In admitting, though, that the courageous are spirited (*thumoeideis*), since *thumos* is impetuous in the face of dangers, Aristotle indicates a distinctively human character by borrowing Plato's term for what is *thumos*-like, once spiritedness becomes an ally with calculation (1116b26; cf. *Republic* 440e–441a).

26. The appeal to confidence might seem necessary simply because the deficiency in regard to fear is so rare that Aristotle has to assign it a name, "fearlessness," not at work in ordinary language (1115b24–26), while the commonly labeled vice of "rashness" can readily be understood as an excess of confidence. In the case of moderation, however, the deficiency in regard to desire for pleasure is so rare among human beings that here too Aristotle must assign a name, "insensibility," not at work in ordinary language (1119a5–11); but while the sphere of moderation also includes two feelings—not only pleasures of a certain sort, but also pain created by their absence—the two are not contraries, like fear and confidence, where an excess of one belongs together with a deficiency of the other.

27. It is striking that *sōphrosunē* is never called an "*aretē*" in the *Charmides*. Its identification as scientific knowledge, in fact the architectonic knowledge, is a position espoused not by Socrates but by Critias, future member of the Thirty

Tyrants, who has found in Socratic principles the promise of a justification for tyrannical political power.

28. The *kalon* appeared previously in the remark that the moderate person pursues pleasures that lead to health and good condition, and other pleasures as well if they are not impediments to those ends or not contrary to the *kalon* (1119a16–18). The concern for nobility, as Susan Collins observes, is hardly at the forefront of moderation ("The Moral Virtues in Aristotle's *Nicomachean Ethics*," p. 136). It is, on the other hand, moderation that makes most explicit the relation in which all the ethical virtues stand to philosophy, and it does so through its aspiration to the *kalon* as the beautiful.

29. It is in this light that Socrates could propose the paradoxical identification of the true virtue of moderation with a kind of madness (cf. *Phaedrus* 249d, 254e).

30. In characterizing the private character of liberality—or, rather, its related vices—in contrast with its public counterpart, Aristotle speaks rather surprisingly, as Stuart Warner has brought to my attention, of the tyrant: however lavish the tyrant may be in spending, he is not said to be prodigal, since he does not outstrip his own resources, nor is he said to exhibit the vice of meanness, however unjust or impious he may be in acquiring wealth (1120b25–27, 1122a3–7).

31. The philosophical nature, Socrates explains to Adeimantus, could never partake of illiberality, since pettiness (*smikrologia*) is most contrary to a soul that always seeks the whole, and magnificence (*megaloprepeia*) would be exhibited most of all by an intellect concerned with the contemplation of all time and all being (*Republic* 486a; cf. 487a, 490c, 494b).

32. The magnificent person, who seems to be some kind of expert in contemplating the fitting and in spending tastefully on great things (1122a34–35), is bound to be someone of great wealth, ancestry, and renown (1122b29–35), who always considers how to carry out his project most beautifully and splendidly (1122b8–10), to accomplish a big and beautiful *ergon* (1122b15–16).

33. The science sought for in the *Metaphysics* is primary either because it is of the highest being or because it is a universal science of being as such (see, esp., 1026a24–33). The beautiful stands to the just, one might then say, as theology does to ontology. The analogy is not merely a formal one: the great-souled person is, Aristotle implies, like a god in the city (1123b17–20), even if it is equally puzzling in both cases what need such a being would have for the honor that can be offered to him or the benefit he could receive from it.

34. The *megalopsuchos* is said to be unable to live in relation to another, except a friend (1124b31–1125a1), but the problematic character of friendship for such an individual is suggested by the discussion of self-love in Chapter 8 of Book IX. See Jacob Howland's analysis of the great-souled man, whose unwillingness to acknowledge his dependence on anyone results in his proneness to "tragic error" ("Aristotle's Great-Souled Man," pp. 38, 47–53).

35. The term occurs in the *Nicomachean Ethics* only here and once in the last chapter, with the claim that speeches are insufficient to turn the many toward *ka-*

lokagathia (1179b10). The last chapter of the *Eudemian Ethics*, in contrast, is devoted to an extended analysis of *kalokagathia* as perfect or complete virtue (1249a17).

36. Thucydides' Alcibiades, urging the Athenians to undertake the grand adventure of the Sicilian expedition under his leadership, begins his speech this way: For someone who thinks big (*mega phronounta*), it is not unjust to be unwilling to be equal (*Peloponnesian War* VI.16.4). In *Alcibiades II*, Socrates speaks of Alcibiades' *megalopsuchia*, which he calls "one the most beautiful names of folly" (140c, 150c).

37. See *Symposium* 216e, 218d; and my discussion in "Socratic *Eironeia*," pp. 143–50. Alcibiades and Socrates appear together, as Martin Sitte first called to my attention, in the *Posterior Analytics*, when Aristotle offers *megalopsuchia* as an example of the problem of defining a genus with several species. In thinking of the great-souled man, one might have in mind Alcibiades or Achilles or Ajax, all of whom cannot bear to be insulted, or perhaps Socrates or Lysander, whose characteristic is to be unaffected by good or bad fortune; but if these traits have nothing in common, there must be two *eidē* of *megalopsuchia* (97b18). Cf. Howland, "Aristotle's Great-Souled Man," pp. 32–33.

38. *Megalopsuchia* had been introduced on the model of the body, which could be beautiful only if big. Its magnitude, however, can prevent what is big from appearing beautiful to those who look up from below and afar, who would see distorted proportions. To overcome that problem requires what Plato calls an art of phantastics, able to adjust the proportions of what is big so as to appear well formed from the perspective of the viewer (*Sophist* 235d–236c). The *eironeia* practiced by the great-souled person might be thought of as just such an art, practiced on one's own person.

39. Aristotle singles out the disposition of sincerity to confirm our *trust* that every virtue is a mean state between two extremes (1127a16–20). The special status of sincerity as a virtuous mean might make sense from within the horizon of ethical virtue; but if Aristotle wants to sanction that horizon, he makes a funny choice to do so by appealing to the case that treats the admittedly graceful Socratic practice of *eironeia* as a vice (1127b22–26).

40. See appendix 2.

41. *Aidōs*, as a feeling of respect, which is found to be suitable for youth, is replaced in midsentence by *aischunē*, as a feeling of disgrace, which no one would praise in the mature, on the grounds that the decent person (*ho epieikēs*) would not "voluntarily" do the base things that arouse it (1128b19–22). After the extended analysis of "the voluntary" with which Book III began, this remark is the only time in the entire discussion of the virtues that the term appears. The description of the *epieikēs* here is transferred to the *phronimos* in Book VII, when Aristotle considers the opinion that it would be strange if the same person could be prudent and akratic, since no one would say that the *phronimos* does base things voluntarily (1146a5–7).

42. See *Rhetoric* 1384a, where the subject of discussion is *aischunē*, while *aidōs* is mentioned only in a proverb, "Shame is in the eyes."

43. Hegel holds up Sophocles' *Oedipus Tyrannus* as the paradigmatic ancient drama on just these grounds (*Vorlesungen über die Aesthetik,* pp. 545–46).

44. See *Poetics* 1452b34–36, and Benardete's discussion of the point in connection with *Oedipus Tyrannus,* in "On Greek Tragedy," in *The Argument of the Action,* pp. 134–35.

45. See my discussion of this *pathos* in "Ethical Reflection and Righteous Indignation: *Nemesis* in the *Nicomachean Ethics,*" pp. 127–40.

46. If, the point is first argued, the just is the equal—as it seems to everyone without any *logos*—and the equal is a mean, the just would be some sort of mean (1131a13–15). In the case of distributive justice, this is the proportionate (1131b10–12); in the case of corrective justice, the just is a mean between greater and lesser in accordance with arithmetic proportion, while the judge himself, who is "justice ensouled," is some sort of mean between disputing parties (1132a24–30). In exchange, money is in some sense a mean, since it measures all things, and so excess and deficiency (1133a20–21). Finally, doing justice (*dikaiopragma*) is a mean between doing injustice and suffering injustice (1133b30–32), though these hardly look like vices of excess and deficiency relative to the mean.

47. The turn from the virtues of character to justice recalls the movement of the *Republic* from the music education, designed to mold the guardians' character, to the ordering of institutions, such as the abolition of private property, which suggests that the education was not sufficient.

48. As Fred Miller argues, however, Aristotle's treatment of justice contains the grounds for a defense of certain rights of the individual: distributive justice determines in a distribution the just claim or right of each person to a portion of the whole, corrective justice determines in a dispute "the right (*to dikaion*) of each party, that is, what is his own (*to hauton*)," and reciprocal justice determines in an exchange "the right of each party to the value of their commodity" (*Nature, Justice, and Rights in Aristotle's "Politics,"* pp. 71–74). Douglas Den Uyl and Douglas Rasmussen undertake the project of developing a theory of rights based on Aristotelian natural-end ethics in *Liberty and Nature: An Aristotelian Defense of Liberal Order* (see, esp., pp. 58–76).

49. It is because Aristotle's treatment of justice is to such a large extent an "abstraction from the soul," Joseph Cropsey argues, that the later discussion of friendship is required (see "Justice and Friendship in the *Nicomachean Ethics,*" p. 265). Delba Winthrop examines several respects in which friendship, as described in Books VIII and IX, seems to fulfill what justice alone cannot (see "Aristotle and Theories of Justice"; and, on it, chap. 6, n. 20, below).

50. Socrates supports his separation of *thumos* as a part of the soul distinct from the desiring part by telling the story of Leontius, whose longing for justice turns into self-hatred in the conflict between his desire to see criminality punished and his revulsion at the ugliness of that desire, when justice should be beautiful (*Republic* 439e–440a). The second step of Socrates' analysis, which is supposed to separate *thumos* from the calculating part of the soul, is based on the inner conflict Odysseus

experiences in carrying out his aim to punish the suitors (see my discussion in "The Thumotic Soul," pp. 151–67). When Aristotle finally admits, at the end of Book V, that injustice could be understood as an inner disorder, and justice as an inner order, he speaks of the relation between the rational and nonrational parts of the soul but says nothing about *thumos*.

51. Even if justice, as the lawful, does aim at the common advantage, it "accords with human flourishing or the good order of the soul," Susan Collins concludes, "only inasmuch as that order preserves or contributes to the common good" ("Justice and the Dilemma of Moral Virtue in Aristotle's *Nicomachean Ethics*," p. 120).

52. See *Politics* 1264b15–21. When Adeimantus protests that Socrates' guardians, deprived of all private property, are not being allowed much happiness, Socrates responds that while it would not be wondrous if the guardians' way of life did turn out happy, their purpose in constructing the city was to aim for the happiness not just of a part but of the whole (*Republic* 419e–420d).

53. Thomas Aquinas discusses the view of Bias, one of the seven wise men, that legal justice aims at performing actions useful to another, either the community or the ruler, in contrast with other virtues, like moderation, that aim to achieve the good of the individual (*Commentary on Aristotle's "Nicomachean Ethics"* 909; p. 286).

54. The personified laws of Athens warn Socrates that if he were to escape to a well-governed city, he would be considered a corrupter of the laws and would confirm the jurors at his trial, since whoever is a corrupter of laws might be thought somehow a corrupter of young and mindless human beings (*Crito* 53b–c).

55. Reflecting on Socrates' ambivalence in the *Minos* about the status of law as a political community's decree and the necessary variability of law that entails, Christopher Bruell comments: "For a treatment of comparable delicacy, one would have to turn to Aristotle's discussion of general justice (the justice that consists in law-abidingness) in the first part of the fifth book of the *Nicomachean Ethics*" (*On the Socratic Education*, p. 9).

56. See *Politics* 1282b14–24. This is the only use of the precise phrase "political philosophy" (*philosophia politikē*) in either the *Ethics* or the *Politics*. It comes at the culmination of an examination of the disagreement among various regimes, each with a partial understanding of justice, and in particular the passionate debate between democrat and oligarch on what counts as equal (*Politics* 1280a17–25; cf. 1281a15–17, 1281b17–22).

57. Punishment, altogether absent from corrective justice, has a place in reciprocity, which takes into consideration whether the offense was voluntary or not. Compelling a thief to restore what he took, Aquinas comments, is enough to reestablish the equality of justice; but he should in addition be punished for the offense, which would be greater if it were voluntary (*Commentary on Aristotle's "Nicomachean Ethics"* 970; p. 308).

58. It is as if the Athenian Stranger were putting to work for his penal code the division Plato's Eleatic Stranger introduces, in his hunt for the sophist, when he separates hunting, as a furtive action, from combat, which is out in the open. The

sophist first shows up as a hunter, but the philosopher falls into that furtive class as well until some further feature can disentangle them (*Sophist* 219c–e, 222b–223b).

59. See 1131a7 and appendix 3, "Categories of Justice."

60. Describing his art of psychic midwifery to Theaetetus, Socrates speaks of the pride female midwives take in their art of matchmaking (*promnēstikē*), though they must avoid or conceal it out of fear of being accused of unjust and artless pandering (*progagōgia*); Socrates reveals his own version of the art when he goes on to describe how he sends off some of the young men, whom he cannot benefit, to be together with one of the "wise and inspired men," like Prodicus (*Theaetetus* 149d–150a, 151b). In Xenophon's *Symposium*, Socrates justifies his practice of procuring (*mastropeia*), while he praises Antisthenes for the related practice of pandering (*proagōgeia*), by which he brought together, for example, Callias and Prodicus (IV.56–64). Cf. Nalin Ranasinghe's discussion of Socratic pandering, in *The Soul of Socrates*, pp. 151–52. The case that precedes *proagōgeia* on the list of furtive actions in *Ethics* V is *pharmakeia*, which Socrates mentions as an instrument of the midwife (*Theaetetus* 149d) and which serves in the *Phaedrus* as an image for the dangerous power of the written word (274e–275b).

61. To explain how reciprocity could be a necessary foundation for the political community and not just for the exchange of goods, Bernard Yack calls our attention to the notion of reciprocal equality applied in *Politics* II (1261a30) to the requirement for ruling and being ruled in turn (see *The Problems of a Political Animal*, pp. 136–40). Jill Frank analyzes the ways in which reciprocal justice, which involves phronetic judgment, "presupposes and teaches freedom, that is, it presupposes and teaches equality and distinction among its practitioners and, thus, opens the way to their friendship" (*A Democracy of Distinction: Aristotle and the Work of Politics*, pp. 100–101).

62. In discussing the causes of faction in *Politics* V, Aristotle observes that everyone understands "the just simply" to be that in accordance with worth, though they disagree radically about the application of the principle (1301b36–39; cf. 1282b14–20). The Athenian Stranger identifies "the political just itself," which should be the aim of every legislator, with the kind of equality that distributes more to the greater and less to the smaller, giving the right measure to each according to nature (*Laws* 757b–d).

63. One might think of the earlier reference to "the *phusis* of justice and injustice" at the conclusion of the discussion of the just as the equal (1134a15) and the later reference to "the *phusis* of the equitable" (1137b27). On Aquinas's interpretation of the equitable in connection with the just by nature, see *Commentary on Aristotle's "Nicomachean Ethics"* 1086–7, and n. 67 below.

64. "For Aristotle," Strauss observes, "political philosophy is primarily and ultimately the quest for the political order that is best according to nature everywhere" (*The City and Man*, p. 17; cf. his *Natural Right and History*, pp. 156–57). Yack develops a plausible interpretation of Aristotle's conception of natural right by connecting it with his understanding of the political community as natural. Natural right, Yack

argues, is not a matter of nature supplying us with determinate standards of political justice, or an innate disposition to act justly; but it does dispose us to form political communities in which we argue about the intrinsically correct standards of political justice (*The Problems of a Political Animal*, pp. 59, 147).

65. Aristotle's formula brings to mind the image Socrates offers in the *Cratylus* for the names legislated by the "namegiver": while *pharmaka* embroidered with different colors and smells appear other to laymen, although they are in fact the same, to the physician investigating their *dunamis* they do appear the same. The expert who investigates the *dunamis* of names, likewise, should not be surprised if letters are added or transposed or subtracted or even if the underlying power appears in altogether different letters: the letters of the alphabet other than the vowels, for example, get names, which allow them to be pronounced by adding other letters (e.g., *beta*), but that addition doesn't prevent the name from revealing the nature of the letter—the silent *b*—intended by the lawgiver (393d–394b). Conventional laws, by analogy, would appear, in all their variety, other to the layman; but the expert investigating them might recognize an underlying *dunamis* that is one and the same, which would be just by nature.

66. In the *Minos*, Socrates' interlocutor appeals to sacrifices and burial as exemplary of the changing character of the lawful things (315b–d). Maimonides uses the example of sacrifices to address the claim that the commandments have been given merely for the sake of something being ordered. That is true of the details, he grants, but not of the general principles: although the offering of sacrifices has in itself a great and manifest utility, no cause will ever be found for the fact that one particular sacrifice consists in a lamb and another in a ram or that the victims should be one particular number or another (*The Guide of the Perplexed* III.26; 2:509).

67. As Aquinas interprets the passage, the superiority of the right hand by nature means that this is the case for the most part, though ambidexterity is an occasional exception: it is, analogously, just by nature that a deposit be returned in most cases, but there may be exceptions. Thinking, perhaps, of the counterexample Socrates presents to Cephalus, Aquinas sets legal justice, which is valid only for the most part, against the just by nature, which he links with equity. He has to prepare for this, however, by a paraphrase of Aristotle's text that changes "become" to "be"—"Now by nature the right hand is stronger, although some people *are* ambidextrous"—so the point is no longer about transformation of a potential (*Commentary on Aristotle's "Nicomachean Ethics"* 1028; p. 327).

68. See *Laws* 794d–e. The digression on right-handedness sets in motion an indirect path—which passes through the issues of nature and convention, education, war and peace, and the *telos* of the city and of human life—on its way to the problem of the equality of men and women (cf. 805a). The argument for ambidexterity, in Thomas Pangle's words, "is a 'stalking horse' for the sexual arrangement." If, Pangle wonders, ambidexterity stands for "all-around natural perfection," perhaps the argument is in fact a criticism of that standard, which leads to a recognition of society's need for divisions of labor, especially the sexual division (interpretative essay, in *The "Laws" of Plato*, pp. 480–81).

69. In *The Harmonization of the Two Opinions of the Two Sages,* Alfarabi sets out to overturn the prejudices of his time about the differences between Plato and Aristotle. Among those is the belief that Aristotle thought no moral habits are by nature but all undergo change, in contrast with Plato, for whom nature is thought to prevail over habit (par. 42–43; pp. 147–48).

70. In the course of constructing "the best city in speech," Socrates speculates about a philosophical artist who contemplates the just by nature as a pattern that could inform his own soul; but he goes on to consider what would happen if this artist were compelled to reproduce that pattern in public as well as in private (*Republic* 501b2). Glaucon finally comes to agree with Socrates that the model they have constructed can be found nowhere on earth but only in speeches or, perhaps, as a paradigm in heaven, for founding a city in oneself (592a–b).

71. The best regime Aristotle constructs in Book VII of the *Politics* is, Mary Nichols argues, "less an ideal model for politics than a lesson in its imperfection. Aristotle's designation of that regime as the 'best' is surely ironic" (*Citizens and Statesmen: A Study of Aristotle's "Politics,"* p. 145). The "best city" of *Politics* VII is characterized by its autotelic action—action that has its end in itself—and the model, Michael Davis argues, is philosophy; but Book III acknowledged the "obvious" way of transferring this model to the political sphere—awarding rule to those of extraordinary wisdom—only to show that it is impossible (*The Politics of Philosophy: A Commentary on Aristotle's "Politics,"* pp. 61, 126–27).

72. See appendix 3. Comparing this account with the earlier one, Robert Faulkner notes that "Book III's occasional reminders of nature are replaced by Book V's attention to the various regimes that yield various kinds of laws" ("Spontaneity, Justice, and Coercion: in *Nicomachean Ethics* Books III and V," pp. 82–89, esp. 88–89). According to the classification in Book V.8, damage or harm (*blabē*) is divided into error (*hamartēma*), an act committed in ignorance, and injustice (*adikēma*), an act done knowingly, the latter being the expression of an unjust character only when done out of choice. The former class is subdivided into accident (*atuchēma*), where the effect of an action is contrary to reasonable expectation, and culpable error (*hamartēma* in the strict sense). That distinction, Daube notes, is not articulated in Book III (though it is Aristotle's *Rhetoric,* 1374b4–10); but Book V incorporates both classes of involuntary action as species of *hamartēma* in a broad sense, so that, in accordance with Book III, even accident is understood as some kind of ignorance. Daube discusses why the deed from ignorance, as opposed to accident, held such "enormous fascination for the ancients"—both in Greek tragedy and in the Bible (*Roman Law,* pp. 141–42, 147–50).

73. It certainly sounds strange, Aristotle remarks, when Euripides' Alcmaeon, after confessing his deed of matricide, is asked, "each willing, or each not willing?" (1126a10–14). The same drama provided the illustration of a questionable claim for excusing action done under compulsion (1110a28–9).

74. "Does it not seem to you to be a shameful thing," Callicles asks Socrates, "to be in such a condition as I think you and the others are, who are forever pushing

further on in philosophy? For now, if someone seized you or anybody else of that sort of people and carried you off to prison, claiming that you were doing an injustice when you were not, you know that you would not have anything of use to say for yourself . . . and when you stood up in the law court, happening to face a very lowly and vicious accuser, you would die, if he wished to demand the death penalty for you" (*Gorgias* 486a–b, trans. by James Nichols). A similar sentiment animates Crito's effort to persuade Socrates to escape from prison (*Crito* 45c).

75. The proposal about greediness for the *kalon* anticipates the discussion of self-sacrifice in the account of friendship (1168b25–30, 1169a3–6).

76. Aristotle prepares for the discussion of equity with an apparent digression that leads to a radical conclusion (1137a5–26). People think it is in their power to act unjustly and, therefore, that it is easy to be just; but that is not so, Aristotle counters, with quite surprising examples: it is in one's power to commit adultery or offer a bribe, but it is not easy to do those things out of a certain disposition. Likewise, people think it is easy to know what is just simply by following the laws, but those actions are only just by accident; really knowing how to act justly is more difficult than knowing what medical treatment to apply to produce health (1137a4–26). Aristotle suggests that the just person as knower has a capacity as neutral as the physician's; he might choose to do actions for reasons he understands that would otherwise flow from the character of an unjust person and would be bound to look that way from the outside.

77. Plato's Eleatic Stranger takes up the nonmathematical measure and its claim to meet the standard of the precise in the *Statesman* (see esp. 283e–284e; cf. chap. 2, nn. 10 and 25, above).

78. The Athenian Stranger sets down as punishment for suicide that the tomb must be in an isolated spot without any headstone or name on it (*Laws* 873c–d).

CHAPTER 4

1. After presenting this portrait in the central interlude of the *Theaetetus*, Socrates addresses Theodorus: "This is the person raised in freedom and leisure, whom *you* call a philosopher" (see, esp., 173c–175e; cf. introduction, n. 4, above).

2. The argument of the *Ethics* is called down from the heavens as philosophy was by the Socratic turn (cf. Cicero *Tusculan Disputations* V.4.10–11). The segment from the end of Book VI to the beginning of Book VII contains the greatest density of references to Socrates in the *Ethics* (see appendix 1).

3. See chap. 1, nn. 41–45, above; and chap. 7, nn. 20–24, below.

4. Book VI strengthens the doctrine of the mean, Richard Kraut argues, by identifying two ultimate ends, excellent theoretical reasoning and excellent practical reasoning, which can supply a standard for decision making (*Aristotle on the Human Good*, pp. 300–301). But practical reasoning is instrumental and serves an end other than itself, either the end supplied by ethical virtue or *sophia*.

5. This is the assumption Socrates articulates at the end of the fifth book of the *Republic*, which he adopts as the basis for his image of the divided line (cf. *Republic* 478c, and *Ethics* 1139a7–12).

6. This account is developed in *De anima* (431b20–432a4). Cf. Martin Heidegger's analysis of this conception of truth (see *Plato's "Sophist,"* p. 17; and n. 10 below).

7. Socrates' construction of the tripartite soul in *Republic* IV requires just such a sequence: after separating the calculating from the desiring part of the soul, he marks off a third part by first separating *thumos,* in its alliance with calculation, from the desiring part, and then separating it from calculation, through its association with desire (437b–441c; cf. chap. 3, n. 50, above). From the point of view of desire, *thumos* and calculation look like a unitary whole; from the point of view of calculation *thumos* and desire do.

The unfolding of the psychology of the *Ethics* in two steps—first in Book I, then in Book VI—echoes that sequence. But in comparison with the psychology of the *Republic,* Aristotle's double account extends the range of the human soul both lower and higher, while taking *thumos* out from the middle.

Republic IV:	*epithumētikon—thumos—logistikon*	
Ethics I /VI:	*threptikon—epithumētikon—*	*—logistikon—epistēmonikon*

8. It is at the moment Aristotle confronts the question of this relation, at the end of the sixth book, that he refers, for the first and only time in the *Ethics,* to four parts of the human soul (1144a9–10).

9. Aristotle's understanding of the nature of the human poses the question, in Richard Velkley's words, of the human composite—"how is it a whole, and why as a problematic whole does it seldom attain its natural end?" But, as Velkley goes on to observe, "*theōria* concerning the human composite receives no mention in the account of the intellectual virtues in *Nicomachean Ethics,* book 6, in keeping with its failure to mention philosophy as such." The activity involved in producing that account goes unnamed in it (*Being after Rousseau: Philosophy and Culture in Question,* pp. 35, 161 n. 12).

10. Heidegger considers the way each particular mode of being in the truth uncovers (*alētheuein*) beings of a particular character. The basis for the privileging of *sophia* over *phronēsis,* he argues, is the ranking of the correlative classes of the beings in themselves, of which those that always are have ontological priority for the Greeks (*Plato's "Sophist,"* pp. 22–23, 94). Aristotle, he implies, is simply a spokesman for the presuppositions of his epoch and culture. But when Aristotle claims that we *suppose* knowledge in the strict sense to be of the unchanging beings, he is speaking not of the beings in themselves but of a dominant opinion about them, which he is not engaged in defending.

11. Aristotle's analysis of *technē* adopts the principle Thrasymachus introduces in the first book of the *Republic,* when he appeals to "the precise" in order to argue that just as a doctor who makes a mistake is no doctor at all, the would-be ruler who fails to lay down laws in his own interest is not truly a ruler (340d–341a).

12. This development of the notion of *sophia* echoes the problem Aristotle brings to light in the second chapter of the *Metaphysics,* in his survey of our opinions about the wise person: we think of such an individual as someone who has

comprehensive knowledge as well as the most precise knowledge (982a8–14), without reflecting on whether these standards are compatible.

13. Plato's Eleatic Stranger, supposedly rebuking young Socrates for his manly separation of humans from beasts, objects that if there were some other *phronimos* animals, such as the crane is thought to be, it would do the same and put its own species into one class, separated from all the rest of the animals, including humans, in the other (*Statesman* 263d).

14. See *Phaedo* 97b–98c; cf. *Metaphysics* 984b15–19 and 985a18–22.

15. This passage (1141b16–22) should be compared with two passages in the account of *akrasia* (see 1146b36–1147a10 and 1147a24–b3, together with the discussion in chap. 5, "Practical Reasoning and Its Failure").

16. Aristotle follows the same strategy, one might say, in the opening chapter of the *Metaphysics*, where he presents an exaggerated account of the separation of theoretical knowledge of universals from experience of particulars in order to establish how much we admire theoretical knowledge entirely apart from any practical benefits (981a14–30).

17. *Phronēsis* is the same disposition as *politikē*, Aristotle asserts, but what it is to be for each is not the same (1141b23–24). They are the same and not the same, Steven Salkever proposes, the way that the road from Athens to Thebes is the same and not the same as the road from Thebes to Athens—in this case, the path from a particular good to the human good and back again; and this is possible insofar as theorizing is an activity of seeing the universal in the particulars before us (*Finding the Mean: Theory and Practice in Aristotelian Political Philosophy*, pp. 101–2, 106).

18. In relation to the primary sense of *phronēsis*, politicians look like busybodies (*polupragmones*) who interfere in the lives of others: Socrates, who is put on trial for not minding his own business, admits that it is hard to understand the strange way he is a busybody not in public but only in private (*Apology* 31c; cf. *Apology* 19b, and *Republic* 433a–434c, 444a–b).

19. The Eleatic Stranger, practicing his method of division, locates *politikē* within the class of gnostic, as opposed to practical, arts—but within that as a commanding art (*epitaktikē*), not a judging art (*kritikē*) (*Statesman* 260b–c; cf. Seth Benardete, "The Plan of Plato's *Statesman*," in *The Argument of the Action*, pp. 371–72).

20. Practical wisdom, as Douglas Den Uyl puts it, "exhibits reason in action because deliberation, perception, experience, insight, judgment, understanding, and action are distinct but not separable components of the exercise of practical wisdom" (*The Virtue of Prudence*, p. 78). The kind of experience that makes this possible involves confronting "particulars in context, that is, with an eye towards their relationship to our final good" (p. 68).

21. It was in arguing for an alternative to the universal *idea* of the good that Aristotle first spoke of an analogy between *nous* in the soul and sight in the body (1096b29).

22. In its capacity to grasp the definitions from which reasoning proceeds, *nous* was at first contrasted with *phronēsis*, which apprehends the ultimate particular in practical reasoning (1142a25–30); but finally *nous* is credited with grasping

"both ultimates," not only definitions but also the particulars in practical reasoning (1143a36–b5). As Reeve puts it, while demonstration begins with a universal abstracted from particulars, practical reason ends with a universal being applied to a particular (*The Practices of Reason*, p. 59). On Heidegger's analysis of this double direction of *nous,* see *Plato's "Sophist,"* p. 108.

23. Alfarabi argues for the necessity of positing natural virtue by developing a dilemma that follows either from the deliberative virtue being independent of the moral virtues or from their being inseparable. The consequence is that the deliberative virtue either must be itself the virtue of goodness—an alternative never explicitly rejected—or it must be accompanied by some other virtue that enables the individual to wish for a good and virtuous end. Since that virtue cannot be the product of will (or there would be an infinite regress), it must be natural—parallel to the natural deliberative virtue, cleverness. Alfarabi goes on to argue for a difference among individual natures, leading to the conclusion that "the prince occupies his place by nature and not merely by will" ("The Attainment of Happiness," ii.35–37, in *The Philosophy of Plato and Aristotle,* pp. 33–34).

24. Discussing the philosopher's nature and the harmful effects of the wrong environment, Socrates asserts in *Republic* VI the general principle that the stronger the nature, the worse the result when corrupted (491a–c).

25. This is the solution, Aristotle claims, to the "dialectical argument" about the separability of the virtues (cf. *Protagoras* 329c). There is a hierarchical order, Jaffa argues, from natural virtue, which is only a particular kind of propensity toward virtue, to ethical virtue, which is a development of that potentiality through habituation, and, finally, to genuine virtue, when practical wisdom is added, with the true dividing line between moral virtue and strict virtue (*Thomism and Aristotelianism,* pp. 92–93). But once that line is drawn, it is not so obvious that natural virtue is of lower rank than the dispositions produced by habituation.

26. This is, in fact, what Plato's Socrates does assert when, before stating the conclusion that virtue is *phronēsis,* he draws the more moderate inference that the states ordinarily praised as virtues do not prove beneficial and, hence, should not count as virtues unless guided by *phronēsis* (*Meno* 88c–89a). Aristotle's description of the necessary unity of genuine virtue, in contrast with the separability of the natural virtues, might make us wonder whether he can move as close as he does to the position he ascribes to Socrates without fully endorsing it.

27. Thornton Lockwood reflects on the significance of this passage by considering the disputants Aristotle might have in mind (see "Is Virtue a *logos, kata ton logon,* or *meta tou orthou logou?*").

28. In sliding from one formulation to the other, Aristotle follows the strategy of Plato's Socrates himself, who, after setting out to prove to Meno that virtue is *epistēmē,* since it would then be teachable, reaches the conclusion that what makes any of the so-called virtues beneficial is *phronēsis* (*Meno* 87c, 88c). Cf. Bruell's discussion of the argument (*On the Socratic Education,* pp. 179–80).

29. Having argued that wisdom "seizes upon happiness in truth" whereas prudence seizes on the means to it, Alfarabi concludes: "These two, therefore, are the

two mutual assistants in perfecting the human being—wisdom being what gives the ultimate goal, and prudence being what gives the means by which that goal is attained" (*Selected Aphorisms* 53, in *Alfarabi: The Political Writings*, p. 35).

30. And philosophy would be the practice of dying and being dead (cf. *Phaedo* 64a)?

31. The problem raised by the contrast between health of soul as construed at the end of Book VI and the *akrasia* discussion in Book VII echoes the problem in the Eleatic Stranger's account of the "art of purification." In applying that art to the soul, the Stranger divides wickedness, as a condition of internal faction (*stasis* between opinions and desires, *thumos* and pleasures, *logos* and pains) from ignorance, as a condition of disproportion in aiming at the target of the truth but falling short. The metaphor for the first is disease; for the second, ugliness. The greatest ignorance is found to consist in the pretense to wisdom, which is treated by a practice of refutation that induces shame; and the image for that treatment is the doctor who must purify the body before it can benefit from food, but ignorance was supposed to be a matter of psychic ugliness, not disease (*Sophist* 227e–230d).

CHAPTER 5

1. Considerations of praise and blame do come up in the initial survey of common opinions about self-restraint and the lack of it, but that only highlights the subsequent disappearance of concern with what is praiseworthy and blameworthy, which is replaced by the question of what is curable or not. The one exception is in the discussion of *akrasia* in regard to *thumos*, which is said to be more shameful and more unjust than in regard to bodily pleasures (see 1149b18–20, and the discussion in "*Akrasia* Extended" later in this chapter).

2. It is especially striking that there is no occurrence of *phusis* or related terms throughout the analysis of the ethical virtues in Book IV, whereas there are forty-three occurrences, if I am not mistaken, in Book VII. The closest contenders are Book III, with sixteen occurrences (including eight in the discussion of *thumos*), and Book V, with seventeen occurrences (including ten in the discussion of natural justice).

3. While "incontinence" and "weakness of will" are common translations of *akrasia*, "lack of self-restraint" or "lack of self-mastery" captures most literally the notion of the divided self that is the subject of this experience.

4. The issues are interwoven in Plato's *Protagoras*, where Socrates examines the opinions of the many through the Sophist as their spokesman (352a–357e). Since, according to Protagoras, the many have no other good in mind besides pleasure, Socrates demonstrates that if they call some pleasures bad, they can mean only that pursuing them fails in the end to maximize pleasure. But they contradict themselves if they maintain that it is possible for one's knowledge of the good to be overcome by pleasure while admitting that pleasure is the good. Precisely on the basis of their hedonism, they are compelled to reinterpret akratic action as a product of ignorance of the good.

5. "It would not be surprising," Strauss reasons, "if the primeval equation of the good with the ancestral had been replaced, first of all, by the equation of the good with the pleasant. For when the primeval equation is rejected on the basis of the distinction between nature and convention, the things forbidden by ancestral custom or the divine law present themselves as emphatically natural and hence intrinsically good. The things forbidden by ancestral custom are forbidden because they are desired, and the fact that they are forbidden by convention shows that they are not desired on the basis of convention; they are then desired by nature. Now what induces man to deviate from the narrow path of ancestral custom or divine law appears to be the desire for pleasure and the aversion to pain. The natural good thus appears to be pleasure. Orientation by pleasure becomes the first substitute for the orientation by the ancestral" (*Natural Right and History*, pp. 108–9).

6. This is the metaphor by which Socrates conveys to Protagoras the opinion of the many, while taunting the Sophist to come out in the open as a member of their camp or to take his stand against them (*Protagoras* 352b).

7. The explicit agreement with Socrates on the surface of Aristotle's discussion seems merely formal, as David Schaefer notes, and does not in itself reveal the deeper understanding they share of the kind of knowledge that would be resistant to *akrasia* ("Wisdom and Morality: Aristotle's Account of *Akrasia*," pp. 232, 247).

8. There are correlative states we praise and blame with regard to resisting the pressures of pain: softness (*malakia*) in yielding to such pressures against one's better judgment, and endurance (*karteria*) in resisting them. This pair requires, we later discover, a sympathetic standard of evaluation: we blame for softness only someone who yields to pains the many could resist, and we praise the endurance of one who conquers pains to which the many yield. Once that standard is introduced in regard to pain, it is applied in turn to the struggle against pleasure (1150a9–16).

9. The task of the dialectician, as Terence Irwin puts it, is "to see how far we must go from the common beliefs if we defend the counterintuitive view"—like that of Socrates against the possibility of *akrasia*—and the consideration of dialectical puzzles plays a crucial role in this process (*Aristotle's First Principles*, pp. 38–43).

10. On the role of opinion in the explanation of *akrasia*, cf. 1145b32–1146a4, 1146b24–30, and 1147b9–11.

11. The *phronimos* here takes the place of the "decent person" (*ho epieikēs*), to whom the same standard was applied at the conclusion of the discussion of the ethical virtues in order to show why shame should not be considered a virtue (1128b28–29).

12. See, e.g., *Meno* 77b–78a; *Protagoras* 358c–d; and *Apology* 25c–26a.

13. This reasoning is illustrated in *De anima*, where the universal premise "Such and such a kind of man should do such and such a kind of act" is followed by a twofold particular premise: "This is an act of the kind meant, and I a person of the kind meant" (434a16–19). Schaefer shows why this is the appropriate model for reasoning about moral action where differences in character play a crucial role ("Wisdom and Morality: Aristotle's Account of *Akrasia*," pp. 238–41; cf. n. 16 below).

14. See *De anima* 403a29–403b1. Aristotle alluded in Book I of the *Ethics* to the difference between political science's practical concern with the human good and a more precise, theoretical science of the soul (1102a18–26); it is the controversial pyschology of *akrasia* that seems to push the argument of the *Ethics* in the direction of that more precise science.

15. In his initial presentation of the parallel between practical reasoning and theoretical reasoning, Aristotle spoke of a point at which "one comes to be" out of the two premises, upon which action follows (1147a26–28). As Amélie Rorty reasons, if the akratic does think about what he is doing, he misperceives the particular case before him, or if he gets it right, he fails to connect it with his general principles, and therefore fails to draw the right conclusion ("*Akrasia* and Pleasure: *Nicomachean Ethics* Book 7," p. 273). It looks as if he does both, misperceiving the feature of the particular case that concerns his own good because of connecting it with one general principle, not the correct one but the one formulated by desire for pleasure.

16. The akratic has the opinion that sweets are forbidden and the particular opinion that "this is a sweet." The knowledge he does not possess, Schaefer concludes, is that of the class character of the food, which would explain why it is harmful; the analogous situation would be that of someone whose virtue is a mere product of habituation, not guided by prudence ("Wisdom and Morality," pp. 233–36). The understanding of what is beneficial or harmful, which belongs to prudence, might seem to require some kind of theoretical inquiry; but if it really "presupposes the possession of theoretical wisdom," as Schaefer proposes (p. 246), prudence would be no more available than *sophia*. The real question raised by the whole discussion seems to be how *phronēsis* is related not to *sophia* but to philosophy.

17. The argument comes back to this thread when it later differentiates two different forms of *akrasia*, the impetuous (*propeteia*) and the weak (*astheneia*): in the case of the impetuous akratic, passion takes over at the beginning to prevent him from reasoning at all; in the case of the weak, passion takes over in the end to prevent his perfectly correct reasoning from being translated into action (1150b19–28). It is not clear how either case fits the account of practical reasoning that locates a moment of ignorance or error in the akratic's deliberation.

18. See appendix 4, "Classifications of Pleasure." Kathryn Sensen analyzes the problematic status of the appeal to *phusis* in these various distinctions among pleasure in "On Nature as a Standard: Book VII of Aristotle's *Ethics*," pp. 8–17.

19. The classifications return in the end to this division, between necessary and nonnecessary pleasures (1150a15–18), in order to compare our attraction to pleasures with our aversion to pain. It is at this point that the charitable standard by which we measure endurance of pain—what most people can take—is adopted for self-restraint and its absence in relation to pleasure (1150b1–6).

20. With their translation of Aristotle's *Poetics*, Seth Benardete and Michael Davis include an appendix citing the account in *Ethics* VII of the range of human

possibilities from divine virtue to bestiality, along with the subsequent discussion of bestial dispositions (*Aristotle: On Poetics*, pp. 87–89). In his study of Sophocles' *Antigone*, Benardete calls attention to the chorus describing Antigone as "the savage offspring of a savage father," using a word applied to the flesh-eating dogs she tried to keep away from her brother's corpse: "They sense that her devotion is incompatible with civility. The law, whose political effect is mansuetude, shows itself through Antigone as the instrument of bestialization" (*Sacred Transgressions*, p. 63).

21. At the conclusion of a list of what is supposed to be diseaselike behaviors acquired by habit (plucking out one's hair, biting one's nails, eating cinders), Aristotle slips in, without any argument at all, homosexuality (practicing the *aphrodisia* with males). He then notes that some of these conditions are by nature, while others result from habit, as in cases of childhood abuse, though he introduces the contrast, it seems, only to conclude, surprisingly, that just as a condition given by nature would not be considered akratic, neither would one produced by habit. Does this mean it would not count as behavior that can be blamed? Or that it would not be a possible case of desire overcoming one's better judgment? Perhaps the point is only, as the passage goes on to explain, that such behaviors could not be akratic simply, since they lie outside the sphere of vice and, hence, of *akrasia* proper (1148b27–1149a4).

Plato's Athenian Stranger issues a complicated, not to say highly qualified, statement on the subject. Discussing the customary common meals and gymnasia of Crete and Sparta, he admits that they have been beneficial in some respects; but his interlocutors' cities, he goes on, might be held responsible for having corrupted, through this practice, the lawful thing from long ago concerning the aphrodisiac pleasures, which are according to nature not only for humans but for beasts as well. One should have in mind, the Stranger recommends, whether in jest or seriously, that in the uniting by nature of the female with the nature of males for generation, the pleasure involved seems to be in accordance with nature, but of males with males or females with females, contrary to nature, and the daring of those first engaged in it seems to be because of lack of self-restraint (*akrateia*) in pleasure (*Laws* 636b–c).

22. In response to a question Dante poses about where certain groups of sinners are to be found, Virgil explains: "Rememberest thou not the words with which thy *Ethics* expounds the three dispositions which are against the will of Heaven, incontinence, malice, and mad brutishness, and how incontinence offends God less and incurs less blame?" (Dante, *Inferno* XI.79–85).

23. The text of this much-disputed passage is unclear. While it makes some sense to think of bestiality as the complete absence of reason, that would make *akrasia* in regard to bestial desires and pleasures impossible, although the discussion is presumably trying to argue for the possibility in such cases of *akrasia* in a qualified sense.

24. One wonders if Aristotle is thinking of Plato's understanding of *thumos*— which he seems, in turn, to have learned, from Homer—as a passion inclined to

express itself in poetic figures—in particular, personification, which treats inanimate things as if they were alive and had a will of their own (see, esp., *Republic* 439e–440a, 441b–c).

25. Of course, the "Oedipal" evidence Aristotle supplies—sons who beat their fathers on the grounds that they had beaten their own fathers (1149b6–14)—is rather strange support for the more natural status of *thumos* over desire.

26. Socrates describes in Homer's words the peculiar pleasure that comes with the satisfaction of anger (*Philebus* 47e; *Iliad* XVIII.109). No one suffers pain, Aristotle asserts, in committing an act of *hubris*, unlike an act done in anger (1149b20–24): why, one wonders, if he wants to separate anger from pleasure, should he use *hubris* here to mean, presumably, a lustful act, when it first referred to the insult arousing *thumos* (1149a34)? See Paul Ludwig's analysis of *hubris* and its "nexus of violation, arrogant superiority, and the deliberate humiliation of others" (*Eros and Polis: Desire and Community in Greek Political Theory*, pp. 171–72; cf. 50–51).

27. From his analysis of the soul in *Republic* IV (439e–441c; cf. chap. 3, n. 50, and chap. 4, n. 7, above), Socrates draws the conclusion that justice is present in the soul when each part does its own thing—when the rational part rules and the spirited part obeys, serving as its ally in presiding over desire (441d–442a).

28. In Chapter VI of *Eight Chapters*, Maimonides acknowledges an apparent contradiction between the teaching of "the philosophers," for whom virtue, or the harmonious relation of desire and reason, is superior to self-restraint, and the view of the sages, who admire the struggle in which obedience to law prevails over the desire for pleasure. Maimonides proposes a "wonderful reconciliation" of the two views by differentiating the kinds of actions assumed in the two cases: while the philosophers have in mind the things considered bad according to generally accepted opinions, the sages are thinking of actions that are not bad in themselves but only because of the prohibitions of traditional laws. (I discuss this in "Self-Restraint and Virtue: Sages and Philosophers in Maimonides' *Eight Chapters*.") Contrasting the self-restrained person with one possessing the virtue of moderation, Alfarabi ranks the two with regard to different classes of individuals: natural virtue is preferable for the ruler; restraining oneself in accordance with what *nomos* requires is preferable for the ruled (*Selected Aphorisms* 14–15, in *Alfarabi: The Political Writings*, p. 19).

29. Tessitore rightly calls attention to the importance of this single reference to political philosophy, and its replacement of the role previously assigned to political science (*Reading Aristotle's Ethics*, pp. 63–64), as does Marc Guerra ("Aristotle on Pleasure and Political Philosophy," p. 172). But, on reflection, it is certainly puzzling that "political philosophy" should make its first appearance to introduce an account that seems to stand at such a distance from ethical and political concerns, looking through the eyes of a biologist at pleasure and pain.

30. The notion, as Benardete puts it, "that the constraints that any set of laws impose on man are originally painful before they become second nature and any release from their constraints will be experienced as pleasure" leads to "the corol-

lary that the life without the law is the life of pleasure" (*The Tragedy and Comedy of Life*, p. 89).

31. A. J. Festugière finds the account of pleasure in Book X to be Aristotle's more mature version but one that repeats too much from the earlier account to serve a purpose in the same work (*Aristote: Le Plaisir*, pp. xxiv–xliv). "Traditionally," G. E. L. Owen observes, "the question has been whether the two accounts are too divergent to be compatible," but he sets out to show that in fact "they are too divergent to be incompatible." They are not competing answers to the same question, Owen argues, but address two different questions: the first, an issue about what is *enjoyed* or *enjoyable;* the second, about the character of *enjoying* or *taking pleasure* ("Aristotelian Pleasures," pp. 93, 102–3).

32. Upon completing its investigation of how virtue is acquired (1105b19), Book II turned to the question, What is it? It is interesting, though, that the discussion began by apparently demoting the concern with that question: "It is not in order that we may know what it is that we are investigating virtue, but in order that we might become good" (1103b27–28).

33. See J. C. B. Gosling and C. C. W. Taylor, *The Greeks on Pleasure*, p. 202. Aristide Tessitore provides a helpful analysis of the difference in context of the two accounts, emphasizing the rhetorical purposes at work in Book X ("A Political Reading of Aristotle's Treatment of Pleasure in the *Nicomachean Ethics*," p. 260). Of course, the discussion in Book X is still concerned with the question of the nature of pleasure and its relationship to activity, though it comes to that question separate from and after a discussion of what should be taught about pleasure as good or bad.

34. On this notion of pleasure as a *genesis,* see *Philebus* 54d.

35. "Nature" seems to be identified here with the nondefective state of the organism, not with the whole cycle of corruption and restoration in the life of an animal (cf. *Philebus* 31d and 42c–d).

36. This is the argument that will be attributed to Eudoxus in Book X (1172b9–15, cf. 1172b35–1173a5).

37. Aristotle uses this strategy systematically in *Politics* I, developing an argument implicitly by alluding to the context of the lines he cites from the poets, with conspicuous omissions (cf. 1252b8, 11, 23; 1253a6; 1260a30–31). See the discussion of these passages by Davis, *The Politics of Philosophy*, pp. 16–17, 25–26; and by Nichols, *Citizens and Statesmen*, p. 31.

38. Although everyone may think or say they are seeking different pleasures, "nevertheless," Thomas Aquinas comments, "everyone is inclined by nature to the same pleasure as the highest, namely, the contemplation of rational truth inasmuch as all men naturally desire to know" (*Commentary on Aristotle's "Nicomachean Ethics"* 1511; p. 468).

39. The passage that began by referring to "all"—humans and beasts—as a neuter plural, slides into "all" as a masculine plural when it speaks of the pleasures we believe or would say we are pursuing; but it concludes again with "all" in the neuter

plural, as evidence for pursuit of the same pleasure being the mark of something divine (1153b25–32). While he does say pleasure is the natural end of all animate beings, Aristotle is not a hedonist, Julia Annas maintains, since he cannot hold that pleasure is one single independently specifiable end that everyone pursues ("Aristotle on Pleasure and Goodness," p. 288). Yet that seems to be what Aristotle is proposing at this moment.

40. "And the pastime (*diagōgē*) [of the highest being] is such as the best for us in a short time. For thusly that one is always, which is impossible for us, since its *energeia* is also pleasure, and because of that, waking, perception, thinking are most pleasant. . . . And life also belongs [to god]; for the *energeia* of mind is life, and god is that *energeia*" (*Metaphysics* 1072b15–18, b27–28). On the relation of all living things to this highest being, see Jonathan Lear, *Aristotle: The Desire to Understand*, p. 295.

41. See Euripides *Orestes* 234. The denial of positive pleasure implied here is echoed in the dark view of friendship expressed in the same drama, to which Book IX will allude (cf. *Ethics* 1168b7, and *Orestes* 1046; and *Ethics* 1169b8, and *Orestes* 665).

42. Tessitore speaks of "a sober teaching on the limited human capacity for pleasure" (*Reading Aristotle's "Ethics*," p. 69); Francis Sparshott, of "a blackly pessimistic point" (*Taking Life Seriously: A Study of the Argument of the "Nicomachean Ethics*," p. 262).

CHAPTER 6

1. On Aristotle's justification for his critical examination of the *idea* of the good, see chap. 1, n. 32, above.

2. When Book IX ends by characterizing friendship as a matter of "sharing in discussion and thought" (1170b11–14), which is the activity of those who "philosophize together" (1172a5), Aristotle implies, as Judith Swanson puts it, "that friendship can be the midwife of truth" (*The Public and the Private in Aristotle's Political Philosophy*, p. 200).

3. Mind is described, at *De anima* 413b25–28, as "another genus of soul" that alone may turn out to be capable of separability.

4. Homer conveys this understanding of mind through the profound pun he has Odysseus put to work in his encounter with the Cyclops. After experiencing the terrible sight of his companions being devoured, Odysseus sets a plan in motion by first plying Polyphemus with wine. When the drunken Cyclops demands the Stranger's name, Odysseus replies, "No one" (*outis, Odyssey* 9. 366). After Odysseus has blinded Polyphemus, the other Cyclopes hear him shouting and call into his cave, "Surely no one (*mē tis*) can be killing you by guile or by force?," to which Polyphemus responds, "No one (*outis*) is killing me by guile not by force" (406–9). If no one (*mē tis*) is doing violence to you, they conclude, you must be struck by sickness from Zeus (410–11). And as they went their way, Odysseus narrates, his heart laughed at the way he had deceived them by his name and his cunning (*mētis*, 413–14), which are of course the same. This is the anonymity of mind Odysseus loses when he finally sails away and "in the anger of his heart" boasts to the Cyclops

that it was Odysseus, son of Laertes, who blinded him (IX.501–5). Back in Ithaca in disguise, Odysseus holds himself back from striking out in anger at the slave girls by remembering how he endured in the cave of the Cyclops until he found a way out by *cunning* (*mētis*, 20.18–21). Seth Benardete finds a key to the *Odyssey* in this pun, which raises the question of the relation between individuating anger and impersonal rationality (see *The Bow and the Lyre*, pp. 74–79).

5. Self-sufficiency was redefined, in that context, as the characteristic of an activity that by itself would make life lacking nothing (1097b16–17). Friendship is not held up to that standard, but it is presented as a necessity so vital that no life could be sufficient without friends (1155a5–6).

6. The same phrase is put to equally problematic use when Aristotle quotes it in the third book of the *Politics* (1287b10), in the context of considering the limitations of monarchy. Cf. Socrates' citation of this Homeric passage at *Protagoras* 348c.

7. Aristotle considers such threats to political stability in Book V (Chaps. 2–7) of the *Politics*. In Plato's *Symposium*, Pausanias speaks of the threat to tyrants posed by subjects whose "big thoughts" are inspired by "strong friendships and communities," like "the eros of Aristogeiton and the *philia* of Harmodius" that led to the overthrow of the Peisistratids (182c; cf. Thucydides *Peloponnesian War* VI.54). Aristophanes confirms the point in the *Symposium* in his mythical account of eros as an attempt to restore our "ancient nature," which led the original whole human beings, with their "big thoughts," to assault the heavens in rebellion against the Olympian gods (190b–c).

8. This weighing of claims takes up an especially long segment of the discussion of friendship (from Chap. 9 of Book VIII through Chap. 3 of Book IX; see, esp., 1159b36–1160a8; see also n. 22 below). It ends with the admission that friendships based on character, though more stable than those based on pleasure or utility, are nevertheless subject to change, raising difficulties about how one should act toward a former friend in such a situation.

9. Friendship in its highest form is rare, it will be argued, because there are so few individuals capable of it and because it takes time to develop such a relationship (1156b25–32); hence, being a friend in the fullest sense is as exclusive as loving, or nearly so (1158a10–16, 1171a10–13).

10. Cf. *Lysis* 214a–b and 215e, where a cosmological account evokes the notion of *philia* as a relationship between either likes or opposites.

11. The contrast is especially evident in the case of courage, where the genuinely virtuous overcoming of fear for the sake of the beautiful was restricted to the narrowest possible circumstances and the true excellence understood precisely by excluding the range of states that merely resemble it. The equivalent to the present analysis of friendship would have been to speak of those states as *eidē* of courage, however much they might fall short of the perfect form.

12. In the *Lysis*, Socrates questions the necessity of reciprocity if it means there is no possibility of "friends of wine" or "friends of gymnastics," any more

than "friends of wisdom" (*philosophoi*) as long as wisdom does not return their affection (212d–e). If the question the *Lysis* raises "were to be put linguistically," Benardete remarks, "one could ask whether it was just an accident that *philosophia* had not been designated *erotosophia*" ("On Plato's *Lysis*," in *The Argument of the Action*, p. 200).

13. See Chap. 13 of Book VIII, esp. 1162b5–21.

14. This ambiguity first appeared in the characterization of happiness as *teleios* (1097a28–b1), then as a characterization of *teleia* virtue in connection with the human good (1098a16–18).

15. Aristotle's account of the three species of friendship, with two falling short of perfect *philia*, exemplifies Robert Berman's analysis of the "virtuosity model" of class membership, which admits a comprehensive class while singling out a paradigm case within it. An "exclusivist model," in contrast, would exclude everything but the friendship of virtue, while an "inclusivist model" would admit all three kinds as equally members of the class (see "Ways of Being Singular: The Logic of Individuality," pp. 112–15). On the application of this analysis to Aristotle's account of primary and secondary happiness, see chap. 7, n. 48, below.

16. The account of the friendship of the good has not, or not yet, addressed the questions Socrates raises in the *Lysis:* How could that which is like be useful or beneficial to its like? And, if it could not, how could two persons insofar as they are alike treasure each other? If their likeness, moreover, consists in being good, but the good person is self-sufficient, and that means in want of nothing, so he would not treasure anything and, hence, not like it, how could the good be friends to the good? (See *Lysis* 214e–215c; cf. David Bolotin, *Plato's Dialogue on Friendship*, pp. 130–34).

17. According to Aristotle's teaching, as Lorraine Pangle puts it, "virtuous people ... can be whole in themselves, and it is those who have such wholeness who can be the best friends." In contrasting love affairs, based on the attraction of opposites, to the finest friendships, Aristotle "does not present eros," Pangle remarks, "as Aristophanes does in Plato's *Symposium,* as 'finding one's missing half'—one who in a lasting way complements and completes what is lacking in one's soul" (*Aristotle and the Philosophy of Friendship*, p. 41).

18. In the first book of the *Republic*, Polemarchus interprets the formula for justice as "giving to each his due" to mean helping friends and harming enemies (332d). Enmity (*echthra*) appears in the discussion of friendship in the *Ethics* only at the beginning of Book VIII, where the legislator is said to be concerned with promoting concord, which is like friendship, and driving out faction, which is enmity (1155a24–26). The term had come up once before, in the description of the great-souled person, who doesn't stoop to speaking ill even of his enemies, unless as a matter of *hubris* (1125a8–9); he had just been described as incapable of living in relation to another, unless a friend.

19. As the *Ethics* moves through various "levels of morality," in Jaffa's terms, justice "is carried to a higher degree by friendship" (*Thomism and Aristotelianism*, pp. 142–43).

20. Justice, Winthrop cautions, "even if it is the whole of virtue to others, should not be mistaken for the whole of virtue, moral and intellectual," whereas friendship calls for and makes possible the practice of the whole of virtue ("Aristotle and Theories of Justice," p. 1211). Aristotle's account may indeed be meant, as Winthrop argues, to draw us away from the dangerous idealism of a search for perfect justice. But it is not so obvious that "the teaching on friendship is meant to replace rather than supplement the theory of justice" (p. 1214). In what way, exactly, can friendship furnish a "nonpolitical solution" (p. 1215) to the problems that lead us to seek justice?

21. It is only by laying down laws, the Athenian Stranger advises, that the legislator can implement his goal of making the city "a friend of itself," as well as free and sensible (*Laws* 693b–c; cf. 743c).

22. In *Politics* VII, discussing the desirability of a thumoeidetic (as well as dianoetic) nature in the citizens of the best regime, Aristotle makes a similar observation about the demands being greater the closer the relationship: *thumos* is aroused more, he explains, if one deems oneself slighted by friends than by strangers, which leads in that context to the identification of *thumos* as the source of affectionate feeling (*to philētikon*; 1327b39–1328a4). Ludwig discusses the relation of *philia* to anger and aggression in *Eros and Polis* (see, esp., pp. 194–95). *Thumos* is especially prone to being inflamed, it seems, in erotic relationships precisely because eros is not, or not necessarily, reciprocal. The way "the justified indignation about injustice shifts insensibly into the unjustified indignation about unrequited love" is, Strauss once suggested, "perhaps the deepest secret of spiritedness" ("The Origins of Political Science and the Problem of Socrates," pp. 192–93).

23. In this tension, Pierre Aubenque finds "le destin tragique de l'amitié" ("Sur l'amitié chez Aristote," in *La Prudence chez Aristote*, p. 180).

24. Aristotle's implication about the nature of philosophical friendship calls to mind Plato's choice of never representing a conversation between two interlocutors of equal philosophical status. A dialogue between equals, Strauss notes, would be unable to show a teaching adjusted by the main speaker to fit his particular audience; it would, therefore, not assign the reader the task of determining whether and how that teaching is valid beyond the circumstances of the conversation in question (*The City and Man*, pp. 54–55). Of course, that is a problem concerning the representation of dialogue in a written work, while Aristotle is presumably speaking of actual relationships.

25. See, especially, *Politics* 1279a22–b10 for the classification of regimes assumed here. According to the analogy proposed in *Ethics* VIII.10, kingship is parallel to the relationship between father and son; tyranny, as its perversion, to the relationship of master and slave or to a despotic paternal relationship like that found among the Persians. The likeness of aristocracy can be seen in the proper relationship of husband to wife; that of oligarchy, as a perversion of aristocracy, in a relationship in which the husband interferes in the wife's sphere of competence or one in which, because of family wealth, the wife, rules. Timocracy, in which equal citizens are supposed to rule in turn, has its counterpart in the relationship between brothers; and democracy, in a household with no master or a weak one.

26. While the relationship between husband and wife only *appears* aristocratic in form (1160b33), and that between brothers only *seems* timocratic (1161a4), the father's relation to the child is said not merely to seem or appear kingly but to "have the *schēma* of kingship" (1160b25). Aristotle's *Politics* begins with a critique of those who consider the difference between *polis* and *oikos* merely a matter of degree and not a difference in kind (1252a7–14). In the account that follows of the emergence of the *polis* as the most fully developed community, Aristotle observes that the first cities were ruled by kings as a mere extension of the household, under the royal rule of the eldest; he points to the meaning of this collapse of household and city when he invokes Homer's Cyclops to illustrate royal rule (1252b20–28; cf. chap. 7, n. 39, below).

27. In the first book of the *Politics*, Aristotle defends the view of Gorgias, ranking the types of virtue in accordance with the hierarchy of roles in the household and city over against Socrates' search for a universal definition of human virtue (1260a15–34; cf. *Meno* 71e–73a).

28. While the analysis of the various sorts of kinship based on their similarity to political regimes takes its bearings from the point of view of the city, Aristotle reconsiders the family, Tessitore observes, by focusing on "the natural source of these relationships as they spring from the act of generation, something that is not dependent upon a particular kind of regime" (*Reading Aristotle's "Ethics,"* pp. 82–83).

29. Aristotle finds an illustration of this principle in the phenomenon of the benefactor's care for his beneficiary, which seems to be greater, surprisingly, than the recipient's affection (1167b16–68a10). One might assume that the benefactor wishes his beneficiary well because he awaits a return, like a lender who wants his debtor preserved in order to get his money back. Aristotle does not simply reject this view—any more than he rejects the same explanation for parents' love of their children (1163b24–25). But the "more natural" model, he proposes, is the artist in relation to his work (*ergon*): the *energeia* of the maker lies in his product; hence, he cares for it so much out of attachment to his own being, and the beneficiary is in a sense the *ergon* of the benefactor.

30. If, one wonders, such an individual deceives himself and in fact harbors desires that are not in his true interest, would he be able to possess anything like the inner harmony of the truly decent person? Kathryn Sensen discusses this question in "On the Nature of Friendship in Aristotle's *Nicomachean Ethics,"* pp. 9–10.

31. *Psychē*, which has by this point in the inquiry been replaced by mind (*nous*), appears only in this statement about the decent person and, once again, to contrast the base person, whose soul is in a state of faction (1166b20). *Psychē* occurred just once in Book VIII, in an aside comparing the relation of master to slave with that of body to soul (1161a35); it will appear again in Book IX only in the proverbial formula "one soul" (1168b7) and in the description of the blameworthy lover of self who indulges the nonrational part of his soul (1168b20). Its rare appearance in the whole discussion of friendship makes one realize that it has, in fact, more or less disappeared after Book VI. In Book VII—where we might have expected

to see it most—it makes only one, rather odd, appearance, in the description of syllogistic reasoning and its counterpart in action: once the major premise about a universal is joined with the minor premise about a particular, the soul must affirm the conclusion, just as in practice one must act immediately (1147a25–28). *Psychē* will be conspicuously absent from the description of the contemplative life, appearing only once in Book X, in the last chapter, with the claim that it is necessary to cultivate the soul, just as one must cultivate the soil before planting seeds (1179a25).

32. The "true self," Germaine Walsh observes, is identified in Chap. 8 of Book IX with the practical intellect and in Chap. 7 of Book X with the theoretical intellect, whereas in Chap. 4 of Book IX, it includes both the practical and theoretical aspects of the intellect; and that understanding of the true self is implicitly preserved by the discussion in Chap. 9 of Book IX of the intellectual activity perfected in friendship (review of *Reading Aristotle's "Ethics,"* by Aristide Tessitore, p. 733).

33. This difference between the treatment of soul and the treatment of mind recalls Klaus Brinkmann's analysis of the distinction, in Aristotle's *Metaphysics*, between the *konstitutionstheoretische* conception of substance, as a compound whole of parts, and the *bestimmtheitstheoretische* conception, concerned with the relation between being and essence (*Aristoteles allgemeine und spezielle Metaphysik*, pp. 80, 103–4). Maimonides concludes his analysis of the human soul, including the rational part, with the claim that "this single soul, whose powers or parts are described above, is like matter, and the intellect is its form" (*Eight Chapters*, Chap. I; p. 64).

34. Thus "self" is, as Suzanne Stern-Gillet puts it, an achievement word: it "constitutes an ideal toward which we should strive but which we may not reach" (*Aristotle's Philosophy of Friendship*, p. 29).

35. The psychology underlying the account of *philia* is one, Julia Annas charges, that Aristotle takes over from the *Lysis* and fails to integrate into the system of the *Ethics* as a whole: the crucial argument about self-love is partly based on the Platonic premise, according to which good men are internally consistent and unified, and bad men are internally conflicted, which "does not fit happily into Aristotle's *Ethics*" ("Plato and Aristotle on Friendship and Altruism," p. 553). Rejecting the unlikely assumption that Aristotle is unaware of the problem, we must infer that the movement of the argument has led to this revision and that, accordingly, the psychology required for the analysis of virtue no longer suffices for the understanding of the self.

36. As Socrates maintains in the sixth book of the *Republic*, every soul pursues the good and does everything for its sake, divining that it is something, though perplexed and unable to grasp what it is sufficiently (505e).

37. If being in a state of inner faction is utter misery, we should strive to avoid it, Aristotle concludes, in order to have friendly feelings for ourselves and become a friend to another (1166b27–29). This is a unique point, Franz Dirlmeier notes, at which Aristotle steps out of the frame of his scientific perspective and says

"you should" (*Aristoteles Nikomachische Ethik*, p. 546). While presenting a "morally edifying contrast between the decent and the base," which concludes with a "rare moral exhortation," Aristotle has begun at the same time, Tessitore observes, "to lay bare the psychological root for friendship" by pointing to "the primary importance of self-love" (*Reading Aristotle's "Ethics,"* pp. 84–85).

38. The real possibility of loving another for his own sake even if that individual is not aware of being loved had been illustrated by the case of mothers' love for their children (1159a28–34; cf. 1161b27–28, 1168a25–27). Aristotle is now trying to argue that the best friend whom one should love in this way is oneself, and the problematic character of this claim is reflected in the grammatical structure of the statement supporting it: in the middle of the sentence, the object—the best friend one should love most—turns into the subject, who wishes another well for his own sake (1168b2–3).

39. When Diotima asks Socrates what the lover of the beautiful things desires, he responds, "that they come to be his"; but he is altogether unable to answer when she asks him what one would have in that case (*Symposium* 204d–e). The verb Aristotle uses to express the attempt at procuring the beautiful for oneself (*peripoiein;* 1168b27, 1169a22) occurs in the *Ethics* in only one other context: in contrast with contemplation, from which nothing further results, practical activities are engaged in to procure something beyond the action itself—in particular, the politician seeks to procure something beyond being politically active in itself (1177b1–4, 13–16).

40. The only appearance of the *kalon* in Book V came in Aristotle's discussion of the decent person's equitable action, which might seem to be an act of injustice toward himself; but in taking less than his fare share, Aristotle proposes, he could perhaps be construed as greedy for a larger share of another good, like reputation or the beautiful (1136b21–23).

41. This paradoxical structure reappears in Book X's characterization of theoretical activity, with the pre-Socratic philosopher as representative: even if it is in fact in the highest interest of the one engaged in it, the *energeia* of *theōria* cannot be pursued out of that motivation and still be what it is (see chap. 7, nn. 49–51, below).

42. Orestes, with his life under threat, exhorts his uncle Menelaus to come to his aid, admitting quite explicitly that one turns to friends only when one cannot help oneself (Euripides *Orestes* 665). Kinship proves to mean nothing to Menelaus once he calculates his own future interests; and Orestes' comrade, Pylades, who proclaims himself ready to do anything for his friend, only leads him into deeper confusion and danger.

43. That honor is the greatest of external goods is the view, Thomas Smith proposes, of the ambitious men who make up Aristotle's audience, whose perspective he attempts to correct when he identifies friendship as the greatest external good (*Revaluing Ethics,* p. 185).

Harry Jaffa addresses the apparent contradiction between the two claims about the greatest external good by considering the status of philosophical activity as the perfection of the activity of friendship (see n. 66 below). If, he reasons, "we raise the question as to why the magnanimous man is primarily concerned with honor and not with friendship, the answer would seem to be connected with the fact that the magnanimous man, not being a philosopher, cannot be a party to a perfect friendship . . . and for that reason *honor is said to be*, with respect to him, the greatest of external goods" (*Thomism and Aristotelianism*, p. 126).

44. The point about continuity helps prepare for the conclusion of Book X, where that characteristic is one of the criteria for ranking activities in their claim to the title of happiness (1177a22–23); only, there, it serves to pick out the activity, and the life devoted to it, that supposedly stand in the least need of being carried on with others.

45. On this account of benefactor and beneficiary, see 1167b29–1168a10, and n. 29 above.

46. This role, which the *spoudaios* has been called upon to play throughout the *Ethics,* is especially obvious when he is appealed to in the tenth book, which attempts to establish the status of real pleasures by identifying them with the things that appear pleasant to the serious person (1176a17–22).

47. This argument will be complemented by the account in Book X of pleasure as an experience that accompanies the natural activities of perceiving and thinking (1174b14–1175a3).

48. The "Pythagorean" principle of the determinate (*bōrismenon*) stands in contrast to the indefinite or infinite—the one associated with the good, the other with the bad. These principles first showed up in the account of the mean, in which the single target in feelings or actions is set over against the unlimited excess and deficiency that fall short of that standard (1106b29–34). When Book X takes up the argument that pleasure cannot be good because the good is definite (*bōrismenon*) and pleasure, which admits the more and less, is indefinite, Aristotle does not question the standard but only the description of pleasure: if health admits the more and less, yet it is definite (*bōrismenē*), why shouldn't pleasure be like that (1173a16–29)? In the *Philebus*, Socrates analyzes health as a product of the right mixture of the unlimited with the limit (25e–26b), appealing to these Pythagorean principles after previously introducing his own procedure of analysis of *eidē*. This is an unfamiliar Socrates, Benardete comments, who engages unexpectedly in pre-Socratic cosmology, albeit in apparent subordination to the issue of the human good (*The Tragedy and Comedy of Life,* pp. 89–90).

49. Because happiness is an activity of life that is reflexive, Michael Pakaluk comments, there can be an analogous relationship to others that would be desirable in just the way life is (see *Aristotle's "Nicomachean Ethics" Books VIII and IX,* p. 216). Whether it would show up, or show up equally, in all forms of friendship is another question (p. 226): if the reflexive character of friendship is realized through sharing speeches and thoughts, it would seem to belong essentially and above all to the activity of friends who philosophize together.

50. "Consciousness of the other," as John Cooper puts it, "is a kind of overflow from the good man's self-consciousness" ("Friendship and the Good," in *Reason and Emotion,* p. 340).

51. The argument applies some version of the principle of self-sufficiency introduced in Book I as a criterion for happiness: without friendship, life would not be "lacking nothing" (1097b16–17). The deficiency that would result if the happy person did not have this awareness of a friend's life is, Thomas Aquinas explains, contrary to the notion of happiness that calls for sufficiency (*Commentary on Aristotle's "Nicomachean Ethics"* 1912, p. 578).

52. The conclusion of the argument does not appear to require, as Sparshott puts it, its "portentous-looking premises." But the argument, as Sparshott goes on to note, by locating the value of friendship in the extended awareness it brings, provides the basis for finding the intellectual life characteristic of the highest friendship (*Taking Life Seriously*, pp. 299–300).

53. "Perceiving together" (*sunaisthanesthai*) anticipates the concluding description of activities in which friends participate jointly, which ends with "philosophizing together" (*sumphilosophousin;* 1172a4–7).

54. Commenting on the centrality of eros in Plato's thought, Seth Benardete observes: "With Plato, for the first time, man becomes a metaphysical problem, and love a metaphysical passion" (*Socrates and Plato: The Dialectics of Eros,* p. 19). The apparent absence or unimportance of eros in the *Ethics* has a parallel in the absence of *thumos* and the punitive impulse it inspires from Aristotle's discussion of justice.

55. This is the subject of my essay "Hunting Together or Philosophizing Together: Friendship and Eros in Aristotle's *Nicomachean Ethics,*" pp. 37–60. A version of the discussion, with reference to Stanley Rosen's articles on the nonlover in the *Phaedrus,* appears in Ranasinghe, *Logos and Eros: Essays Honoring Stanley Rosen,* pp. 105–17.

56. References to eros or related terms appear in Book VIII at 1155b3–4, 1156b2–3, 1157a6–13, 1158a11–12, 1159b15–17, and in Book IX at 1164a3–8, 1167a4–6, 1171a11–12, and 1171b29–31, with a very different treatment up to the first chapter of Book IX from that which appears after the fifth chapter of Book IX (the last three references listed above). Words related to *eros* show up outside Books VIII and IX in only two passing remarks: one in the inscription at Delos that declares what one loves most pleasant (1099a28); the other in a denial that seeking death to escape the pangs of unrequited love is courage (1116a10).

57. The relationship is even more unstable, Aristotle remarks, when lover and beloved exchange pleasure for gain, although that relationship looks indistinguishable from what was previously depicted as an exchange of pleasures, albeit pleasures of diverse sorts (cf. 1157a12–14 and 1164a3–12).

58. Cf. *Phaedrus* 233c–d, in contrast with 255a–b, 256c–d.

59. See *Phaedrus* 231c–d and 240e–241a.

60. See *Phaedrus* 233d–234b.

61. See *Phaedrus* 231a–b, 240c–d, and 241a–b. Intimacy with the nonlover, Socrates warns at the end of his second speech, is mixed with "mortal and thrifty economizing," which begets a lack of freedom in the soul (*Phaedrus* 256e).

62. If he were to contemplate the beautiful itself, Diotima tells Socrates, he would realize how far it surpasses the beautiful boys and youths so astonishing to

him now that he would do without food or drink, if possible, only to gaze on them and be together with them (*Symposium* 211d–e). Aristophanes, in his description of two halves who long for nothing but fusion into one, takes one of these aspects to the extreme (192d–e); Diotima, in her account of the ascent to contemplation of the beautiful itself, emphasizes the other (210–211d)—though she ends her account by speaking of a way of life that involves contemplating the beautiful itself and being together with it (212a). See Steven Berg's discussion, in "On Socrates' Speech in Plato's *Symposium*," p. 212.

63. The lover's sight of the godlike face of his beloved or "some *idea* of the body," Socrates explains, inspires his recollection of beauty itself as he once glimpsed it among the "hyperuranian beings" (*Phaedrus* 251a), and the *kalon* is the only such being that shows up in a concrete particular this way (250d–e). Aristotle, one should admit, while suggesting such an ascent, has not exactly offered a "playful mythic hymn," as Socrates does, praising the divine madness of the lover's winged flight from the beautiful sight of the beloved to the beautiful itself. For one thing, the beautiful, which was identified as the *telos* of virtue (1115b12–13), has not been reinterpreted, explicitly, as the object of eros; in the whole discussion of friendship, *kalon* appears with the greatest density in the description of the noble lover of self who sacrifices himself for its sake (see Chap. 8 of Book IX).

64. Diotima identifies Eros as a "terrible hunter," who philosophizes throughout life but is at the same time a sorcerer and a sophist (*Symposium* 203d–e). The Eleatic Stranger, hunting with his net of divisions, tries to capture the sophist in the category of hunting, which contains, at the same time, Socrates' practice of an erotic art (*Sophist* 222d–e). The Athenian Stranger turns to hunting after supposedly completing his discussion of education but only after his reflections on hunting are the laws about education said to have a *telos* (*Laws* 822d–823b). Hunting, which stands in here for philosophy or dialectic, represents, as Benardete puts it, "the Stranger's first foray into law as wanting to be the discovery of the beings, and it prepares the way for what the Stranger has long postponed, the question of eros" (*Plato's "Laws": The Discovery of Being*, pp. 226–27).

65. A gathering of men drinking together provides the setting in the *Symposium* for the speeches on eros. It is through the construction of a model of law-governed *symposia*, in the first two books of Plato's *Laws*, that the Athenian Stranger introduces his discussion of laws and, in particular, the problem of how the law can open up a window for its own examination. Dialectics is a game of draughts played with words (*Republic* 487b). Socrates transforms the meaning of gymnastics when he announces, in *Republic* VI, that "the most precise guardians" must be the philosophers and that those few with the rare combination of the requisite natural capacities must "exercise" (*gumnazein*) in many studies and be tested for their capacity to endure the greatest studies (503b–504a).

66. "Only in a philosophic friendship," Jaffa observes, "are the discussion and thought which characterize friendship not derivative from other activities; thus only in a philosophic friendship is the activity of friendship self-contained in the activity of discussion and thought" (*Thomism and Aristotelianism*, p. 126).

67. Book IX ends with the human equivalent, one might say, to the appearance of eros in *Metaphysics* Λ—a cosmological principle of movement toward *nous* as awakeness or awareness, which discloses, as Davis puts it, the inseparability of thinking from longing (see *The Autobiography of Philosophy*, p. 65 n. 9).

CHAPTER 7

1. It is striking, in light of this concern, that Book X is the one book of the *Ethics* in which the word "*aporia*" and related words do not appear.

2. Book VII presented this argument as plausible grounds for identifying pleasure as the good (cf. 1153b25–26 and 1172b36–1173a5). Like the position ascribed here to Eudoxus, the hedonistic thesis ascribed to Philebus in Plato's dialogue is a claim about pleasure as the good for all animals, while Socrates is concerned with the good for "all those able to participate in it" (*Philebus* 11b–c, 60a).

3. The reference to Plato here—the third and last in the *Ethics*—confirms how much the criteria Aristotle holds up for happiness have been borrowed from the *Philebus* (cf. *Philebus* 20e–21e, 60c–e, and *Ethics* 1097b14–20). Aristotle uses the Platonic argument against Eudoxus to reject the claim of pleasure to be *the* good, but at the same time to confirm that it is a good. He arrives at the same conclusion from a critical examination of antihedonist arguments, which can all be found in the *Philebus*. If, Aristotle argues, the characterization of pleasure as indeterminate just means that it allows for more or less, that doesn't prevent other indeterminate things, like health, from being considered good (see 1173a15–17, 24–28; and *Philebus* 24e–25a, 27e–28a, 31a). Those who identify pleasure as a *genesis* or *kinēsis*, hence incomplete and therefore not good, do not seem to speak beautifully, Aristotle charges (see 1173a29–31, and *Philebus* 53c–55a). If they are assuming that pleasure is the replenishment of the natural state of the organism, while pain is a defective state, those are bodily processes, which is not what pleasure seems to be. While pleasure might be an experience accompanying a process of replenishment, like the pleasure of eating when hungry, there are at least certain pleasures not preceded by pain, so that should not be an argument against the goodness of pleasure as such (see 1173b7–20, and *Philebus* 51b–52b).

4. "How long is the present?" Eva Brann asks, explaining that "by 'present' I here mean that moment which Aristotle calls 'now' in the *Physics*, when the world is before the soul and they touch each other" (*What, Then, Is Time?* p. 45).

5. See *De anima* 418a3–6, 425b26–426a2, 429a10–17.

6. Aristotle first approaches the problem with an analogy: the difference between the way pleasure completes the *energeia* and the way the sense faculty and its object do is like the difference between health and the doctor as a cause of being healthy (1174b23–26). Now, pleasure presumably does not complete the *energeia* the way the doctor produces health; but if it is to be understood as the very form of the *energeia*, as health is of being healthy, that would seem to confirm the definition of pleasure in Book VII as itself an "unimpeded *energeia*."

7. See J.C. Gosling and C. C. Taylor, *The Greeks on Pleasure*, p. 212. Pleasure either perfects the activity as an added peak, or it completes it in the sense that it prevents it from missing something that belongs to it as a whole: the verb *teleioō* meaning either "to complete" or "to perfect" has been imbued with the same ambiguity that from the outset haunted the adjective (*teleios*) as a characterization of happiness.

8. Aristotle's formulation of this question is replete with ambiguity. "Because of" (*dia*) could indicate that for the sake of which we choose what we do or, rather, the cause in some other sense that explains why we choose what we do. Then there is the problematic language of "choice": if it is used as defined in Book III, its object can only be the means to an end (1113b3–5), but that restriction disappeared in Book VI, when "choice" was understood as "desiring mind" or "intellectual desire," which could be oriented to an end. There is a difference, moreover, as Robert Berman points out to me, between an account of an agent deliberating and intentionally choosing means to an end and an account of a cause, which could be at work bringing about a result behind the back of an agent. The first alternative, then—we choose to live because of pleasure—could mean: (1a) we choose life as a means for the sake of pleasure or, on the other hand, (1b) we seek life as an end, and pleasure—perhaps as a ruse of nature—fosters that striving. The other alternative—we choose pleasure because of living—could mean: (2a) pleasure, whether we choose it or nature uses it, is for the sake of living or, on the other hand, (2b) being alive is a condition that causes one to seek pleasure. Each of the alternatives Aristotle poses thus allows for two different interpretations, which leaves open whether pleasure is the end and life serves it or life the end and pleasure serves it.

9. Tessitore finds an indication of the rhetorical and pedagogical horizon of Book X in Aristotle's dismissal of this question, which he interprets this way: "What constitutes the fundamental standard for human beings? Is it pleasure or is it a certain way of life characterized by a noble disregard for questions of this sort?" ("A Political Reading of Aristotle's Treatment of Pleasure in the *Nicomachean Ethics*," p. 261). The question Aristotle is putting aside at the moment, though, about the relation between pleasure and life, seems to be one that could be raised about all living things, even if being alive is something different in different cases.

10. In the *Philebus*, Socrates examines the strange notion that the pleasure accompanying a false opinion is itself a false pleasure (36c–38a).

11. The titles of the three parts of this study—"The Human Good," "The Beautiful and the Just," and "The Return to the Good"—are meant to capture the movement of the argument of the *Ethics*, as it sets out in Book I from *the* good, which becomes the human good; traverses the territory of the beautiful and the just in Books II–V; then enters a return path in the course of Books VI–X. But the title of part 3 speaks only imprecisely of a "return to the good," since the inquiry does not get back to that exact starting point.

12. Mary Nichols called my attention to this moment of Aristotelian playfulness.

13. Under the class of "plaything," the Eleatic Stranger includes—along with *kosmos—graphikē* and all the imitations produced by it, which would include the Platonic dialogue (*Statesman* 288c). Socrates addresses the difference between the serious and the playful use of speeches at the conclusion of his conversation with Phaedrus. On the model of the difference between seeds seriously sown in fitting ground, in accordance with the agricultural art, and those playfully planted in flowerpots, whose beautiful blossoms we enjoy contemplating, Socrates considers one whose "seeds" are knowledge of the just, the beautiful, and the good things. Apparently contrasting the seriousness of conversation with the playfulness of writing as such, what he in fact finds lacking in seriousness is, more specifically, planting in a river of ink speeches that cannot defend themselves. Planting the garden of written words may be playful, but the playful, then, cannot exclude the serious if that is the characteristic of the dialectical art; for Socrates' description of it—planting and sowing in a fitting soul speeches with knowledge, able to save themselves and the one who planted them, while in turn generating new seeds in others—looks like a wonderful description of the Platonic dialogue (*Phaedrus* 276b–277a).

14. Finding no appearance of this thesis earlier in the *Nicomachean Ethics*, René Gauthier and Jean Yves Jolif speculate that it is a reference to the *Protrepticus* (*L'Éthique à Nicomaque*, 2: 876). The conclusion reached in Book X had not been stated explicitly in the earlier books, W. F. R. Hardie acknowledges, though it was prepared for by the end of Book VI (*Aristotle's Ethical Theory*, p. 337; cf. John Cooper, *Reason and Human Good in Aristotle*, p. 156). Book VI, in the context of the investigation of virtue, identified happiness with the virtue of *sophia*—at least it concluded that *sophia* produces happiness the way health produces health (1144a3–5); it did not develop an argument about the identity of the human being and the *energeia* that most perfectly fulfills it.

15. Cf. 1097b1–7, 1097b14–21, and 1177a27–b4. And see Howard Curzer's discussion of how the criteria for happiness in Book X differ from those in Book I, despite Aristotle's own suggestion that he is using the original standards to determine in the end what happiness is ("Criteria for Happiness in *Nicomachean Ethics* I 7 and X 6–8," pp. 421–32).

16. See *Metaphysics* 982b11–23, cf. 983a11–20. *Metaphysics* Λ returns to the wondrous in its description of the activity of the highest being (1072b25–26).

17. The "divine science" desired for its own sake, Aristotle admits at the outset of the *Metaphysics*, might be thought to be beyond human power; but if so, it would not be, as the poets claim, because envious gods willfully prohibit it but because human nature is in many ways slavish (982b29–983a11; cf. Seth Benardete, "On Wisdom and Philosophy: The First Two Chapters of Aristotle's *Metaphysics A*," in *The Argument of Action*, p. 406.) To explain human limitations, or to encourage self-limitation, by appealing to divine jealousy, as Solon does in his understanding of human happiness (see nn. 28 and 29 below), would be to ascribe to the gods a form of *nemesis*, or indignation at the undeserved good fortune of others, which,

though it may be a mean state, should not count as a virtue (see 1108a35–b6, and chap. 3, n. 45, above).

18. The shifting identification of the human in *Ethics* X exhibits the tension generally at work between a comprehensive account and one that takes its bearings from the highest part of a whole or the highest instance of a kind. That tension underlies the whole project of the *Metaphysics*: it sets out in search of a science of being qua being, distinguished from all particular sciences by its comprehensive status (1003a20–32); but once theology is ranked as the highest of the theoretical sciences, "one might be perplexed whether first philosophy is universal or about some genus and some one nature." If there is some being that is unchangeable, Aristotle responds, the study of it would be first philosophy—and universal insofar as it is primary (1026a24–33). The problem recurs when *Metaphysics* Λ raises the question whether "the good and the best" are to be found in "the nature of the whole" or "separated itself by itself." That is like asking whether the well-being of an army resides in the order of the whole or in the general, to which Aristotle responds: it resides in both, though more in the general, since the order depends on him and not the other way around (1275a12–16).

19. As Gabriel Richardson Lear puts it, "though *nous* is not *merely* human, it is *most truly* human"; the human activity of contemplating is a matter of "approximating" the divine activity but precisely in doing so, realizing our human nature to the fullest extent possible (*Happy Lives and the Highest Good*, pp. 192–93). It is hard to understand, though, how approximation to divine activity could be the grounds for the happiness attributed to morally virtuous action and the political life devoted to it (*Happy Lives and the Highest Good*, pp. 193–195), when it is the absurdity of imagining gods engaged in just, courageous, liberal, or moderate actions that leads Aristotle to the conclusion that *theōria* is the only activity fitting for a god (1178b8–21).

20. See, e.g., Anthony Kenny, *The Aristotelian Ethics: A Study of the Relationship between the "Eudemian" and the "Nicomachean Ethics,"* pp. 202–6; and Cooper, *Reason and the Human Good in Aristotle,* pp. 155–80. The account of *eudaimonia* in *Ethics* X, Chaps. 7–8, is a kind of "ethical Platonism," Nussbaum argues, which does not fit into the argument of the *Ethics* and even seems problematic in this very context; the passage was probably composed separately, she speculates, and most likely inserted in its present position by someone other than Aristotle (*The Fragility of Goodness,* p. 377).

21. The identification of the individual with theoretical *nous,* and not also with practical *nous,* is a view about personal identity, Jennifer Whiting maintains, from which "strict intellectualism" follows; but it is not, she argues, the view Aristotle in fact accepts ("Human Nature and Intellectualism in Aristotle," p. 72, 87–88). In the *Ethics,* however, the distinction between theoretical reason and practical reason is an internal division of the part of the soul that has *logos*—not of *nous.* Soul can be understood as a whole composed of parts; mind, whatever its different functions, cannot. If one looks to the human being as a composite whole, as Whiting argues,

mind is something divine and cannot be the identity of the human as such; but if identified by that which is "sovereign and better" in it, the human being would be mind, or mind most of all (1177b26–1178a8). One may put the view somewhat paradoxically, in Thomas Nagel's words, "by saying that comprehensive human good isn't everything and should not be the main human goal. We must identify with the highest part of ourselves rather than with the whole" ("Aristotle on *Eudaimonia*," p. 13). There is, as this pattern of thought always seems to demonstrate, an ineradicable tension between these two ways of thinking of the human being (see n. 18 above).

22. The two types of life, Gauthier and Jolif maintain, are meant to lead the same person to happiness (*L'Éthique à Nicomaque*, 2:891). "There is nothing about the practical life," Amélie Rorty remarks, "which prevents its also being contemplative, and even enhanced by being contemplated" ("The Place of Contemplation in Aristotle's *Nicomachean Ethics*," p. 377). But once the theoretical life is defined by *sophia* as its final end, and the practical life by ethical virtue, neither end can be subordinated to the other to define a single type of life. The exercise of the ethical virtues, as Kraut argues, has to be itself a "dominant end," albeit of the life ranked second-best (*Aristotle on the Human Good*, pp. 5–6).

23. "However often he may perform the just or the temperate or liberal deed," as Cooper puts it, "anyone who organizes his life from the intellectualist outlook cannot care about such actions in the way a truly just or temperate or liberal man does" (*Reason and Human Good in Aristotle*, p. 164). Socrates may have done the just and beautiful thing in accepting his death as he did (cf. *Phaedo* 98e–99a); whether he made those choices solely for the sake of the just and the beautiful is another question. In Plato's fiction, in any case, the just and the beautiful coincide perfectly with Socrates' prudential calculation of his good.

24. Book X's admission of the instrumental status of practical activity appears to contradict not only the earlier claim that an ethically virtuous action is one chosen for its own sake (1105a28–32) but, more generally, as Keyt notes, the idea that action (*praxis*), in contrast with production, has its end in itself, in doing or faring well (*eupraxia;* 1140b6–7; "Intellectualism in Aristotle," pp. 364–65). In an effort to minimize the apparent conflict between Book X and the rest of the *Ethics*, Keyt argues that *bios* can refer to one among many aspects of a person's life and that in the best total life, those various aspects form a hierarchy with the higher ones resting on and presupposing the lower (p. 384). But the lower aspects cannot have the same role in a life in which they are alone as they would if subordinated to something higher in a greater whole—and that has particularly important consequences in the case of moral virtue (cf. the reference to Cooper, *Reason and the Human Good*, in n. 23 above).

25. The theoretical inquiry of *De anima*, which should contain that more precise account, only seems to reproduce the tension between separate mind and the inseparable union of body and soul (contrast 403a8–10 and 431a17 with 430a17–19).

26. Pericles represented the prudent man (1140b7–10), Thales and Anaxagoras the wise, who have no interest, supposedly, in the human goods (1141b3–8). In choosing the pre-Socratic cosmologist as representative of the activity of *theōria*, Aristotle appears to ignore the possibility, as Rorty puts it, that "we can contemplate the moral life in activity as well as the starry heaven above" ("The Place of Contemplation in Aristotle's *Nicomachean Ethics*," p. 378). Perhaps, however, we cannot be a mere spectator of the one as we can, presumably, of the other.

27. Here, as elsewhere in Book X, Aristotle, in Tessitore's words, "succeeds in muting, without actually denying, a fundamental tension between philosophy and politics" (*Reading Aristotle's "Ethics*," p. 116). He does so in part through an idealized image of philosophical activity, which is "removed from, and therefore less apparently in conflict with the exigencies of moral and political life" (p. 106)—like the figure Socrates presents in the *Theaetetus*, who could hardly be a threat to the city when he does not even know his way to the marketplace, let alone the courtroom or place of assembly (173c–d).

28. See Herodotus *Histories* I.30–32, and chap. 1, n. 64, above.

29. In Solon's juxtaposition of two ways of life, Benardete finds "the double frame of Greek tragedy: the political in its innocent autonomy and the sacred in its subversion of that innocence" ("On Greek Tragedy," in *The Argument of the Action*, pp. 102–3).

30. Solon's own life—in particular, his presence at the court of Croesus—provides an interesting model for the relation of the theoretical and practical. After laying down laws for the Athenians, Herodotus reports, Solon went abroad for ten years, claiming he traveled to see other cities but, in reality, leaving Athens in order to establish the authority of his laws, having prohibited any changes during his absence (*Histories* I.29); this was the reason Solon found himself in Sardis, Herodotus repeats—though there was *also* his desire to see other places (I.30).

31. See *Theaetetus* 174a–c. Of course, Thales, according to Aristotle, was able to disprove the typical charges against the uselessness of philosophy by demonstrating that his knowledge of the stars could result in procuring a monopoly on winepresses in just the right season (*Politics* 1259a7–17).

32. Socrates wishes the citizens would just laugh at him, as they do at Euthyphro, rather than feeling rage (*Euthyphro* 3b–e). As Socrates explains in his cave image, if someone were to come back into the darkness out of the sunlight and have to contend with the prisoners about the shadows on the wall, he would provoke laughter, but if he tried to release another, the prisoners would want to kill him (*Republic* 516e–517a).

33. On Cicero's description of the Socratic turn, see chap. 4, n. 2, above.

34. That the inquiry, which is a way (*methodos*) to the human good, could become a *prohairesis* was anticipated by the opening statement of the *Ethics*. We were warned in Book I that the end of the inquiry would not be knowledge but action—or, rather, according to Aristotle's revised claim, that the knowledge it provides would be useless if not applied to and enriched by some sort of action (1095a4–9).

35. The twofold form of action recalls the ambiguity of the "true politician" in Book I, who seems to be, on the one hand, the legislator, dedicated to making the citizens good and law-abiding and, on the other hand, the psychic equivalent to the doctor, who must study the whole body in order to heal the eye (1102a7–20).

36. On *kalokagathia*, see chap. 3, n. 35, above. To illustrate the sophistic reduction of the political art to rhetoric, Strauss cites Xenophon's contrast of himself, as a pupil of Socrates in possession of the political art, with Proxenus, a student of Gorgias, whose rhetoric enabled him to rule gentlemen but left him incapable of disciplining his soldiers by instilling respect and fear in them (*The City and Man*, p. 23).

37. Cf. *Laws* 653a–c. The metaphor of tilling the soil in the last chapter of the *Ethics* brings with it the only reference to *psychē* in Book X after the discussion of pleasure.

38. The debate on law in the last chapter of the *Ethics* (1180a14–b28) recalls in manner as well as content Plato's *Statesman* (293e–302b). In the third book of the *Politics* (Chaps. 15–16), a similar debate develops in the context of analyzing kingly rule by contrast with rule by law.

39. See *Odyssey* IX.114. With the same Homeric citation, the argument in *Politics* I points to the cannibalistic Cyclops as the model for what the human being would be in the absence of the city and law (1252b23–24; cf. 1253a35–37). In both the *Politics* and the *Ethics*, Aristotle omits Homer's initial characterization of the Cyclopes as "overweening and lawless (*athemistoi*)" (*Odyssey* IX.106)—the same term Athena uses of the suitors when she urges Odysseus, disguised as a beggar, to go among them and discover who are righteous and who are lawless (XVII.363). Aristotle's omission of this line implicitly raises the question of what it means for the Cyclopes to lay down laws (*themisteuei*) in private. See Ludwig's discussion in *Eros and Polis*, pp. 93–94.

40. The competing paradigms of gymnastics and medicine lead Plato's Eleatic Stranger to the same argument about the law (*Statesman* 294b–295b).

41. This is the problem Socrates takes up in the *Meno*, after Anytus, his future accuser, ominously appears on the scene and the question arises why the great politicians, like Pericles, could not transmit their virtue to their own sons. Meno's own uncertainty whether virtue can be taught is shared by many, Socrates informs him, including the poet Theognis. He cites the line Aristotle quotes here—"many wages and great ones" would justly be won if speeches were sufficient to make people decent—which leads the poet to conclude, "By teaching, you will never make a bad man good." But this is just the opposite of what Theognis implies, Socrates charges, when he recommends spending time with the powerful, for "from the worthy you will be taught worthy things, but if you mingle with the bad, you will destroy whatever sense is present" (*Meno* 95d–e). Aristotle cited the first half of this verse, about the worthy, while leaving out the remark about the bad, as the conclusion of the discussion of friendship in Book IX.

42. Aristotle goes on to criticize the Sophists using the same argument Socrates musters against treatises on the art of rhetoric (*Phaedrus* 268c–269c): someone who

understood politics would not believe it easy to legislate merely by making collections of laws from which selections are to be made, as if such judgment did not require understanding and experience (1181a12–b2). Of course, Aristotle admits, such a collection—which he himself produced—might be very useful for those able to theorize and judge what is beautiful, or the opposite, and what is suitable for what sort of situation. Richard Bodéüs reflects on the connection between this point in the final chapter of the *Ethics* and Aristotle's original characterization of his intended audience: just as he warned at the outset that the inquiry would be of use only for someone who comes to it with the right preparation (1094b27–1095a4), he indicates in the end that his political philosophy has something to teach the potential lawgiver if he brings the right kind of experience to it (*The Political Dimensions of Aristotle's "Ethics,"* pp. 57–69).

43. Carnes Lord connects Aristotle's remark here about the neglected study of legislation with his criticism of the *Laws* in Book II of the *Politics* for having little to say about the actual character of the regime it presents (introduction to *Aristotle: The "Politics,"* p. 21). Discussing the issue of "preludes" in *Laws* IV, Benardete remarks, "There seems to be always something that puts off the beginning of the laws, despite Clinias's impatience to get started and the Stranger's own promises" (*Plato's "Laws,"* p. 134). The replacement of Socrates in the *Laws* by the Athenian Stranger, as an "unofficial legislative adviser," indicates, as Sara Monoson puts it, the dialogue's "deep meditation on the possible political importance of forms of intellectual labor in which the historical Socrates did not engage but in which Plato . . . certainly did" (*Plato's Democratic Entanglements: Athenian Politics and the Practice of Philosophy,* p. 233). Leo Strauss explores what Alfarabi might have had in mind when he first summarizes the content of the *Laws* without saying a word about "laws" as its theme and later attributes the science and art embodied in the *Laws* to Socrates: "It is as if Farabi had interpreted the absence of Socrates from the *Laws* to mean that Socrates has nothing to do with laws, and as if he had tried to express this interpretation by suggesting that if *per impossibile* the *Laws* were Socratic, they would not deal with laws" ("How Farabi Read Plato's *Laws,*" p. 153).

44. The aim to "complete philosophy," which sounds almost like a contradiction in terms, is particularly striking in light of the unfinished character of the *Politics*. If the discussion of music in *Politics* VIII—with its reference, in particular, to *katharsis*—sends us to the *Poetics*, as the *Ethics* sends us on to the *Politics*, Aristotle would have split into three treatises the subject matter Plato's *Republic* brought together in one.

45. See *Politics* 1325b24–33. In the seventh book of the *Politics*, the question of the best life is formulated in a way that determines the answer to it: Which life is more choiceworthy, engaging together in politics and participating in the city or living the life of a stranger (1324a14–15)? The political and active life is set against one "released from externals," some sort of theoretical life—which is said by some, Aristotle adds, to be the only philosophical life (1324a25–29). A complex argument leads, finally, to the conclusion that if happiness is posited to be a condition of

doing and faring well (*eupragia*), the *praktikos bios* would be best for the city and the individual. But such a life, Aristotle immediately adds, is not necessarily in relation to others, as some believe, any more than acts of thinking engaged in for the sake of their consequences are the only practical ones; more truly practical are acts of contemplation and thinking that are ends in themselves, for their *telos* is simply faring well (*eupraxia*) (1325b14–22). The *Politics*, then, might appear to conflict with the *Ethics* in speaking of the superiority of the active life, or the practical life, over some sort of theoretical life, but its characterization of the practical life puts that dichotomy into question.

46. While arguing, in the second chapter of the *Politics*, for the understanding of the human being as a political animal, Aristotle admits that it is possible for an individual to be by nature "citiless" not only in the case of someone below the level of the human as such but also above it—either a beast or a god (1253a1–5, 28–29). Benardete reflects on the "divide between man as man and man as political animal," which philosophy recognizes, but poetry denies (*The Tragedy and Comedy of Life*, p. ix). The issue in the context concerns the status of the prohibitions against "foundational crimes," such as incest, which tragic poetry represents, and whether they are necessary for the human as such or only for the possibility of the city.

47. Alfarabi ends his account of Aristotle by noting the way in which he attempted to "complete the natural philosophy, and the political and human philosophy" ("The Philosophy of Aristotle" xix.99, in *The Philosophy of Plato and Aristotle*, p. 130). Speaking in his own name, in "The Attainment of Happiness," Alfarabi differentiates "the science of man," which investigates "the what and the how of the purpose for which man is made, that is, the perfection that man must achieve," from the investigation of "all the things by which man achieves that perfection or that are useful to him in achieving it," as well as those that obstruct it, which is the work of "political science" (i.20, in *The Philosophy of Plato and Aristotle*, p. 24).

48. If *eudaimonia* is a class that allows two different members but only one that is primary, it would exemplify what Berman designates a "virtuosity" model of class membership, in contrast with an inclusivist or an exclusivist one (see chap. 6, n. 15, above, on Berman, "Ways of Being Singular").

49. This seems to be the argument Aristotle develops in the opening of the *Metaphysics*. After conducting a survey of our opinions about wisdom, the inquiry turns to philosophy and traces its origin to wonder; wonder induces perplexity and that in turn recognition of one's ignorance. So, Aristotle reasons, "If it was because of fleeing ignorance that they philosophized, it is manifest that because of knowing (*eidenai*) they pursued knowing (*epistasthai*), and not for the sake of some use (*chrēsis tis*)." Aristotle finds evidence in human history—when almost all the necessities were present, with regard both to ease and pastime, they began to seek "such a *phronēsis*"; he then concludes, "It is clear that it was not for the sake of some *other use* (*chreia hetera*) they sought it" (982b20–28). Philosophy, then, seeks knowledge that is indeed of some use, just not some extraneous use: the knowledge that is alone "free," like a human being, because it exists for its own sake, is motivated

in fact by need—by the natural desire to know, which defines us as human. This paradoxical structure is present in our opinions about wisdom, which require that the science sought for its own sake be at the same time the science of the good (see Benardete, "On Wisdom and Philosophy: The First Two Chapters of Aristotle's *Metaphysics A,*" in *The Argument of Action,* pp. 401–6). As Velkley puts it, in his analysis of this essay, "Knowing at the highest level would bring together contemplative knowing for its own sake and causal knowing of the good. This would be the self-knowing that knows why knowledge for its own sake is good, and that grasps the reason for the desire to know. . . . In its erotic pursuit of this perplexity, philosophy is a paradoxical combination of the self-regarding and the self-forgetting" ("Being and Politics: Seth Benardete on Aristotle's *Metaphysics,*" pp. 16–17.)

50. See the discussion in "A Friend of Oneself," in chap. 6 above.

51. I take something along these lines to be the meaning of the concluding passage in Alfarabi's "Philosophy of Aristotle," cited as the epigraph to the introduction to this study: "And it has become evident that the knowledge that he [Aristotle] investigated at the outset just because he loved to do so . . . has turned out to be necessary for acquiring the intellect for the sake of which man is made" (xix, in *The Philosophy of Plato and Aristotle* [1962 ed.], p. 130). The revised edition (1969) offers another translation: "It has become evident that the knowledge that he [Aristotle] investigated at the outset just because he loved to do so, and inspected for the sake of explaining the truth about the above-mentioned pursuits, has turned out to be necessary for realizing the political activity for the sake of which man is made," with a note of the translator, Muhsin Mahdi, about the reading of the text on which this is based. I thank Charles Butterworth for explaining the situation to me. The Arabic text has the term *al-'aql* (intellect); but on the basis of a paraphrase by al-Baghdadi that Mahdi discovered after the first edition of this translation, he read *al-'aql* as *al-fi'l* (activity), to which he added the term *al-madani* (political). One point seems to hold on either reading: according to Alfarabi, Aristotle came to see that the knowledge he first thought of as simply for its own sake proved to be necessary for the human being to realize his proper end.

52. Benardete arrives at this designation in reflecting on Strauss's reasoning in *The City and Man:* "Philosophy examines opinions, especially the most authoritative opinions of the city. In subjecting the most authoritative opinions to examination, it denies their authoritativeness and transcends the city. Its transcendence of the city discloses the limitations of the city. . . . The city thus comes to light as a special kind of part: while being the obstacle to philosophy, it alone makes philosophy possible. . . . Political philosophy is the eccentric core of philosophy" ("Leo Strauss' *The City and Man,*" p. 4).

53. Addressing the question of how we become good, which requires coming to know what is truly good for us, Smith responds: "We do the work Aristotle has been doing all along. His pedagogy is not merely an invitation and exhortation to a new way of life. It is also an initiation into that life. By following along with the inquiry, we experience what is necessary in order to become good" (*Revaluing Ethics,* p. 183).

54. Heinrich Meier develops a conception of political philosophy defined by a fourfold task: not only is its subject matter the political things, but its way of proceeding serves the purpose of defending philosophy against external threat, while providing the rational justification of philosophy in itself; in doing so, it becomes the locus of philosophy's self-knowledge (see "Why Political Philosophy?" chap. 4 in *Leo Strauss and the Theologico-Political Problem,* esp. pp. 94, 104). Aristotle's *Ethics* provides an interesting test case for this conception of the features of political philosophy. It investigates the political things and is concerned with the political defense of philosophy, including—or, in particular, through—its final image of the wise one and his divine reward. But it is not so clear whether or how it succeeds in supplying a rational justification of the superiority of the philosophical life: such a justification, the *Ethics* seems to imply, can be accomplished only, if at all, through the deed of one engaged in the activity essential to that life.

55. In "Jerusalem and Athens: Some Preliminary Reflections," speaking of Hermann Cohen's lecture "The Social Ideal in Plato and the Prophets" and his own preference to speak of "Socrates and the prophets," Leo Strauss explains: "We are no longer . . . sure . . . we can draw a clear line between Socrates and Plato. There is traditional support for drawing such a clear line, above all in Aristotle, but Aristotle's statements on this kind of subject no longer possess for us the authority that they formerly possessed"—I would add: or that Aristotle himself intended them to possess for his best reader. "The decisive fact for us," Strauss continues, "is that Plato as it were points away from himself to Socrates. Plato points not only to Socrates' speeches but to his whole life, to his fate as well" (in *Studies in Platonic Political Philosophy,* p. 168; cf. Catherine Zuckert's discussion of the passage in "Primitive Platonism: Strauss's Response to Radical Historicism," in *Postmodern Platos: Nietzsche, Heidegger, Gadamer, Strauss, Derrida,* p. 163).

BIBLIOGRAPHY

CLASSICAL SOURCES

References to Aristotle's *Nicomachean Ethics* are to the page and line numbers in the Oxford Classical Text, edited by I. Bywater, 1894. Unless otherwise noted, translations from Greek texts are my own. For the following sources I have relied primarily on the Loeb Classical Library editions (Harvard University Press):

Aristotle *De anima, Eudemian Ethics, Metaphysics, Nicomachean Ethics, Physics, Poetics, Politics, Posterior Analytics, Rhetoric*
Euripides *Orestes*
Herodotus *Histories*
Hesiod *Works and Days*
Plato *Alcibiades I, Alcibiades* II, *Apology, Charmides, Cratylus, Gorgias, Laches, Laws, Lysis, Phaedo, Phaedrus, Philebus, Protagoras, Republic, Sophist, Statesman, Symposium, Theaetetus*
Thucydides *Peloponnesian War*
Xenophon *Symposium*

OTHER WORKS CITED

Achtenberg, Deborah. *Cognition of Value in Aristotle's Ethics: Promise of Enrichment, Threat of Destruction.* Albany: State University of New York Press, 2002.
Ackrill, J. L. "Aristotle on *Eudaimonia.*" In Rorty, *Essays on Aristotle's "Ethics."*
Alfarabi. *The Harmonization of the Two Opinions of the Two Sages: Plato the Divine and Aristotle and Selected Aphorisms.* In *Alfarabi: The Political Writings,* translated and annotated by Charles E. Butterworth. Ithaca, NY: Cornell University Press, 2001.
———. *The Philosophy of Plato and Aristotle.* Translated and with an introduction by Muhsin Mahdi. New York: Free Press of Glencoe, 1962. Rev. ed., Ithaca, NY: Cornell University Press, 1969.
Anastaplo, George and Laurence Berns, trans. *Plato's "Meno."* Newburyport, MA: Focus Publishing / R. Pullins Co., 2003.

Annas, Julia. "Aristotle on Pleasure and Goodness." In Rorty, *Essays on Aristotle's "Ethics."*

———. "Plato and Aristotle on Friendship and Altruism." *Mind* 86 (1977): 532–54.

Aubenque, Pierre. *La Prudence chez Aristote.* Paris: Presses Universitaires de France, 1976.

Barnes, Jonathan, Malcolm Schofield, and Richard Sorabji, eds. *Articles on Aristotle.* Vol. 2, *Ethics and Politics.* New York: St. Martin's Press, 1978.

Bartlett, Robert C., trans. *Plato: "Protagoras" and "Meno."* With notes and interpretive essays. Ithaca, NY: Cornell University Press, 2004.

Bartlett, Robert C. and Collins, Susan D., eds. *Action and Contemplation: Studies in the Moral and Political Thought of Aristotle.* Albany: State University of New York Press, 1999.

Bechhofer Roberts, C. E. [Ephesian, pseud.]. *Winston Churchill: Being an account of the life of the Right Hon. Winston Leonard Spencer Churchill.* New York: Robert M. McBride & Co., 1928.

Benardete, Seth. *The Argument of the Action: Essays on Greek Poetry and Philosophy.* Edited and with an introduction by Ronna Burger and Michael Davis. Chicago: University of Chicago Press, 2000.

———, trans. *The Being of the Beautiful: Plato's "Theaetetus," "Sophist," and "Statesman."* With commentary. Chicago: University of Chicago Press, 1984.

———. *The Bow and the Lyre: A Platonic Reading of the "Odyssey."* Lanham, MD: Rowman & Littlefield, 1997.

———. *Herodotean Inquiries.* The Hague: Nijhoff, 1969. Rev. ed., South Bend, IN: St. Augustine's Press, 1999.

———. "Leo Strauss' The City and Man." *Political Science Reviewer* 8 (1978): 1–20.

———. "On Wisdom and Philosophy: The First Two Chapters of Aristotle's *Metaphysics* A." *Review of Metaphysics* 32, no. 2 (1978): 205–15. Reprinted in Benardete, *The Argument of the Action.*

———. *Plato's "Laws": The Discovery of Being.* Chicago: University of Chicago Press, 2000.

———. *Sacred Transgressions: A Reading of Sophocles' "Antigone."* South Bend, IN: St. Augustine's Press, 1999.

———. *Socrates and Plato: The Dialectics of Eros / Socrates und Platon: Die Dialektik des Eros.* Parallel texts in English and German. Translated into German by Wiebke Meier. Edited and with an introduction by Heinrich Meier. Munich: C. F. von Siemens Stiftung, 2002. German translation first published in *Über die Liebe: Ein Symposion,* translated by Wiebke Meier, edited by Heinrich Meier and Gerhard Neuman. Munich: Piper Verlag, 2001.

———. *Socrates' Second Sailing: On Plato's "Republic."* Chicago: University of Chicago Press, 1989.

———, trans. *The Tragedy and Comedy of Life: Plato's "Philebus."* With commentary. Chicago: University of Chicago Press, 1993.

Benardete, Seth, and Michael Davis, trans. *Aristotle: On Poetics*. With an introduction, by Michael Davis. South Bend, IN: St. Augustine's Press.

Berg, Steven. "On Socrates' Speech in Plato's *Symposium*." In Velásquez, *Love and Friendship*.

Berman, Robert. "Ways of Being Singular: The Logic of Individuality." *Cardozo Public Law, Policy, and Ethics Journal* 3, no. 1 (2004): 109–24.

Berns, Laurence. "Spiritedness in Ethics and Politics: A Study in Aristotelian Psychology." *Interpretation* 12, nos. 2–3 (1954): 335–48.

Bloom, Allan, trans. *The "Republic" of Plato*. With interpretive essay and notes. New York: Basic Books, 1968.

Bodéüs, Richard. *The Political Dimensions of Aristotle's "Ethics."* Translated by Jan Edward Garrett. Albany: State University of New York Press, 1993.

Bolotin, David. *An Approach to Aristotle's "Physics": With Particular Attention to the Role of His Manner of Writing*. Albany: State University of New York Press, 1997.

———. *Plato's Dialogue on Friendship: An Interpretation of the "Lysis."* With a New Translation. Ithaca, NY: Cornell University Press, 1979.

Brann, Eva. *What, Then, Is Time?* Lanham, MD: Rowman & Littlefield, 1999.

Brinkmann, Klaus. *Aristoteles allgemeine und spezielle Metaphysik*. Berlin: de Gruyter, 1979.

Broadie, Sarah. *Ethics with Aristotle*. Oxford: Oxford University Press, 1991.

Bruell, Christopher. *On the Socratic Education: An Introduction to the Shorter Platonic Dialogues*. Lanham, MD: Rowman & Littlefield, 1999.

Burger, Ronna. "Ethical Reflection and Righteous Indignation: *Nemesis* in the *Nicomachean Ethics*." In *Essays in Ancient Greek Philosophy*, edited by John Anton and Anthony Preus. Vol. 4. Albany: State University of New York Press, 1991.

———. "Hunting Together or Philosophizing Together: Friendship and Eros in Aristotle's *Nicomachean Ethics*." In Velásquez, *Love and Friendship*.

———. *The "Phaedo": A Platonic Labyrinth*. New Haven, CT: Yale University Press, 1984. Reprinted with new preface. South Bend, IN: St. Augustine's Press, 1999.

———. "Self-Restraint and Virtue: Sages and Philosophers in Maimonides' *Eight Chapters*." Paper presented at the Academy of Jewish Philosophy, Eastern Division Meeting of the American Philosophical Association, December 2006.

———. "Socratic *Eironeia*." *Interpretation* 13, no. 2 (1985): 143–50.

———. "The Thumotic Soul." *Epoché: A Journal in the History of Philosophy* 7, no. 2 (2003): 151–68.

———. "Wisdom, Philosophy, and Happiness: On Book X of Aristotle's *Ethics*." *Proceedings of the Boston Area Colloquium on Ancient Philosophy* 6 (1992): 289–307.

Collins, Susan D. "Justice and the Dilemma of Moral Virtue in Aristotle's *Nicomachean Ethics*." In Tessitore, *Aristotle and Modern Politics*.

———. "The Moral Virtues in Aristotle's *Nicomachean Ethics*." In *Action and Contemplation: Studies in the Moral and Political Thought of Aristotle*, edited by Robert C. Bartlett and Susan D. Collins. Albany: State University of New York Press, 1999.

Cooper, John. *Reason and Emotion*. Princeton, NJ: Princeton University Press, 1999.

———. *Reason and Human Good in Aristotle*. Cambridge, MA: Harvard University Press, 1975.

Cox, Richard H. "Aristotle's Treatment of Socrates in the *Nicomachean Ethics*: A Proem." In *Politikos: Selected Papers of the North American Chapter of the Society for Greek Political Thought*, edited by Kent Moors. Pittsburgh: Duquesne University Press, 1989.

Cropsey, Joseph. "Justice and Friendship in the *Nicomachean Ethics*." In *Political Philosophy and the Issues of Politics*, edited by Joseph Cropsey. Chicago: University of Chicago Press, 1972.

Curzer, Howard. "Criteria for Happiness in *Nicomachean Ethics* I 7 and X 6–8." *Classical Quarterly* 40, no. 2 (1990): 421–32.

Dante Alighieri. *Inferno*. Translated by John D. Sinclair. New York: Oxford University Press, 1939.

Daube, David. *Roman Law: Linguistic, Social and Philosophical Aspects*. Edinburgh: Edinburgh University Press, 1969.

Davis, Michael. *The Autobiography of Philosophy*. Lanham, MD: Rowman & Littlefield, 1999.

———. "Father of the *Logos*: The Question of the Soul in Aristotle's *Nicomachean Ethics*." *Epoché: A Journal in the History of Philosophy* 7, no. 2 (2003): 169–87.

———. *The Poetry of Philosophy*. Lanham, MD: Rowman & Littlefield, 1999. Reprint, South Bend, IN: St. Augustine's Press, 1999.

———. *The Politics of Philosophy: A Commentary on Aristotle's "Politics."* Lanham, MD: Rowman & Littlefield, 1996.

Den Uyl, Douglas J. *The Virtue of Prudence*. New York: Peter Lang, 1991.

Den Uyl, Douglas J., and Douglas Rasmussen. *Liberty and Nature: An Aristotelian Defense of Liberal Order*. La Salle, IL: Open Court, 1991.

Dirlmeier, Franz, trans. *Aristoteles Nikomachische Ethik*. Vol. 6, *Aristoteles Werke*. With commentary. Berlin: Akademie Verlag, 1956.

Faulkner, Robert. "Spontaneity, Justice, and Coercion: On *Nicomachean Ethics* Books III and V." In "Coercion", edited by J. Roland Pennock and John W. Chapman. Special issue, *Nomos* 14 (1972): 163–70.

Festugière, A. J. *Aristote: Le Plaisir*. Paris: Librairie Philosophique, 1936.

Fitzgerald, W. *Selections from the "Nicomachean Ethics" of Aristotle*. Dublin: Hodges & Smith, 1853.

Frank, Jill. *A Democracy of Distinction: Aristotle and the Work of Politics*. Chicago: University of Chicago Press, 2005.

Gauthier, René Antoine, and Jean Yves Jolif, trans. *Aristote: L'Éthique à Nicomaque*. 2 vols. With introduction and commentary. Louvain: Publications Universitaires de Louvain, 1958–59.

Gildin, Hilail. "Leo Strauss and the Crisis of Liberal Democracy." In *The Crisis of Liberal Democracy*, edited by Kenneth Deutsch and Walter Soffer. Albany: State University of New York Press, 1987.

Gosling, J. C. B. and Taylor, C. C. W. *The Greeks on Pleasure*. Oxford: Clarendon Press, 1982.

Gourevitch, Victor. "Philosophy and Politics, I–II." *Review of Metaphysics* 22 (1968): 38–84, 281–328.

Grant, Alexander. *The "Ethics" of Aristotle*. 4th rev. ed. 2 vols. With essays and notes. London: Longmans, Green, 1885. Reprinted in 1 vol.; New York: Arno Press, 1973.

Guerra, Marc. "Aristotle on Pleasure and Political Philosophy: A Study in Book VII of the *Nicomachean Ethics*." *Interpretation* 24, no. 2 (1997): 171–82.

Halper, Edward C. *Form and Reason: Essays in Metaphysics*. Albany: State University of New York Press 1993.

Hardie, W. F. R. "Aristotle's Doctrine That Virtue Is a 'Mean.'" In Barnes, Schofield, and Sorabji, *Articles on Aristotle*.

———. *Aristotle's Ethical Theory*. Oxford: Oxford University Press, 1968.

———. "The Final Good in Aristotle's *Ethics*." In *Aristotle: A Collection of Critical Essays*, edited by J. M. E. Moravcsik. Garden City, NY: Doubleday & Co., 1967. Rev. ed., Notre Dame, IN: University of Notre Dame Press, 1974.

Hegel, G. W. F. *Vorlesungen über die Aesthetik*. Vol. 3. Frankfurt am Main: Suhrkamp Verlag, 1970.

Heidegger, Martin. *Plato's "Sophist."* Translated by Richard Rojcewicz and André Schuwer. Bloomington: Indiana University Press, 1997.

Heinaman, Robert. "*Eudaimonia* and Self-Sufficiency in the *Nicomachean Ethics*." *Phronesis* 33, no. 1 (1988): 31–53.

———, ed. *Plato and Aristotle's "Ethics."* Ashgate Keeling Series in Ancient Philosophy. Burlington, VT: Ashgate, 2003.

Höffe, Otfried. "Ethik als praktische Philosophie-Methodische Überlegungen." In *Aristoteles, Die Nikomachische Ethik*, edited by Otfried Höffe. Berlin: Akademie Verlag, 1995.

Howland, Jacob. "Aristotle's Great-Souled Man." *Review of Politics* 64 (2002): 27–56.

Hursthouse, Rosalind. "A False Doctrine of the Mean." In Sherman, *Aristotle's "Ethics": Critical Essays*.

Irwin, Terence, trans. *Aristotle: Nicomachean Ethics*. Indianapolis: Hackett Publishing, 1985.

———. *Aristotle's First Principles*. Oxford: Clarendon Press, 1988.

———. "The Metaphysical and Psychological Basis of Aristotle's *Ethics*." In Rorty, *Essays on Aristotle's "Ethics."*

———. "Permanent Happiness: Aristotle and Solon." In Sherman, *Aristotle's "Ethics": Critical Essays*.

Jaffa, Harry. "Aristotle." In *History of Political Philosophy*, edited by Leo Strauss and Joseph Cropsey. 2nd ed. Chicago: Rand McNally, 1972.

———. *Thomism and Aristotelianism: A Study of the Commentary by Thomas Aquinas on the "Nicomachean Ethics."* Chicago: University of Chicago Press, 1952. Reprint, Westport, CT: Greenwood Press, 1979.

Kenny, Anthony. *The Aristotelian Ethics: A Study of the Relationship between the "Eudemian" and "Nichomachean Ethics" of Aristotle.* Oxford: Oxford University Press, 1978.

Keyt, David. "Intellectualism in Aristotle." In *Essays in Ancient Greek Philosophy*, edited by John Anton and Anthony Preus. Vol. 2. Albany: State University of New York Press, 1983.

Kraut, Richard. *Aristotle on the Human Good.* Princeton, NJ: Princeton University Press, 1989.

———, ed. *The Blackwell Guide to Aristotle's "Nicomachean Ethics."* Oxford: Blackwell, 2006.

Lear, Gabriel Richardson. "Aristotle on Moral Virtue and the Fine." In Kraut, *The Blackwell Guide to Aristotle's "Nicomachean Ethics."*

———. *Happy Lives and the Highest Good.* Princeton, NJ: Princeton University Press, 2004.

Lear, Jonathan. *Aristotle: The Desire to Understand.* Cambridge: Cambridge University Press, 1988.

Lockwood, Thornton C. "Is Virtue a *logos, kata ton logon,* or *meta tou orthou logou*?" Paper presented at the Eastern Division meeting of the American Philosophical Association, December 2006.

———. "A Topical Bibliography of Scholarship on Aristotle's *Nicomachean Ethics*: 1880 to 2004." *Journal of Philosophical Research* 30 (2005): 1–116.

Lord, Carnes, trans. *Aristotle: The "Politics."* With introduction, notes, and glossary. Chicago: University of Chicago Press, 1984.

Ludwig, Paul. *Eros and Polis: Desire and Community in Greek Political Theory.* Cambridge: Cambridge University Press, 2000.

Machiavelli, Niccolò. *The Prince.* Translated and with an introduction by Harvey Mansfield. 2nd ed. Chicago: University of Chicago Press, 1998.

Mahdi, Muhsin S. *Alfarabi and the Foundation of Islamic Political Philosophy.* Chicago: University of Chicago Press, 2001.

Maimonides, Moses. *Eight Chapters.* In *Ethical Writings of Maimonides,* translated by Charles E. Butterworth and Raymond L. Weiss. New York: New York University Press, 1975. Reprint, New York: Dover Publications, 1983.

———. *The Guide of the Perplexed.* Translated by Shlomo Pines, with an introductory essay by Leo Strauss. 2 vols. Chicago: University of Chicago Press, 1963.

Mara, Gerald M. *Socrates' Discursive Democracy: Logos and Ergon in Platonic Political Philosophy.* Albany: State University of New York Press, 1997.

Meier, Heinrich. *Leo Strauss and the Theologico-Political Problem.* Translated by Marcus Brainard. Cambridge: Cambridge University Press, 2006.

Meyer, Susan Sauvé. "Aristotle on the Voluntary." In Kraut, *The Blackwell Guide to Aristotle's "Nicomachean Ethics."*

Miller, Fred D. *Nature, Justice, and Rights in Aristotle's "Politics."* Oxford: Clarendon Press, 1997.

————. Review of *Reason and Human Good in Aristotle*, by John M. Cooper. *Reason Papers*, no. 4 (Winter 1978): 111–14.

Monoson, Sara. *Plato's Democratic Entanglements: Athenian Politics and the Practice of Philosophy*. Princeton, NJ: Princeton University Press, 2000.

Nagel, Thomas. "Aristotle on *Eudaimonia*." In Rorty, *Essays on Aristotle's "Ethics."*

Nichols, James, trans. *Plato "Gorgias."* Ithaca, NY: Cornell University Press, 1988.

————. *Plato: Laches*. In *The Roots of Political Philosophy: Ten Forgotten Socratic Dialogues*. Translated, with Interpretative Studies. Edited by Thomas L. Pangle. Ithaca, NY: Cornell University Press, 1987.

Nichols, Mary P. *Citizens and Statesmen: A Study of Aristotle's "Politics."* Lanham, MD: Rowman & Littlefield, 1992.

————. *Socrates and the Political Community*. Albany: State University of New York Press, 1987.

Nussbaum, Martha. *The Fragility of Goodness: Luck and Ethics in Greek Tragedy and Philosophy*. Cambridge: Cambridge University Press, 1986.

Owen, G. E. L. "Aristotelian Pleasures." In Barnes, Schofield, and Sorabji, *Articles on Aristotle*.

Pakaluk, Michael, trans. *Aristotle's "Nicomachean Ethics" Books VIII and IX*. With commentary. Oxford: Clarendon Press, 1998.

Pangle, Lorraine. *Aristotle and the Philosophy of Friendship*. Cambridge University Press, 2002.

Pangle, Thomas, trans. *The "Laws" of Plato*. With interpretative essay. New York: Basic Books, 1980. Reprint, Chicago: University of Chicago Press, 1988.

Parens, Joshua. *An Islamic Philosophy of Virtuous Religions: Introducing Alfarabi*. Albany: State University of New York Press, 2006.

Ranasinghe, Nalin, ed.. *Logos and Eros: Essays Honoring Stanley Rosen*. South Bend, IN: St. Augustine's Press, 2006.

————. *The Soul of Socrates*. Ithaca, NY: Cornell University, 2000.

Reeve, C. D. C. *The Practices of Reason: Aristotle's "Nicomachean Ethics."* Oxford: Clarendon Press, 1992.

Roche, Timothy. "*Ergon* and *Eudaimonia* in *Nicomachean Ethics* I: Reconsidering the Intellectualist Interpretation." *Journal of the History of Philosophy* 26, no 2 (1988): 175–94.

Rogers, Kelly. "Aristotle's Conception of *To Kalon*." *Ancient Philosophy* 13, no. 2 (1998): 355–72.

Rorty, Amélie Oksenberg. "*Akrasia* and Pleasure: *Nicomachean Ethics* Book 7." In Rorty, *Essays on Aristotle's "Ethics."*

————, ed. *Essays on Aristotle's "Ethics."* Berkeley: University of California Press, 1980.

————. "The Place of Contemplation in Aristotle's *Nicomachean Ethics*." In Rorty, *Essays on Aristotle's "Ethics."*

Ross, W. D. *Aristotle*. London: Methuen, 1949. Reprint, New York: Meridian Books, 1960.

Sachs, Joe, trans. *Aristotle: Nicomachean Ethics*. With introductory essay and glossary. Newburyport, MA: Focus Publishing / R. Pullins, 2002.

Salkever, Steven. *Finding the Mean: Theory and Practice in Aristotelian Political Philosophy*. Princeton, NJ: Princeton University Press, 1990.

Saxonhouse, Arlene W. *Athenian Democracy, Modern Mythmakers, and Ancient Theorists*. Notre Dame, IN: University of Notre Dame, 1996.

Schaefer, David. "Wisdom and Morality: Aristotle's Account of *Akrasia*." *Polity* 21, no. 2 (1988): 221–52.

Scott, Dominic. "Aristotle and Thrasymachus." *Oxford Studies in Ancient Philosophy* 19 (2000): 225–52.

Sensen, Kathryn. "On Nature as a Standard: Book VII of Aristotle's *Ethics*." Paper presented at the annual meeting of the Northeastern Political Science Association, November 2006.

———. "On the Nature of Friendship in Aristotle's *Nichomachean Ethics*." Paper presented at the annual meeting of the New England Political Science Association, May 2006.

Sherman, Nancy, ed. *Aristotle's Ethics: Critical Essays*. Lanham, MD: Rowman & Littlefield, 1999.

———. *The Fabric of Character: Aristotle's Theory of Virtue*. Oxford: Oxford University Press, 1989.

Smith, Thomas W. *Revaluing Ethics: Aristotle's Dialectical Pedagogy*. Albany: State University of New York Press, 2001.

Sparshott, Francis. *Taking Life Seriously: A Study of the Argument of the "Nicomachean Ethics."* Toronto: University of Toronto Press, 1996.

Speliotis, Evanthia. "Women and Slaves in Aristotle's *Politics* I." In *Nature, Woman, and the Art of Politics*, edited by Eduardo A. Velásquez. Lanham, MD: Rowman & Littlefield, 2000.

Stern-Gillet, Suzanne. *Aristotle's Philosophy of Friendship*. Albany: State University of New York Press, 1975.

Strauss, Leo. *The City and Man*. Charlottesville: University Press of Virginia, 1964. Reprint, Chicago: University of Chicago Press, 1978.

———. "How Farabi Read Plato's *Laws*." Chap. 5 in *What Is Political Philosophy? and Other Studies*. NY: Free Press, 1959. Reprint, Westport, CT: Greenwood Publishers, 1973.

———. *Natural Right and History*. Chicago: University of Chicago Press, 1953.

———. "On Classical Political Philosophy." Chap. 4 in *The Rebirth of Classical Political Rationalism: An Introduction to the Thought of Leo Strauss; Essays and Lectures by Leo Strauss*, selected and introduced by Thomas L. Pangle. Chicago: University of Chicago Press, 1989.

———. "The Origins of Political Science and the Problem of Socrates." Edited by David Bolotin, Christopher Bruell, and Thomas Pangle. *Interpretation* 23, no. 2 (1998).

———. *Studies in Platonic Political Philosophy*. With an introduction by Thomas L. Pangle. Chicago: University of Chicago Press, 1983.

Swanson, Judith. *The Public and the Private in Aristotle's Political Philosophy*. Ithaca, NY: Cornell University Press, 1992.

Tessitore, Aristide, ed. *Aristotle and Modern Politics: The Persistence of Political Philosophy*. Notre Dame, IN: University of Notre Dame Press, 2002.

———. "Aristotle's Political Presentation of Socrates in the *Nicomachean Ethics*." *Interpretation* 16, no. 1 (1988): 3–22.

———. "A Political Reading of Aristotle's Treatment of Pleasure in the *Nicomachean Ethics*." *Political Theory* 17, no. 2 (1989): 247–65.

———. *Reading Aristotle's "Ethics": Virtue, Rhetoric, and Political Philosophy*. Albany: State University of New York Press, 1996.

Thomas Aquinas, Saint. *Commentary on Aristotle's "Nicomachean Ethics."* Translated by C. I. Litzinger, OP. 2 vols. Chicago: Henry Regnery, 1964. Rev. ed. in 1 vol, Notre Dame, IN: Dumb Ox Books, 1993.

Urmson, J. O. "Aristotle's Doctrine of the Mean." In Rorty, *Essays on Aristotle's "Ethics."*

Velásquez, Eduardo A., ed. *Love and Friendship: Rethinking Politics and Affection in Modern Times*. Lanham, MD: Rowman & Littlefield, 2003.

Velkley, Richard. *Being after Rousseau: Philosophy and Culture in Question*. Chicago: University of Chicago Press, 2002.

———. "Being and Politics: Seth Benardete on Aristotle's *Metaphysics*." *Political Science Reviewer* 34 (2005): 7–21.

Walsh, Germaine Paulo. Review of *Reading Aristotle's "Ethics,"* by Aristide Tessitore. *Political Theory* 91, no. 3 (1997): 732–33.

Ward, Lee. "Nobility and Necessity: The Problem of Courage in Aristotle's *Nicomachean Ethics*." *American Political Science Review* 95, no. 1 (2001): 71–83.

Welldon, J. E. C., trans. *Aristotle: The Nicomachean Ethics*. Amherst, NY: Prometheus Books, 1987.

Wilkes, Kathleen. "The Good Man and the Good for Man in Aristotle's *Ethics*." In Rorty, *Essays in Aristotle's "Ethics."*

Whiting, Jennifer. "Human Nature and Intellectualism in Aristotle." *Archiv für Geschichte der Philosophie* 68 (1986): 70–95.

Winthrop, Delba. "Aristotle and Theories of Justice," *American Political Science Review* 72 (1978): 1201–15.

Yack, Bernard. *The Problems of a Political Animal*. Berkeley: University of California Press, 1993.

Zuckert, Catherine H. *Postmodern Platos: Nietzsche, Heidegger, Gadamer, Strauss, Derrida*. Chicago: University of Chicago Press, 1996.

INDEX